Innovative Teaching Strategies and New Learning Paradigms in Computer Programming

Ricardo Queirós
Polytechnic Institute of Porto, Portugal

A volume in the Advances in Higher Education
and Professional Development (AHEPD) Book
Series

Managing Director:	Lindsay Johnston
Managing Editor:	Austin DeMarco
Director of Intellectual Property & Contracts:	Jan Travers
Acquisitions Editor:	Kayla Wolfe
Production Editor:	Christina Henning
Development Editor:	Erin O'Dea
Typesetter:	Cody Page
Cover Design:	Jason Mull

Published in the United States of America by
Information Science Reference (an imprint of IGI Global)
701 E. Chocolate Avenue
Hershey PA, USA 17033
Tel: 717-533-8845
Fax: 717-533-8661
E-mail: cust@igi-global.com
Web site: http://www.igi-global.com

                    Library of Congress Cataloging-in-Publication Data

CIP Data

Innovative teaching strategies and new learning paradigms in computer
programming / Ricardo Queiros, editor.
      pages cm
  Includes bibliographical references and index.
   ISBN 978-1-4666-7304-5 (hardcover) -- ISBN 978-1-4666-7305-2 (ebook) -- ISBN 978-1-4666-7307-6 (print & perpetual access) 1. Computer programming--Study and teaching. I. Queiros, Ricardo, 1975- editor.
   QA76.6.I523 2015
   005.1071--dc23
                    2014036851

This book is published in the IGI Global book series Advances in Higher Education and Professional Development (AHEPD) (ISSN: 2327-6983; eISSN: 2327-6991)

British Cataloguing in Publication Data
A Cataloguing in Publication record for this book is available from the British Library.

For electronic access to this publication, please contact: eresources@igi-global.com.

Advances in Higher Education and Professional Development (AHEPD) Book Series

Jared Keengwe
University of North Dakota, USA

ISSN: 2327-6983
EISSN: 2327-6991

MISSION

As world economies continue to shift and change in response to global financial situations, job markets have begun to demand a more highly-skilled workforce. In many industries a college degree is the minimum requirement and further educational development is expected to advance. With these current trends in mind, the **Advances in Higher Education & Professional Development (AHEPD) Book Series** provides an outlet for researchers and academics to publish their research in these areas and to distribute these works to practitioners and other researchers.

AHEPD encompasses all research dealing with higher education pedagogy, development, and curriculum design, as well as all areas of professional development, regardless of focus.

COVERAGE

- Adult Education
- Assessment in Higher Education
- Career Training
- Coaching and Mentoring
- Continuing Professional Development
- Governance in Higher Education
- Higher Education Policy
- Pedagogy of Teaching Higher Education
- Vocational Education

IGI Global is currently accepting manuscripts for publication within this series. To submit a proposal for a volume in this series, please contact our Acquisition Editors at Acquisitions@igi-global.com or visit: http://www.igi-global.com/publish/.

Titles in this Series

For a list of additional titles in this series, please visit: www.igi-global.com

New Voices in Higher Education Research and Scholarship
Filipa M. Ribeiro (University of Porto, Portugal) Yurgos Politis (University College Dublin, Ireland) and Bojana Culum (University of Rijeka, Croatia)
Information Science Reference • copyright 2015 • 316pp • H/C (ISBN: 9781466672444) • US $185.00 (our price)

Professional Development Schools and Transformative Partnerships
Drew Polly (UNC Charlotte, USA) Tina Heafner (UNC Charlotte, USA) Marvin Chapman (UNC Charlotte, USA) and Melba Spooner (UNC Charlotte, USA)
Information Science Reference • copyright 2015 • 363pp • H/C (ISBN: 9781466663671) • US $195.00 (our price)

Models for Improving and Optimizing Online and Blended Learning in Higher Education
Jared Keengwe (University of North Dakota, USA) and Joachim Jack Agamba (Idaho State University, USA)
Information Science Reference • copyright 2015 • 320pp • H/C (ISBN: 9781466662803) • US $175.00 (our price)

Advancing Higher Education with Mobile Learning Technologies Cases, Trends, and Inquiry-Based Methods
Jared Keengwe (University of North Dakota, USA) and Marian B. Maxfield (Ashland University, USA)
Information Science Reference • copyright 2015 • 364pp • H/C (ISBN: 9781466662841) • US $195.00 (our price)

Handbook of Research on Higher Education in the MENA Region Policy and Practice
Neeta Baporikar (Ministry of Higher Education, Oman)
Information Science Reference • copyright 2014 • 527pp • H/C (ISBN: 9781466661981) • US $315.00 (our price)

Advancing Knowledge in Higher Education Universities in Turbulent Times
Tanya Fitzgerald (La Trobe University, Australia)
Information Science Reference • copyright 2014 • 337pp • H/C (ISBN: 9781466662025) • US $195.00 (our price)

Cases on Teacher Identity, Diversity, and Cognition in Higher Education
Paul Breen (Greenwich School of Management, UK)
Information Science Reference • copyright 2014 • 437pp • H/C (ISBN: 9781466659902) • US $195.00 (our price)

Handbook of Research on Trends in European Higher Education Convergence
Alina Mihaela Dima (Bucharest Academy of Economic Studies, Romania)
Information Science Reference • copyright 2014 • 516pp • H/C (ISBN: 9781466659988) • US $315.00 (our price)

Overcoming Challenges in Software Engineering Education Delivering Non-Technical Knowledge and Skills
Liguo Yu (Indiana University South Bend, USA)

www.igi-global.com

701 E. Chocolate Ave., Hershey, PA 17033
Order online at www.igi-global.com or call 717-533-8845 x100
To place a standing order for titles released in this series, contact: cust@igi-global.com
Mon-Fri 8:00 am - 5:00 pm (est) or fax 24 hours a day 717-533-8661

Editorial Advisory Board

Table of Contents

Section 1
State of the Art

Anabela de Jesus Gomes, Coimbra Institute of Engineering, Portugal & University of
Coimbra, Portugal
António José Mendes, University of Coimbra, Portugal
Maria José Marcelino, University of Coimbra, Portugal

Amine V. Bitar, University of Balamand, Lebanon
Antoine M. Melki, University of Balamand, Lebanon

Sema A. Kalaian, Eastern Michigan University, USA
Rafa M. Kasim, Indiana Tech University, USA

J. Ángel Velázquez-Iturbide, Universidad Rey Juan Carlos, Spain
Ouafae Debdi, Universidad Rey Juan Carlos, Spain
Maximiliano Paredes-Velasco, Universidad Rey Juan Carlos, Spain

Section 2
Teaching Strategies

Section 3
Frameworks and Tools

Detailed Table of Contents

Section 1
State of the Art

Chapter 1

*Anabela de Jesus Gomes, Coimbra Institute of Engineering, Portugal & University of
Coimbra, Portugal*
António José Mendes, University of Coimbra, Portugal
Maria José Marcelino, University of Coimbra, Portugal

This chapter aims to present and summarize a variety of research areas that directly or indirectly have influenced Computer Science Education Research, particularly associated to the teaching and learning of programming. It is known that many students encounter a lot of difficulties in introductory programming courses. Possible reasons for these difficulties are discussed and some existing proposals in the literature are presented. Based on this discussion, the chapter also includes a description of work done at the University of Coimbra, trying to define more adequate pedagogical strategies for introductory programming courses. The results obtained and their implementation in a common undergraduate course are presented and discussed. The authors conclude that this new strategy makes learning more stimulating for the students, minimizes dropout intentions, and makes the students learn more and better. The chapter ends with suggestions of future research opportunities within the topic of teaching and learning of programming.

Chapter 2

Amine V. Bitar, University of Balamand, Lebanon
Antoine M. Melki, University of Balamand, Lebanon

Social computing systems such as Social Network Sites have become more powerful. In some universities, SNSs have been adopted as a communication method between teachers and students. In addition, educational institutions have started the initiative of using open source social networking application. This chapter discusses the benefits of adopting open source SNS in education. It is organized as follows: 1) a literature review to properly define the terms, 2) a discussion of the effect of open source social networking technologies on education systems, 3) an overview of Elgg, followed by a comparison with different social learning platforms, 4) a case study of implementing Elgg at the Computer Science Department at the University of Balamand, 5) an exhibition of the requirements for the Next Generation SCORM, 6) a case study using Tin Can API with open source SNSs (Elgg), and 7) a conclusion wrapping up the chapter.

Sema A. Kalaian, Eastern Michigan University, USA
Rafa M. Kasim, Indiana Tech University, USA

The focus of this meta-analytic chapter was to quantitatively integrate and synthesize the accumulated pedagogical research that examined the effectiveness of one of the various small-group learning methods in maximizing students' academic achievement in undergraduate computer science classrooms. The results of the meta-analysis show that cooperative, collaborative, problem-based, and pair learning pedagogies were used in college-level computer science classrooms with an overall average effect-size of 0.41. The results of the multilevel analysis reveal that the effect sizes were heterogeneous and the effects were explored further by including the coded predictors in the conditional multilevel model in efforts to explain the variability. The results of the conditional multilevel model reveal that the effect sizes were influenced significantly by both instructional duration and assessment type of the studies. The findings imply that the present evidence-based research supports the effectiveness of active small-group learning methods in promoting students' achievement in computer science classrooms.

J. Ángel Velázquez-Iturbide, Universidad Rey Juan Carlos, Spain
Ouafae Debdi, Universidad Rey Juan Carlos, Spain
Maximiliano Paredes-Velasco, Universidad Rey Juan Carlos, Spain

Algorithmics is an important core subject matter in computer science education. In particular, optimization algorithms are some of the most difficult to master because their problem statement includes an additional property, namely optimality. The chapter contains a comprehensive survey of the teaching and learning through practice of optimization algorithms. In particular, three important issues are reviewed. Firstly, the authors review educational methods which partially or completely address optimization algorithms. Secondly, educational software systems are reviewed and classified according to technical and educational criteria. Thirdly, students' difficulties and misunderstandings regarding optimization algorithms are presented. The chapter intends to consolidate current knowledge about the education of this class of algorithms for both computer science teachers and computer science education researchers.

Section 2
Teaching Strategies

Chapter 5

Ana M. Pessoa, Polytechnic Institute of Porto, Portugal
Luis Coelho, Polytechnic Institute of Porto, Portugal
Ruben Fernandes, Polytechnic Institute of Porto, Portugal

Massive Open Online Courses (MOOC) are gaining prominence in transversal teaching-learning strategies. However, there are many issues still debated, namely assessment, recognized largely as a cornerstone in Education. The large number of students involved requires a redefinition of strategies that often use approaches based on tasks or challenging projects. In these conditions and due to this approach, assessment is made through peer-reviewed assignments and quizzes online. The peer-reviewed assignments are often based upon sample answers or topics, which guide the student in the task of evaluating peers. This chapter analyzes the grading and evaluation in MOOCs, especially in science and engineering courses, within the context of education and grading methodologies and discusses possible perspectives to pursue grading quality in massive e-learning courses.

Chapter 6

Štefan Korečko, Technical University of Košice, Slovakia
Ján Sorád, Technical University of Košice, Slovakia

Because of the current trend of massification of higher education, motivation of students is a serious issue, especially in courses closely related to mathematics. The ones that undoubtedly belong to this group are courses dealing with formal methods for software development, such as Z notation, B-Method, or VDM. The chapter shows how a customized simulation game can be used to bring a domain typical for utilization of formal methods, the railway domain, to students and thus motivate them to learn these sophisticated ways of software development. By means of two examples, it demonstrates that such a tool, despite its limited scope, can be used to teach a variety of concepts related to formal methods. It also discusses related approaches to teaching formal methods, describes the customized game and its application in teaching, and evaluates experience with the application.

Chapter 7

Maria João Varanda Pereira, Instituto Politécnico de Bragança, Portugal
Nuno Oliveira, Universidade do Minho, Portugal
Daniela da Cruz, Universidade do Minho, Portugal
Pedro Rangel Henriques, Universidade do Minho, Portugal

All of us that teach Language Processing topics are aware that a great part of the students face big difficulties and a lack of motivation inherent to the concept abstraction level and to the technical capacities required to implement efficient processors. In order to overcome this problem, a starting point is to identify the main concepts involved in Language Processing subject and to consider that a person learns when he/she is involved in a process. The authors argue that motivation is a crucial factor to engage students in the course work, and it is highly dependent on the languages used to work on during the course. Therefore, they discuss the characteristics that a language should have to be a motivating case study. The authors think that LP teachers should be very careful in their choices and be astute in the way they explore the underlying grammars along the course evolution.

Chapter 8

M. Costa Neves, SportTools – Technology for Sport Company, Portugal
M. Ramires, SportTools – Technology for Sport Company, Portugal
J. Carvalho, Polytechnic Institute of Setúbal, Portugal
M. Piteira, Polytechnic Institute of Setúbal, Portugal
J. Santos, Polytechnic Institute of Setúbal, Portugal
N. Folgôa, Polytechnic Institute of Setúbal, Portugal
M. Boavida, Polytechnic Institute of Setúbal, Portugal

Learning computer programming is for most of the new students a difficult task. Besides the computer language learning of the syntax and all the aspects related with the compiler or the IDE environment, programming also has its artistic counterpart, where the individual personality is indissociable of the way he programs. Therefore, the main difficulties identified in students are closely related with aspects of their personality: self-confidence, resiliency, creativity, and autonomy. The sports science approach emerged naturally as all the authors were involved in high performance training for several years. The personality characteristics one needs to develop in students are similar to elite sports athletes in order to cope with the stress associated with their activity. In this chapter, the authors present a case study that took place at the Polytechnic Institute of Setubal with 28 students with different backgrounds and a workload of 8 hours per day.

Section 3
Frameworks and Tools

Chapter 9

Ricardo Queirós, Polytecnic Institute of Porto, Portugal & University of Porto, Portugal
José Paulo Leal, CRACS & INESC-Porto LA, Faculty of Sciences, University of Porto, Porto, Portugal

Currently, the teaching-learning process in domains, such as computer programming, is characterized by an extensive curricula and a high enrolment of students. This poses a great workload for faculty and teaching assistants responsible for the creation, delivery, and assessment of student exercises. The main goal of this chapter is to foster practice-based learning in complex domains. This objective is attained with an e-learning framework—called Ensemble—as a conceptual tool to organize and facilitate technical interoperability among services. The Ensemble framework is used on a specific domain: computer programming. Content issues are tacked with a standard format to describe programming exercises as learning objects. Communication is achieved with the extension of existing specifications for the interoperation with several systems typically found in an e-learning environment. In order to evaluate the acceptability of the proposed solution, an Ensemble instance was validated on a classroom experiment with encouraging results.

Chapter 10

M. Antón-Rodríguez, University of Valladolid, Spain
M. A. Pérez-Juárez, University of Valladolid, Spain
M. I. Jiménez-Gómez, University of Valladolid, Spain
F. J. Díaz-Pernas, University of Valladolid, Spain
M. Martínez-Zarzuela, University of Valladolid, Spain
D. González-Ortega, University of Valladolid, Spain

The challenge to prepare the graduates for working in a constantly changing environmen like software engineering requires an effective learning framework. This chapter presents a tool, integrated in the Moodle learning management system, that allows students to train the process of designing relational databases. The tool also allows them to practice with SQL queries that are executed over relational databases previously designed. This chapter also describes the result of a qualitative analysis of its use in an engineering course offered at the University of Valladolid and focused on the teaching of the Web applications development. The results of the refereed study reveal that the tool was found useful by both students and teachers to support the teaching and learning process of relational databases.

Chapter 11

André Baltazar, Catholic University of Portugal, Portugal
Luís Gustavo Martins, Catholic University of Portugal, Portugal

Computer programming is not an easy task, and as with all difficult tasks, it can be faced as tedious, impossible to do, or as a challenge. Therefore, learning to program with a purpose enables that "challenge mindset" and encourages the student to apply himself in overcoming his handicaps and exploring different theories and methods to achieve his goal. This chapter describes the process of programming a framework with the purpose of achieving real time human gesture recognition. Just this is already a good challenge, but the ultimate goal is to enable new ways of Human-Computer Interaction through expressive gestures and to allow a performer the possibility of controlling (with his gestures), in real time, creative artistic events. The chapter starts with a review on human gesture recognition. Then it presents the framework architecture, its main modules, and algorithms. It closes with the description of two artistic applications using the ZatLab framework.

Chapter 12

Teaching and learning computer programming is as challenging as it is difficult. Assessing the work of students and providing individualised feedback is time-consuming and error prone for teachers and frequently involves a time delay. The existent tools prove to be insufficient in domains where there is a greater need to practice. At the same time, Massive Open Online Courses (MOOC) are appearing, revealing a new way of learning. However, this paradigm raises serious questions regarding the monitoring of student progress and its timely feedback. This chapter provides a conceptual design model for a computer programming learning environment. It uses the portal interface design model, gathering information from a network of services such as repositories, program evaluators, and learning management systems, a central piece in the MOOC realm. This model is not limited to the domain of computer programming and can be adapted to any area that requires evaluation with immediate feedback.

Foreword

Computer science is an emergent, scientific, and practical approach that deals with the theoretical foundations of information and computation, combined with techniques for their implementation and application. As a discipline, computer science ranges from theoretical studies of algorithm correctness and complexity to the practical issues of implementing computing systems.

Computing Sciences Accreditation Board (CSAB)—represented by the Association for Computing Machinery (ACM) and the IEEE Computer Society (IEEE-CS)—identifies four key areas to the discipline of computer science: theory of computation, algorithms and data structures, programming methodology and languages, and computer elements and architecture. In addition to these four areas, CSAB also identifies other important fields of computer science such as software engineering, artificial intelligence, computer networking and telecommunications, database systems, parallel and distributed computation, computer-human interaction, computer graphics, and operating systems.

Major growth in the European Union is expected to occur in services based on information, finance, communications technology, electronic commerce, mobile applications, and games. These types of applications demand computer science skills to strengthen the field as one of the most important in the new century, as well justifying its inclusion in the curricula of all levels of education in schools.

Despite the importance of computer science, high failure and dropout rates are very common in introductory programming courses in many education institutions worldwide. This situation affects mostly novice students, since those courses are usually placed at the beginning of the curricula. Many causes for the learning difficulties have already been identified, from subject complexity to teaching methodologies and pedagogical strategies. Other causes are also identified related with the student background knowledge.

Several approaches have been proposed in the literature, ranging from psychological studies to computer-based teaching tools. The introduction of specialised services to automate tasks traditionally made by teachers (for instance, evaluation) is one of the biggest trends, but its use is not yet widespread, primarily due to interoperability issues and the scarce number of available programming exercises. In addition, worldwide initiatives have also been appearing to try to motivate young people to learn to program computers, therefore reducing the gap regarding student background knowledge. Despite all these efforts, the situation remains mostly unchanged.

This book provides a valuable window on information for computer science teachers presenting different solutions to foster computer science education. These solutions include the use of new strategies and approaches for teaching computer programming and the use of new frameworks and e-learning tools to motivate novice students to break the barrier of learning computer programming.

The first section, titled "State of the Art," presents several reviews regarding the teaching and learning of programming, more precisely, pedagogical strategies for introductory programming courses, the use of open source networks in education, and the adoption of small-group versus competitive learning in computer science classrooms.

Follows a section, "Teaching Strategies," presents different perspectives on how teachers can foster computer science education. One such strategy is using the emergent concept of Massive Open Online Courses (MOOC) to facilitate the access, dissemination, and communication of knowledge using the Web as the main vehicle. Other trend strategies use simulation games as educational approaches to motivate students to learn by using video game design and game elements in learning environments. The goal is to maximise enjoyment and engagement through capturing the interest of learners and inspiring them to continue learning.

Finally, the third section focuses on "Frameworks and Tools" and presents several models to help with the computer programming teaching-learning process. Many of the solutions presented rely on specialised Web services responsible by the storage, dissemination, evaluation, and classification of the students' progress. These 24x7 services are essential for the 21st century novice students. One such service is the assessment system that allow students to practice programming, anytime and anywhere. This feature represents the cornerstone of computer programming learning, since often one of the major barriers to learning computing is related to the lack of monitoring and feedback from teachers outside of class periods. These automatic evaluators analyse the resolution of students and provide readable and relevant feedback guiding students in a more autonomous manner.

In conclusion, in my point of view, all the pedagogical and technological strategies presented in the book are excellent educational contributions for the challenging field of computer science, more precisely, for one of its main areas, computer programming.

Alberto Simões
Universidade do Minho, Portugal

Alberto Simões *is a PhD in Natural Language Processing affiliated with the Polytechnic Institute of Cávado and Ave (Portugal) and works as a researcher at the Centre for Humanistic Studies of the University of Minho. His research interests focus on parallel corpora alignment, probabilistic translation dictionaries, and bilingual terminology extraction. Some of his major publications are "NATools: A Statistical Word Aligner Workbench," in Procesamiento del Lenguaje Natural, 31 (2003), "Makefile: Parallel Dependency Specification Language," in Anne-Marie Kermarrec, Luc Bougé, and Thierry Priol, editors, Euro-Parl 2007, volume 4641, and "Portuguese English Word Alignment: Some Experiments," in LREC 2008 – The 6th Language and Resources Evaluation Conference, Marrakech (2008).*

Preface

Everybody should learn how to program a computer because it teaches you how to think. - Steve Jobs

Computer Science is the study of computers and algorithmic processes, including their principles, their hardware and software designs, their applications, and their impact on society (Tucker, 2006).

In the education context, Computer Science encompasses several topics such as algorithmic problem-solving, computing and data analysis, human-computer interaction, programming, security, Web design, robotics, and many others. In Computer Science courses, students develop computational and critical thinking skills and how to create, not simply use, new technologies. This fundamental knowledge is crucial to prepare students for the 21st century, eager for people with this training, regardless of their ultimate field of study or occupation, such as:

- **Arts:** Designing, developing, and composing digital music and special effects for movies;
- **Finances:** Designing and overseeing automated trading services;
- **Healthcare:** Designing and developing security and privacy for medical records or new remote monitoring systems for patients;
- **Information Technology:** Designing and developing software and hardware systems for mobile communication devices, networks, applications, and games;
- **Manufacturing:** Designing, developing, and using simulations to improve products;
- **Retail:** Analyzing data to predict trends and improve inventory management;
- **Weather Forecasting:** Designing, developing, and interpreting models to predict the behavior of the weather (for instance, hurricanes).

In fact, the United States Bureau of Labor Statistics predicts that one in every two Science, Technology, Engineering, and Math (STEM) jobs will be in computing in 2020, with more than 150k job openings annually, making it one of the fastest growing occupations. The other important point is that these jobs will pay 75 percent more than the national median annual salary.

These predictions and the breadth of new ways in which computing knowledge prepares people for multiple careers demands even more the inclusion of foundational computer science courses in all levels of education, such as K–12. These courses aims to teach the basic and core concepts of computing, such as abstraction, creativity, algorithms, programming, and Internet, that are fundamental to computer science and also suitable to many others disciplines.

In this context, several organizations are bringing Computer Science classes to every K-12 school. One that stands out is Code.org. This non-profit organization, led by brothers Hadi and Ali Partovi, aims to motivate people, especially school students in the United States, to learn to code. Their website includes free coding lessons and encourages them to include more computer science classes in the curriculum. On December 2013, Code.org launched the Hour of Code 2013 challenge nationwide to promote computer science. Some of the most important tech companies and their founders, including Bill Gates and Mark Zuckerberg, have put up about $10 million for Code.org.

THE CHALLENGES

Despite the need to learn Computer Science by every student in every school, there are many issues that must be addressed.

Introductory programming courses are characterized by an extensive curricula and a high enrolment of students. This poses a great workload for faculty and teaching assistants responsible for the creation, delivery, and assessment of student exercises. These courses are also regarded as difficult and often have high failure and dropout rates. Researchers have pointed out several causes for these rates from teaching methods (lectures on programming language syntaxes), from the lack of feedback to the subject complexity. In fact, learning how to program means integrating knowledge of a wide variety of conceptual domains, such as computer science and mathematics, while developing expertise in problem understanding, problem solving, unit testing, and other skills. Additionally, students peter out when they need to understand and apply abstract programming concepts like control structures or when they need to create algorithms that solve concrete problems. All these issues pose huge challenges in the computer programming teaching-learning process.

Some key points for the success of this process are practice and feedback. For someone to acquire, improve, or even maintain a complex skill, it is necessary to practice it on a regular basis (Gross & Powers, 2005; Eckerdal, 2009). The amount of practice required depends on the nature of the activity and on each individual. How well an individual improves with practice is directly related with her or his inherent aptitudes, previous know-how, and on the feedback. If feedback is either non-existent or inappropriate, then the practice tends to be ineffective or even detrimental to learning.

There are several complex skills that require constant practice, where exercise solving is a key component, such as management, health sciences, and electronics. Playing business games in management courses, or simulating a human patient in life sciences courses, or simulating an electronic circuit in electronics courses are examples of learning processes that require the use of special authoring, rendering, and assessment tools. These tools should be integrated into instructional environments in order to provide a better learning experience. However, these tools would be too specific to incorporate in an e-learning platform. Even if they could be provided as pluggable components, the burden of maintaining them would be prohibitive to institutions with few courses in those domains.

This book reflects yet another domain with complex evaluation: computer programming. Introductory programming courses are generally regarded as difficult and often have high failure and dropout rates (Ala-Mutka, 2005; O'Kelly & Gibson, 2006; Robins, Rountree, & Rountree, 2003). Researchers pointed out several causes for these rates (Esteves, Fonseca, Morgado, & Martins, 2010). The most consensual are:

- **Teaching Methods:** Lectures and programming language syntaxes (Lahtinen, Ala-Mutka, & Jarvinen, 2005; Schulte, Carsten, & Bennedsen, 2006);
- **Subject Complexity:** Learning how to program means integrating knowledge of a wide variety of conceptual domains such as computer science and mathematics while developing expertise in

problem understanding, problem solving, unit testing, and others. Additionally, students petered out when they needed to understand and apply abstract programming concepts like control structures or to create algorithms that solve concrete problems (Esteves et al., 2010).

- **Student Motivation:** The public image of a "programmer" as a socially inadequate "nerd" (Jenkins, 2002) and the reputation of programming courses as being extremely difficult negatively affects the motivation of the students (Gomes & Mendes, 2007).

Many educators claim that "learning through practice" is by far the best way to learn computer programming and to engage novice students (Gross & Powers, 2005; Eckerdal, 2009). Practice in this area boils down to solving programming exercises. Nevertheless, solving exercises is only effective if students receive an assessment on their work. An exercise solved wrong will consolidate a false belief, and without feedback, many students will not be able to overcome their difficulties.

Assessment plays a vital role in learning (Ala-Mutka, 2005). However, automatic assessment of exercises other than multiple choice can be a rather complex task. This kind of evaluation differs significantly from evaluations supported by most LMSs, encoded in the IMS Question and Test Interoperability (IMS QTI) specification. The data model of QTI was designed for questions with a set of pre-defined answers and cannot handle evaluation domains with specialized requirements such as the computer programming. For instance, the assessment of programming exercises requires tests cases, program solutions, compilation lines, and other data that cannot be encoded in QTI. Besides the lack of a formal description for programming exercises, the interaction of assessment tools with other systems is not mature enough since there is no communication specifications as stated in several surveys (Leal & Queirós, 2010; Queirós & Leal, 2011).

Automatic assessment in computer programming domains can be applied in two distinct learning contexts: curricular and competitive learning.

Introductory programming courses are part of the curricula of many engineering and sciences programs. These courses rely on programming exercises, assignments, and practical examinations to consolidate knowledge and evaluate students. The enrolment in these courses is usually very high, resulting in a great workload for the faculty and teaching assistants responsible for assessing student programs.

While the concept of "winners and losers" can hinder the motivation of students (Vansteenkiste & Deci, 2003), competitive learning is a learning paradigm that relies on the competitiveness of students to increase their programming skills (Burguillo, 2010; Siddiqui, Khan, & Akhtar, 2008). This is the common goal of several programming contests where students at different levels compete, such as the International Olympiad in Informatics (IOI) for secondary school students, the ACM International Collegiate Programming Contest (ICPC) for university students, and the IEEExtreme for IEEE student members. In this context, several tools are used to allow students to train or participate in programming contests. These tools, such as Programming Contests Management Systems (PCMS) and Online Judges (OJ), rely also on the assessment of programming exercises.

In both scenarios, the manual assessment of programming assignments poses significant demands on the time of teachers (Douce, Livingstone, & Orwell, 2005). Apart from being time-consuming, manual assessment hinders the consistency and accuracy of assessment results as well as allowing unintended biases and a diverse standard of marking schemes (Romli, Sulaiman, & Zamli, 2010). This demand stimulated the development of automated learning and assessment systems in many universities (Ala-Mutka, 2005) as a means for grading the programming exercises of students as well as giving feedback on the quality of their solutions (Tremblay, Guérin, Pons, & Salah, 2008; Spacco, Hovemeyer, & Pugh,

2006). This feedback support is crucial for the computer programming learning (Wang & Wong, 2008; Mory, 2007), especially for first-year students who need to be adequately engaged in order to learn programming (Jena, 2002). Furthermore, immediate feedback motivates students to continue practising (Daly, 1999; Truong, 2007).

Beyond the automatic assessment, another relevant topic in this domain is the availability of programming exercises. It is important that an e-learning system provides a collection of exercises covering a course syllabus and with different levels of difficulty. It has been shown that this can improve the performance of students and their satisfaction levels (Wang & Wong, 2008). Students with lower computer skills can begin by solving easier problems in order to learn progressively and to stay motivated to solve the harder problems later. At the same time, this gives them experience, which is one of the factors that has a large influence on student success in learning programming. In recent years, a large number of programming exercises have been developed and published mostly for use in programming contests. These exercises are generally stored in proprietary systems (e.g. Online Judges) for their own use. Despite some efforts (Queirós & Leal, 2012) to define a common format to describe programming exercises, each of these systems has its own exercise format, making it difficult to share among instructors and students. This poses several issues on the interoperability of the assessment systems with other e-learning systems.

A number of learning tools and environments have been built to assist both teachers and students in introductory programming courses. Rongas, Kaarna, and Kalviainen (2004) established a classification for these tools dividing them into four categories:

1. Integrated development interfaces,
2. Visualization tools,
3. Virtual learning environments, and
4. Systems for submitting, managing, and testing exercises.

To the best of the editor's knowledge, no e-learning environment described in the literature integrates all these facets (Verdú, Regueras, Verdú, Leal, Castro, & Queirós, 2011; Gomes & Mendes, 2007; Esteves et al., 2010).

Several systems (Jena, 2008; Verdú et al., 2011; Xavier & Coelho, 2011; Guerreiro & Georgouli, 2008) try to address this issue allowing the integration of automatic assessment tools with course management systems, but these approaches rely on ad hoc solutions or proprietary plug-ins rather on widely accepted international specifications for content description and communication among systems.

DESCRIPTION AND ORGANIZATION OF THE BOOK

This book presents a comprehensive and recent view of the issues of learning computer programming and shows different pedagogical and technological strategies to address these issues. At the same time, it identifies new trends on this topic from pedagogical strategies to technological approaches.

The book is organized into 12 chapters. A brief description of each of the chapters follows:

Chapter 1 presents and summarizes a variety of research areas that directly or indirectly have influenced Computer Science Education Research, particularly associated to the teaching and learning of programming. The chapter also includes a description of work done at the University of Coimbra, trying to define more adequate pedagogical strategies for introductory programming courses.

Chapter 2 discusses new trends on Computer Science Education, such as the use of open source social networking in education. A comparison with different social learning platforms and new e-learning standards and specifications is made to clarify the benefits of their adoption.

Chapter 3 discusses the effectiveness of one of the various small-group learning methods in maximizing students' academic achievement in undergraduate computer science classrooms. The findings imply that the present evidence-based research supports the effectiveness of active small-group learning methods in promoting students' achievement in computer science classrooms.

Chapter 4 contains a comprehensive survey of the teaching and learning through practice of optimization algorithms. In particular, three important issues are reviewed: educational methods, educational software systems, and students' difficulties. The survey intends to consolidate current knowledge about the education of this class of algorithms for both computer science teachers and computer science education researchers.

Chapter 5 analyzes the grading and evaluation in Massive Open Online Courses (MOOC), especially in science and engineering courses, within the context of education and grading methodologies, and discusses possible perspectives to pursue grading quality in massive e-learning courses.

Chapter 6 shows how a customized simulation game can be used to bring a domain typical for utilization of formal methods, the railway domain, to students and thus motivate them to learn these sophisticated ways of software development. By means of two examples, it demonstrates that such a tool, despite its limited scope, can be used to teach a variety of concepts related to formal methods. It also discusses related approaches to teaching formal methods, describes the customized game and its application in teaching, and evaluates experiences with the application.

Chapter 7 identifies the difficulties that lead students of Language Processing (LP) courses to fail: the level of abstraction associated with some of the basic concepts in the area and the technical capacities required to implement efficient processors, which negatively affect the students' motivation to learn the main topics. It also discusses the characteristics that a language should have to be a motivating case study.

Chapter 8 presents a sports science approach to address the difficulties of learning computer programming closely related with aspects of personality: self-confidence, resiliency, creativity, and autonomy. The sports science approach emerged naturally as all the authors were involved in high performance training for several years, as coaches, athletes, or psychologists of an elite Women's Match Racing Team. The chapter presents a case study that took place at the Polytechnic Institute of Setubal with 28 students with different backgrounds and a workload of 8 hours per day.

Chapter 9 presents an e-learning framework defined as a conceptual tool to organize and facilitate technical interoperability among systems and services in domains that use complex evaluation. These domains need a diversity of tools, from the environments where exercises are solved to automatic evaluators providing feedback on the attempts of students, not forgetting the authoring, management, and sequencing of exercises. The Ensemble framework is used on a specific domain, computer programming, and its acceptability is validated on a classroom experiment with encouraging results.

Chapter 10 presents a tool, integrated in the Moodle learning management system, that allows students to train the process of designing relational databases. The tool also allows them to practice with SQL queries that are executed over relational databases previously designed. This chapter also describes the result of a qualitative analysis of the tool's use in an engineering course offered at the University of Valladolid and focused on the teaching of the Web applications development. The results of the refereed study reveal that the tool was found useful by both students and teachers to support the teaching and learning process of relational databases.

Chapter 11 describes the process of programming a framework with the purpose of achieving real time human gesture recognition. This is already a challenge, but the ultimate goal is to enable new ways of Human-Computer Interaction trough expressive gestures and to allow a performer the possibility of controlling (with his gestures), in real time, artistic events.

Chapter 12 provides a conceptual design model for a computer programming learning environment. This environment uses the portal interface design model gathering information from a network of services such as repositories and program evaluators. The design model includes integration with learning management systems, a central piece in the MOOC realm, endowing the model with characteristics such as scalability, collaboration, and interoperability.

CONCLUSION

This book presents innovative teaching strategies and new learning paradigms in the computer programming domain. The main contribution of the book is that it can be summarized as a valuable resource for practitioners and as a reference for research scholars and computer science teachers and students pursuing computer science-related subjects.

This book clearly impacts the field and contributes with new trends to foster computer science education. In a world where technological advances appear at a dizzying pace, all computer science educators must keep up with these changes and adapt teaching methodologies in order to enhance the study of computer programming and motivate students to achieve this complex but exciting and emerging area.

Ricardo Queirós
Polytechnic Institute of Porto, Portugal

REFERENCES

Ala-Mutka, K. (2005). A survey of automated assessment approaches for programming assignments. *Journal of Computer Science Education, 15*(2), 83–102. doi:10.1080/08993400500150747

Burguillo, J. C. (2010). Using game theory and competition-based learning to stimulate student motivation and performance. *Computers & Education, 55*(2), 566–575. doi:10.1016/j.compedu.2010.02.018

Daly, C. (1999). Roboprof and an introductory computer programming course. *SIGCSE Bulletin, 31*(3), 155–158. doi:10.1145/384267.305904

Douce, C., Livingstone, D., & Orwell, J. (2005). Automatic testbased assessment of programming: A review. *Journal of Educational Resources in Computing, 5*.

Eckerdal, A. (2009). *Novice programming students' learning of concepts and practice*. (Unpublished doctoral dissertation). Uppsala University, Uppsala, Sweden.

Esteves, M., Fonseca, B., Morgado, L., & Martins, P. (2010). Improving teaching and learning of computer programming through the use of the Second Life virtual world. *British Journal of Educational Technology*. doi: doi:10.1111/j.1467-8535.2010.01056.x

Gomes, A., & Mendes, A. J. (2007). Learning to program – Difficulties and solutions. In *Proceedings of the International Conference on Engineering Education*. Academic Press.

Gross, P., & Powers, K. (2005). Evaluating assessments of novice programming environments. In *Proceedings of the First International Workshop on Computing Education Research* (pp. 99-110). New York: ACM. doi: doi:10.1145/1089786.1089796

Guerreiro, P., & Georgouli, K. (2008). Enhancing elementary programming courses using e-learning with a competitive attitude. *International Journal of Internet Education*.

Jena, S. (2008). *Authoring and sharing of programming exercises*. (Unpublished Master's Thesis). San Jose State University.

Jenkins, T. (2002). On the difficulty of learning to program. In *Proceedings of 3rd Annual Conference of LTSN-ICS*. Retrieved from http://www.ics.ltsn.ac.uk/pub/conf2002/tjenkins.pdf

Lahtinen, E., Ala-Mutka, K., & Jarvinen, H.-M. (2005). A study of the difficulties of novice programmers. *SIGCSE Bulletin, 37*(3), 14–18. doi:10.1145/1151954.1067453

Leal, J. P., & Queirós, R. (2010). *E-learning frameworks: A survey*. Paper presented at the International Technology, Education and Development Conference. Valencia, Spain.

Mory, E. H. (2007). *Feedback research revisited*. Association for Educational Communications and Technology.

O'Kelly, J., & Gibson, J. P. (2006, June). Robocode & problem based learning: A non-prescriptive approach to teaching programming. *SIGCSE Bulletin, 38*(3), 217–221. doi:10.1145/1140123.1140182

Queirós, R., & Leal, J. P. (2011). A survey on elearning content standardization. In *Proceedings of World Summit on the Knowledge Society*. Springer Verlag.

Queirós, R., & Leal, J. P. (2012). Petcha - A programming exercises teaching assistant. In *Proceedings of ACM SIGCSE 17th Annual Conference on Innovation and Technology in Computer Science Education*. ACM Press.

Robins, A., Rountree, J., & Rountree, N. (2003). Learning and teaching programming: A review and discussion. *Computer Science Education, 13*(2), 137–172. doi:10.1076/csed.13.2.137.14200

Romli, R., Sulaiman, S., & Zamli, K. Z. (2010). Automatic programming assessment and test data generation: A review on its approaches. [ITSim]. *Proceedings of Information Technology, 3*, 1186–1192.

Rongas, T., Kaarna, A., & Kalviainen, H. (2004). Classification of computerized learning tools for introductory programming courses: Learning approach. In *Proceedings of ICALT*. IEEE Computer Society. doi:10.1109/ICALT.2004.1357618

Schulte, C., & Bennedsen, J. (2006). What do teachers teach in introductory programming? In *Proceedings of the Second International Workshop on Computing Education Research* (ICER '06) (pp. 17–28). New York: ACM. doi:10.1145/1151588.1151593

Siddiqui, A., Khan, M., & Akhtar, S. (2008). Supply chain simulator: A scenario-based educational tool to enhance student learning. *Computers & Education, 51*(1), 252–261. doi:10.1016/j.compedu.2007.05.008

Spacco, J., Hovemeyer, D., Pugh, W., Emad, F., Hollingsworth, J. K., & Padua-Perez, N. (2006). Experiences with marmoset: Designing and using an advanced submission and testing system for programming courses. *SIGCSE Bulletin, 38*(3), 13–17. doi:10.1145/1140123.1140131

Tremblay, G., Guérin, F., Pons, A., & Salah, A. (2008). Oto, a generic and extensible tool for marking programming assignments. *Software, Practice & Experience, 38*(3), 307–333. doi:10.1002/spe.839

Truong, N. K. D. (2007). A *web-based programming environment for novice programmers*. (PhD thesis). Queensland University of Technology, Brisbane, Australia.

Tucker, A. (Ed.). (2006). A model curriculum for K-12 computer science: Final report of the ACM K-12 task force curriculum committee (2nd ed.). New York: Association for Computing Machinery (ACM).

Vansteenkiste, M., & Deci, E. L. (2003). Competitively contingent rewards and intrinsic motivation: Can losers remain motivated? *Motivation and Emotion, 27*(4), 273–299. doi:10.1023/A:1026259005264

Verdú, E., Regueras, L. M., Verdú, M. J., Leal, J. P., Castro, J. P., & Queirós, R. (2011). A distributed system for learning programming on-line. *Computers & Education*.

Wang, F. L., & Wong, T.-L. (2008). Designing programming exercises with computer assisted instruction. In *Proceedings of the 1st International Conference on Hybrid Learning and Education* (ICHL '08), (pp. 283-293). Berlin: Springer-Verlag. doi:10.1007/978-3-540-85170-7_25

Xavier, J., & Coelho, A. (2011). Computer-based assessment system for e-learning applied to programming education. In *Proceedings of ICERI* (pp. 3738-3747). IATED.

Acknowledgment

I would like to acknowledge the help of all the people involved in this project and, more specifically, the authors and reviewers who took part in the review process. Without their support, this book would not have become a reality.

First, I would like to thank each one of the authors for their contributions. My sincere gratitude goes to the chapter authors who contributed their time and expertise to this book.

Second, I wish to acknowledge the valuable contributions of the reviewers regarding the improvement of quality, coherence, and content presentation of chapters. Most of the authors also served as referees; I highly appreciate their double task.

Third, I would like to express my thanks to the publishing team at IGI Global for their expert support and guidance, more precisely, to Erin O'Dea, Assistant Managing Editor of the Book Development Division.

This book is dedicated to my wife Márcia and my daughter Gabriela.

Ricardo Queirós
Polytechnic Institute of Porto, Portugal

Section 1
State of the Art

Chapter 1
Computer Science Education Research:
An Overview and Some Proposals

Anabela de Jesus Gomes
Coimbra Institute of Engineering, Portugal & University of Coimbra, Portugal

António José Mendes
University of Coimbra, Portugal

Maria José Marcelino
University of Coimbra, Portugal

ABSTRACT

This chapter aims to present and summarize a variety of research areas that directly or indirectly have influenced Computer Science Education Research, particularly associated to the teaching and learning of programming. It is known that many students encounter a lot of difficulties in introductory programming courses. Possible reasons for these difficulties are discussed and some existing proposals in the literature are presented. Based on this discussion, the chapter also includes a description of work done at the University of Coimbra, trying to define more adequate pedagogical strategies for introductory programming courses. The results obtained and their implementation in a common undergraduate course are presented and discussed. The authors conclude that this new strategy makes learning more stimulating for the students, minimizes dropout intentions, and makes the students learn more and better. The chapter ends with suggestions of future research opportunities within the topic of teaching and learning of programming.

INTRODUCTION

High failure and dropout rates are common in introductory programming courses in many high education institutions worldwide (Jenkins, 2002; Lahtinen, Ala-Mutka, & Järvinen, 2005; Lister, Simon, Thompson, Whalley, & Prasad, 2006). This is a situation that affects mostly novices as those courses are usually placed at the beginning of the curricula (Djisktra, 1989; Lee, Rodrigo, Baker,

DOI: 10.4018/978-1-4666-7304-5.ch001

Sugay, & Coronel, 2011; Lister, 2000). Many causes for the learning difficulties have already been identified (Bennedsen & Caspersen, 2006; Byrne & Lyons, 2001; Carbone, Ceddia, Simon, & Mason, 2013; Cook et al., 2012; Gray, Goldberg, & Byrnes, 2007; Jenkins, 2002; Lahtinen, Ala-Mutka, & Järvinen, 2005; Milne & Rowe, 2002; Stachel et al., 2013). It is possible to argue that difficulties are mainly related with the students' background knowledge, the nature of programming, the learning methods and study attitudes and the pedagogical strategies commonly used in introductory programming courses (Gomes & Mendes, 2007; Gomes & Mendes, 2008; Pacheco, Henriques, Almeida, & Mendes, 2008).

Different solutions have been proposed in the literature, but the situation remains mostly unchanged, as many novices continue to struggle to learn basic programming. Research in this field includes efforts in several areas, from psychological studies to computer-based tools. There are also some well-established journals and conferences devoted to this wide field. Fincher and Petre (2004) made a significant contribution to structure the Computer Science Education Research field, identifying several subareas that in some way orient and give focus to researchers in their studies (Kaufman, 2013; Porter, 2013).

We will also use Fincher and Petre work to organize this chapter, namely when we try to understand the developments on Computer Science Education Research that may help the process of teaching and learning programming to novices. This will be the focus of the chapter in its next section. The chapter progresses with a discussion about the factors, which make it difficult to learn introductory programming, leading to the proposal of some pedagogical principles that have been tested and put into practice with some success at our university. Some views on future trends in this field are also included before the chapter conclusion.

BACKGROUND ON COMPUTER SCIENCE EDUCATION RESEARCH AREAS

Research in education (teaching and learning) in computer science now covers a wide variety of topics. In order to explore issues related to the teaching and learning of programming, we must first situate them in the broader Computer Science Education Research area. We start with an overview of related research, structured according to the main research subfields defined in the book Computer Science Education Research, edited by Sally Fincher and Marian Petre (2004). In this book, the authors identified several major areas concerning education in computer science. Although the areas are not disjointed, this classification can be a useful tool for a better positioning when investigating a topic related to the teaching/learning of computer science. The mentioned areas are: Student Understanding; Animation, visualization and simulation; Teaching methods; Assessment; Educational Technology; Transferring professional practice into the classroom; Transferring from presence education to distance education; Recruitment and retention; Construction of the discipline.

Student Understanding

Research conducted in the student understanding area focuses mainly on the mental and conceptual models that students have about a particular subject matter and their conceptions and misconceptions about it. Many of the studies in this area try to understand why students have problems with a particular topic, concept or construction. Also in this area there are various studies related to skills, behaviours and attitudes that distinguish good students from poor students. The differences in terms of understanding and awareness between beginner students and experts are therefore objects of study in this area. The range of investigated topics is also vast and may include broader topics such as

"What program planning and design skills students have?" or "How students learn certain programming paradigms?" to more specific issues such as "How students learn recursion?" Existing research in this area is not specific to computer science, but rather conceived as a multidisciplinary research, often integrating aspects of science and cognitive psychology. We can cite PPIG (Psychology of Programming Interest Group) as a group with major developments in this area. Within this field, it is also worth considering the subareas that this group considers: psychological studies, conceptions and misconceptions, phenomenografic studies, behaviour of beginners in computer science and understanding of the educator. Psychological studies about programming were initiated in the 70s in the twentieth century. In the 80s, motivated by the growth of cognitive science, many researchers conducted surveys on the performance of novice programmers and the problems students faced in learning to program. Studies conducted by various authors, among which stood out Soloway and Spohrer, concluded that novice programmers can learn the syntax and semantics of individual instructions, but do not know how to combine them in order to produce valid programs (Soloway, 1986; Spohrer & Soloway, 1986). Spohrer and Soloway (1986) distinguish between difficulties based on the composition (difficulties in putting all the pieces together) and difficulties based on the construction (misconceptions about the structures of the language). These studies showed that students' difficulties are mostly due to composition problems and not to construction problems. The authors concluded that educators could help to improve the performance of their students by teaching them composition strategies. This result is consistent with previous studies by other researchers (Linn & Dalbey, 1985; Mayer, 1981) who analyzed the distinction between the ability to interpret programs (program understanding) and the ability to write or compose programs (program generation). The findings of Spohrer and Soloway were confirmed by similar research conducted in

the 90s. According to these, the ability to solve a problem requires skills that go beyond the syntax and semantics of a programming language. The errors in students' programs are generally not related to syntax but to poor problem-solving strategies and insufficient planning (Anjaneyulu, 1994; Scholtz & Wiedenbeck, 1992; Shackelford & Badre, 1993; Wiedenbeck, Fix, & Scholtz, 1993). Winslow (1996) states that students can learn the syntax and semantics of individual statements, but do not know how to combine them in order to generate valid programs. The same author concluded that there is very little correlation between the ability to write a program and the ability to interpret it. More recent studies confirm the persistence of these problems (Carbone, Ceddia, Simon, & Mason, 2013; Hawi, 2010; Kinnunen & Malmi, 2006; Lee, Rodrigo, Baker, Sugay, & Coronel, 2011; Stachel et al., 2013). According to the authors, the explanation for this failure is the lack of students' knowledge and skills to solve problems. That is, students are not able to break down a problem into sub problems, implement them and then merge all sub solutions in a complete solution. The working group "ITiCSE 2004" studied an alternative explanation. They argue that the students' knowledge is fragile in both basic programming principles and also in systematically carrying out routine programming tasks such as interpreting code (Lister et al., 2004). A continuation of the study regarding the understanding of programs is documented in Lister et al. (2006) using the SOLO taxonomy (Biggs & Collis, 1982). In this article the authors report the use of this taxonomy to test the programming knowledge of inexperienced programmers. The authors argue that teachers should use appropriate evaluation strategies, testing students at all levels of the taxonomy. A student should not only be able to interpret isolated lines of code, but should also know how to integrate them into a coherent structure and use that structure to solve the task: "... Students should be prepared to see the forest and not just the trees ...". According to these authors, students often lack the ability to interpret code and describe it in relational terms. So in these situations they are not intellectually equipped to write similar code. Other studies have concluded that students could not generate programs, understand them or project them to acceptable levels (Mead et al., 2006). Robins et al. (2003) provide a detailed review of the literature regarding the psychological/educational study of programming, reaching the following conclusion: "The main recommendation emerging from the literature is that education should focus not only on learning the characteristics of a specific programming language, but also the combination of those features and especially the underlying problem in the project of basic programs. One way of achieving this could be to introduce many examples as these programs are developed, discussing the used strategies as part of this process". Soloway suggested essentially the same twenty years ago (Soloway, 1986). Research shows that even with such a time lapse, students continue to fail to learn to program, particularly with the composition side of programming – how to link different programming pieces together.

Animation, Visualization, and Simulation

Many researchers in Computer Science Education are programmers who dedicate themselves to building systems, computer programs, in order to improve student learning. There are a wide variety of tools; most of them dedicated to the animation and visualization of algorithms and data structures (Ben-Ari, 2011; Naps et al., 2003). There were several classification proposals for these systems, such as the proposal of Kelleher and Pausch (2005). The underlying motivation to this area is to appeal to the potential of the human visual system. Thus, since the dynamics of computer programs can be difficult to grasp when presented in textual format, it is expected

that animated graphical formats can contribute to a better understanding.

After some enthusiasm around animation and visualization tools the attention of many researchers was directed towards its educational effectiveness (Salleha, Shukura, & Judib, 2013; Stone & Clark, 2013). We can cite, for example, studies by Hundhausen and colleagues concerning the effectiveness of algorithms visualizations. In these studies, they presented a comprehensive review of 24 controlled experiments, including a classification and analysis concerning learning theories underlying the various visualization types (Hundhausen, Douglas, & Stasko, 2002). The general conclusion was that the use of these tools seemed to have a high impact and educational effectiveness, allowing students to engage actively in the learning process. These authors add that students often make "what if" analysis of the algorithm behaviour, engaging in predicting exercises. The positive effect of using visualization of programs was also later documented (Ebel & Ben-Ari, 2006).

Teaching Methods

There are several aspects that motivate researchers in this area. Examples of how educators can "build bridges" for the students, providing better learning, are seen in the following. The work of Sopher and his colleagues (Sopher, Soloway, & Pope, 1985) on programming plans is a good example. Also the work on case studies conducted by Linn and Clancy had a major impact in this area (Linn & Clancy, 1992). These authors explain how some important program design principles can be applied in the creation of reasonably complex programs, and how they can help students develop important programming skills. The use of patterns is another example of efforts in this area, as documented in Astrachan and colleagues (1998). There is also some work motivated by findings in other areas where psychology and sociology stand out, relating to issues such as "active learning", "cognitive styles", "learning styles", among others. This is a very large area that Caspersen divided into six subareas: education centered on the learner/student, constructivism, case studies and learning, inverted curriculum, patterns and teaching/learning of object-oriented concepts (Caspersen, 2007).

Assessment

This area can be divided into three subfields: methods/types of evaluation, automated assessment and validity of the assessment. Some of the issues addressed in these areas relate to different types of evaluation. Trying to understand which ones are best suited for certain objectives or particular contexts, as well as what makes them effective. Research on automatic program evaluation systems can also be included in this area. For example, Ala-Mutka discussed a large number of these tools, detailing the strengths and weaknesses of each of them (Ala-Mutka, 2005). Other researchers look to understand if an assessment method actually assesses the type of knowledge or skills that the educator wants to evaluate (Fincher & Petre, 2004). Other issues under investigation in this area concern the authenticity of examinations and work done by students, as well as plagiarism (Dick et al., 2003; Lancaster & Culwin, 2004).

Educational Technology

In this context different types of tools have been developed, including special purpose integrated development environments (IDEs), microworlds for learning, algorithm animation systems, among other tools (Krushkov, Krushkova, Atanasov, & Krushkova, 2009; Roebling, 2012; Verdú, Regueras, Verdú, Leal, & Castro, 2012). Kelleher and Pausch (2005) made an extensive classification of such tools, developed over the past years and for different needs. Another study describes prelimi-

nary results of research related to programming teaching tools (Salleha, Shukura, & Judib, 2013).

Another aspect also prominent, but less explored in this area, relates to the use of more recent technologies in the context of the classroom. It is worth mentioning the use of tablet PCs and Personal Digital Assistants (PDAs) (Anderson et al., 2004; Denning, Griswold, Simon, & Wilkerson, 2006). Their results seem to indicate that the use of these technologies enhances learning (Koile & Singer, 2006). The authors report several improvements: an increase of student interest and attention in class; immediate feedback to the student and to the teacher (on the students' doubts); adjustment of the materials in real time according to the student's questions and answers and an increase of the student's satisfaction.

Also in this area it is particularly interesting to mention the use of robots, like LEGO Mindstorms robots and other types of robots to support programming learning with different purposes and in diverse contexts (Fagin & Merkle, 2003; McGill, 2012). Some authors use robots to motivate and involve students in algorithm design, trying to overcome the student's lack of problem solving skills, allowing them to manipulate real entities, making the algorithm concrete instead of completely abstract (Davis, Wellman, Anderson, & Raines, 2009; Lauwers, Nourbakhsh, & Hamner, 2009; Martin & Hughes, 2011; McWhorter & O'Connor, 2009). Other authors propose the use of robots as a communication tool, fostering the interpersonal communication and the interactions between groups (trying to stimulate the students to relate to each other, sharing experiences/ideas and building knowledge) (Almeida, 2012). A recent Systematic Literature Review investigated the use of robots to attract and motivate students and concluded, in fact, that the majority of the studies reported that robots are effective when used to teach introductory programming (Major, Kyriacou, & Brereton, 2012). The studies covered the use of both physical and simulated robots.

There are also some approaches using Arduino, applied to Engineering classes for freshman traditionally focused on problem solving, engineering graphics and computer programming (Brock, Bruce, & Reiser, 2009; Greenberg, Kumar, & Xu, 2012; Soule & Heckendorn, 2011). The idea is to enable the development of problem solving skills through a more creative, motivating and engaging way. The microcontroller platform provides the context and motivation for students to learn computer programming. Writing programs to make lights blink, read sensor data, control DC motors, among other features, students develop important programming skills in a real way. As the outcome of these programs is tangible and evident to anyone, regardless of their familiarity with programming, students will have a more positive programming experience this way. Even though these approaches bring positive results there are other opinions. For instance, in Beug (2012) there is a study comparing the use of Arduino and Scratch to teach introductory programming concepts. Teachers conclude that in some classes Arduino appears to be overly complicated for teaching introductory programming concepts to beginners. There are also other approaches to introduce the fundamentals of computing by giving students the capability for programming a device, the SenseBoard, which has built-in input/output and sensors. Programming is done in Sense, an extension of Scratch, which supports programming, but reduces the syntax details.

Another recent approach is that of Crunchzilla (Linden, 2013), developed to build educational games. It is also an online environment including different interactive tutorials for kids of different ages and adults. They can play with code, experiment, build and learn. Players learn step-by-step, building fun graphics, animations, and even fractals and simple games. Players build right away using code and learn about coding by coding. Important programming concepts like variables, loops, conditionals, expressions, and functions are introduced by exemplifying.

Different types of games approaches have also been developed to engage students in the process of learning. Kazimoglu et al. (2012) discuss computer video games and game-like environments as one strategy to use as a motivational tool to engage students in learning programming. Several studies also point out that a game based learning (GBL) environment for programming learning is more enjoyable and motivational to students than a traditional teaching environment (Eagle & Barnes, 2009; Yeh, 2009). In Adamo-Villani, Oania and Cooper (2012) it is reported that the development and initial evaluation of a serious game, in conjunction with appropriately designed matching laboratory exercises, can be used to teach secure coding and Information Assurance concepts across a range of introductory computing courses. In Kazimoglu et al. (2011) the design of an innovative educational game framework focused on the development of Computational Thinking (CT) skills is described. The authors used a serious game, based on their framework, and describe how a limited number of key introductory computer programming concepts have been mapped onto the game-play, and how an equivalent set of skills characterizing CT can be acquired through playing the game. It is important to emphasize that programming is not only coding, but also thinking computationally. For this, students need to acquire different types of skills enabling them to develop solutions. These solutions could be solved in a different way from the one a computer does. Wing (2006) describes CT as a problem solving approach that combines logical thinking with CS concepts, and that it can be used to solve a problem in any discipline regardless of where the problem lies. Several studies outline the necessity of students to become trained in thinking computationally before learning programming (Guzdial, 2008; Wing, 2008; Lu & Fletcher, 2009; Qualls, Grant, & Sherrell, 2011). We also agree with this point of view.

Transferring Professional Practice into the Classroom

The transfer of professional practice into the context of the classroom may be another approach to follow (Fincher & Petre, 2004). The topics of design patterns and frameworks, extreme programming, agile software development and test-driven development are examples of that subarea (Beck, 2000; Beck, 2003; Cockburn, 2002; Christensen, 2004; Fowler, 1999; Gamma, Helm, Johnson, & Vlissides, 1995; Martin, 2003). It is also worth mentioning the OOPSLA (Object-Oriented Programming Systems, Languages and Applications) conference that aims to join industry participants and academics, to promote discussions about interesting topics, such as the best way to teach design patterns in introductory programming courses (Alphonce, 2003). However, other authors have questioned the utilization of design patterns in introductory programming courses (Astrachan, Mitchener, Berry, & Cox, 1998; Clancy & Linn, 1999; Gelfand, Goodrich, & Tamassia, 1998; Nguyen & Wong, 1999; Preiss, 1999). Some authors also mention the use of agile software development methods for program development (Williams & Tomayko, 2002), while others proposed the use of extreme programming (Bergin, Caristi, Dubinsky, Hazzan, & Williams, 2004; Williams & Kessler, 2001). Several educators also suggest the use of test-driven development (Edwards, 2004; Janzen & Saiedian, 2006; Jones, 2004). These authors mentioned that instead of using a trial and error approach to find their programming errors, students develop a set of skills including reflection, understanding, analysis and hypothesis testing.

Transferring from Presence Education to Distance Education

Like many other courses, computing is increasingly being taught at a distance. Edwards and colleagues refer to a workshop on "Establish-ing a Distance Education Program" (Edwards, Thompson, Halstead-Nussloch, Arnow, & Oliver 2000) and Gersting (2000) reports experiments on using distance education in computer science. Bennedsen and Caspersen describe an introductory programming course based on the world wide web, where the technology and the course organization intend to allow some flexibility to compensate the disadvantages of this type of education (Bennedsen & Caspersen, 2003).

In Mobbs (2011), a new undergraduate module for novice students, conducted entirely through distance learning, My Digital Life (TU100), is presented. The module has been designed to lower the barriers of creating programs that interact with the world. TU100's materials have been designed to excite, encourage, reassure and support learners who explore the novel topic of ubiquitous computing through playful experimentation.

Recruitment and Retention

One of the major issues this area addresses concerns the search for indicators of success and reasons for failure in programming courses. In the first case, several variables have been investigated, including the mathematical skills (Bennedsen & Caspersen, 2005a; Butcher & Muth, 1985; Ventura, 2005), performance in previous programming courses (Chamillard, 2006), the abstraction ability (Bennedsen & Caspersen, 2006), personal perceptions of students (Wilson & Shrock, 2001) or emotional factors (Cegielski & Hall, 2006). Efforts have been made to develop instruments that can measure programming skills or the aptitude to the field. Examples include the APTS (Aptitude Profile Test Series) (Morgan, Stephanou, & Simpson, 2000) and a test developed by the Middlesex University (Dehnadi, 2006). Various aspects are studied regarding the causes of failure. For example, Beaubouef and Mason (2005) investigated the possible causes for the high failure rates and the dropout of computer science students. The authors invoke various factors, including: bad advice to students in order to attend courses for which they have no skills; weak math and problem solving skills; students with weak project planning skills; laboratory disciplines poorly planned/scheduled; lack of time to provide appropriate feedback to students; poorly prepared teachers; poor choice of teaching languages, among others. The issue of attractiveness of programming courses for women is another question often discussed. Studies attribute the lack of interest and discouragement of females due to the existence of stereotypes that consider programming courses as uncreative, asocial, without applicability, unfriendly and intimidating (Margolis & Fisher, 2003).

Construction of the Discipline

This category covers questions about the constitution of courses in computer science. Essentially considered in this theme are issues about which are the basic teaching/learning concepts, the elementary courses, the fundamental principles that should be covered, the advanced and optional curricular areas. ACM (Association for Computing Machinery) and IEEE (Institute of Electrical and Electronics Engineer) created a Joint Task Force on Computing Curricula that has been producing recommendations for some decades. Many universities worldwide use these recommendations when they plan their courses. The latest recommendation from this Task Force is the 2013 Curriculum Guidelines for Undergraduate Degree Programs in Computer Science (ACM, 2013).

"INNOVATIVE TEACHING STRATEGIES" AND "NEW LEARNING PARADIGMS"

Issues, Controversies, Problems

It is well known that teaching programming to students who have never had any previous experience in the field is difficult. The literature shows that not only students experience difficulties in programming learning, but also teachers find programming teaching to novices a challenging task (Bennedsen, Caspersen, & Kolling, 2008; Mathews, Hin, & Choo, 2009; Stone & Clark, 2011). Several authors have discussed diverse reasons that may be in the origin of the difficulties felt by students (Gray, Goldberg, & Byrnes, 2007; Jenkins, 2002; Lahtinen, Ala-Mutka, & Järvinen, 2005). We will discuss this important issue considering four factors, namely the students' background knowledge and skills, the teaching methods, the learning methods and the nature of programming.

The Students' Background Knowledge and Skills

Often teachers complain that many students do not have the abilities and attitudes required to learn to program. The authors own experience points in the same direction, as it is frequent to find students who don't have basic problem solving skills that should have been developed earlier in their education. This seems to be a major issue, as the main difficulty for many students is to create algorithms that solve specific problems. In other words, for these students the main difficulty is to devise and formalize a solution and not its codification in a particular programming language. Our experience also shows that student's problem solving difficulties are not specific of typical introductory programming problems, but more general, as they often lack generic problem solving skills. We believe that many students do not know how to create algorithms, mainly because they do not know how to solve problems.

Problem solving requires multiple abilities that students often do not have (Gomes & Mendes, 2007), namely:

1. **Problem Understanding:** Many times the students try to solve a problem without completely understanding it. Sometimes

this happens because they have difficulties interpreting the problem statement and others simply because they are too anxious to start writing code and do not read and interpret correctly the problem description.

2. **Relating Knowledge:** Many students do not establish correct analogies with past problems and do not transfer prior knowledge to new problems. They tend to group problems that have the same superficial characteristics instead of the same principle. Consequently, many times students base their solutions on unrelated problems, leading to incorrect solutions.

3. **Reflection about the Problem and the Solution:** Students have a tendency to write an answer without thinking carefully about it. Many times testing is done superficially and they are satisfied just because the program works with a data set, without making more extensive testing.

Problem solving difficulties often appear together with a lack of mathematical and logical knowledge (Byrne & Lyons, 2001; Gomes & Mendes, 2008; Pacheco, Gomes, & Mendes, 2008; Tomai & Reilly, 2014). Some students' programming difficulties are aggravated by misconceptions about common programming structures (Kaczmarczyk, East, Petrick, & Herman 2010). It is also common that students show many difficulties in detecting simple syntactical and logical errors in their own code. Many students also do not show a good attitude when they struggle to learn to program. They often give up solving a problem if they do not quickly find a possible solution. Usually solving programming problems demands effort and persistence. However, when facing difficulty, many students prefer to ask for the solution from a colleague or simply give up, instead of trying to solve the problem. This is especially important, since learning is more effective when students find the solution, instead of simply reading the solution. Recent discussions about

diverse perspectives and approaches to engage students on problem solving can be consulted in the literature (Adamo-Villani, Oania, & Coope, 2012; Hwang, Wu, & Chen, 2012).

The Teaching Methods

The teaching conditions and methods are a second factor often mentioned as part of the introductory programming-learning problem. It would be desirable to have a teacher always available to allow more personalized student supervision. Immediate feedback during problem solving and detailed explanation of less understood aspects could probably help many students. However, in reality, it is often impossible to give this type of support to every student due to time constraints and course sizes.

People learn in different ways and have diverse preferences to approach new materials. In traditional lectures all students must follow the same rhythm and using the teacher's pedagogical strategies, which usually are based on his/her learning style. Different students have normally different learning styles and can have several preferences in the way they learn. Some may regard learning as a solitary process, while others may prefer a more dynamic learning environment, for instance through discussions with their peers. Some individuals prefer to learn in a team, while others work better alone. Some tend to prefer more practical activities and others like to learn by reading and reflecting. Due to the different preferences in the way people perceive and process information, learning styles are a useful instrument to help students and teachers to understand how to improve how they learn and teach respectively. Additionally, some topics may demand a particular learning approach, but, without guidance, students will tend to adopt the style they prefer or which has served them best in the past. It is an important responsibility of the teacher to ensure that the students adopt the most appropriate learning approach for the subject matter at hand.

Another important aspect that should be acknowledged by professors and curricula developers is that programming learning takes time for many students, being a slow and gradual process (Dijkstra, 1998). This time needs to be given, so that students can develop their programing abilities.

Usually students are asked to write simple programs in the course's early stages, and more complex programs as it develops. This strategy might not be adequate for many students, especially weaker ones that are not able to solve even simple problems. That means that the complexity of those problems is too high for those students right from the beginning, leading to frustration, lack of motivation and failure. Maybe the entry level should be easier for those students, so that they can have success in the early learning activities, before they engage in tasks that require complete programs to be created. A taxonomy of educational objectives, such as Bloom's Taxonomy or others (Anderson et al., 2001; Bloom, Engelhart, Furst, Hill, & Krathwohl, 1956; Fuller et al., 2007), can be a good reference to deal with this issue. In fact, as pointed out by Lister (2000), "This traditional approach jumps to the fifth and sixth levels of Bloom's Taxonomy of Educational Objectives, when these last two levels depend upon competence in the first four levels". So, maybe students with difficulties should be first directed to easier tasks, instead of just insisting in the development of complete programs, no matter how simple they may be. Also, as stated by Lister (2000), "students should first be taught to read programs before they write programs. As children, in our early school years, the ability to read and understand our native language outstripped our capacity to write fragments of that language".

Another criticism often mentioned is the tendency of many teachers to concentrate more on teaching a programming language and its syntactic details, than on promoting problem solving using a programming language. In our view, the purpose of an introductory programming course should be to increase students' programming abilities. It is important to recognize that the language should only serve as a tool to express ideas and algorithms. However, an enormous amount of syntactic details are often taught, even before the students have a good understanding of some important and basic programming concepts. It is also important to note that programming involves dynamic concepts that often are taught using static materials (projected presentations, verbal explanations, diagrams, board drawings, texts, and so on). This means that students have to abstract program dynamics from textual materials, which may be a serious problem for some of them.

In summary, traditional teaching methods, based on lectures with a big number of students, can also be part of the introductory programming-learning problem. Especially the lack of consideration of individual needs and characteristics, with the uniformity of approaches, rhythms and activities do not contribute to a good learning environment to all students.

The Learning Methods

The study methods used by many students are often considered inappropriate for learning in general and for programming learning in particular. Many students are used to solving other courses' problems through memorization of formulas or procedures that are many times applied without a complete understanding of the underlying concepts. They just know that a particular formula should be used to solve some type of problem. Programming requires a different study method. It should be essentially practical and very intensive, quite different from what is required in many other courses (more based in theoretical knowledge, implying reading and some memorization). Some students believe that they can learn to program mostly through a textbook, failing to understand that their main activity should be solving as many programming problems as possible.

Another relevant issue is that many students do not work hard enough to acquire programming competences. They are used to courses where assisting classes and studying by a textbook is enough. However programming demands intense extra class work. We believe that teachers should try to show to students the different nature of programming, convincing them that studying a textbook or problems solved by others is not enough to promote the necessary learning.

The Nature of Programming

It is important to recognize that learning to program is difficult also due to its own characteristics. Programming requires a hierarchy of skills, like abstraction, generalization, transfer and critical thinking, among others. These skills are hard to develop and students usually show a clear lack of training in this respect. Experience has also shown that the problem starts, in general, in the initial learning phase, when students are expected to understand and apply abstract programming concepts, like control structures, to solve problems. Most programming languages used in introductory courses are professional languages, usually with a complex syntax, that were developed for professional use and not to support learning. Common languages are extensive and have many complex syntactic details to become familiar with. That complexity requires that students have to concentrate simultaneously in algorithm construction and complex syntactic rules. The same often happens with the Integrated Development Environments used, normally developed for professional use and far too complex for inexperienced students.

In conclusion, it is possible to say that all these four groups of factors play a role in the difficulties many students feel when they face introductory programming courses. We believe that to be successful any pedagogical strategy must take into consideration all these factors, and try to give answers to as many as possible, so that its effect is minimized for most students. This has been the main objective of our research group in the

past few years. Part of that work and the results obtained so far are presented in the next section.

Solutions and Recommendations

Our research group started its work in Computer Science Education Research with the development of some tools that might help students in their early programming stages (Santos, Gomes, & Mendes, 2010). However, considering the issues discussed in the previous section we added a new trend to our work, looking for new pedagogical strategies that might be more effective than the traditional format we used for many years in our Department. The work developed by our research group in this field led to deep changes in the form in which programming courses are taught at the Informatics Engineering Department of University of Coimbra. So, it is relevant to describe the more recent part of this work, the changes introduced and some results obtained so far.

In the 2008/2009 academic year we started a set of experiments trying to identify conditions that may make programming learning more stimulating, minimizing dropout intentions and making the student learn more and better. This work was developed during three years in the context of the Programming course included in the Design and Multimedia Master degree (DMM) at the University of Coimbra. The aim of this course is to develop basic programming knowledge that may allow students to follow other courses that require some programming knowledge. Although it is a Master, most students didn't have any relevant programming experience, as they come from design and arts areas. The main objective of this work was to create a course context that could strengthen the student's motivation and provide a supportive environment for learning. We used several instruments to measure the success of the different components of the proposed strategy (e.g. questionnaires, interviews, success rates in the course), and from year to year we introduced several improvements in the overall strategy and in some of its individual components. Further details of this work can be found in Martins, Figueiredo and Mendes (2012).

The success obtained in our experiments gave us confidence to propose the adoption of a similar approach in all introductory programming courses of the department. As the student's results in these courses used to be far from satisfactory, the Department decided to support this proposal. The changes decided at management level were essentially organizational: to create separate courses for students following different degrees and to modify the course class structure. However, these decisions created the opportunity to make crucial changes at the pedagogical level.

The rest of this section will describe the changes and the results obtained in the academic year 2011/12 in one of the courses, "Introduction to Programming and Problem Solving" that is offered to novice Design and Multimedia students (we will call it IPPS-DMD from now on).

The Design and Multimedia Degree was offered for the first time in the academic year of 2008/2009. Since then, the introductory programming course included in each week a 2 hour lecture with all the students together, 3 hour lab classes in groups of 24 students and 2 hour free tutorial classes in groups of about 60 students. The new class structure includes only one type of class, with students divided in groups of about 24 students. Each group has 5 hours of classes per week, divided in two different days, one with 2 hours and the other with 3 hours. The same teacher is responsible for all classes of a particular group during the semester. Each class can consist of the presentation of theoretical aspects and/or practical programming assignments applying the concepts just presented. The rationale behind the changes made included a better use of class time, as traditional lectures were not being as useful as they should (class rhythm, examples, and activities were not suited to many students due to the dimension and the very heterogeneous nature of the group). Also, the new class structure would allow the presentation and immediate practice of the different concepts, eliminating problems that used to arise due to the separation in time between lectures and the different lab groups (even more clear in the case of students who missed lectures and arrived to the lab without a clue about the relevant concepts for that day).

The separation of students (of the Design and Multimedia degree from the Informatics Engineering degree) allowed us to shape the course considering the interest most Design and Multimedia students have in design and digital art issues. This was the main reason in choosing the Processing language for the course, instead of Python that was previously used in the joint course. The reason was not language simplicity (on the contrary), but its ability to easily support the development of applications that display drawings, animations and art works. Most programming class activities, homework assignments, and exam questions had a visual nature, while involving programming concepts usual in an introductory course (e.g. selection, repetition, arrays, and an introduction to object oriented programming). A recurrent question of IPPS-DMD students in previous years was: Why should they learn to program? Many of them did not have any motivation to face the inherent difficulties, because they did not feel a sense of utility to their future life. As motivation is very important for student involvement in learning activities we addressed this question in the first class. However, instead of telling them how important programming can be, we gave them an assignment that asked each student to make a web search about applications made in Processing. Each of them had to select a project to present in the next class. This activity had a very positive impact, as many students came to the second class saying they wanted to learn programming, because they also would like to create projects like those they had found.

The separation of students following different degrees in separate courses also reduced the number of students in each of them. The possibility to work with small groups of students and the increase of time available (5 hours of class per week), allowed the teachers to know each student well, her/his difficulties, preferences and reactions to teacher interactions. To reinforce the teacher–student relationship we used a less conventional activity in programming courses: students had to write a reflection about their learning every two weeks. Reflections were written in the course Learning Management System (Moodle) and were accessible only to the teacher. This activity allowed a better knowledge about each student, as many of them seemed to find it easier to write about their problems than to speak about them. It was possible to identify and address some learning issues that were causing difficulties to some students, and also prevent some dropouts through direct interventions with the specific students.

To keep students as committed as possible some other strategies were used:

- In several assignments students were allowed to include a more creative component. For example, the teacher defined the minimum visual requirements for the assignment (e.g. it has to include a windmill with rotating sails), but the rest of the specification was left open, allowing each student to design and program other components that she/he felt interesting;
- Teachers often tried to encourage students, praising their efforts and achievements. Errors were always presented as learning opportunities, showing that all programmers make mistakes (including the teacher). It was important to make students conscious of their own progresses, so that they could learn if they commit enough;
- Assignments given to a particular student took into consideration her/his current level as much as possible. This means that in the same class different students could be working in different programs;

- Students were made aware of their role in learning, namely the necessary attitude and commitment to be successful. The teachers frequently reminded students about the importance of an active and pro-active attitude towards learning;
- Teachers closely followed students' progress, trying to early detect any difficulties. This allowed teachers to provide early corrective actions, both to small groups sharing similar problems and at an individual level.

Although the changes made in the course structure were essentially organizational, their consequences were mostly pedagogical. There was a better learning context, more suitable to the student's characteristics, and a higher degree of consideration of individual difficulties. All this resulted in more motivation and a deeper student involvement that had a positive impact in their final results. The results were measured using three different sources of information: the student's final grades, the results of the university official pedagogical survey, and the results of a questionnaire directed to the students that were repeating the course.

To evaluate the impact of the innovations introduced in the course, we compared the course final information with what had happened in the two previous years. The data is presented in Table 1. For each year it shows the number of enrolled students, the number of students who followed the course until the end (including the final exam), the number of approved students, the rate of assessed students (assessed/registered), the success rate (approved/assessed), the approved rate (approved/registered) and the final marks average (expressed in the scale 0 – 20 used in Portugal).

It is easy to conclude that there was a very positive evolution in most fields, especially in success rate and approved rate. The percentage of approved students went from 26.6% and 19.8% in the previous years to 57.3% in 2011/12. Consider-

Table 1. Comparative data in the three analysed years

All Students							
	Enrolled Students	**Assessed Students**	**Approved Students**	**Assessed Students Rate**	**Success Rate**	**Approved Rate**	**Final Marks Average**
2011/12	103	82	59	79.6	72.0	57.3	12.9
2010/11	91	78	18	86.8	23.1	19.8	12.1
2009/10	64	57	17	89.1	29.9	26.6	12.0

ing only the students that were present in the final exam, the approved percentage rose to 72% versus 29.9% and 23.1% in the previous years.

At the end of each semester the university pedagogical services conduct an anonymous survey about all courses of the different degrees offered by the university. The survey included questions about the general conditions of learning (spaces, library, and so on) and questions specific to each of the courses the students followed in the semester. The survey uses a Likert type scale with five points (1 to 5), where higher marks mean a better opinion. The first point to mention is the fact that 90% of IPPS-DMD students answered the survey (a high number when compared with other courses). The survey includes 11 questions about each course the student followed, including questions that ask the student to:

- Appreciate the average quality of learning in the course.
- Classify her/his own learning.
- Rate her/his own participation in learning activities.
- Globally classify her/his own performance in the course.

The average marks to the 11 questions were between 4.0 and 4.3, reflecting a positive view about the course. Considering the highest possible mark is 5, this means that most students had a positive view about the course and what they were able to learn. It is interesting to compare IPPS-

DMD results in the survey with the average of the results of all courses in the Design and Multimedia degree in the same survey. The average marks for all courses were between 3.7 and 3.9. This means that IPPS-DMD was rated above average in all questions included in the survey. This is more significant considering that many other courses could be more appealing to the students, as they are more design and multimedia oriented. It is also significant to note that in the previous year the same survey had already been used, and the average of the student answers about the course were between 2.9 and 3.8, clearly below 2011/12 results. The university survey also includes some questions to allow the students to give their opinion about the teachers. The averages were between 4.0 and 4.7 for the three course teachers. This means that most students liked the course and appreciated the efforts the teachers made to promote learning.

To have a deeper insight on the way students reacted to the changes made in the course, we asked the non-freshmen to answer a specific questionnaire, as they had followed the course in both models, the old model in 2010/11 and the new model in 2011/12. The questionnaire included some questions; which were to be answered in a Likert type scale while other questions were for free text answers. It was put online and the teacher sent an email to the 58 non-freshmen asking them to give their answers anonymously. Only 30 students answered the questionnaire (17 male and 13 female). Answers were given before students knew their final grades. The first question asked the students if they consider the activities used in class more or less adequate to promote learning than those used in the previous year. It was a free text answer, but the answer was unanimous. In a way or another, students expressed their agreement with the changes made. They appreciated the use of Processing and considered visual oriented programming activities more interesting and adequate to them. Some also wrote that it was easier to understand the effect of the programming instructions as they had a visual effect. Finally, some students appreciated the fact that teachers often allowed them to progress at their own pace, giving different exercises to students in different learning stages. The survey also asked students to indicate how often they had gone to the different types of classes (lectures, labs and free tutorials) the year before and how often they went to classes in the current year. The answers showed that:

- Most of these students did not attend the free tutorials, as more than 80% of them went to less than 50% of those classes. Although the students had learning difficulties (they were unsuccessful in the course), it seems that this type of class failed to be relevant to them.
- More than half of the respondents (56.67%) attended less than 50% of lectures.
- Most students (86.67%) attended 50% or more labs.

From these numbers, it seems clear that the labs were the only classes that attracted these students. As they had difficulties in learning to program, we could expect that they would take advantage of all classes to improve their situation. However, that wasn't the case, maybe because they did not feel lectures and free tutorials useful for them. On the contrary, in 2011/12 60% of the students attended more than 75% of classes, showing that they felt them useful for their learning.

The questionnaire also included a question to differentiate dropout situations. The answers show a big difference between the two years, as only 33.3% of the respondents did not drop out in 2010/11. That number grew to 96.7% in 2011/12. For those students who did drop out, the questionnaire included a question about the reasons for that decision. The students mentioned several reasons. The most frequent one was related to failure to achieve the minimum allowed grade in the course project or in some mini tests that existed in the course evaluation schema. Some students mentioned that they found the course uninteresting, especially lectures. They found them difficult to follow, and useless to clarify doubts, as there was an excessive number of students. The separation between lectures and labs was also mentioned. In the labs it was expected that the students had understood the concepts and examples presented in lectures. When that did not happen labs were not very useful, as students could not solve the exercises or even understand the solutions presented by colleagues or the teacher. The time between lectures and labs was also pointed out as a reason for drop out, as some students mentioned that they could hardly remember the lectures when they started the labs. Some students simply said that they dropped out because they could not keep up with the course pace. Analyzing the student's justifications for dropping out in the previous year, we may think that the course structure and activities failed to motivate students to get involved and make the necessary effort to learn. This lack of commitment is obvious when students mention the time between lectures and labs. Of course, teachers expected some autonomous study in that time, but that simply did not seem to have happened in the case of the respondents.

The questionnaire included the question "What are the major advantages/disadvantages of the new course structure?" Some statements were included and the students had to classify each of them in a five point scale: -2 = "strongly disagree", -1 = "disagree", 0 = "neither agree nor disagree", 1 = "agree" and 2 = "strongly agree". The statements were:

1. There was a better connection between theory and practice.
2. There was a higher proximity between student and teacher.
3. The teacher monitored students more closely.
4. There was more time to clarify doubts.
5. The teaching was more personalized.
6. There was more time to practice programming.
7. It was more tiring due to more practical and intensive work.
8. Time was better organized.
9. The reduction of contact hours (7 hours per week in 2010/11 to 5 hours in 2011/12) was disadvantageous.
10. There was more motivation to program.

The results obtained were very positive, expressing a very good opinion about the changes introduced in the course. In statements a) to f), h) and j) almost no student expressed disagreement, and even neutral positions were a small minority. This means that for the respondents there were clear advantages in the changes made. Statement g), which asked if the new approach was more tiring to students, got more disperse answers, as 40% of the students were neutral, 46.6% expressed disagreement (saying it wasn't more tiring) and 13.4% expressed agreement. We see this as natural, as the new approach requires a much more active attitude from the students, both in classes and outside classes. Possibly some student saw this as tiring, while others liked it, since they were learning better than before and thought the extra work was worthwhile. The new model implied a reduction of the number of contact hours. Previously, there were 7h per week (2h lectures, 3h labs and 2h free tutorials), while in the new model the number was reduced to 5h (mostly due to staff constraints, as in the new model all classes were in small groups, creating the need to use more staff hours). Nevertheless, considering the answers to statement i), 56.7% of the students did not consider that a problem, while 33.3% were neutral. So, it seems that, for these students, the changes in the

pedagogical strategy compensate the reduction of contact hours.

The questionnaire also included space to allow students to mention other advantages and/or disadvantages of the new model. Apart from the issues already covered in the statements a) to j) the students also mentioned as advantages:

- The change to the Processing programming language, as it allowed more interesting activities and is a language used in the creative industries.
- The separation of the Design and Multimedia students from the Informatics Engineering students, as they felt that previously the course was essentially thought for those students.
- The students felt more motivated with the learning context, as some of them explicitly mentioned the quality of the teachers and the supportive environment in classes.

As for disadvantages some students mentioned:

- As each group only has one teacher, it is possible that different teachers have different assessment criteria.
- It is possible that different programming issues are presented and practiced differently in the various groups, creating an unbalanced situation when those issues appear in the final exam.

Finally, the questionnaire gave each student the possibility to include any other remark not covered before. Some students used that possibility to reinforce some ideas previously mentioned. Others asked that this experiment and its pedagogical approach to be extended to other courses in the degree. One student expressed the hope that the better programming knowledge acquired in the course would be helpful in other courses. Some students wanted to stress the pedagogical difference they saw in that specific year when compared with the previous year.

Considering the positive results and feedback obtained, it was decided that class structure and methodology should be maintained in the following years. The results obtained in 2012/13 continued to be positive, and much better than before the changes were introduced.

FUTURE RESEARCH DIRECTIONS

Computer Science Education Research is a very wide area, including very diverse contributions and approaches. Consequently research in this area will likely continue to be very diversified and multidisciplinary. The integration of different subareas in common work might be one of the most interesting trends, as the different contributions may lead to better tools and methodologies that may be effective to support learning. We believe that motivation and cognitive skills development, and an individualized support will be very important for learning. So we will focus our attention in these areas.

Motivation and Cognitive Skills

It is common to find references to students that develop their programming competences without difficulties, while others struggle, even though participating in the same classes and using the same materials. What makes the difference? Although there have been studies trying to compare fast learners with struggling students there are no clear answers. In this context, it would be useful to have a good definition of the cognitive skills more relevant to programming learning. With that definition, it is important to know how to develop those skills, considering the different types of students.

Many studies acknowledge the importance of student motivation for learning. How can this motivation be developed and kept during all learning stages? How does intrinsic motivation influence the student's study strategies? How do these strategies relate with student's characteristics and learning? These questions deserve further attention from the researchers in this field.

Individualized Support

It seems clear that a close teacher monitoring can be a positive factor to learning. Often this is not feasible due to time constraints and class sizes. This opens the field for research on computer-based tools that support teachers, for example giving diagnostic information about each student or replacing teachers in some tasks, such as automatic feedback about student work.

A more comprehensive environment that might diagnose student's needs in each learning stage and propose adequate learning activities considering his/her characteristics, preferences and past learning behaviour would be very useful. However this is a very complex task, needing a multidisciplinary approach that might not be possible as a whole in the near future. However, it is likely that some steps are taken in this direction, looking to answer questions like in what learning context and for which students is a particular learning activity adequate? Can we define taxonomy of introductory exercises that may be used to define individual learning paths? Some steps have been made in this direction (Santos, Gomes, & Mendes, 2013), but a lot of work is still necessary before the final objectives may be reached.

CONCLUSION

The Computer Science Education Research field in general and the programming-learning field in particular are very complex, as they deal with individuals acquiring complex and abstract knowledge and skills. There is a wide diversity of factors affecting learning, which also creates a large number of research approaches when they are considered individually. Maybe a more integrated research approach, with contributions from several fields, may be necessary for the definition of more successful pedagogical strategies and tools.

In this chapter we provided an overview of the field based on the areas defined by Fincher and Petre (2004). We also presented some work done at the University of Coimbra, especially in the definition of alternative pedagogical strategies to support introductory programming learning. This work has been a basis for some changes in our courses, which so far produced positive results. From that work it is possible to argue that student motivation and a very close student support might be fundamental. To support such pedagogical strategies, it would be very important to have adequate tools that might automatize part of the teachers job, reducing the amount of work that is implicit in the pedagogical strategy we proposed and use. Maybe the development of such tools is the next step for the field.

REFERENCES

ACM. (2013). *Computing Science Curricula 2013: Curriculum Guidelines for Undergraduate Degree Programs in Computer Science* (Report from The Joint Task Force on Computing Curricula). Retrieved from Recommendations - Association for Computing Machinery: http://www.acm.org/education/CS2013-final-report.pdf

Adamo-Villani, N., Oania, M., & Cooper, S. (2012). Using a Serious Game Approach to Teach Secure Coding in Introductory Programming: Development and Initial Findings. *Journal of Educational Technology Systems, 41*(2), 107–131. doi:10.2190/ET.41.2.b

Ala-Mutka, K. M. (2005). A Survey of Automated Assessment Approaches for Programming Assignments. *Computer Science Education, 15*(2), 83–102. doi:10.1080/08993400500150747

Almeida, C. (2012). *Mindstorms na aprendizagem da algoritmia e programação*. (Master Thesis). Universidade de Aveiro, Areiro, Portugal.

Alphonce, C. G. (2003). *"Killer Examples" for Design Patterns and Objects First*. Retrieved from http://www.cse.buffalo.edu/~alphonce/KillerExamples/OOPSLA2002/

Anderson, L., Krathwohl, D., Airasian, P., Cruikshank, K., Mayer, R., & Pintrich, P. et al. (2001). *A Taxonomy for Learning and Teaching and Assessing: A Revision of Bloom's Taxonomy of Educational Objectives*. New York: Addison Wesley Longman, Inc.

Anderson, R., Simon, B., Wolfman, S. A., VanDeGrift, T., & Yasuhara, K. (2004). Experiences with a tablet PC based lecture presentation system in computer science courses. *SIGCSE Bulletin, 36*(1), 56–60. doi:10.1145/1028174.971323

Anjaneyulu, K. S. (1994). Bug analysis of Pascal programs. *SIGPLAN Notices, 29*(4), 15–22. doi:10.1145/181761.181762

Astrachan, O., Mitchener, G., Berry, G., & Cox, L. (1998). Design patterns: An essential component of CS curricula. *SIGCSE Bulletin, 30*(1), 153–160. doi:10.1145/274790.273182

Beaubouef, T., & Mason, J. (2005). Why the high attrition rate for computer science students: Some thoughts and observations. *SIGCSE Bulletin, 37*(2), 103–106. doi:10.1145/1083431.1083474

Beck, K. (2000). *Extreme programming explained: Embrace change*. Boston, MA: Addison-Wesley Longman, Inc.

Beck, K. (2003). *Test-Driven Development: By Example*. Boston, MA: Addison-Wesley Longman, Inc.

Ben-Ari, M., Bednarik, R., Levy, R., Ebel, G., Moreno, A., Myller, N., & Sutinen, E. (2011). A decade of research and development on program animation: The Jeliot experience. *Journal of Visual Languages and Computing, 22*(5), 375–384. doi:10.1016/j.jvlc.2011.04.004

Benaya, T., & Zur, E. (2008). Understanding Object Oriented Programming Concepts in an Advanced Programming Course. In R. Mittermeir & M. Syslo (Eds.), *Informatics Education - Supporting Computational Thinking* (pp. 161–170). Berlin: Springer-Verlag. doi:10.1007/978-3-540-69924-8_15

Bennedsen, J., & Caspersen, M. E. (2003). Rationale for the Design of a Web-based Programming Course for Adults. In *Proceedings of the International Conference on Open and Online Learning (ICOOL'03)*. University of Mauritius.

Bennedsen, J., & Caspersen, M. E. (2005a). An investigation of potential success factors for an introductory model-driven programming course. In *Proceedings of the first International workshop on Computing Education Research (ICER'05)* (pp. 155-163). Seattle, WA: ACM. doi:10.1145/1089786.1089801

Bennedsen, J., & Caspersen, M. E. (2006). Abstraction ability as an indicator of success for learning object-oriented programming? *SIGCSE Bulletin, 38*(2), 39–43. doi:10.1145/1138403.1138430

Bennedsen, J. B., Caspersen, M. E., & Kölling, M. (2008). *Reflections on the Teaching of Programming: Methods and Implementations*. Springer Publishing Company, Inc. doi:10.1007/978-3-540-77934-6

Bergin, J., Caristi, J., Dubinsky, Y., Hazzan, O., & Williams, L. (2004). Teaching software development methods: The case of extreme programming. *SIGCSE Bulletin, 36*(1), 448–449. doi:10.1145/1028174.971452

Beug, A. (2012). *Teaching Introductory Programming Concepts: A Comparison of Scratch and Arduino*. (Master Thesis). California Polytechnic State University, San Luis Obispo, CA.

Biggs, J. B., & Collis, K. F. (1982). *Evaluating the quality of learning: the SOLO taxonomy (structure of the observed learning outcome)*. New York: Academic Press.

Bloom, B. S., Engelhart, M. D., Furst, E. J., Hill, W. H., & Krathwohl, D. R. (1956). *Taxonomy of Educational Objectives, Handbook I: Cognitive Domain*. London, UK: Longmans, Green and Co Ltd.

Brock, J., Bruce, R., & Reiser, S. (2009). Using Arduino for introductory programming courses. *Journal of Computing Sciences in Colleges, 25*(2), 129–139.

Butcher, D. F., & Muth, W. A. (1985). Predicting performance in an introductory computer science course. *Communications of the ACM, 28*(3), 263–268. doi:10.1145/3166.3167

Byrne, P., & Lyons, G. (2001). The effect of student attributes on success in programming. *SIGCSE Bulletin, 33*(3), 49–52. doi:10.1145/507758.377467

Carbone, A., & Ceddia, J., Simon, D'Souza, & Mason, R. (2013). Student Concerns in Introductory Programming Courses. In *Proceedings of the fifteenth Australasian Computing Education conference (ACE'13)* (pp. 41-50). Adelaide, Australia: ACE.

Caspersen, M. E. (2007). *Educating novices in the skills of programming*. (PhD Thesis). University of Aarhus, Aarhus, Denmark.

Cegielski, C. G., & Hall, D. J. (2006). What makes a good programmer? *Communications of the ACM, 49*(10), 73–75. doi:10.1145/1164394.1164397

Chamillard, A. T. (2006). Using student performance predictions in a computer science curriculum. *SIGCSE Bulletin, 38*(3), 260–264. doi:10.1145/1140123.1140194

Christensen, H. B. (2004). Frameworks: Putting design patterns into perspective. *SIGCSE Bulletin, 36*(3), 142–145. doi:10.1145/1026487.1008035

Clancy, M. J., & Linn, M. C. (1999). Patterns and pedagogy. *SIGCSE Bulletin, 31*(1), 37–42. doi:10.1145/384266.299673

Cockburn, A. (2002). *Agile software development*. Boston, MA: Addison-Wesley Longman Inc.

Cook, C., Drachova, S., Hallstrom, J., Hollingsworth, J., Jacobs, D., Krone, J., & Sitaraman, M. (2012). A Systematic Approach to Teaching Abstraction and Mathematical Modeling. In *Proceedings of the 17th ACM Annual Conference on Innovation and Technology in Computer Science Education (ITiCSE'12)* (pp. 357-362). Haifa, Israel: ACM. doi:10.1145/2325296.2325378

Davis, J., Wellman, B., Anderson, M., & Raines, M. (2009). Providing robotic experiences through object-based programming (PREOP). In *Proceedings of the 2009 Alice Symposium*, (pp. 1-5). Durham, NC: ACM. doi:10.1145/1878513.1878520

Dehnadi, S. (2006). Testing Programming Aptitude. In P. Romero, J. Good, E. A. Chaparro, & S. Bryant. In *Proceedings of the 18th Annual Workshop of the Psychology of Programming Interest Group (PPIG'06)* (pp. 22-37). Brighton, UK: PPIG.

Denning, T., Griswold, W. G., Simon, B., & Wilkerson, M. (2006). Multimodal communication in the classroom: What does it mean for us? *SIGCSE Bulletin, 38*(1), 219–223. doi:10.1145/1124706.1121410

Dick, M., Bareiss, C., Carter, J., Joyce, D., Harding, T., & Laxer, C. (2003). Addressing student cheating: Definitions and solutions. *SIGCSE Bulletin, 35*(2), 172–184. doi:10.1145/782941.783000

Dijkstra, E. W. (1989). On the Cruelty of Really Teaching Computing Science. *Communications of the ACM, 32*(12), 1388–1404.

Eagle, M., & Barnes, T. (2009). Experimental evaluation of an educational game for improved learning in introductory computing. In *Proceedings of the 40th ACM Technical Symposium on Computer Science Education (SIGCSE'09)* (pp. 321-325). Chattanooga, TN: ACM. doi:10.1145/1508865.1508980

Ebel, G., & Ben-Ari, M. (2006). Affective effects of program visualization. In *Proceedings of the second International workshop on Computing Education Research (ICER'06)* (pp. 1-5). Canterbury, UK: ACM.

Edwards, H. M., Thompson, J. B., Halstead-Nussloch, R., Arnow, D., & Oliver, D. (2000). Report on the CSEET '99 Workshop: Establishing a Distance Education Program. *Computer Science Education, 10*(1), 57–74. doi:10.1076/0899-3408(200004)10:1;1-P;FT057

Edwards, S. H. (2004). Using software testing to move students from trial-and-error to reflection-in-action. *SIGCSE Bulletin, 36*(1), 26–30. doi:10.1145/1028174.971312

Fagin, B., & Merkle, L. (2003). Measuring the effectiveness of robots in teaching computer science. *SIGCSE Bulletin, 35*(1), 307–311. doi:10.1145/792548.611994

Fincher, S., & Petre, M. (2004). *Computer Science Education Research*. RoutledgeFalmer, Taylor & Francis Group.

Fowler, M. (1999). *Refactoring: Improving the Design of Existing Code*. Boston, MA: Addison-Wesley Longman Inc.

Fuller, U., Johnson, C. G., Ahoniemi, T., Cukierman, D., Hernán-Losada, I., & Jackova, J. (2007). Developing a computer science-specific learning taxonomy. *SIGCSE Bulletin*, *39*(4), 152–170. doi:10.1145/1345375.1345438

Gamma, E., Helm, R., Johnson, R., & Vlissides, J. (1995). *Design Patterns: Elements of Reusable Object-Oriented Software*. Boston, MA: Addison-Wesley Longman Inc.

Gelfand, N., Goodrich, M. T., & Tamassia, R. (1998). Teaching data structure design patterns. *SIGCSE Bulletin*, *30*(1), 331–335. doi:10.1145/274790.274324

Gersting, J. L. (2000). Computer Science Distance Education Experience in Hawaii. *Computer Science Education*, *10*(1), 95–106. doi:10.1076/0899-3408(200004)10:1;1-P;FT095

Gomes, A., & Mendes, A. J. (2007). Learning to program - difficulties and solutions. In *Proceedings of the International Conference on Engineering Education, (CD-ROM)*. Coimbra, Portugal: Academic Press.

Gomes, A., & Mendes, A. J. (2008). A study on student's characteristics and programming learning. In *Proceedings of the World Conference on Educational Multimedia, Hypermedia and Telecommunications (EDMEDIA'08)* (pp. 2895-2904). Vienna, Austria: AACE.

Gray, W., Goldberg, N., & Byrnes, S. (2007). Novices and programming: Merely a difficult subject (why?) or a means to mastering metacognitive skills? *Journal of Educational Resources in Computing*, *9*(1), 131–140.

Greenberg, I., Kumar, D., & Xu, D. (2012). Creative coding and visual portfolios for CS1. In *Proceedings of the 43rd ACM technical symposium on Computer Science Education* (SIGCSE'12) (pp. 247-252). Raleigh, NC: ACM. doi:10.1145/2157136.2157214

Gudzial, M. (2008). Education: Paving the way for computational thinking. *Communications of the ACM*, *51*(8), 25–27. doi:10.1145/1378704.1378713

Hadjerrouit, S. (2008). Towards a Blended Learning Model for Teaching and Learning Computer Programming: A Case Study. *Information in Education*, *7*(2), 181–210.

Hawi, N. (2010). Causal attributions of success and failure made by undergraduate students in an introductory-level computer programming course. *Computers & Education*, *54*(4), 1127–1136. doi:10.1016/j.compedu.2009.10.020

Hundhausen, C. D., Douglas, S. A., & Stasko, J. T. (2002). A Meta-Study of Algorithm Visualization Effectiveness. *Journal of Visual Languages and Computing*, *13*(3), 259–290. doi:10.1006/jvlc.2002.0237

Hwang, G.-J., Wu, P.-H., & Chen, C.-C. (2012). An online game approach for improving students' learning performance in web-based problem-solving activities. *Computers & Education*, *59*(4), 246–1256. doi:10.1016/j.compedu.2012.05.009

Janzen, D. S., & Saiedian, H. (2006). Test-driven learning: Intrinsic integration of testing into the CS/SE curriculum. *SIGCSE Bulletin*, *38*(1), 254–258. doi:10.1145/1124706.1121419

Jenkins, T. (2002). On the difficulty of learning to program. In *Proceedings of 3rd Annual LTSN-ICS Conference* (pp. 53-58). Loughborough University.

Jones, C. G. (2004). Test-driven development goes to school. *Journal of Computing Sciences in Colleges*, *20*(1), 220–231.

Kaczmarczyk, L., East, J. P., Petrick, E. R., & Herman, G. L. (2010). Identifying Student Misconceptions of Programming. In *Proceedings of the 41st ACM Technical Symposium on Computer Science Education (SIGCSE'10)* (pp. 107-111). Milwaukee, WI: ACM. doi:10.1145/1734263.1734299

Kazimoglu, C., Kiernan, M., Bacon, L., & MacKinnon, L. (2011). Understanding Computational Thinking before Programming: Developing Guidelines for the Design of Games to Learn Introductory Programming through Game-Play. *International Journal of Game-Based Learning*, *1*(3), 30–52. doi:10.4018/ijgbl.2011070103

Kazimoglu, C., Kiernan, M., Bacon, L., & Mackinnon, L. (2012). A Serious Game for Developing Computational Thinking and Learning Introductory Computer Programming. *Procedia-Social and Behavioral Journal*, *47*, 991–1999.

Kelleher, C., & Pausch, R. (2005). Lowering the barriers to programming: A taxonomy of programming environments and languages for novice programmers. *ACM Computing Surveys*, *37*(2), 83–137. doi:10.1145/1089733.1089734

Kinnunen, P., & Malmi, L. 2006. Why students drop out CS1 course? In *Proceedings of the second International workshop on Computing Education Research (ICER'06)* (pp. 97-108). Canterbury, UK: ACM.

Koile, K., & Singer, D. (2006). Improving learning in CS1 via tablet-PC-based in-class assessment. In *Proceedings of the Second International Workshop on Computing Education Research (ICER'06)* (pp. 119-126). Canterbury, UK: ACM. doi:10.1145/1151588.1151607

Krushkov, H., Krushkova, M., Atanasov, V., & Krushkova, M. (2009). A computer –based tutoring system for programming. In *Proceedings of Mathematics and Mathematical Education*. Academic Press.

Lahtinen, E., Ala-Mutka, K. A., & Järvinen, H. M. (2005). A Study of the difficulties of novice programmers. In *Proceedings of 10th Annual SIGSCE Conference on Innovation and Technology in Computer Science Education* (pp. 14-18). Monte da Caparica, Portugal: ACM. doi:10.1145/1067445.1067453

Lancaster, T., & Culwin, F. (2004). A Comparison of Source Code Plagiarism Detection Engines. *Computer Science Education*, *14*(2), 101–112. doi:10.1080/08993400412331363843

Lauwers, T., Nourbakhsh, I., & Hamner, E. (2009). CSbots: design and deployment of a robot designed for the CS1 classroom. In *Proceedings of the 40th ACM Technical Symposium on Computer Science Education (SIGCSE'09)*. Chattanooga, TN: ACM. doi:10.1145/1508865.1509017

Lee, D., Rodrigo, M., Baker, R., Sugay, J., & Coronel, A. (2011). Exploring the relationship between novice programmer confusion and achievement. In *Proceedings of the 4th International Conference on Affective Computing and Intelligent Interaction (ACII'11)* (pp. 175-184). Memphis, TN: Springer-Verlag. doi:10.1007/978-3-642-24600-5_21

Linden, G. (n.d.). *Learning JavaScript Crunchzilla Code Monster*. Retrieved from http://www.crunchzilla.com/

Linn, M. C., & Clancy, M. J. (1992). The case for case studies of programming problems. *Communications of the ACM*, *35*(3), 121–132. doi:10.1145/131295.131301

Linn, M. C., & Dalbey, J. (1985). Cognitive consequences of Programming Instruction: Instruction, Access and Ability. *Educational Psychologist*, *20*(4), 191–206. doi:10.1207/s15326985ep2004_4

Lister, R. (2000). On blooming first year programming and its blooming assessment. In *Proceedings of the Australasian Conference on Computing Education (ACSE'00)* (pp. 158-162). Melbourne, Australia: ACM. doi:10.1145/359369.359393

Lister, R., Adams, E. S., Fitzgerald, S., Fone, W., Hamer, J., & Lindholm, M. et al. (2004). A multinational study of reading and tracing skills in novice programmers. *SIGCSE Bulletin*, *36*(4), 119–150. doi:10.1145/1041624.1041673

Lister, R., Simon, B., Thompson, E., Whalley, J. L., & Prasad, C. (2006). Not seeing the forest for the trees: Novice programmers and the SOLO taxonomy. *SIGCSE Bulletin, 38*(3), 118–122. doi:10.1145/1140123.1140157

Lu, J., & Fletcher, G. (2009). Thinking about computational thinking. In *Proceedings of the 40th ACM technical symposium on Computer Science Education (SIGCSE'09)* (pp. 260-264). Chattanooga, TN: ACM. doi:10.1145/1508865.1508959

Major, L., Kyriacou, T., & Brereton, O. (2012). Systematic literature review: Teaching novices programming using robots. *IET Software, 6*(6), 502–513. doi:10.1049/iet-sen.2011.0125

Margolis, J., & Fisher, A. (2003). *Unlocking the Clubhouse: Women in Computing.* Cambridge, MA: The MIT Press.

Martin, C., & Hughes, J. (2011). Robot dance: edutainment of engaging learning. In *Proceedings of the 23rd Psychology of Programming Interest Group (PPIG'11)*. York, UK: PPIG.

Martin, R. C. (2003). *Agile Software Development: Principles, Patterns, and Practices.* Upper Saddle River, NJ: Prentice Hall.

Martins, S., Mendes, A. J., & Figueiredo, A. D. (2012). A Context for Learning Programming Based on Research Communities. *Cadernos de Pedagogia do Ensino Superior, 4*, 3–22.

Matthews, R., Hin, H., & Choo, K. (2009). Multimedia learning object to build cognitive understanding in learning introductory programming. In *Proceedings of the 7th International Conference on Advances in Mobile Computing and Multimedia (MoMM'09)* (pp. 396-400). Kuala Lumpur, Malaysia: ACM. doi:10.1145/1821748.1821824

Mayer, R. E. (1981). The Psychology of How Novices Learn Computer Programming. *ACM Computing Surveys, 13*(1), 121–141. doi:10.1145/356835.356841

McGill, M. (2012). Learning to program with personal robots: Influences on student motivation. *ACM Transations on Computers Education, 12*(1), 4.

McWhorter, W., & O'Connor, B. (2009). Do LEGO® Mindstorms® motivate students in CS1? In *Proceedings of the 40th ACM technical symposium on Computer Science Education (SIGCSE'09)* (pp. 438-442). Chattanooga, TN: ACM. doi:10.1145/1508865.1509019

Mead, J., Gray, S., Hamer, J., James, R., Sorva, J., Clair, C., & Thomas, L. (2006). A cognitive approach to identifying measurable milestones for programming skill acquisition. *SIGCSE Bulletin, 38*(4), 182–194. doi:10.1145/1189136.1189185

Milne, I., & Rowe, G. (2002). Difficulties in learning and teaching programming – views of students and tutors. *Education and Information Technologies, 7*(1), 55–66. doi:10.1023/A:1015362608943

Mobbs, R. (n.d.). *TU100: Sense and the Sense-Board, an introduction.* Retrieved from http://www.youtube.com/watch?v=xmYS1slSUuM

Morgan, G., Stephanou, A., & Simpson, B. (2000). *Aptitude Profile Test Series: Manual.* Retrieved from http://www.acer.edu.au

Motil, J., & Epstein, D. (2000). *JJ: a Language Designed for Beginners (Less Is More).* Retrieved from http://www.ecs.csun.edu/~jmotil/TeachingWithJJ.pdf

Moura, I., & van Hattum-Janssen, N. (2011). Teaching a CS introductory course: An active approach. *Computers & Education, 56*(2), 475–48. doi:10.1016/j.compedu.2010.09.009

Muller, O., Haberman, B., & Ginat, D. (2007). Pattern-Oriented Instruction and its Influence on Problem Decomposition and Solution Construction. In *Proceedings of the 12th Annual Conference on Innovation and Technology in Computer Science Education (ITiCSE'07)* (pp. 151-155). Dundee, UK: ACM. doi:10.1145/1268784.1268830

Naps, T., Rößling, G., Anderson, J., Oshkosh, W., Cooper, S., & Koldehofe, B. et al. (2003). Evaluating the educational impact of visualization. *SIGCSE Bulletin, 35*(4), 124–136. doi:10.1145/960492.960540

Nguyen, D., & Wong, S. B. (1999). Patterns for decoupling data structures and algorithms. *SIGCSE Bulletin, 31*(1), 87–91. doi:10.1145/384266.299693

Pacheco, A., Henriques, J., Almeida, A. M., & Mendes, A. J. (2008). A study on basic mathematics knowledge for the enhancement of programming learning skills. In *Proceedings of the IEEIII08 - Informatics Education Europe III*. Venice, Italy: Academic Press.

Preiss, B. R. (1999). Design patterns for the data structures and algorithms course. *SIGCSE Bulletin, 31*(1), 95–99. doi:10.1145/384266.299696

Qualls, J., Grant, M., & Sherrell, L. (2011). CS1 Students' Understanding of Computational Thinking. *Journal of Computing Sciences in Colleges, 26*(5), 62–71.

Rankin, Y., Gooch, A., & Gooch, B. (2008). The impact of game design on students' interest in CS. In *Proceedings of the 3rd international conference on Game development in computer science education (GDCSE'08)* (pp. 31-35). Miami, FL: ACM. doi:10.1145/1463673.1463680

Robins, A., Rountree, J., & Rountree, N. (2003). Learning and Teaching Programming: A Review and Discussion. *Computer Science Education, 13*(2), 137–172. doi:10.1076/csed.13.2.137.14200

Robotiky – Play & Learn. (n.d.). Retrieved from robotiky.com

Rößling, G. (2010). A Family of tools for supporting the learning of programming. *Algorithms, 3*, 168-182. Retrieved from http://www.mdpi.com/1999-4893/3/2/168/pdf

Salleha, S., Shukura, Z., & Judib, H. (2013). Analysis of Research in Programming Teaching Tools: An Initial Review. In *Proceedings of 13th International Educational Technology Conference*, (pp. 127 – 135). Kuala Lumpur, Malasya: Science Direct, Elsevier. doi:10.1016/j.sbspro.2013.10.317

Santos, A., Gomes, A., & Mendes, A. J. (2010). Integrating New Technologies and Existing Tools to Promote Programming Learning. *Algoritms, 3*(2), 183–196. doi:10.3390/a3020183

Santos, A., Gomes, A., & Mendes, A. J. (2013). A taxonomy of exercises to support individual learning paths in initial programming learning. In *Proceedings of the 43rd Annual Frontiers in Education (FIE'13) Conference*. FIE. doi:10.1109/FIE.2013.6684794

Scholtz, J., & Wiedenbeck, S. (1992). The role of planning in learning a new programming language. *International Journal of Man-Machine Studies, 37*(2), 191–214. doi:10.1016/0020-7373(92)90085-Y

Shackelford, R. L., & Badre, A. N. (1993). Why can't smart students solve simple programming problems? *International Journal of Man-Machine Studies, 38*(6), 985–997. doi:10.1006/imms.1993.1045

Soloway, E. (1986). Learning to program = learning to construct mechanisms and explanations. *Communications of the ACM, 29*(9), 850–858. doi:10.1145/6592.6594

Soule, T., & Heckendorn, R. (2011). COTSBots: Computationally powerful, low-cost robots for Computer Science curriculums. *Journal of Computing Sciences in Colleges*, *27*(1), 180–187.

Spohrer, J. C., & Soloway, E. (1986). Novice mistakes: Are the folk wisdoms correct? *Communications of the ACM*, *29*(7), 624–632. doi:10.1145/6138.6145

Spohrer, J. C., Soloway, E., & Pope, E. (1985). A goal/plan analysis of buggy pascal programs. *Human-Computer Interaction*, *1*(2), 163–207. doi:10.1207/s15327051hci0102_4

Stachel, J., Marghitu, D., Brahim, T., Sims, R., Reynolds, L., & Czelusniak, V. (2013). Managing Cognitive Load in Introductory Programming Courses: A Cognitive Aware Scaffolding Tool. *Journal of Integrated Design and Process Science. Computer Science*, *17*(1), 37–54.

Stone, J., & Clark, T. (2011). The Impact of Problem-Oriented Animated Learning Modules in a CS1-Style Course. In *Proceedings of the 42th ACM technical symposium on Computer Science Education (SIGCSE'11)* (pp. 51-56). Dallas, TX: ACM. doi:10.1145/1953163.1953182

Stone, J., & Clark, T. (2013). Engaging Students with Animated Learning Modules for Introductory Computer Science. In *Proceedings of the World Conference on E-Learning in Corporate, Government, Healthcare and Higher Education*. Las Vegas, NV: Association for the Advancement of Computing in Education (AACE).

TIOBE Programming Community Index for April. (2014). Retrieved from http://www.tiobe.com/index.php/content/paperinfo/tpci/index.html

Tomai, E., & Reilly, C. (2014). The impact of math preparedness on introductory programming (CS1) success. In *Proceedings of the 45th ACM Technical Symposium on Computer Science Education (SIGCSE'14)* (pp. 711-711). Atlanta, GA: ACM. doi:10.1145/2538862.2544292

Ventura, P. R. Jr. (2005). Identifying predictors of success for an objects-first CS1. *Computer Science Education*, *15*(3), 223–243. doi:10.1080/08993400500224419

Verdú, E., Regueras, L., Verdú, M., Leal, J., & Castro, J. (2012). A distributed system for learning programming online. *Computers & Education*, *58*(1), 1–10. doi:10.1016/j.compedu.2011.08.015

Wiedenbeck, S., Fix, V., & Scholtz, J. (1993). Characteristics of the mental representations of novice and expert programmers: An empirical study. *International Journal of Man-Machine Studies*, *39*(5), 793–812. doi:10.1006/imms.1993.1084

Williams, L. A., & Kessler, R. R. (2001). Experiments with Industry's "Pair-Programming" Model in the Computer Science Classroom. *Computer Science Education*, *11*(1), 7–20. doi:10.1076/csed.11.1.7.3846

Williams, L. A., & Tomayko, J. (2002). Agile Software Development. *Computer Science Education*, *12*(3), 167–168. doi:10.1076/csed.12.3.167.8613

Wilson, B. C., & Shrock, S. (2001). Contributing to success in an introductory computer science course: A study of twelve factors. *SIGCSE Bulletin*, *33*(1), 184–188. doi:10.1145/366413.364581

Wing, J. (2008). Five deep questions in computing. *Communications of the ACM*, *51*(1), 58–60. doi:10.1145/1327452.1327479

Wing, J. M. (2006). Computacional Thinking. *Communications of the ACM*, *49*(3), 33–35. doi:10.1145/1118178.1118215

Winslow, L. E. (1996). Programming pedagogy—a psychological overview. *SIGCSE Bulletin*, *28*(3), 17–22. doi:10.1145/234867.234872

Yeh, K. C. (2009). Using an Educational Computer Game as a Motivational Tool for Supplemental Instruction Delivery for Novice Programmers in Learning Computer Programming. In *Proceedings of the Society for Information Technology & Teacher Education International Conference* (pp. 1611-1616). Charleston, SC: AACE.

Zeil, S. J. (2011). *ALGAE - Algorithm Animation Engine, Reference Manual Version 3.0, 2011*. Retrieved from http://www.cs.odu.edu/~zeil/AlgAE/referenceManual.pdf

ADDITIONAL READING

Abdul-Rahmana, S.-S., & Boulayb, B. (2014). Learning programming via worked-examples: Relation of learning styles to cognitive load. *Computers in Human Behavior, 30,* 286–298. doi:10.1016/j.chb.2013.09.007

Ahmad, K., & Gestwicki, P. (2013). Studio-Based Learning and App Inventor for Android in an Introductory CS Course for Non-Majors. In *Proceedings of the 44th ACM technical symposium on Computer Science Education (SIGCSE'13)* (pp. 165-170). Denver, Colorado, USA: ACM New York, NY, USA. doi:10.1145/2445196.2445286

Assiter, K. (2012). Introvert Educators: Techniques to be Effective in the Traditional Face-to-Face CS classroom. In *Proceedings of the 17th ACM annual conference on Innovation and Technology in Computer Science Education (ITiCSE'12)* (pp. 381-381). Haifa, Israel: ACM New York, NY, USA. doi:10.1145/2325296.2325397

Bennedsen, J., & Caspersen, M. (2012). Persistence of elementary programming skills. *Computer Science Education, 22*(2), 81–107. doi:10.1080/08993408.2012.692911

Brito, M., & Sá-Soares, F. (2014). Assessment frequency in introductory computer programming disciplines. *Computers in Human Behavior, 30,* 623–628. doi:10.1016/j.chb.2013.07.044

Bryce, R., Mayo, Q., Andrews, A., Bokser, D., Burton, M., Day, C., et al. (2013). In *Proceedings of the 44th ACM technical symposium on Computer Science Education (SIGCSE'13)* (pp. 513-518). Denver, Colorado, USA: ACM New York, NY, USA.

Cámara, L., Velasco, M., & Iturbide, J. (2012). Evaluation of a Collaborative Instructional Framework for Programming Learning. In *Proceedings of the 17th ACM annual conference on Innovation and Technology in Computer Science Education (ITiCSE'12)* (pp. 162-167). Haifa, Israel: ACM New York, NY, USA.

David Ginat, D., & Shmalo, R. (2013). Constructive Use of Errors in Teaching CS1. In *Proceedings of the 44th ACM technical symposium on Computer Science Education (SIGCSE'13)* (pp. 353-358). Denver, Colorado, USA: ACM New York, NY, USA. doi:10.1145/2445196.2445300

Denner, L., Werner, L., & Ortiz, E. (2012). Computer games created by middle school girls: Can they be used to measure understanding of computer science concepts? *Computers & Education, 58*(1), 240–249. doi:10.1016/j.compedu.2011.08.006

Dorn, B., & Tew, A. (2013). Becoming Experts: Measuring Attitude Development in Introductory Computer Science. In *Proceedings of the 44th ACM technical symposium on Computer Science Education (SIGCSE'13)* (pp. 189-194). Denver, Colorado, USA: ACM New York, NY, USA. doi:10.1145/2445196.2445252

Eckerdal, A. (2009). Novice Programming Students' Learning of Concepts and Practise. PhD Thesis, Department of Information Technology, Upsalla University, Sweeden.

Ferreira, D. (2013). Fostering the Creative Development of Computer Science Students in Programming and Interaction Design. *Procedia Computer Science, 18,* 1446–1455. doi:10.1016/j.procs.2013.05.312

Hazzan, O., Lapidot, T., & Ragonis, N. (2011). *Guide to teach Computer science: An Activity-Based Approach.* Springer Publishing Company, Inc. doi:10.1007/978-0-85729-443-2

Hertz, M., & Ford, S. (2013). Investigating Factors of Student Learning in Introductory Courses. In *Proceedings of the 44th ACM technical symposium on Computer Science Education (SIGCSE'13)* (pp. 165-170). Denver, Colorado, USA: ACM New York, NY, USA. doi:10.1145/2445196.2445254

Jermann, P., Nussli, M.-A., Dillenbourg, P., & Sharma, K. (2012). Gaze Evidence for Different Activities in Program Understanding. In *Proceedings of Psychology of Programming Interest Group (PPIG'12).* London, United Kingdom: London Metropolitan University.

Jurado, F., Redondo, M., & Ortega, M. (2012). Using fuzzy logic applied to software metrics and test cases to assess programming assignments and give advice. *Journal of Network and Computer Applications, 35*(2), 695–712. doi:10.1016/j.jnca.2011.11.002

Mason, R. (2012). *Designing introductory programming courses: the role of cognitive load.* PhD Thesis, Southern Cross University, Lismore, NSW.

Nandigam, D., & Bathula, H. (2013). Competing Dichotomies in Teaching Computer Programming to Beginner-Students. *American Journal of Educational Research, 1*(8), 307–312. doi:10.12691/education-1-8-7

Oliveira, M. G., Ciarelli, P., & Oliveira, E. (2013). Recommendation of programming activities by multi-label classification for a formative assessment of students. *Expert Systems with Applications, 40*(16), 6641–6651. doi:10.1016/j.eswa.2013.06.011

Pears, A., Seidman, S., Malmi, L., Mannila, L., Adams, E., & Bennedsen, J. et al. (2007). A survey of literature on the teaching of introductory programming. *SIGCSE Bulletin, 39*(4), 204–223. doi:10.1145/1345375.1345441

Porter, L., & Simon, B. (2013). Retaining nearly one-third more majors with a trio of instructional best practices in CS1. In *Proceedings of the 44th ACM technical symposium on Computer Science Education (SIGCSE'13)* (pp. 165-170). Denver, Colorado, USA: ACM New York, NY, USA. doi:10.1145/2445196.2445248

Ragonis, N., & Shilo, G. (2013). What Is It We Are Asking: Interpreting Problem-Solving Questions in Computer Science and Linguistics. In *Proceedings of the 44th ACM technical symposium on Computer Science Education (SIGCSE'13)* (pp. 189-194). Denver, Colorado, USA: ACM New York, NY, USA. doi:10.1145/2445196.2445253

Rubio-Sánchez, M., Kinnunen, P., Pareja-Flores, C., & Velázquez-Iturbide, A. (2014). Student perception and usage of an automated programming assessment tool. *Computers in Human Behavior, 31,* 453–460. doi:10.1016/j.chb.2013.04.001

Serrano-Cámara, L., Paredes-Velasco, M., Alcover, C.-M., & Velazquez-Iturbide, J. (2014). An evaluation of students' motivation in computer-supported collaborative learning of programming concepts. *Computers in Human Behavior, 31,* 499–508. doi:10.1016/j.chb.2013.04.030

Sheard, J., Hamilton, M., & Lönnberg, J. (2009). Analysis of research into the teaching and learning of programming. In *Proceedings of the fifth International workshop on Computing Education Research (ICER'09)* (pp. 93-104). Berkeley, CA, USA: ACM New York, NY, USA. doi:10.1145/1584322.1584334

Simon, C., A., Raadt, M., Lister, R., Hamilton, M., & Sheard, J. (2008). Classifying computing education papers: process and results. In *Proceedings of the fourth International workshop on Computing Education Research (ICER'08)* (pp. 161-172). Sydney, Australia: ACM New York, NY, USA. doi:10.1145/1404520.1404536

Sorva, J. (2012). *Visual program simulation in introductory programming education*. PhD Thesis, Department of Computer Science and Engineering, Aalto University School of Science, Espoo, Finland.

Stachel, J., Marghitu, D., Brahim, T., Sims, R., Reynolds, L., & Czelusniak, V. (2013). Managing Cognitive Load in Introductory Programming Courses: A Cognitive Aware Scaffolding Tool. *Journal of Integrated Design and Process Science. Computer Science*, *17*(1), 37–54.

Tew, E., & Dorn, A. (2013). The Case for Validated Tools in Computer Science Education Research. *Computer*, *46*(9), 60–66. doi:10.1109/MC.2013.259

Thies, R., & Vahrenhold, J. (2013). On Plugging "Unplugged" into CS Classes. In *Proceedings of the 44th ACM technical symposium on Computer Science Education (SIGCSE'13)* (pp. 365-370). Denver, Colorado, USA: ACM New York, NY, USA. doi:10.1145/2445196.2445303

Utting, I., Tew, A. E., McCracken, M., Thomas, L., Bouvier, D., Frye, R., et al. (2013). A Fresh Look at Novice Programmers' Performance and Their Teachers' Expectations. In *Proceedings of the 18th annual conference on Innovation and Technology in Computer Science Education (ITiCSE'13)* (pp. 15-32). Canterbury, Kent, UK: ACM New York, NY, USA. doi:10.1145/2543882.2543884

Velazquez-Iturbide, J., Debdi, O., Esteban-Sanchez, N., & Pizarro, C. (2013). GreedEx: A Visualization Tool for Experimentation and Discovery Learning of Greedy Algorithms. *IEEE Transactions on Learning Technologies*, *6*(2), 130–143. doi:10.1109/TLT.2013.8

KEY TERMS AND DEFINITIONS

Animations and Visualizations: Are computer programs intended to help students to understand concepts related to programming. They help to concretize the abstract nature of programming concepts and structures through visual elements. Some of them enable student interaction.

Computational Thinking: Is a fundamental way of thinking and problem solving for computer science individuals. It is a very important set of skills of thinking applicable to nearly any subject. Specific computational thinking includes techniques such as problem decomposition, pattern recognition, abstractions definition, algorithm design or data analysis.

CS1 and CS2: Are general terms used by the ACM Computing Curricula to designate the introductory sequence of a computer science major. These abbreviations are still used nowadays. The term CS1 is used to refer to the introductory programming course. The term CS2 is used to refer to the second programming course.

Learning Styles: Are combinations of the individuals' preferred approaches of learning. They are based on the idea that individuals differ in how they learn and the way they approach learning. They are an individual's natural or habitual pattern of acquiring and processing information in learning situations.

Misconceptions: Are wrongly or imperfectly preconceived ideas, notions, concepts or beliefs. This term means a mismatch between the student's comprehension and the real meaning of a concept.

Programming Structures: Are different types of elements needed to create a program using a programming paradigm language aimed at improving the clarity of a computer program by making extensive use of control structures, functions and other programming blocks.

Serious Games: Are games designed for a primary purpose other than only entertainment. They have learning and pedagogical principles embedded and the adjective "serious" means that they usually have real purposes (education, training, scientific experimentation…).

Chapter 2
Open Source Social Networks in Education

Amine V. Bitar
University of Balamand, Lebanon

Antoine M. Melki
University of Balamand, Lebanon

ABSTRACT

Social computing systems such as Social Network Sites have become more powerful. In some universities, SNSs have been adopted as a communication method between teachers and students. In addition, educational institutions have started the initiative of using open source social networking application. This chapter discusses the benefits of adopting open source SNS in education. It is organized as follows: 1) a literature review to properly define the terms, 2) a discussion of the effect of open source social networking technologies on education systems, 3) an overview of Elgg, followed by a comparison with different social learning platforms, 4) a case study of implementing Elgg at the Computer Science Department at the University of Balamand, 5) an exhibition of the requirements for the Next Generation SCORM, 6) a case study using Tin Can API with open source SNSs (Elgg), and 7) a conclusion wrapping up the chapter.

INTRODUCTION

Human-to-Human communication environment has changed in the last few years. Social networking sites have been used as important tools and interactive means which connect people with others around the world. Such technologies provide institutions and organizations with community building competences. In particular, open source social networks present lot of features that allow people to build social relations between each other. Moreover, these media supply institutions with enhanced learning capabilities which have been used by students and teachers in their daily communications. In progression, higher educational institutions have started to implement open source social networking sites as a mean to improve students' academic performance. The main purpose of adopting such techniques is to allow teachers and

DOI: 10.4018/978-1-4666-7304-5.ch002

students benefit from online services to achieve high level of cooperative learning platform.

The aim of this chapter is to show the advantage of using open source social networks in higher educational institutions. It presents an overview about open source software in general, then open source social networking in particular and their effects on education systems. In Lebanon, 80% of higher educational institutions have adopted learning management systems, like Moodle, to provide both students and teachers with online interactive learning opportunities. Moodle is limited to some basic features (user collaboration, group discussions, file sharing…). A comparison among different social learning platforms is followed which clearly emphasizes on the most included features that Elgg offers and makes it a right choice to be a good social learning tool for institutions. Elgg offers a lot of features that make it a good choice to be considered as a powerful social learning tool for institutions. The department of Computer Science at the University of Balamand has implemented Elgg as a social networking engine. A questionnaire survey was conducted on teachers and students in order to assess the effectiveness of using Elgg as an open source learning platform. The results of the survey obviously show a good satisfaction from all participants of using Elgg which offers them all the important features of a learning management system. On the other hand, Elgg does not comply with Sharable Content Object Reference Model (SCORM), so its lack of course management might be made for with the integration with Moodle. In contrast, SCORM has some limitations to achieve the necessities of today's online educational system. Consequently, a solution is proposed in this chapter to integrate Tin Can API with Elgg as a replacement to the Elgg/Moodle integration solution to form a complete learning management system.

BACKGROUND

Open Source Software

In definition, open source is a software free code available for free where any person can modify, extend, and improve the code. According to GNU project, free software can be defined as "a matter of the users' freedom to run, copy, distribute, study, change and improve the software". Open source software – software delivered with its source code – is an outcome of the convergence of information and communication technologies (Van Rooij, June 2009).

Developers of open source software are also the users of the software where they participate in the collaborative development process. One of the benefits of open source philosophy is that open source software is more secure, because weaknesses and code bugs are easier for users to find and fix due to the large number of people examining the software ((Raymond, 2001), (Stallman,1999), (Weber, 2004). Moreover, open source software is less expensive to use than proprietary software because there are no license fees for the source code.

Consequently, the world is moving towards open education by adopting online teaching. Open education is a new social process that is beginning to act as complete substitute for traditional face-to-face class (Hiltz & Turoff, 2005). It refers to the educational institutions where knowledge and learning materials should be free and open to use by students. Open education resources have much in common with open source software where software has better performance and more customizable than proprietary software. The use of open source software in open education allows better performance and more customizable than proprietary software. By adopting open education, institutions can benefit from a wide range of advantages such as: cost-saving, improving reputation and visibility, developing education strategies, increasing community collaborations.

Open Source Social Networking Technologies

Institutions are moving towards open education by adopting online teaching. Open education is when knowledge and learning materials should be free and open to use by students (Hiltz & Turoff, 2005)). The use of open source software in open education allows better performance and more customizable than proprietary software which allows institutions to benefit from a wide range of advantages such as: increasing community collaborations, developing education strategies, and cost-saving.

An open source social networking technology can be defined as an online site or platform which can be used by people to build social relations among them. People use social networking sites to make connections with friends and new people they meet through the site, as well as for a number of purposes: sharing photos, discussions, activities, ideas, events, and interests. As an example, Facebook, Diaspora and Elgg are open source social networking site that provide many popular features which allow users to interact over the internet such as: users' interactions, instant messaging, shared blogs, file sharing, forums, and news feeds.

In the past few years, institutions have adopted open source social networking applications like social networking sites and course management systems as an online medium for education. The goal behind such transition is that institutions consider open source social networking technology as a free means to deliver education online for many reasons: cost reducing, vendor dependency and rapid fixing of open source software bugs and problems. The benefits of the open source model are increased quality, greater stability, superior performance, and improved functionality (Siemens, 2003).

In their research paper on next-generation social networking media, Jafari, McGee and Carmean show the interest of students in social networking media and course management systems where these systems have much in common with the systems they use socially in their daily communication life (Jafari, McGee, & Carmean, 2007). Furthermore, students use some of these systems in their daily social communication life. Students want systems that place them at the epicenter, rather than being course-focused (Garett, Thoms, Soffer, & Ryan, 2007).

A number of academic researches have been conducted on the importance of deploying open source social networking media as methods for online education in classrooms.. These researches focus on the interest of using blogs to create informal student-centered spaces. The greatest benefits of such deployment are to promote student reflection, engagement, portfolio, and high-level synthesizing activities (Berscia & Miller M, 2006). Additionally, the use of these medias as methods for online education allows students to present themselves to others and to reflect on their learning (Barrett, 2005).

Accordingly, open source social networking provides institutions with the capability to enhance the learning process ((Schlenkrich & Sewry, 2012; Clyde, 2005). Furthermore, open source social networking platforms offer a numerous number of positive effects on enhancing the educational process such as: increased productivity, cost saving, advanced collaboration, research support, creative teaching atmosphere, increased libraries visibilities, motivated students and enhanced learning opportunities.

Effect of Open Source Social Networking Technologies on Education Systems

Open source social networking presents may opportunities, which may be exploited by institutions to enhance learning (Schlenkrich & Sewry, 2012). Furthermore, open source social networking platforms offer a numerous number of positive effects on enhancing the educational process:

- **Increase Productivity:** Open source social networking sites allow students to work on projects and assignments online with their colleagues. Also, teachers can communicate with other international teachers and researchers which result in effective products in less time.

- **Cost Saving:** Institutions adopt open source social networking platforms to reduce cost of ownership and maintenance. Educational institutions can customize open source technologies to meet their needs.

- **Advanced Collaboration:** Open source social networking technologies allow an increasing activity among teachers and students. Students can communicate with other students from their community or other communities, link to resources, and share personal files. Also, teachers can locate expertise, collaborate with other researchers, and expand the range of their professional relationships.

- **Research Support:** Open source social networking allows researchers the possibility to support their researches and developments. Researchers can explore their ideas and researches interest with researchers outside of their community.

- **Motivate Students and Enhance Learning Opportunities:** Students can build online collaboration to enhance their learning capabilities. They can post, and share their ideas. Also, they can receive feedback from others which allow them to improve and develop their ideas.

- **Creative Teaching Atmosphere:** Teachers use social networking sites to go beyond the institution walls (Clyde, 2005). In this way, students can achieve high level of motivation and access large amounts of information anytime and anywhere. Moreover, teachers can track their students in an effective learning system.

- **Increase Libraries Visibilities:** Library in an institution can benefit from open social networking sites to increase their visibility and research assistance. Information grabbing could me much easier when library services are open and convenient for all communities.

- **Fruitful Conversations:** Students can engage into online conversations and post comments on the site. Teachers can use such useful information to keep track of their students' activities, interact and give proper help.

MAIN FOCUS OF THE CHAPTER

Elgg

Elgg is an award-winning social networking engine, delivering the building blocks that enable businesses, schools, universities and associations to create their own fully-featured social networks and applications (Elgg). Elgg has a lot of social features that makes it a right choice for educational institutions. It combines a set of features which provide an attractive environment for institutions and students to create their own learning network. Furthermore, it can be used to allow students to collaborate in an online learning community. It can be integrated with other learning management systems such as Moodle to produce e-learning software specifically for education.

Being adopted as online social networking software, Elgg offers university students the opportunity to create an online learning environment including a set of features: weblogs, bookmarks, instant messaging, files repository, resources publishing, sharing and linking with others.

Elgg provides students with full control over their online profiles where they can maintain their own file gallery, blog, and personal customized templates. Besides, Elgg provide its users with a full control over others in the community who

Table 1. Elgg features and their corresponding descriptions

Features	Description
Social Networking	Find, link and share knowledge and resources with others
Weblog	Personal and friends web logging system which can link to items in repository and shared with others
Bookmark	Bookmark users favorite pages and groups
Instant Messaging	Allow users to carry on conversations and message each others instantly
Files Repository	Include different types of files
Access Control	Powerful access system feature which provides privacy to all users characteristics
Tagging	Search and find other users of similar interest
Customization	Users can customize their own groups and templates
XML-RPC	Use external blogging clients to post to an Elgg site
Community Building	Creating users own communities around shared interests

can view their content. Wiki add-in component makes Elgg more practical for an academic course community which allows several students to have their own pages with same name.

Table 1 shows a set of features with their corresponding descriptions that Elgg combines.

Elgg has been adopted by different international organizations and institutions: Australian government, British government, New Zealand ministry of education, the World Bank, UNESCO, NASA, Harvard University and many others.

In this chapter, a comparison has been made among different social networking sites such as: Elgg, Moodle, Drupal, JomSocial, and Chamilo. The selection of these social networking sites was made based on their popular usage among millions of members. These applications have been used in many institutions as a social networking mean for educational purpose to provide both teachers and students with a motivated framework and cooperative online platform.

Moodle is an open source community-based course management system (CMS). It is a free web application that educators can use to create social effective learning sites (Moodle). Moodle has been widely used in many educational institutions to deliver online materials with the aim of enhancing students' learning experiences. It

allows students/teachers to study/create and teach online courses. Both, teachers and students can participate into forums, events, and discussions.

Drupal is an open source software maintained and developed by a community of 630,000+ users and developers (Drupal). Using Drupal, people can easily organize, manage and publish their content with a diversity of customization. It encourages modularity, standards, collaboration, ease-of-use, and more.

JomSocial is a social networking component that allows people to create their own social network with photo and video gallery, event management, activity stream and other features (Joomla). JomSocial can be easily integrated with Facebook to get additional features. It has a lot of social features which make it a good social network platform. These features include: user file management, events management, groups interaction, functionalities extensibility, privacy control and files sharing.

Chamilo is a fully-fledged open source e-learning system. It aims at bringing the best e-learning and collaboration platform in the open source world (Chamilo). It is currently used by thousands of users, like governments, companies, universities, NGOs, and other organizations. Chamilo

Table 2. Comparison of the offered features by different social learning platforms

	Elgg	Moodle	Drupal	JomSocial	Chamilo
Open Source	Yes	Yes	Yes	Yes	Yes
Discussion Forum	Yes	Yes	Yes	Yes	Yes
Discussion Management	Yes	Yes	Yes	Yes	Yes
Personal File Sharing	Yes	No	No	Yes	No
Entire Class Single E-Mailing	No	No	No	Yes	Yes
Real-Time Chat	Plug-in	Yes	Plug-in	Yes	No
Community Networking	Yes	Yes	Plug-in	No	Yes
Full Administrative Tools	Yes	No	No	No	No
Full Course Management	Yes	No	No	Yes	Yes
Full Course Delivery Tool	Yes	No	No	No	Yes
Full Students Tracking	Yes	No	No	No	Yes
Multiple Institutions Support	Yes	Yes	No	No	No
Real-Time Notifications	Yes	No	No	No	No
Create Groups	Yes	No	No	Yes	No
Create Pages	Yes	No	No	Yes	No
Third-Part Integration	Yes	No	Yes	Yes	No
SCORM	No (Yes, with Moodle integration)	Yes	No	No	Yes

provides its users the possibility to manage from live training to full distant learning.

A comparison among the above described social learning platforms is listed in Table 2 to focus on the features of each one.

Based on the most included features listed in Table 2 that Elgg offers, and some limitations of the remaining social learning platforms, Elgg could be considered as the most powerful social network component for higher education institutions to improve student's interaction and flexibility in learning.

Case Study

As mentioned earlier, Elgg has been used in a wide range of applications across different institutions and organizations. In this chapter, we have implemented Elgg, a social networking system, as a platform to create an online community in the Department of Computer Science at the University of Balamand – Lebanon. The goal of adopting Elgg as a social networking platform is to enhance community among students taking the course and provide both, teachers and students, with a full set of features that are an asset for the educational process. Also, this motivated framework will lead to a cooperative online platform.

Implementation

As a matter of fact, Elgg has been implemented in the department since Spring 2012 semester. A set of different courses were created. In this chapter, we have selected an example consisting of creating one course in Elgg with a number of enrolled students. The main goal of adopting Elgg is to enhance learning community among students and teachers.

A sample of different screenshots shows the creation of one course, "Introduction to Computers & Programming". These screenshots focus on the importance of perceived learning of students and the academic activities in a cooperative learning community.

In Figure 1, the Introduction to Computers & Programming class has been created. Obviously, a description about the course and the course instructor appear on the top of the above figure, In addition, group members show the students enrolled in this class. In the remaining part of the above screenshot, a set of features that Elgg offer could be identified. These features are: weblog, posted files, homework and projects. A list of group activities records the activity history performed by the group members. Lastly, a log of discussions among community members is shown.

Figure 2 lists the activities and comments performed by the group members. A detailed history is shown for each member's activity within the community.

A snapshot on weblog is shown in Figure 3. Students get into collaboration with each others in solving their projects and commenting on others' solutions.

Figure 4 shows a sample of class discussion between teacher and students. Students use this feature to engage into class discussions, involve in solving their homework and coordinate in their projects. Members can post to either a single community blog or diversity of outside communities.

Figure 1. Introduction to computers and programming class

Figure 2. Activities and comments performed by the group members

Figure 3. Snapshot on weblog

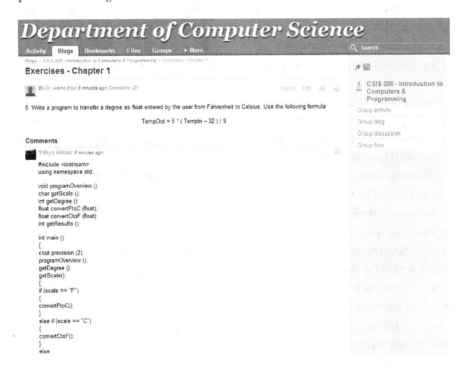

Figure 4. Sample of class discussion between teacher and students

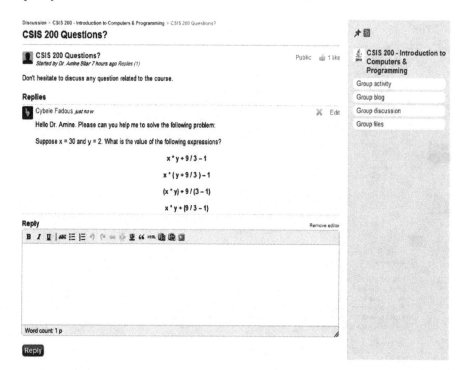

Survey Questionnaire

As we have mentioned previously, Elgg has been adopted as a social networking platform to provide computer science students at the University of Balamand with an efficient tool to create a collaborative learning community. Teachers used Elgg to communicate with their students, post information, and keep track of their students' online activities. On the other hand, students used such technology for social learning and interaction, build communications and make new connections.

In order to assess the effectiveness of using Elgg in higher educational institutions as an open source learning platform, a questionnaire survey was conducted for this purpose. The survey covered 7 teachers and 210 students from the Computer Science Department with a total of 217 participants. Teachers/students have given/taken courses using Elgg as a social learning platform over two consecutive semesters in year 2012 where both have previous experiences in using social networking sites such as Facebook, Moodle, and Drupal.

The survey contained questions related to the usefulness of Elgg listed features in Table 2. A five-point rating scale ranging from 1 (totally disagree) to 5 (totally agree) was used for this purpose. Questions were asked about features related to people communication, file repository, blogs, customizability, instant messaging, resource publishing, discussions, and group collaboration.

Discussion of Results

Table 3 summarizes the Elgg's features with their corresponding number of teachers and students in each rating scale.

Table 3 shows the number of participants in the corresponding scale of each Elgg's feature. Overall results show that majority of participants had an encouraged feedback for using Elgg as an open source for social learning. A positive

Table 3. Corresponding Elgg's features rating-points of the questionnaire survey

Features	1	2	3	4	5
Customizations	0	0	3	58	156
Discussion Forum	0	0	15	59	143
Discussion Management	0	0	11	85	121
Personal File Sharing	0	0	13	60	144
Entire Class Single E-Mailing	0	0	17	49	151
Instant Messaging	0	0	13	57	147
Blogs	0	0	9	67	141
Resource Publishing	0	0	11	70	136
Full Course Management	0	0	8	71	138
Create Groups	0	0	12	79	126
Create Pages	0	0	13	77	127
More Interaction than Class	0	0	10	59	148
More Group Collaboration	0	0	15	43	159

response was received from students using such a powerful media for social education.

The main factor behind this positive feedback is that Elgg can be used, as any other social networking site, in their daily communication life to communicate with their classmates, share interests, share news, share personal files, and meet new friends from other communities. Add to that, they can use such a tool to collaborate in their classes, post files, solve assignments, get involved into class discussions, and coordinate with others in their projects. This model will lead to better collaboration and high level of expertise achievement in an enhanced learning educational system.

Basically, students from different classes used Elgg in major different ways. In some courses, students mostly used community public blogs and comments features to share ideas. Other groups used personal blogs to post their files. Others have used the wiki feature for projects' coordination. Similarly, teachers' contributions vary from member to another. Such adoption shows that students have more interests in learning and have achieved better results in their learning progression.

In general, using Elgg, teachers can reach a high level of collaborative research with other colleagues from one side and can get into enthusiastic learning system with students from another side. As well, students can benefit from such an interactive environment to improve themselves and communicate with their remaining colleagues.

As a result, this model will lead to better collaboration and high level of expertise achievement in an enhanced learning educational system. Most teachers and students show interest in using Elgg as a social networking in their educational process. The results promise that Elgg can be considered as an efficient tool that can be adopted as an open source social networking platform to enhance education. Based on such satisfaction, Elgg can be adopted as an online social learning platform in education by other universities.

Requirements for Next Generation SCORM

To have an access to online materials, a course based system requires course management characteristics such as: file access control, user levels and many different features. By definition, "Sharable Content Object Reference Model (SCORM) is a set of technical standards for e-learning software products. It is the de facto industry standard for e-learning interoperability" (SCORM). The main goal of SCORM is to manage the communication process between online learning content and learning management systems (LMSs). It is mainly supported by many LMSs and Virtual Learning Environments.

In online education, learning system could be synchronous or asynchronous. A synchronous learning system is an environment where learning occurs at the same time and place. On the other hand, asynchronous learning system is an environment where time and place are not constraints. SCORM provides synchronous and asynchronous online learning system with basic course management features. In contrast, it has a lot of disadvantages: complicated format, lot of internet bandwidth usage, high storage space usage, limited selection of activities, long time download of learning interactions, web browser dependent, limited tracking capabilities, LMS dependent, no availability of cross domain content and platform transition, and no support for offline mode.

The above listed requirements are introduced as new features and possibilities in Tin Can API. It is classified to be the next generation solution of 10 years old SCORM which eliminates all the limitations and weaknesses of previous e-learning systems (SCORM).

Tin Can API is a new tool for learning systems which allow the possibility of collecting data in a consistent format about various experiences a person has (online and offline) from numerous technologies (Tin Can API). In addition to the above requirements, Tin Can API offers many solutions such as: complete control over content (materials, files...), social and collaborative learning, mobile applications, virtual worlds, games tracking and simulations, real-world performance and offline learning tracking.

A comparison between SCORM and Tin Can API is shown in Table 4 which highlights the most included features of each one.

Table 4 shows some SCORM limitations of primitive features. Consequently, Tin Can API offers more advanced features and could be considered as a replacement for previous e-learning standards.

Requirements Importance for Elgg

On the other hand, Elgg lacks some features of course management system: no course creating, no instructors mentioning, and no grading system and scheduling availability. Add to that, Elgg does not comply with SCORM. In order to include the most features of a course based system, Elgg could be integrated with other LMSs (like Moodle).

Moodle is SCORM compliant but limited to some basic features like: user collaboration, group discussions, and file sharing.... These features might be complemented through the integration of a powerful social networking tool like Elgg.

Based on the above comparison in Table 4 which shows the lack of advanced features in SCORM and provided by Tin Can API, therefore, we suggest the integration of Elgg with next generation SCORM to form a complete learning management system. Tin Can API is LMS independent; it provides all the advanced features as a next generation SCORM to Elgg without the use of LMS (like Moodle).

Proposed Solution

As mentioned earlier, we propose to integrate Tin Can API with Elgg as a solution to replace Elgg/Moodle integration. Tin Can API presents an open source client libraries which are available in four main languages: Objective C, Javascript, .Net and Java. Such solution can be developed under any platform. In addition to that, it provides large open source software community support through

Table 4. Comparison of the offered features by SCORM and Tin Can API

	SCORM	Tin Can API
Completion tracking	Yes	Yes
Time tracking	Yes	Yes
Students pass/fail tracking	Yes	Yes
Single score reporting	Yes	Yes
Multiple score reporting	No	Yes
Detailed test results	No	Yes
Solid security	No	Yes
No LMS required	No	Yes
Complete control over content	No	Yes
No limitation for cross-domain	No	Yes
Mobile apps usage for learning	No	Yes
Platform transition	No	Yes
Games tracking	No	Yes
Simulations tracking	No	Yes
Informal learning tracking	No	Yes
Real-world performance tracking	No	Yes
Offline learning tracking	No	Yes
Interactive learning tracking	No	Yes
Adaptive learning tracking	No	Yes
Blended learning tracking	No	Yes
Long-term learning tracking	No	Yes
Team-based learning tracking	No	Yes

GitHub which is a collaborative repository of open source projects.

Tin Can API integration with Elgg can be completed and achieved through a Learning Record Store (LRS). A LRS is a learning records repository of Tin Can API activities which can be accessed by Elgg, reporting tools, or any other LMSs. LRS can provide with read/write accessibilities to its data which are stored as individual learning records or entire records.

There are two available integrations: In the first one, LRS can be installed on local servers in an institution along with Elgg which is installed locally also. In the second one, LRS can be installed on cloud servers where Elgg is installed

locally in the institution. In this integration, LRS can communicate with Elgg through the network.

Having any of the above integrations in an educational institution allows teachers with better understanding of their students. Moreover, it provides teachers with the capabilities to track and monitor online/offline students activities. Unlike SCORM and other e-learning standards which store a limited amount of data and learning materials, Tin Can API allows LRS to store all data, logs, and reporting process of students.

According to Figure 5, it shows a complete integration of Elgg with Tin Can API through LRS. LRS acts as middleware between Elgg and Tin Can features. Learning data and activities (Tin

Figure 5. Complete integration of Elgg with tin can API through LRS

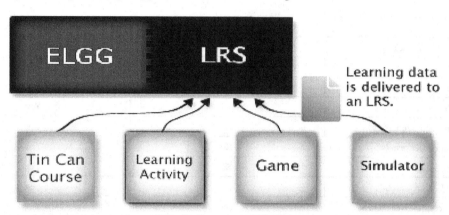

Can course, game, simulator…) are delivered to Elgg through LRS. An Elgg plug-in should be developed as a Tin Can client to communicate with the LRS.

In the above proposed system, a course, game, quiz, or any learning activity are created through the Elgg interface which are stored in the LRS and managed by the Tin Can API. When students access the activities, the LRS stores and record their actions. LRS reports actions to teachers who can monitor and track students' activities with all the provided Tin Can features.

FUTURE RESEARCH DIRECTIONS

As future work, a Tin Can Client Elgg plug-in is planned for development. Educational institutions and organizations which started the adoption of Elgg can implement the resulting system as a complete learning management system.

Tin Can Client Elgg Plug-in provides a set of functionalities that adds more featured components for the system. The user can interact directly with these functionalities of the plug-in. Such interaction will result in automatic and quick forwarding of Tin Can messages to the LRS.

CONCLUSION

In conclusion, open source social networking platforms have been adopted in many institutions and organizations. Using open source social networking sites in education has a lot of advantages and enhances the learning process and collaboration in institutions. A comparison was made between different social networking sites which has emphasized on the most features that Elgg offer to be a social learning tool and has shown some limitations for other social networking sites.

In this chapter, we have presented a case study of implementing Elgg at the Department of Computer Science at the University of Balamand. The results show the importance of adopting such an open source social networking platform as an efficient tool to enhance education.

Elgg, has shown to be an effective social networking platform that empowers the learning process with a set effective features that facilitate online communications among teachers and students. Elgg can be used into different ways as a class social networking. Each institution can integrate it into their courses using the most suitable way. Thus, Elgg can be considered as a fully-featured powerful tool for social class education which can improve students' social learning and teachers' satisfactions.

In contrast, Elgg is not Sharable Content Object Reference Model (SCORM) compliant, so its lack of course management might be made for with the integration with Moodle. SCORM offers some basic and primitive features for e-learning. A comparison was made between SCORM and Tin Can API which is the next generation SCORM. The compared table shows the most advanced features that Tin Can API offers which make it a replacement for the e-learning standards.

In this chapter, we have proposed a solution to integrate Elgg with Tin Can API through a Tin Can Client Elgg plug-in. The proposed system, being a combination of social media with the latest e-learning technologies, promises to present an alternative of traditional LMS and e-learning standards.

REFERENCES

Barrett, H. (2005). *Researching Electronic Portfolios and Learning Engagement: The REFLECT Initiative*. TaskStream Inc.

Berscia, W., & Miller, M. (2006). *What's Worth? The Perceived Benefits of Instructional Blogging. Electronic Journal for the Integration of Technology in Education.*

Clyde, L. A. (2005). Educational Blogging. *Teacher Librarian*, *32*(3), 43–45.

Elgg. (n.d.). Retrieved May 14, 2014 from http://www.elgg.org

Garett, N., Thoms, B., Soffer, M., & Ryan, T. (2007). Extending the Elgg Social Networking System to Enhance the Campus Conversation. In *Proceedings of DESRIST 2007*. DESRIST.

Hiltz, S. R., & Turoff, M. (2005). Education Goes Digital: The Evolution of Online Learning and The Revolution in Higher Education. *Communications of the ACM*, *48*(10), 59–63. doi:10.1145/1089107.1089139

Jafari, A., McGee, P., & Carmean, C. (2007). *A Research Study on Current CMS and Next Generation E-Learning Environment*. Next Generation Course Management System Group.

Raymond, E. S. (2001). *The Cathedral and the Bazaar: Musings on Linux and Open Source by an Accidental Revolutionary*. Cambridge, MA: O'Reilly & Associates.

Schlenkrich, L., & Sewry, D. A. (2012). Factors for Successful Use of Social Networking Sites in Higher Education. *Journal of Social Studies Research*, *5*.

SCORM. (n.d.a). Retrieved May 15, 2014 from http://scorm.com/scorm-explained/

SCORM. (n.d.b). Retrieved May 15, 2014 from http://scorm.com/tincan/

Siemens, G. (2003). *Open Source Content in Education: Part 2 – Developing, Sharing, Expanding Resources*. Retrieved May 12, 2014, from http://www.elearnspace.org/Articles/open_source_part_2.htm

Stallman, R. (1999). *The GNU Project*. Retrieved May 12, 2014, from http://www.gnu.org/gnu/thegnuproject.html

TinCanAPI. (n.d.). Retrieved May 16, 2014 from http://tincanapi.com/overview/

Van Rooij, S. (2009, June). Adopting Open-Source Software Applications in Higher Education: A Cross-Disciplinary Review of the Literature. *Review of Educational Research*, *79*(2), 682–701. doi:10.3102/0034654308325691

Weber, S. (2004). *The Success of Open Source*. Cambridge, MA: Harvard University Press.

ADDITIONAL READING

Bach, P., DeLine, R., & Carroll, J. (2009). *Designers Wanted: Participation & The User Experience in Open Source Software Development*. ACM. doi:10.1145/1518701.1518852

Barton, M., & Maranto, G. (2010). Paradox and Promise: MySpace, Facebook, and The Sociopolitics of Social Networking in the Writing Classroom. *ScienceDirect.*, *27*, 36–47.

Begel A. & Deline R. (2010). Social Media for Software Engineering. FOSER. 33-37.

Berg, J., Berquam, L., & Christoph, K. (2007). Social Networking Technologies: A "Poke" for Campus Services. *EDUCAUSE Review*, (March/April): 32–44.

Boyd, D. M., & Ellison, N. B. (2008). Social Network Sites: Definition, History, and Scholarship'. *Journal of Computer-Mediated Communication*, *13*(1), 210–230. doi:10.1111/j.1083-6101.2007.00393.x

Christensen, R. (2002). Effects of Technology Integration Education on the Attitudes of Teachers and Students. *Journal of Research on Technology in Education*, *34*(4), 411–433. doi:10.1080/1539 1523.2002.10782359

Correas, J. M., Correas, I., & Lopez, P. (2006). Designing Third-Generation Web-Based Systems for Distance Learning: Influence and Contributions From Open Source. *Proceedings of the 6th WSEAS*, 16-19.

Downes, S. (2004). Educational Blogging. Educause Review. http://www.downes.com

Gourley B. & Lane A. (1009). Re-Invigorating Openness at the Open University: The Role of Open educational Resources. Open Learning: The Journal of Open, Distance & E-Learning. 24 (1), 57-65.

Grosseck G. (2009). To Use or Not To Use Web2.0 in Higher Education? ScienceDirect. 478-482.

Hemmi, A., Bayne, S., & Landt, R. (2009). The Appropriation and Repurposing of Social Technologies in Higher Education. *Journal of Computer Assisted Learning*, *25*(1), 19–30. doi:10.1111/j.1365-2729.2008.00306.x

Koohang, A., & Harman, K. (2005), Open Source: A Metaphor for E-Learning. Informing Science Journal. http://gatortracks.pbworks.com/f/facebook+changes+in+use.pdf

Lampe C., Ellison L. & Steinfield C. (2008), Changes in Use and perception of Facebook. CSCW'08.

Littauer R., Scheidel A., Schulder M., & Ciddi S. (2012). Crowd Sourcing The Classroom: Interactive Applications in Higher Learning. Proceedings of Edulearn12 Conference, 1473-1481.

Mazer, J. P., Murphy, R. E., & Simonds, C. J. (2007). I'll See You On "Facebook": The Effects of Computer-Mediated Teacher Self-Disclosure on Student Motivation, Affective Learning, and Classroom Climate. *Communication Education*, *56*(1), 1–17. doi:10.1080/03634520601009710

Morelli, R., & De Lanerolle, T. (2009). *FOSS 101: Engaging Introductory Students in The Open Source Movement*. SIGCSE. doi:10.1145/1508865.1508977

Schlenkrich L. & Sewry DA. (2012). Factors for Successful Use of Social Networking Sites in Higher Education. SACJ. no. 49, 12-24.

Snyder, J., Carpenter, D., & Slauson, G. J. (2007). MySpace.com – A Social Networking Site and Social Contract Theory. *Information Systems Education Journal*, *5*(2), 3–11.

Storey MA., Van Deursen A., & Cheng T. (2010). The Impact of Social Media on Software Engineering Practices and Tools. FOSER. 359-363.

Watsan, R., Boudreau, M. C., York, P., & Greiner, M. (2008). Opening The Classroom. *Journal of Information Systems Education*, *19*(1), 75–85.

KEY TERMS AND DEFINITIONS

CMS: A course management system is a set of software tools that provide online course management.

GitHub: It is a web based repository for software projects. It offers social networking functionalities (such as: wikis, feeds).

GNU Project: It is a free software that gives the users the freedom rights to run, test, modify and share the software.

LMS: Learning management system is used for e-learning educational purposes. It offers creating, administrating, tracking of online courses.

LRS: Learning Record Store is a repository to store learning records and activities in e-learning systems.

Plug-In: It is a set of components that can be added to software which adds more customizable features.

Tin Can API: It is a specification for e-learning software that records and tracks learning content in learning systems.

OSS: Open source software is a software where its code is available for any user to run, modify, and distribute to other users in the community.

Chapter 3
Small-Group vs. Competitive Learning in Computer Science Classrooms:
A Meta-Analytic Review

Sema A. Kalaian
Eastern Michigan University, USA

Rafa M. Kasim
Indiana Tech University, USA

ABSTRACT

The focus of this meta-analytic chapter was to quantitatively integrate and synthesize the accumulated pedagogical research that examined the effectiveness of one of the various small-group learning methods in maximizing students' academic achievement in undergraduate computer science classrooms. The results of the meta-analysis show that cooperative, collaborative, problem-based, and pair learning pedagogies were used in college-level computer science classrooms with an overall average effect-size of 0.41. The results of the multilevel analysis reveal that the effect sizes were heterogeneous and the effects were explored further by including the coded predictors in the conditional multilevel model in efforts to explain the variability. The results of the conditional multilevel model reveal that the effect sizes were influenced significantly by both instructional duration and assessment type of the studies. The findings imply that the present evidence-based research supports the effectiveness of active small-group learning methods in promoting students' achievement in computer science classrooms.

INTRODUCTION

For the last three decades, there have been numerous and consistent calls for instructional reforms and innovations in science, technology, engineering, and mathematics (STEM) education by the national and federal agencies as well as professional organizations such as the American Association for the Advancement of Science (2005), National Science Foundation (1996), National Research Council (2001), and the Accreditation Board of Engineering and Technology (2008).

DOI: 10.4018/978-1-4666-7304-5.ch003

In their publications and recommendations, they emphasized the need to examine the existing teaching methods and student-learning processes. They also emphasized the need to develop and explore innovative teaching practices that require the implementation of one of the various forms of active methods of small-group learning pedagogies in STEM college classrooms including computer science classrooms. Cooperative learning, collaborative learning, pair programming, problem-based learning, and team-based learning are examples of such innovative active small-group pedagogies. In addition, these calls emphasized the requirement that the graduates from these various STEM disciplines including computer science fields of study to have the ability to communicate effectively, think reflectively and critically, and function effectively in cooperative and collaborative multidisciplinary team-based educational settings, which mirror the real STEM including computer science related workplace environments. Thus, teamwork has long been an important component of computer science education since it models the way computer programing and software development in industrial settings nationwide and throughout the world. The global software development (GSD) industry is an example of such contextual setting.

In response to these numerous calls and recommendations for educational reform, many STEM educators, including computer science instructors and educators have been developing, experimenting, adopting, and/or implementing different forms of the various innovative active small-group learning methods in their classrooms. As a result of developing and using these active learning methods, many empirical primary studies have been conducted to examine and evaluate the effectiveness of these active small-group learning pedagogies compared to the traditional competitive instructional methods such as lecture-based instruction and individualized instruction in increasing the students' achievement across all levels of schooling (K-12 and college).

BACKGROUND

Small-group learning is defined as an instructional method in which small groups of students work together to accomplish a shared common learning goal. These small-group learning methods stem from both of the cognitive and social constructivist philosophies of learning. These philosophies view that each individual in a learning group actively and collaboratively constructs knowledge based on previously learned conceptual knowledge and through his or her experiences and social interactions with the other learners in their teams. Cooperative learning, collaborative learning, pair learning/programming, problem-based learning, inquiry-based learning, and team-based learning are such systematic forms of active small-group learning methods. In collaborative learning environments, students perceive that they can reach their common learning goals if they work collaboratively with the other group members. In competitive environments, students perceive that they can reach their goals if and only if the other students in the classroom cannot achieve their learning goals (Johnson & Johnson 1989; Johnson, Johnson, & Stanne, 2000; Johnson & Johnson, 2009; Qin, Johnson, & Johnson, 1995).

Inspired by many studies focusing on the effectiveness of various forms of small-group methods, computer science instructors have begun to shift from the use of traditional competitive lecture-based pedagogies and individualized learning to innovative methods of learning/teaching, which encourage collaboration, cooperation, self-motivation, and self-direction. For example, McDowell, Werner, Bullock, & Fernald (2002) stated that collaboration is an effective pedagogy for teaching introductory programming because pair programming (a) produces more efficient and bug free codes, (b) leads to better team communication and comprehension of the programming problems, and (c) enhances programmers' satisfaction, enjoyment, and confidence in their programming solutions. The increased popularity of small-group learning pedagogies including pair programming has led to an increase in the number of empirical studies conducted in both industrial as well as in educational contexts nationwide and globally to examine the effectiveness of these different pedagogies compared to the traditional methods (e. g., solo programming, competitive learning, or individualized learning) across different organizational settings and all levels of schooling including college level.

Dyba, et al. (2007) conducted a systematic literature review to investigate whether existing empirical evidence supports the claims that pair programing is more advantageous than solo programming. They reviewed 15 primary studies that examined the effectiveness of pair programming compared to solo programming in educational and industrial settings. Thus, their research sample included both students and software developers as subjects in the meta-analytic review. The general aspects investigated were related the effectiveness of pair programming, including programming duration, effort, and quality of the final programming product. They concluded that pair programming is more effective than solo programming in terms of programming quality and the time to complete the programming tasks. But, they concluded that pair programming requires more effort (i.e., more total person hours).

As an extension of the systematic literature review conducted by Dyba et al. (2007), Hannay, Dyba, Arisholm, and Sjøberg (2009) conducted a quantitative meta-analytic review of the existing primary studies that examined the effects of pair versus solo programming of professional and student programmers on three outcome constructs (quality, duration, and efforts). Thus, as their previous review, their extended research sample also included both students and software developers as subjects. They included 18 primary studies in their meta-analytic review. The results of their extended meta-analysis showed a small positive overall effect of pair programming on quality, a medium positive overall effect on duration, and

a medium negative overall effect on effort. They concluded that the results of the meta-analysis suggest that pair programming is not uniformly effective and the variability among the effect sizes of the primary studies is high.

Salleh, Mendes, and Grundy (2011) conducted a systematic literature review (SLR) of the empirical studies of pair programming effectiveness and/or pair compatibility in higher education settings. Their review included 73 primary studies measuring pair programming effectiveness, which classified into technical productivity, program/design quality, academic performance, and satisfaction. Their results showed that paired students usually completed the assigned tasks in less time and were more satisfied than solo students. Their meta-analytic results also showed that pair programing had no significant advantage in improving students' performance in final exams over solo programming (effect size = 0.16). In contrast to this finding, their results showed that pair programming was effective in helping students obtaining better scores in their assignments (effect size = 0.67). They suggested that further research needs to be conducted to investigate whether pair programming can be an effective pedagogical tool to learn computer science and software engineering (e.g., software design/modeling) in topics other than coding and application development.

These three systematic literature reviews were conducted to examine the effectiveness of only pair programming as a pedagogical tool used in computer programming, coding, or application development and not in higher education general computer science and/or software modeling and software engineering courses. As far as we know, no meta-analytic review has been conducted to examine the impact of various active small-group learning pedagogies on students' achievement in computer science including computer programming in undergraduate college context. Therefore, as of today there is a need to survey, review, integrate, and synthesize the existing research on the effectiveness of the various small-group learning methods compared to competitive and individualized instruction in college computer science classrooms including computer programing classrooms.

The main purpose of this study was to conduct a meta-analytic review of the existing empirical literature on the effectiveness of collaborative small-group learning in comparison to competitive and individualized learning on student achievement in college computer science including computer programing classrooms. The meta-analytic review was guided by the following research questions:

1. Do active small-group learning pedagogies promote better student achievement than competitive and individualized instruction in college computer science and computer programing classrooms?
2. Are the various forms of small-group learning methods have similar effects on students' achievement? In other words, which one of the various small-group learning methods promotes better achievement?
3. What features of the primary studies moderate the effects of using the small-group learning pedagogies in general computer science including computer programing classrooms?

META-ANALYSIS METHODOLOGY

Meta-analysis is a statistical method for quantitatively synthesizing and integrating the related research (address the same research question and hypothesis) findings using the reported descriptive summary statistics from the accumulated scientific literature in a specific field of study (Glass, 1976; Hedges & Olkin, 1985; Kalaian & Kasim, 2008). The multilevel meta-analysis, which are also known as mixed-effects or random-effects regression methods (Kalaian & Kasim, 2008; Kalaian & Kasim, 2013; Kalaian & Kasim, 2014; Raudenbush & Bryk, 2002) were used to

synthesize and integrate the accumulated computer science literature on the effectiveness of the various forms of active small-group learning on undergraduate students' achievement in college computer science classrooms. The main steps that were taken to conduct the meta-analytic review for the present study are:

1. Identification of the Relevant Primary Studies

The primary studies that were used in this meta-analysis had been located through a comprehensive search of publicly available literature to identify the published and unpublished primary studies that have focused on and investigated the effectiveness of the various forms of the small group learning methods compared to competitive learning instruction (e.g., individualized solo instruction) in college computer science classrooms. The search strategies included the following:

1. Electronic searches were performed up through June 2010 via the following electronic databases: JSTOR, ProQuest Dissertations and theses, International Dissertation Index, ABI, PsycINFO, and Education Resources Information Center (ERIC).
2. Manual searches were performed in individual print and electronic computer science and technology journals such as "Computer Science Education", "Computers and Education", "Journal of Science Education and Technology", and "Journal of Technology Education".
3. Manual examination of the reference lists of the primary studies included in the present review and the previously conducted meta-analytic reviews (e.g., Dyba, et al., 2007; Hannay, et al., 2009; Salleh, Mendes, & Grundy, 2011) to identify additional relevant computer science primary studies that have the potential to be included in the present meta-analytic review.

4. Web searches using standard search engines, such as "Bing", "Google", and "Google Scholar".

5. Searching several conference proceedings, including the proceedings of the "Association for the Advancement of Computing in Education", the "American Educational Research Association", "ACM Technical symposium on Computer Science Education", and the "Annual Meeting of the National Association for Research in Science Teaching".

The keywords that were used in this study included "cooperative learning", "collaborative learning", "Problem-based learning", "pair programming", "small-group learning", "Peer learning", Team-based learning" representing the key alternative learning pedagogies combined with "programming" or "Computer" subject matters descriptors. Every effort was made to include both published and unpublished primary sources in this meta-analytic review to minimize the possibility of publication bias.

2. Inclusion/Exclusion Criteria

Stringent inclusion criteria were developed and used to determine whether a primary study was qualified to be included in the meta-analytic review. Therefore, each primary study had to meet the following inclusion criteria:

1. It had to focus on empirical comparisons of one of the many different forms of small-group learning pedagogies, with lecture-based instruction on college students' achievement in undergraduate computer science college classrooms. Therefore, the primary studies with a single pre-post treatment group with no comparison group (individualized learning group or competitive learning group) were excluded from the review.

2. It had to report the descriptive summary statistics of the measured achievement outcomes such as the means and variances of the achievement scores for both comparison groups (the group that was instructed using one of the forms of the small-group learning methods and the group that was instructed using competitive and individualized instruction). These reported descriptive summary statistics are needed to calculate the effect size for each primary study in the review. Therefore, the primary studies that did not report one of the following three quantitative summary data, were excluded from the review:

    a. Descriptive summary statistics (mean, standard deviation, and sample sizes for the two comparison groups).

    b. Raw primary data.

    c. Calculated effect size.

3. It had to be conducted in undergraduate college classrooms. Therefore, the primary studies that were conducted in graduate level and high-school classrooms were excluded from the review.

With these preset criteria, we identified 18 computer science primary studies that focused on comparing various active small-group learning pedagogies to the traditional competitive instruction such as individualized solo instruction) in maximizing the achievement of college students in computer science classrooms.

3. Coding of Study Features and Outcome Measures

Based on reviewing some of the collected primary studies, a coding instrument was designed and developed to cover the methodological and substantive features of the identified primary studies that can be used to code across all primary studies (e.g., research design, publication year, sample characteristics, contextual study features, instructional duration, and performance test type). The study features of the 18 primary studies were coded by two coders to examine the methodological and substantive characteristics that may contribute to the variations in the findings of the primary studies. The coding of the study features was based on the available information in the primary studies under review. For example, if it is reported in the primary study that collaborative learning had been implemented in the classroom, then collaborative learning method of instruction had been coded for that specific study. Publication year, publication type, institution type, course period, use of computers in the classrooms, location, method of placing students in small groups, size of small-group, and grade level (a majority freshmen students vs. not majority freshmen students) were examples of the coded characteristics of the primary studies. The coding discrepancies between the two coders were discussed, and sources of the disagreements were identified and resolved through consensus.

4. Outcome Measures and Effect Size Calculation

Achievement measures are the outcome (dependent) variables that were used in the present meta-analytic review. Specifically, measures such as students' scores on standardized tests, teacher-made tests, quizzes, assignments, or a combination of these measures that assessed the extent to which students had achieved the learning objectives of a course (e.g., acquisition of a particular computer related content knowledge) have been used as outcomes in this review.

One or more effect sizes per primary study were extracted from each primary study: If a primary study reported the results of only one sample (classroom), which is the case for most of the studies, then one effect size was extracted from the study; and if a primary study reported the results of two or more independent samples in the same study (e.g., Barak, et al., 2007; Crooks & Klein, 1998; Soh, 2006), then two or more effect

sizes were extracted per primary study. On the other hand, if multiple effect sizes provided by the same students for different categories of the same outcome measure (e.g., assignment grades, mid-term exams, final exams, quizzes, and project grades) per primary study (e.g., Kacer, 1990; McDowell, et. al, 2002; Williams, et. al 2002), the dependent effect sizes from such measures were averaged and a single effect size was extracted.

Therefore, in this study, twenty three independent effect sizes were estimated and calculated from the 18 primary studies. An effect size is an index measure of the effectiveness of a small group learning instruction compared to a competitive and individualized instruction on the academic achievement of college students in computer science courses. Each of the effect size indices for this meta-analytic review were calculated by taking the difference between the means of achievement scores of the two instructional groups of students (the group who had been instructed using one of the various forms of small-group learning methods and the group that had been instructed using competitive and individualized learning methods) and dividing the difference by the two groups' pooled standard deviation (Hedges & Olkin, 1985; Kalaian & Kasim, 2008; Kalaian & Kasim, in press).

5. Multilevel Modeling via HLM

Multilevel modeling for meta-analysis via Hierarchical Linear Modeling (HLM) was used to analyze the meta-analytic data for the present study. The analysis was done in two stages. At the first stage, the effect sizes extracted from all the primary studies were integrated and an overall weighed average effect size were estimated and tested for statistical significance using the basic unconditional multilevel model (within-study model) via the HLM6 software. In general, the unconditional multilevel model, where no explanatory predictor variables are included in the model, helps the meta-analyst to estimate and examine the heterogeneity in the primary studies' effect sizes in order to assess the need for modeling this heterogeneity in the subsequent second stage modeling. At the second stage, the coded predictor variables were included in the multilevel model to analyze the meta-analytic data using the conditional multilevel models (between-studies models) to model and explain the variability in the effect sizes (Kalaian & Kasim, 2008; Kalaian & Kasim, 2013; Kalaian & Kasim, 2014; Raudenbush & Bryk, 2002).

RESULTS

The results of our meta-analysis are organized into two sections. In section 1 with the "Description of the Coded Characteristics of the Primary Studies" subheading, we describe the coded characteristics of the primary studies in the review. In section 2 with the "Results of the Multilevel Analyses via HLM" subheading, we report the results of the multilevel analyses, which were applied to the calculated effect sizes and the coded characteristics of the computer science primary studies.

Section 1: Description of the Coded Characteristics of the Studies

Table 1 lists the 18 primary studies that were included in the present meta-analytic review and the 23 effect sizes that were extracted from them. Table 1 also lists the coded sample sizes of the two groups of students (the group who were instructed using one of the various forms of small-group learning methods and the group that were instructed using competitive and individualized learning methods), the four coded small-group learning methods that were used, and the coded instructional duration (hours) of the computer science classrooms for each of the primary studies in the review. Examining the instructional duration column of Table 1 indicates that there is a great variability in the instructional duration for the 18 primary studies, which ranged from an hour

to 83 hours of instruction. Also, as is shown in Table 1, the 18 primary studies included in this meta-analysis review were published between 1990 and 2010. The values of the 23 independent effect sizes ranged from -0.34 to +1.37 with an average effect size of 0.41. Out of these 23 effect sizes, 19 were positive favoring small-group learning methods in increasing students' achievement scores, while four effect sizes were negative favoring competitive and individualized learning instruction in computer science courses including computer programming courses.

Table 2 summarizes the major characteristics of the 18 primary studies. Also, it shows the breakdowns (subcategories) of the major characteristics, the number of the primary studies, the average effect size, and the number of effect sizes for each subcategory for all the studies included in the review. As is shown in Table 2, eight (44%) of the primary studies were published in 2000 or earlier with an average effect size of 0.32. The remaining ten studies (56%) were published in 2001 or later with a larger average effect-size of 0.49. These results indicate that the primary studies that were published in 2001 or later yielded larger effect of the various small-group learning methods than the studies that were published in 2000 or earlier.

In regards to the type of the publications, the majority of the studies (10 studies, 55%) were articles published in refereed peer-reviewed journals with an average of effect size of 0.32. Three (17%) were dissertations with an average effect size of 0.34. The remaining five (28%) of the 18 studies were conference proceedings with much higher average effect size of 0.70 than the other publication types. These results indicate the differential effects of the type of the publication on the small-group effect sizes.

In regards to the research design of the primary studies, Table 2 shows that far more primary studies (14 studies, 74%) were non-experimental comparative studies (two-group post-only design) with much higher average effect-size of 0.44 than

Table 1. The primary studies, effect sizes, sample sizes, small-group learning methods, and the instructional duration of the studies in the meta-analytic review

Author (Publication Year)	Small Group (n)	Lecture Group (n)	Duration (Hours)	Small-Group Learning Method	Effect Size
Baker (1995)	33	35	3	Collaborative	-0.02
Barak et al. (2007)	181	151	83	Collaborative	0.44
Barak et al. (2007)	170	151	83	Collaborative	0.52
Baturay & Bay (2010)	43	35	38	Problem-based	0.33
Beck & Chizhik (2008)	34	37	38	Cooperative	0.88
Crooks & Klein (1998)	50	25	36	Cooperative	-0.20
Crooks & Klein (1998)	50	25	36	Cooperative	0.30
Gonzalez (2006)	5	13	45	Cooperative	1.00
Howles (2007)	32	130	27	Collaborative	-0.34
Ivers & Barron (1998)	50	52	1	Pair	0.15
Kacer, et al. (1990)	10	4	3	Pair	0.46
Kacer, et al. (1990)	10	3	3	Pair	-0.09
Kacer, et al. (1990)	14	8	3	Pair	0.58
Keeler & Anson (1995)	15	18	40	Cooperative	0.51
McDowell, et al. (2002)	172	141	37	Pair	0.50
Mehta (1993)	21	10	45	Cooperative	1.37
Priebe (1997)	24	25	81	Cooperative	0.34
Quinn & McCune (1996)	14	15	15	Pair	0.80
Sendag & Odabasi (2009)	20	20	24	Problem-based	1.01
Seymour (1994)	57	57	15	Pair	0.12
Soh (2006)	12	17	6	Cooperative	0.01
Soh (2006)	12	17	6	Cooperative	0.22
Williams, et al. (2002)	44	69	42	Pair	0.47

the combined five (28%) primary studies, which included the three randomized experimental studies and the two quasi-experimental studies with an average effect-size of 0.32. The lack of experimental studies is something expected in educational research because of the difficulty of conducting randomized experimental research in college settings.

In regards to the small-group learning methods that were used in computer science classrooms, cooperative learning methods had been implemented in seven primary studies (39%) with an average effect-size of 0.49. Three studies (17%) had used collaborative learning methods in the computer science classrooms with an average effect-size of 0.15. Two studies (11%) had implemented problem-based leaning methods with an average effect-size of 0.67. The remaining six studies (32%) had implemented pair learning with an average effect size of 0.37. Although the four small-group learning methods yielded positive mean effect sizes, the unstructured collaborative learning method with more than two students in each of the groups appears to be less effective in

Table 2. Summary of the categories of the characteristics of the primary studies, number of primary studies, and the average effect sizes

Study Charactersistics	# of Studies (%)	Average Effect Size (# of Effect Sizes)
Publication Year		
2000 or Earlier	8 (44%)	0.32 (11)
2001 or Later	10 (56%)	0.49 (12)
Publication Type		
Journal	10 (55%)	0.32 (15)
Dissertation	3 (17%)	0.34 (3)
Conference Proceeding	5 (28%)	0.70 (5)
Research Design		
Experimental and Quasi	5 (28%)	0.32 (6)
Non-Experimental	13 (72%)	0.44 (17)
Small-Group Learning Method		
Cooperative	7 (39%)	0.49 (9)
Collaborative	3 (17%)	0.15 (4)
Problem-Based Learning	2 (11%)	0.67 (2)
Pair Learning	6 (33%)	0.37 (8)
Duration of Instruction		
27 Hours or Less	7 (39%)	0.32 (10)
More than 27 Hours	11 (61%)	0.47 (13)
Use of Computers in Instructions		
Yes	14 (78%)	0.39 (19)
No	4 (22%)	0.47 (13)
Classroom Instructor		
Investigator	13 (72%)	0.38 (17)
Other	5 (28%)	0.50 (6)
Assessment Type		
Standardized Test	4 (22%)	1.01 (4)
Teacher Made Test	14 (78%)	0.28 (19)
Placement into Small Groups		
Random	7 (39%)	0.35 (8)
Ability Grouping	5 (28%)	0.43 (6)
Self-Selected	6 (33%)	0.44 (9)
Small-Group Size		
2 Students	8 (44%)	0.25 (11)
3 Students	5 (28%)	0.55 (6)
4 Students	4 (22%)	0.58 (4)
10 Students	1 (6%)	0.48 (2)

continued on following page

Table 2. Continued

Study Charactersistics	# of Studies (%)	Average Effect Size (# of Effect Sizes)
Classroom Level		
First Year	9 (50%)	0.32 (10)
Not First Year	9 (50%)	0.48 (13)
Classroom Setting		
Laboratory	8 (44%)	0.28 (12)
Classroom	10 (56%)	0.55 (11)
Study Location		
U.S.	15 (83%)	0.37 (20)
Other Countries	3 (17%)	8.48 (3)

increasing the achievement of college students in computer science courses than the other three small-group learning pedagogies.

Seven primary studies (39%) had 27 hours or less on instruction with an average effect-size of 0.32. The remaining 11 studies (61%) had instructional durations of more than 27 hours with an average effect-size of 0.47. Therefore, the longer the hours of instruction in the college computer science classrooms, the more effective was the implemented small-group learning method in increasing the achievement scores of students.

In the majority of studies (12 studies), the investigators of the primary studies were also the instructors of the computer science classrooms with an average effect-size of 0.38. In the remaining five studies (28%) the investigators of the primary studies were not the instructors of the computer science classrooms. These five studies yielded an average effect-size of 0.50.

In regards to the methods that had been used for assigning students to the small groups, six studies (33%) had reported that the placement of students into small groups was accomplished through self-selection with an average effect-size of 0.44. Seven primary studies (39%) had randomly placed students into small groups with an average effect size of 0.35. In the remaining five studies (28%), the placement of students into

small groups was done by assigning students into groups based on their abilities (e.g., Grade Point Average scores) with an average effect size of 0.43. These results indicate that placing the students in small-groups either randomly or self-selection was equally effective in increasing the achievement of the college students. Also, the results show that these two placement strategies were more effective than the ability grouping method of placement.

Regarding the size of the small groups, in eight primary studies (44%) the size of the small groups was two students with an average effect size of 0.25. In five studies (28%), the size of the groups in the computer science classrooms was three students with an average effect size of 0.55. In four (22%) studies, the size of the groups in the computer science classrooms was four students with an average effect size of 0.58. In the remaining one study, the size of the small groups was ten students with an average effect size of 0.48. The results indicate that regardless of the size of the group, the grouped students achieved significantly more than the students in ungrouped classes. These results also indicate that the various forms of small-group learning methods were more effective with three- to four- member group teams.

In regards to the college class level, nine (50%) studies had reported that the majority of the students in the computer sciences courses were

Table 3. Results of the unconditional and conditional multilevel meta-analysis via HLM

Models and Parameters	Fixed Effects			Random Effects		
	Coefficient	T-Ratio	P-Value	S.D.	Chi-Square	P-Value
Unconditional HLM Model						
Intercept	0.35	4.47	0.000	0.24	42.63	0.005
Conditional HLM Model						
Intercept	0.08	0.75	0.461	0.13	21.31	0.379
Instructional Duration	0.01	2.34	0.030			
Assessment Type	0.72	3.57	0.002			

first year students (freshmen) with an average effect size of 0.32. The remaining nine studies had reported that the majority of the students in the computer sciences courses were not first year students (sophomore, junior, and senior) yielding an average effect size of 0.48. These results indicate that the small-group learning methods were more effective for advanced undergraduate college students (sophomore, junior, and senior) than the introductory freshman level students.

As is shown in Table 2, the majority of the primary studies in this review were conducted at universities and colleges in the United States (15 primary studies) with an average effect size of 0.37. The remaining three studies were conducted at universities in other countries (one study in Canada and two studies in Turkey) with an average effect size of 0.48. Therefore, the various forms of small-group methods were more effective in increasing the achievement scores of college students at universities in other countries than in the United States.

Section 2: Results of the Multilevel Analyses via HLM

As indicated earlier in the Multilevel Modeling via HLM section of this chapter, multilevel modeling for meta-analysis is typically conducted in two stages (unconditional and conditional

multilevel modeling). The results are obtained by fitting the multilevel model (Kalaian & Kasim, 2008; Kalaian & Kasim, 2013; Raudenbush & Bryk, 2002) via hierarchical linear modeling using HLM6 software (Raudenbush, et al. 2004). Table 3 lists the results of fitting the unconditional (no predictors in the multilevel model) and simple conditional models (one predictor in each of the multilevel models) to the meta-analytic data. Simple conditional modeling was used in this study because of the limited number of primary studies.

The unconditional results (see Table 3) show that the overall weighted average of the 23 effect sizes from the 18 computer science primary studies was 0.35 across the four small-group learning methods (cooperative, collaborative, problem-based, and pair learning methods). An average effect size of 0.35 indicates that the use of the four different small-group pedagogies can lead to more than one-third standard deviation increase in students' achievement in college computer science classrooms.

The random-effects test of the unconditional multilevel results also show that the effect sizes were heterogonous (Standard Deviation = 0.24, Chi-square = 42.63, p = 0.005). A significant Chi-square value indicates the existence of a significant amount of variability in the 18 effect sizes. Therefore, a significant Chi-square value indicates a need to proceed further by exploring and fitting the conditional multilevel models by including the coded variables from the primary studies as predictors in the multilevel model to explain some of the variability in the effect sizes.

The results of fitting the conditional multilevel model that included the instructional durations in hours and the type of assessment methods (standardized tests or teacher-made tests) used in the primary studies as predictors show that the duration of instruction in hours controlling for assessment type had a significant positive effect on the achievement effect sizes (beta coefficient = 0.01, t = 2.34, p = 0.03). This significant positive effect of the instructional duration indicates that the longer the hours of instruction, the more effective was the various small-group methods in increasing the achievement scores of the students in the college computer science classrooms. The results also show that the type of assessment controlling for instructional duration in hours had a significant positive effect on the achievement effect sizes (beta coefficient = 0.72, t = 3.57, p = 0.002). This significant positive effect indicate that measuring achievement by instructor developed tests or by standardized tests in computer science subjects can produce significantly different small-group effects.

In addition, the multilevel results show that these two exploratory predictors explained most of the variations in the effect sizes, which was evident by the non-significant random-effect Chi-square test (Standard Deviation = 0.13, Chi-square = 21.31, p = 0.379). The remaining predictor variables (e.g., study's research design, instructional duration, study's location, use of computers in the classrooms) were also tested using different conditional multilevel models and were not statistically significant. These non-significant results might be due to the limited number of primary studies in this review, which led to low statistical power of the statistical tests.

FUTURE RESEARCH DIRECTIONS

In the near future, we are expected to witness a renaissance in the adoption and use of the various forms of small-group pedagogies across a broad variety of disciplines and fields of study including computer science and computer programing. It is also expected that the quality of the research design and the reporting of the results of future research in this area will be improved to better understand the small-group processes in college classrooms and facilitate the future meta-analytic integration of the emerging empirical studies that examine the effectiveness of small-group pedagogies. In addition, it is expected that new and innovative teaching/learning pedagogies will emerge to promote deep conceptual understanding of the general computer science subject areas including computer programming, which hopefully will lead to better achievement and persistence in college computer science classrooms. Further, we will witness the phenomena of new textbooks and supplementary instructional materials to be published that include small-group activities and exercises that can be used in college computer science classrooms.

Furthermore, we will witness increased use of e-collaboration and virtual teams that rely on technology-mediated communications and computer supported collaborative learning (CSCL) rather than face-to-face interactions to accomplish their common learning goals. Similar to face-to-face small-group instruction, virtual (e-collaboration) small-group teams and online groups that are designed and implemented effectively can maximize achievement, performance, and harness talent to solve computer science problems including computer programming. The increased use of synchronous and asynchronous online and virtual learning/teaching using small collaborative face-to-face groups and virtual teams will lead to conducting more primary studies that focus on evaluating the effectiveness of the virtual teams in cyber learning settings.

In sum, future and emerging trends will include the increased adoption and utilization of various small-group learning pedagogies by college instructors in science, technology, engineering, and mathematics (STEM) including computer science instructors for face-to-face and online classrooms. Therefore, we are expecting to witness a shift in paradigm from lecturing and competitive individualized learning to collaborative and cooperative learning in the college classrooms. The instructor's role will shift from being the transmitters of knowledge to facilitators of learning. Based on these changes, the need for faculty development seminars that focus on the effective use of these various small-group pedagogies will increase.

CONCLUSION

This study had quantitatively synthesized the literature on the effectiveness of the various forms of small-group learning pedagogies on student achievement in college computer science classrooms. The results complement and greatly extend the findings of the previously conducted systematic reviews and meta-analysis studies (Dyba et al., 2007; Hannay, et al., 2009; Salleh, Mendes, & Grundy, 2011).

The results of our meta-analysis showed that four different small-group learning pedagogies were used in college computer science classrooms, where students are grouped in small groups to learn different computer science subject matters such as computer programing, computer languages, computer hardware designs, and computer software developments. The four teaching pedagogies were: Cooperative learning; Collaborative learning; Problem-based learning; and Pair Learning (e.g., Pair Programming) methods. The definitions of these four small-group learning methods are provided in the key terms and definitions section in this chapter.

In addition, our research showed that collectively the use of the various forms of small-group pedagogies had significant positive effects in maximizing students' academic achievement in college computer science classrooms with an overall effect size of 0.41, and this is true regardless of the four forms of the small-group pedagogy that was used in a college computer science course. Indeed, the use of cooperative learning, problem-based learning, and pair learning pedagogies led to more than one-third standard deviation increase in students' achievement in college computer science classrooms. These results are consistent with the previous research evidence in STEM education including computer programming, which clearly supports various forms of active small-group learning methods including pair programming as effective instructional pedagogy in higher education.

The unconditional results of the multilevel analysis revealed that collectively the weighted effect size of the 24 effect sizes, which was extracted from the 18 primary studies, was 0.35 favoring the effectiveness of the small-group methods in comparison to competitive and individualized instruction in college computer classrooms. The unconditional results of the multilevel analysis also revealed that the effect sizes were heterogeneous. Therefore, the effect sizes were explored further by including the coded predictors in the conditional multilevel model to explain the variability in the effect sizes. The results of the conditional multilevel model revealed that both of the coded instructional duration and assessment type predictors explained the variability in the effect sizes.

This meta-analytic review revealed that the number of primary studies was fairly small, which indicates a shortage of primary empirical studies investigating the effectiveness of the various forms of small-group learning methods including pair learning (e.g., pair programming) for software design/modeling and application development courses. This clearly indicates that further primary research needs to be conducted to investigate whether various forms of small-group learning methods are effective pedagogical tools to learn different computer science and software engineering topics. This shortage of the primary research may be somewhat limiting factor with respect to our ability to draw strong conclusions regarding the effectiveness of small-group learning in college computer science classrooms.

Our quantitative meta-analytic study is noteworthy given that no previous meta-analytic research had been conducted to examine the effectiveness of various forms of active small-group learning pedagogies compared to competitive and individualized learning (solo learning) on the achievement of college students in all computer science courses and not just computer programming courses, which was the focus of previously conducted reviews. Also, our meta-analytic study findings might significantly contribute to (a) computer science researchers and educators who would benefit from a systematic meta-analytic review of the existing primary studies of the effectiveness of various small-group learning pedagogies in comparison to competitive and individualized instruction on academic achievement in undergraduate college classrooms, and (b) computer science educators who wish to make sound recommendations and provide advice on best and most effective pedagogical practices in college computer classrooms.

ACKNOWLEDGMENT

This project is a subset of a larger Science, Technology, Engineering, and Mathematics (STEM) meta-analytic project, which has been supported by a grant from the Research and Evaluation in Science and Engineering (REESE) Program of the National Science Foundation (Award # 0815682). The views expressed herein do not necessarily represent those of the National Science Foundation.

REFERENCES

Accreditation Board of Engineering and Technology. (2008). *Criteria for accrediting engineering programs: Effective for evaluations during the 2008-2009 accreditation cycle.* Baltimore, MD: ABET Engineering Accreditation Commission.

American Association for the Advancement of Science. (2005). *Invention and impact: Building excellence in undergraduate science, technology, engineering, and mathematics (STEM) education.* Retrieved from http://www.aaas.org/publications/books_reports/CCLI

Baker, L. J. (1995). *The effect of cooperative study groups on achievement of college-level computer science programming students.* (Unpublished doctoral dissertation). University of Texas, Austin, TX.

Barak, M., Harward, J., Kocur, G., & Lerman, S. (2007). Transforming an introductory programming course from lectures to active learning via wireless laptops. *Journal of Science Education and Technology, 16*(4), 325–336. doi:10.1007/s10956-007-9055-5

Baturay, M. H., & Bay, O. F. (2010). The effects of problem learning on the classroom community perceptions and achievement of web-based education students. *Computers & Education, 55*(1), 43–52. doi:10.1016/j.compedu.2009.12.001

Beck, L. L., & Chizhik, A. W. (2008). An experimental study of cooperative learning in CS1. In *Proceedings of SIGCSE of ACM Technical Symposium on Computer Science Education,* (pp. 205-209). ACM. doi:10.1145/1352135.1352208

Crooks, S. M., Klein, J. D., Savenye, W., & Leader, L. (1998). Effects of cooperative and individual learning during learner-controlled computer-based instruction. *Journal of Experimental Education, 66*(3), 223–244. doi:10.1080/00220979809604406

Dyba, T., Arisholmk, E., Sjoberg, D. I. L., Hannay, J. E., & Shull, F. (2007). Are two heads better than one? On the effectiveness of pair programming. *IEEE Software*, *24*(6), 12–15. doi:10.1109/MS.2007.158

Glass, G. V. (1976). Primary, secondary, and meta-Analysis. *Educational Researcher*, *5*(10), 3–8. doi:10.3102/0013189X005010003

Gonzalez, G. (2006). A systematic approach to active and cooperative learning in CS1 and its effects on CS2. In *Proceedings of SIGCSE of ACM Technical Symposium on Computer Science Education*, (pp. 133 – 137). ACM. doi:10.1145/1121341.1121386

Hannay, J. E., Dybå, T., Arisholm, E., & Sjøberg, D. I. K. (2009). The effectiveness of pair programming: A meta-analysis. *Information and Software Technology*, *51*(7), 1110–1122. doi:10.1016/j.infsof.2009.02.001

Hedges, L. V., & Olkin, I. (1985). *Statistical methods for meta-analysis*. Orlando, FL: Academic Press.

Howles, T. (2007). *A study of attrition and the use of student learning communities in the computer science introductory programming sequence*. (Unpublished doctoral dissertation). Nova Southeastern University.

Ivers, K. S., & Barron, A. E. (1998). Using paired learning conditions with computer-based instruction to teach preservice teachers about telecommunications. *Journal of Technology and Teacher Education*, *6*(2-3), 183–191.

Johnson, D., Johnson, R., & Smith, K. (1998). Cooperative learning returns to college: What evidence is there that it works? *Change*, *30*(4), 26–35. doi:10.1080/00091389809602629

Johnson, D. W., & Johnson, R. T. (1989). *Cooperation and competition: Theory and research*. Interaction Book Company.

Johnson, D. W., & Johnson, R. T. (2009). An educational psychology success story: Social interdependence theory and cooperative learning. *Educational Researcher*, *38*(5), 365–379. doi:10.3102/0013189X09339057

Johnson, D. W., Johnson, R. T., & Stanne, M. B. (2000). *Cooperative learning methods: A meta-analysis*. Retrieved from http://www.tablelearning.com/uploads/File/EXHIBIT-B.pdf

Kacer, B., Weinholtz, D., & Rocklin, T. (1990). Individual versus small group instruction of computer applications: A quantitative and qualitative comparison. *Journal of Computing in Teacher Education*, *9*(1), 6–12.

Kalaian, S., & Kasim, R. (2013). Multilevel Meta-Analysis: Effectiveness of Small-Group Learning Methods Compared to Lecture-Based Instruction in Science, Technology, Engineering, and Mathematics College Classrooms. In SAGE Research Methods Cases. London: SAGE Publications. doi:10.4135/978144627305014531371

Kalaian, S. A., & Kasim, R. M. (2008). Applications of Multilevel Models for Meta-analysis. In A. O'Connell & B. McCoach (Eds.), *Multilevel Analysis of Educational Data* (pp. 315–343). Charlotte, NC: Information Age Publishing, Inc.

Kalaian, S. A., & Kasim, R. M. (2014). A meta-analytic review of studies of the effectiveness of small-group learning methods on statistics achievement. *Journal of Statistics Education*, *22*(1). Retrieved from www.amstat.org/publications/jse/v22n1/kalaian.pdf

Keeler, C. M., & Anson, R. (1995). An assessment of cooperative learning used for basic computer skills instruction in the college classroom. *Journal of Educational Computing Research*, *12*(4), 379–393. doi:10.2190/1E43-Y7G4-PXRV-KHDC

McDowell, C., Werner, L., Bullock, H., & Fernald, J. (2002). The effects of pair-programming in an introductory programming course. In *Proceedings of the 33rd ACM Technical Symposium on Computer Science Education*. ACM. doi:10.1145/563351.563353

Mehta, J. I. (1993). *Cooperative learning in computer programming at the college level*. (Unpublished doctoral dissertation). University of Illinois, Chicago, IL.

National Research Council. (2001). *Educating teachers of science, mathematics, and Technology: New practices for the new millennium*. Washington, DC: National Academy of Sciences. Retrieved from http://www.nap.edu

National Science Board. (2003). *The science and engineering workforce realizing America's potential* (NSB 03-69). Retrieved from http://www.nsf.gov/nsb/documents/2003/nsb0369/nsb0369.pdf

National Science Foundation. (1996). *Shaping the future: New expectations for undergraduate education in science, mathematics, engineering, and technology*. Washington, DC: Advisory Committee to the National Science Foundation Directorate for Education and Human Resources.

Office of Science and Technology Policy. (2006). *American competiveness initiative*. Domestic Policy Council. Retrieved from http://ostp.gov/html/ACIBooklet.pdf

Priebe, R. (1997). *The Effects of cooperative learning in a second-semester university computer science course*. Paper presented at the Annual Meeting of the National Association for Research in Science Teaching. New York, NY.

Qin, Z., Johnson, D. W., & Johnson, R. W. (1995). Cooperative versus competitive efforts and problem solving. *Review of Educational Research, 65*(2), 129–143. doi:10.3102/00346543065002129

Quinn, J., Pena, C., & McCune, L. (1996). The effects of group and task structure in an instructional simulation. In *Proceedings of the 1996 National Convention of the Association for Educational Communications and Technology*. Indianapolis, IN: Academic Press.

Raudenbush, S. W., & Bryk, A. S. (2002). *Hierarchical linear models: Applications and data analysis methods* (2nd ed.). Thousand Oaks, CA: Sage Publications, Inc.

Raudenbush, S. W., Bryk, A. S., Cheong, Y., & Congdon, R. T. (2004). *HLM 6: Hierarchical linear and nonlinear modeling*. Chicago, IL: Scientific Software International.

Salleh, N., Mendes, E., & Grundy, J. C. (2011). Empirical studies of pair programming for CS/SE teaching in higher education: A systematic literature review. *IEEE Transactions on Software Engineering, 37*(4), 509–525. doi:10.1109/TSE.2010.59

Sendag, S., & Odabasi, H. F. (2009). Effects of an online problem based learning course on content knowledge acquisition and critical thinking skills. *Computers & Education, 53*(1), 132–141. doi:10.1016/j.compedu.2009.01.008

Seymour, S. R. (1994). Operative computer learning with cooperative task and reward structures. *Journal of Technology Education, 5*(2), 40–51.

Soh, L. (2006). Implementing the jigsaw model in CS1 closed labs. In *Proceedings of the ACM Technical Symposium on Computer Science Education*. Bologna, Italy: ACM. doi:10.1145/1140124.1140169

Springer, L., Stanne, M. E., & Donovan, S. S. (1999). Effects of small-group learning on undergraduates in science, mathematics, engineering, and technology: A meta-analysis. *Review of Educational Research, 69*(1), 21–51. doi:10.3102/00346543069001021

Williams, L., Wiebe, E., Yang, K., Ferzli, M., & Miller, C. (2002). In support of pair programming in the introductory computer science course. *Computer Science Education*, *12*(3), 197–212. doi:10.1076/csed.12.3.197.8618

ADDITIONAL READING

Andersson, R., & Bendix, L. (2006). Extreme teaching: A framework for continuous improvement. *Computer Science Education*, *16*(3), 175–184. doi:10.1080/08993400600912335

Barkley, E. F., Cross, K. P., & Major, C. H. (2004). *Collaborative learning techniques: A handbook for college faculty*. San Francisco, CA: Jossey-Bass.

Cook-Sather, A., Bovill, C., & Felton, P. (2014). *Engaging students as partners in learning and teaching: A guide for faculty*. San Francisco, CA: Jossey-Bass.

Cooper, H., Hedges, L. V., & Valentine, J. C. (2009). The handbook of research synthesis and meta-analysis (Ed.). New York, NY: Russell Sage Foundation.

Cooper, J. L., MacGregor, J., Smith, K. A., & Robinson, P. (2000). Implementing small-group instruction: Insights from successful practitioners. *New Directions for Teaching and Learning*, *81*, 64–76.

Cooper, J. L., & Robinson, P. (2000). Getting started: Informal small-group strategies in large classes. *New Directions for Teaching and Learning*, *81*(81), 17–24. doi:10.1002/tl.8102

Fee, S. B., & Holland-Minkley, A. M. (2010). Teaching computer science through problems, not solutions. *Computer Science Education*, *20*(2), 129–144. doi:10.1080/08993408.2010.486271

Goggins, S. P. Jahnke, Isa, & Wulf, V. (2013). Computer-supported collaborative learning at the workplace: CSCL@Work (Computer-Supported Collaborative Learning Series) (Ed.). New York, NY: Springer Science-Business Media.

Hedges, L. V., & Olkin, I. (1985). *Statistical methods for meta-analysis*. Orlando, Florida: Academic Press.

Hmelo-Silver, C. E., Chinn, C. A., Chan, C., & O'Donnell, A. M. (2013). International handbook of collaborative learning (Ed.). New York, NY: Routage.

Hrastinski, S. (2008). What is online learner participation? A literature review. *Computers & Education*, *51*(4), 1755–1765. doi:10.1016/j.compedu.2008.05.005

Johnson, D. W., & Johnson, F. P. (2000). *Joining together: Group theory and group skills* (7th ed.). Boston, MA: Allyn & Bacon.

Johnson, D. W., Johnson, R. T., & Smith, K. A. (1991). *Active learning: Cooperation in the college classroom*. Edina, MN: Interaction Book Company.

Johnson, D. W., Johnson, R. T., & Smith, K. A. (1998). Cooperative learning returns to college: What evidence is there that it works? *Change*, *30*(4), 26–35. doi:10.1080/00091389809602629

Jordan, M. H., Field, H. S., & Armenakis, A. A. (2002). The relationship of group process variables and team performance. *Small Group Research*, *33*(1), 121–150. doi:10.1177/104649640203300104

Kalaian, S. A. (2008). Multilevel modeling methods for e-collaboration data. In N. Kock (Ed.), *Encyclopedia of e-collaboration* (pp. 450–456). Hershey, PA: IGI Global.

Kalaian, S. A., & Kasim, R. M. (2008). Applications of multilevel models for meta-analysis. In A. O'Connell & B. McCoach (Eds.), *Multilevel Analysis of educational data* (pp. 315–343). Charlotte, NC: Information Age Publishing, Inc.

Kalaian, S. A., & Kasim, R. M. (2014). A Meta-analytic review of studies of the effectiveness of small-group learning methods on statistics achievement. *Journal of Statistics Education*, *22*(1). Retrieved from www.amstat.org/publications/jse/v22n1/kalaian.pdf

Kock, N. (2008). Encyclopedia of e-collaboration (Ed.). Hershey, PA: IGI Global.

Michaelson, L. K., Knight, A. B., & Fink, L. D. (2004). *Team-based learning: A transformative use of small groups in college teaching*. Sterling, VA: Stylus Publishing.

Oetzel, J. G. (2001). Self-construals, communication processes, and group outcomes in homogeneous and heterogeneous groups. *Small Group Research*, *32*(1), 19–54. doi:10.1177/104649640103200102

Prince, M. J., & Felder, R. M. (2007). The many faces of inductive teaching and learning. *Journal of College Science Teaching*, *36*(5), 533–568.

Savin-Baden, M., & Wilkie, K. (2006). *Problem-based learning online*. New York, NY: Open University Press.

Slavin, R. E. (1995). *Cooperative learning* (2nd ed.). Boston: Allyn & Bacon.

Smith, K. A. (2000). Going deeper: Formal small-group learning in large classes. *New Directions for Teaching and Learning*, *81*(81), 25–46. doi:10.1002/tl.8103

Smith, K. A., Sheppard, S. D., Johnson, D. W., & Johnson, R. T. (2005). Pedagogies of engagement: Classroom-based practices. *The Journal of Engineering Education*, *94*(1), 1–16. doi:10.1002/j.2168-9830.2005.tb00831.x

Williams, L., & Kessler, R. (2002). *Pair programming illuminated*. Boston, MA: Addison-Wesley Longman Publishing Co., Inc.

Wittenbaum, G. M., Vaughan, S. I., & Stasser, G. I. (2002). Coordination in task-performing groups. In R. S. Tindale (Ed.), *Theory and research on small groups* (pp. 177–204). New York: Kluwer Academic. doi:10.1007/0-306-47144-2_9

KEY TERMS AND DEFINITIONS

Collaborative Learning: Is a relatively unstructured form of small-group learning pedagogies that incorporates a wide range of formal and informal instructional methods in which students interactively work together in small groups toward shared common learning goals and objectives.

Competitive Learning: Is an instructional method that emphasizes on individualized competition in which students individually compete to achieve higher grades. In a competitive classroom environment, the students perceive that they can successfully achieve their goals if and only if other students in the classroom did not succeed.

Cooperative Learning: Is a structured, systematic, and teacher-guided small-group instructional strategy in which students work together in small learning groups to maximize their own and each other's common learning goals. It is guided by principles such as positive interdependence, peer interactions, individual and group accountability, and assessment of group functioning.

Meta-Analysis: Is a systematic statistical method for synthesizing and integrating the research findings such as the reported descriptive summary statistics from the accumulated scientific literature (e.g., primary studies) that address and test the same research question and hypothesis.

Multilevel Meta-Analysis: Is a statistical method for analyzing hierarchically structured meta-analytic data, where groups of individuals are nested within the primary studies.

Pair Programming: Is a form of small-group learning in which two students brainstorm and work together collaboratively at one computer on the same programming tasks such as developing algorithms and codes. One of the student-pair is the *driver* who is responsible for typing the algorithm or code at the computer; the other student is the *navigator* who is responsible for watching the work of the driver and identifying algorithmic errors.

Problem-Based Learning (PBL): Is a student-centered instructional method that challenges students to work collaboratively and cooperatively in small learning groups to seek solutions to discipline-specific problems, which are the organizing focus and stimulus for learning.

Small-Group Learning Methods: Are defined as being an umbrella for various forms of active student-centered instructional methods (e.g., collaborative, cooperative) that empower the learners in small learning groups to work collaboratively and cooperatively with the other members of the group in a team-based environment.

Chapter 4
A Review of Teaching and Learning through Practice of Optimization Algorithms

J. Ángel Velázquez-Iturbide
Universidad Rey Juan Carlos, Spain

Ouafae Debdi
Universidad Rey Juan Carlos, Spain

Maximiliano Paredes-Velasco
Universidad Rey Juan Carlos, Spain

ABSTRACT

Algorithmics is an important core subject matter in computer science education. In particular, optimization algorithms are some of the most difficult to master because their problem statement includes an additional property, namely optimality. The chapter contains a comprehensive survey of the teaching and learning through practice of optimization algorithms. In particular, three important issues are reviewed. Firstly, the authors review educational methods which partially or completely address optimization algorithms. Secondly, educational software systems are reviewed and classified according to technical and educational criteria. Thirdly, students' difficulties and misunderstandings regarding optimization algorithms are presented. The chapter intends to consolidate current knowledge about the education of this class of algorithms for both computer science teachers and computer science education researchers.

INTRODUCTION

Curricular recommendations for Computer Science (CS) date back to the late sixties (ACM, 1968). Although subsequent recommendations gave some importance to laboratories, it was not completely recognized until the writing of the Denning Report (Denning, Comer, Gries, Mulder, Tucker, Turner & Young, 1989). The Report argued for a multi-disciplinary nature of CS based on three different knowledge traditions: mathematics, engineering and science. In particular, the scientific tradition deals with the study of artifacts using the scientific method and experimentation. Laboratories

DOI: 10.4018/978-1-4666-7304-5.ch004

and experimentation attracted the attention in the following years (McCracken, 1989) and since experimentation has attracted the focus now and then (Tichy, 1998; Denning, 2007). Remarkably, some proposals make explicit the relation between experimentation with algorithms and the scientific method (Baldwin, 1992; Matocha, 2002). Some instructors have addressed this issue from a pragmatic point of view for an algorithms course (Sanders, 2002) and even throughout the CS curriculum (Braught, Reed & Miller, 2004; Reed, Miller & Braught, 2000).

Experimentation has probably received the most attention in the field of algorithms. This preeminence is probably due to the fact that algorithms have a clear definition (amenable to formal specification), have well-defined properties, and are small-scale artifacts. Most proposals include experimenting with the running time of different sorting algorithms as well as experimenting with other measures and algorithms. Almost all of these experiences deal with the algorithmic property of efficiency. In addition, we find some experimentation in programming courses, here related to the property of correctness. Experimenting with correctness is called testing. A new instructional approach has recently emerged based on testing, called test-driven development (Shepard, Lamb & Kelly, 2001). We do not deepen here into these forms of experimentation, but the interested reader is referred elsewhere (Velázquez-Iturbide, Pareja-Flores, Debdi & Paredes-Velasco, 2012). Note also that experimentation does not necessarily play an opposite role to formal proofs, but both approaches may complement each other (Coffey, 2013).

The purpose of this chapter is addressing a third property of many algorithms, namely optimality. This property is a variant of correctness which only makes sense for optimization problems. A part of the specification of optimization problems states that not only the solution must be valid, but it must also be optimal (with respect to a given measure). Although not such a general property as correctness or efficiency, optimiza-

tion also is important in algorithmics. Many of the most interesting algorithms are optimization algorithms. Many of the theoretical results about computational complexity involve optimization problems. Several of the most commonly used algorithm design techniques address optimization problems, either exactly or approximately. We are interested in the different issues around practice and experimentation as an approach to teaching optimization algorithms. We do not include here any definitions of algorithms, but the reader is referred to well-known textbooks, e.g. Brassard and Bratley (1996), Cormen, Leiserson, Rivest and Stein (2009), or Sahni (2005).

The structure of the chapter is as follows. The second section presents a brief background on the topics dealt in the chapter with respect to optimization problems: teaching methods, educational software systems, and educational evaluations. The three following sections contain a comprehensive review of these topics in the CS education literature. We classify the experiences included in any of these sections according to three taxonomies given in Section 2, so that the reader may compare them more easily. Furthermore, the section on educational systems presents an original categorization of them. We conclude the chapter with our conclusions and a brief discussion on lines for future research.

BACKGROUND

In this section we introduce the three topics that will form our review of the learning and teaching of optimization algorithms. The topics are very general: teaching methods, learning tools, and educational evaluations. For the sake of brevity, we just give a very brief introduction of them and we outline several frameworks adopted to discuss our subsequent review.

Table 1. Levels of inquiry according to Herron

	Goal	**Materials**	**Method**	**Answer**
Confirmation/verification	Given	Given	Given	Given /open
Structured inquiry	Given	Given part or whole	Open or part given	Open
Guided inquiry	Given	Open	Open	Open
Open inquiry	Open	Open	Open	Open

Teaching Methods

In the last century, education has experienced a huge advancement. Not only a number of educational theories have been proposed, but numerous evaluations have been conducted, giving more or less empirical support to the different theories. We agree with Diana Laurillard (2012) in adopting an eclectic approach. All the relevant theories can play a different role in different situations. For instance, behaviorism may assist in developing basic skills in children (e.g. arithmetic) or in learning physical skills (e.g. swimming). However, we are interested in computer science education at the university level. At this level, theories that argue for more active learning are the most adequate. Not only university students must learn facts by rote but they must acquire and master concepts and methods specific of computer science, as well as develop metacognitive capabilities that will allow them to further learning and training along their professional career.

A number of active learning methods have been proposed. Some of them are well-known, such as problem-based learning or collaborative learning, while others are less known, such as peer instruction. Currently, there is a large body of knowledge about how to conduct them with higher probability of success (Prince, 2004).

A useful classification of learning methods is proposed by Laurillard (2012). Based on an eclectic approach encompassing the main theories of learning, she proposes a framework that describes the learning actors and processes. Laurillard characterizes five categories of learning

through one of the following generic activities: acquisition, inquiry, discussion, practice, and collaboration. All the categories are valuable for some specific educational context. Therefore, the informed teacher should make use of them for designing the most adequate teaching method in his/her situation. Also note that all the categories can benefit from good use of educational software.

If we focus on learning through practice, Herron (1971) proposed a clear classification of four levels of "inquiry-oriented laboratory experiences" for science courses. Each level is characterized by the information and support given to students prior to or as they complete the activity (see Table 1):

Educational Software Systems

The number and variety of educational software systems is overwhelming. Laurillard (2012)'s framework implicitly provides us with a way of classifying educational tools. We are mostly interested in software systems that can function as intellectual partners with the learner in order to engage and facilitate critical thinking and higher-order learning. Kommers, Jonassen and Mayes (1992) coined the term cognitive tools to name systems that "actively engage learners in creation of knowledge that reflects their comprehension and conception of the information rather than replicating the teachers' presentation of information". Cognitive tools amplify students' thinking by transcending their limitations and allow students to reorganize how they think. According to these authors, cognitive tools have three distinctive features: they support students' active engagement, creation of contents, and control.

Systems supporting active learning can be classified according to the specific educational activities they support. Jonassen (2000) characterizes several classes of cognitive tools for school education: semantic organization tools, dynamic modeling tools, interpretation tools, knowledge construction tools, and conversation tools. Thus, dynamic modeling tools help learners to organize dynamic relationships among the concepts they are studying and learning. Examples of this kind of cognitive tools are spreadsheets, expert systems, systems modeling, and microworlds. Another class of cognitive tools comprises interpretation tools that help learners to interpret information they encounter while constructing their knowledge, for instance, intentional information search tools and visualization tools.

We also find classifications of specific kinds of learning systems. For instance, Naps, Roessling, Almstrum, Dann, Fleischer, Hundhausen et al. (2003) propose an engagement taxonomy to characterize the learning activities students must accomplish using algorithm and program visualization systems. However, for the purposes of this chapter, these more specialized taxonomies are not necessary.

Educational Evaluation

Assessing students' outcomes is on the basis of behaviorism. Even if we disagree with this theory of learning, most of us will agree that students must be assessed with respect to their learning outcomes to know if we succeeded in our teaching task. Thus, the most obvious way of evaluating learning methods is evaluating whether students instructed with them learn more than using a well-known teaching method. The same applies to the evaluation of educational systems. We may call educational effectiveness to this desirable effect. It can be measured according to well-known

quantitative research methods of the social sciences (Cohen, 2001).

However, there are other factors also related to success in education. Motivation is a key factor in students' attitude towards learning because motivation concerns energy, direction, persistence and equifinality –all aspects of activation and intention (Ryan & Deci, 2000a). The literature shows a high diversity in terms and approaches about motivation. From these different conceptual models, the self-determination theory (Deci & Ryan, 1985) is a theoretical framework very useful to understand motivation within the educational and academic contexts. Self-determination theory emphasizes the importance of the development of internal human resources for personal development and self-regulation of behavior. Self-determination is based on intrinsic motivation, or prototypical manifestation of the human tendency toward learning and creativity, and on self-regulation, which is concerned with how people assume social values and extrinsic contingencies and progressively transform these into personal values and self-motivation (Ryan & Deci, 2000a).

There are several dimensions of motivation depending on the level of self-determination, ranging through a continuum from more to less self-determination:

1. **Intrinsic Motivation:** Refers to doing something because it is inherently interesting or enjoyable; intrinsic motivation is an important phenomenon for educators because it is a natural wellspring of learning and achievement that can be systematically catalyzed or undermined by instructor practices, and because intrinsic motivation produces results in high-quality learning and creativity (Ryan & Deci, 2000b).

2. **Extrinsic Motivation via Identified Regulation:** A more self-determined or somewhat internal regulation– implies an option as it occurs when the behavior is

considered important for the subject's goals and values.

3. **Extrinsic Motivation via External Regulation:** A less self-determined or more external regulation– refers to doing something because it leads to a separable outcome –to obtain a reward or to avoid a punishment.

4. **Amotivation:** The least self-determined dimension, implies non-regulation and occurs when individuals do not perceive the contingencies between the behavior and its consequences, and behavior has not intrinsic or extrinsic motivators (Ryan & Deci, 2000a).

Another important issue related to educational success is the understanding of students' difficulties and conceptions. We must first distinguish between conceptual and mental models (Norman, 1983). A conceptual model is a representation of knowledge, built by the instructor in order to transmit it to the students. Consequently, a conceptual model must be precise, complete and consistent. On the other hand, a mental model is the presentation that a student builds of a conceptual model, i.e. his/her understanding of it. Consequently, a mental model often is partial and ambiguous. This distinction between conceptual and mental models clearly underlies the definition of education given by Diana Laurillard (1989): "Education is the design of an environment which will help others learn what experts have articulated".

We do not speak about correct mental models because they vary from one person to another. Two students receiving the same instruction may construct different mental models. Therefore, we speak about viable or unviable models, depending on whether they allow explaining and understanding the phenomena under observation. We may speak about conceptual errors or misconceptions to refer to key aspects of a mental model that make it difficult or impossible to be viable. In addition, the term preconception is used to refer to ideas

which are previous to instruction in a subject. From the point of view of constructivism (Ben-Ari, 2001), knowledge is constructed from previous knowledge and instruction. Therefore, pre- and mis-conceptions can be used by the instructor to assist students in a successful construction of their knowledge.

A number of studies have been conducted in computer science education on students' difficulties since the seventies, mainly on learning to program (Clancy, 2004). These studies address different programming paradigms, from procedural or object-oriented programming to functional, logic or concurrent programming. There are fewer studies on preconceptions or misconceptions on algorithms. Haberman, Averbuch and Ginat (2005) noticed the fragile knowledge of students on algorithms. Students hardly distinguish different elements of the algorithm development process, such as the algorithm itself, its underlying design decisions and analyses results. Closely related is the study by Kolikant (2005) on correctness misconceptions. She found that students are more tolerant to bugs than expert programmers, therefore they share a weaker definition of correctness. For brevity, we do not deal here with misconceptions on either efficiency or specific algorithms.

DIDACTIC METHODS FOR TEACHING OPTIMIZATION ALGORITHMS

Most contributions found in the literature about the teaching and learning of algorithms do not deal explicitly with optimization algorithms. We cite here some contributions that either implicitly or explicitly address this class of algorithms. In the former case, we identify the optimization algorithms that they address.

Ginat (2003, 2007, 2008) has reported on a continuous effort to foster rigorous and creative algorithmic thinking in students and to analyze their difficulties. His studies do not deal exclusively with optimization problems, but he illustrates his experiences with non-trivial problems, many of them optimization problems. (We report more extensively on students' difficulties in Section 5.) A consequence of his experience was the refinement a didactic method (Ginat, 2008). Ginat devotes about one quarter of the sessions in an algorithms course to sessions where students are challenged with non-trivial problems. The didactic method capitalizes on a typical process, based on trial and error that students use for problem-solving. He forces students to reflect on their design mistakes and to appreciate the value of trying alternative approaches to faulty designs. As a consequence, students enhance their meta-learning capabilities by learning from their faulty tendencies in algorithm design and from finding input data that prove the incorrectness of their algorithmic solutions. Notice that Ginat's claims are coherent with constructivist theory, as students construct their knowledge on their previous knowledge and new experiences.

Forišek and Steinová (2012) explore and assess the use of metaphors and analogies in teaching algorithms. They present several physical metaphors that may illuminate the understanding of concepts, data structures and algorithms. In particular, they propose a balls-and-strings metaphor for Dijkstra's algorithm and rubber bands for several optimization geometric algorithms. They also warn against some metaphors for explaining exact optimization algorithms, but that could be useful to explain approximation algorithms. They give anecdotal evidence of their proposals and a reasoned judgment of their instructional experience. An advantage of many metaphors is that they can be put into practice with physical devices or, at least, most of us may imagine how they work based on our previous experience with physical objects.

Mehta, Kouri & Polycarpou (2012) present an experience using a matching algorithm for bipartite graphs with two simultaneous purposes: formation of students' groups for the course projects, and reinforcing network flow concepts and algorithms. They also present an exploratory study. The results from the study suggest that groups formed using the proposed algorithm were successful with respect to student satisfaction and effectiveness, and that students consolidated their mastery of network flow modeling.

Coffey (2013) presents a comprehensive and innovative proposal consisting in integrating three traditional courses on discrete structures, data structures and algorithms into two sequential courses with more heterogeneous contents. This integration of theory and practice eases the reinforcement of theoretical contents with experimental studies. Students are required to perform five projects in the second course, three of them dealing with optimization problems. Two projects deal with approximation algorithms (either genetic or greedy), comparing their optimality. The final project deals with dynamic programming as a technique for improving space and time efficiency. The author presents an evaluation of the experience, explaining the methodological difficulty of comparing his experience with the previous implementation of the course. However, he claims that the completion outcomes were at least as good as in previous years, and likely better.

Velázquez-Iturbide (2013) proposes a didactic method for the active learning of selection functions as the key element in the design of greedy algorithms. In brief, the student is given an optimization problem to be solved by a greedy algorithm and a collection of candidate selection functions, and he/she has to decide which of them are optimal. The inquiry process is simple and proceeds according to the scientific method. The student must provide some input data and determine the result of the greedy algorithm resulting from applying each of the selection functions to these input data. For a maximization problem, those selection functions that yield lower values can be discarded; for a minimization problem,

Table 2. Comparison of features of educational methods for optimization algorithms

Authors	Learning Through...	Kind of Inquiry	Evaluation
Ginat	practice	Guided	Q
Forišek & Steinová	acquisition		A
Mehta, Kouri & Polycarpou	discussion		E/S
Coffey	practice	Structured	E
Velázquez-Iturbide	practice	Structured	E/Mi
Velázquez-Iturbide, Paredes-Velasco & Debdi	practice, collaboration	Structured	E/Mo

selection functions that yield higher values can be discarded. The student will repeat this process with new input data until he/she has experimental evidence on which selection functions are optimal, i.e. they always yield optimal values. The didactic method was devised jointly with an interactive system that supports it, called GreedEx. The method and the system were jointly evaluated with respect to educational effectiveness, with statistically significant positive results, and they have been used to identify and remove students' misconceptions. (The GreedEx system and the evaluations are presented in Sections 4 and 5, respectively.)

This didactic method was later extended with a collaborative phase for discussion of the results within small groups (Velázquez-Iturbide, Paredes-Velasco & Debdi, 2013). This collaborative phase is supported by a collaborative extension of GreedEx, called GreedExCol. It was evaluated with respect to educational effectiveness and motivation, with statistically significant positive results in both cases.

Summary

The didactic methods presented above are summarized in Table 2. Each row contains a particular method. Each cell may be in blank (if the classification of the corresponding column does not apply) or may contain one or several abbreviations. The columns represent the different features selected:

- Column "learning through..." classifies the method into one or several of the categories in Laurillard's taxonomy (2012).
- Column "kind of inquiry" classifies those experimental methods into one of the kinds of inquiry proposed by Herron (1971).
- Column "evaluation" shows if any evaluation of the system or the students was held, either anecdotal evaluation (A), qualitative evaluation (Q), educational effectiveness (E), students' satisfaction (S), students' motivation (Mo), or identification of students' misconceptions (Mi). Although some evaluations are not rigorous according to established standards, we do not go deeper into this issue here.

TOOLS FOR PRACTICING WITH OPTIMIZATION ALGORITHMS

In this section, we review systems for practicing with optimization algorithms. We present a number of systems, classified according to the kind of learning activity that they promote, either understanding, checking or comparing. Some distinctions are made among tools intended for the most populated category, namely understanding. We present the systems in each category in chronological order. In the last subsection, we summarize the systems and discuss their features.

Given the huge number of potential systems, we do not include either general purpose systems (e.g.

general purpose algorithm animation systems) or professional systems (e.g. research packages for graph visualization); we include references on these systems in the additional reading section. In other words, we restrict our review to educational systems that were designed taking (at least partially) optimization problems into account.

Understanding Optimization Problems

The systems classified in this category test the students' understanding of problem statements. Typically, a specific instance of a problem is either entered by the student or generated by the system, and is visualized by the system. The student must then give a correct, probably optimal, solution to the problem.

The AλgoVista system (Collberg, Kobourov & Westbrook, 2004) combines functionalities of a search engine, visual queries and algorithm checking. AλgoVista supports about 350 graph, geometric and numeric problems. It relies on a technique for proving correctness known as program checking. Programmers must extend each algorithm with a checker which is in charge of verifying the correctness of the results it computes. The AλgoVista database stores problem descriptions as well as their checkers, called checklets.

Students may draw a visual query in AλgoVista that is translated into a textual query and answered by the database server, where the query is matched against the checklets in the database and a list of the problems whose checklets match the query is returned. AλgoVista can be used by students to check their knowledge of combinatorial concepts, their understanding of problem statements, and the correctness of their algorithms (via checklets).

The PILOT system (Bridgeman, Goodrich, Kobourov & Tamassia, 2000) was designed to assist in learning several graph problems, including minimum cost spanning trees (at least, Prim's algorithm) and shortest paths. The student may select one of the problems supported by PILOT.

The system randomly generates a problem instance, draws it on the screen and the student must interactively enter a correct solution to the problem. When the student considers that a correct solution has been built, the system corrects and grades the solution. If the solution is wrong, PILOT displays the data structure with the incorrect choices highlighted (e.g. edges), along with a score and an explanation of the errors made. The student may ask at any moment for a correct solution.

Checking Optimization Algorithms

Checking whether an optimization algorithm is correct means assessing whether it satisfies its problem statement. An obvious tool for assessing the design of algorithms is automated assessment systems (Ihantola, Ahoniemi, Karavirta & Seppälä, 2009). However, the most common approach to checking algorithm correctness is not directly applicable to optimization problems. In general, an instance of an optimization problem may have several optimal, equivalent solutions. Therefore, a direct comparison of the instructor's solution with the solution generated by the student's algorithm may be misleading.

Several approaches have been adopted for checking students' programs. The automated assessment system Jutge.org (Giménez, Petit & Roura, 2012) incorporates, in addition to a traditional checker, four additional checkers, each one adequate to a particular class of algorithmic problems. External checkers were especially designed for optimization problems. An external checker is a program (written by the problem setter) that, given an input of the problem and given the output of a candidate solution on that input, decides whether this solution is correct or not. The decision involves deciding whether the solution is valid and optimal. The first check can be made without comparing it to any other solution, but by checking that it satisfies given validity conditions; the second check involves comparing the value associated to the solution computed by the student' algorithm with the value of the solution computed by the problem setter.

A similar checking technique was incorporated into AλgoVista (Collberg et al., 2004) and PILOT (Bridgeman et al. 2000). However, these systems only check that the student's solution satisfies given conditions, thus it is doubtful their general applicability. AλgoVista supports many graph algorithms, while PILOT supports minimum spanning tree algorithms.

Understanding Optimization Algorithms by Tutoring

These tools play a similar role to the systems described in the first subsection, but with respect to algorithms instead of problems. We have only found systems that assist in understanding some of the best-known graph optimization algorithms, such as Dijkstra's, Prim's and Kruskal's algorithms. We refer three tutor-like systems; they make use of visualization for better comprehension.

The DIDAGRAPH system (Dagdilelis & Satratzemi, 1998) was in a preliminary stage, only supporting the three predefined algorithms identified above. The student may enter or load a graph and apply a sequence of actions to simulate the algorithm execution. The system gives the student freedom to perform wrong actions until he/she asks whether the actions are correct; DIDAGRAPH gives then an answer and a short explanation. Finally, DIDAGRAPH allows building visualizations of other graph algorithms by using commands available at the menu structure.

PILOT (Bridgeman et al. 2000), briefly described in the first category of systems, allows students to select a specific algorithm for a given problem. Then, he/she must give the exact order of the elements' selection in the solution. Although the authors do not clarify the algorithms supported, this feature is obviously adequate for greedy algorithms. An outstanding feature of PILOT is that it gives partial credit to a student's solution by checking incrementally the solution and adding a penalty for each mistake detected.

The GRAPHs system (Sánchez-Torrubia, Torres-Blanc & Escribano-Blanco, 2010) allows checking the student whether he/she understands several graph algorithms, including Dijsktra's algoritm. The student may visually edit a graph (or load it from a file) and simulate the behavior of the selected algorithm. The internal state of the algorithm is displayed at any instant in both graphical and tabular formats. The execution can proceed in any of three different degrees of detail, in coordination with a code panel where the active code line is highlighted. In the interactive modes, the student must enter the next choice of node and the changes in minimal distances that the algorithm computes, and the system assesses the correctness of these decisions.

Understanding Optimization Algorithms by Visualization

One of the most common ways of trying to understand abstract concepts is by means of visualization. We find hundreds of algorithm animations on the web. The comprehensive portal Algoviz contained 326 algorithm animations (Shaffer, Cooper, Alon, Akbar, Stewart, Ponce & Edwards, 2010), being at least 63 of them were of optimization algorithms: 20 of shortest paths, 17 of minimum-cost spanning trees, 13 of Huffman codes, 9 of dynamic programming, and 4 of network flow. These animations differ much in their educational features, thus their analysis would distract us from a more general overview of systems for optimization algorithms. Therefore, we restrict ourselves to visualization systems explicitly designed to support the learning of optimization algorithms.

The first class of animation systems allow visualizing the execution of graph algorithms; we found two such systems. The DisViz system (Sherstov, 2003) is heterodox compared to typical visualization systems. DisViz displays a graph that mimics the structure of students sitting at the workstations in a classroom. The shape of the graph can be changed by any of the students. Students may launch an algorithm on the graph so defined, with the restriction that only one algorithm can be simultaneously animated in all the workstations. DisViz supports four well-known graph algorithms, including Barůvka's (for the minimum cost spanning tree problem) and Dijkstra's algorithms.

The IAPPGA system (Wu, 2005) allows flexible input of graphs and step-by-step execution of a number of predefined graph algorithms (at least, the Edmonds-Karp algorithm for the maximum flow problem). The system provides both visual and textual feedback about the algorithm execution. The author gives anecdotal experience of its use.

A second, related class of systems is visualization systems or packages that allow the user to build visualizations of his/her own graph algorithms. In most cases, they also include predefined visualizations of well-known algorithms. The EVEGA package (Khuri & Holzapfel, 2001) supports visual editing and random generation of graphs, as well as animation of a predefined set of graph algorithms, at least for the maximum flow problem. The tool provides Java packages for the user interested in creating his/her own visualizations. Moreover, EVEGA supports the graphical display of performance data of one or several algorithms.

GraphMagic (Hansen, Tuinstra, Pisani & McCann, 2003) is a collection of Java classes for visualizing graph algorithms. They support editing or loading graphs and graph visualization with a simple user interface. The authors cite a group of built-in animations developed for well-known algorithms, including Dijkstra's, Prim's and Bellman-Ford's algorithms. They also report on anecdotal experience and on several formal evaluations, with mixed results.

The VisualGraph class (Lucas, Naps & Roessling, 2003) supports flexible generation of graphs and generation of graph animations. VisualGraph generates AnimalScript output and the resulting stream can then be used by the JHAVÉ support system. AnimalScript is then parsed and rendered by the ANIMAL animation system. Consequently, the user interface for walking through visualizations is automatically equipped with a vast array of educational functions provided by ANIMAL.

Although less frequent, we also find visualization systems aimed at understanding other kinds of optimization algorithms. Thus, we find brief descriptions of systems assisting in understanding the simplex algorithm aided by visualization (Lazaridis, Samaras & Zissopoulos, 2003, Papamanthou & Paparrizos, 2003). More interesting from the point of view of a course on algorithms are visualization systems supporting any algorithm design technique. We have found visualization systems supporting techniques based on searching in a state space or the greedy technique.

The INTEGER system (Ramani & Rama Rao, 1994) is intended to solve integer programming problems by using a branch-and-bound technique which has similarities to the technique found in algorithms textbooks. The system generates automatically the visualizations and includes several zooming and details-on-demand functions for greater interactivity. The authors also report on a controlled experiment that showed a statistically significant improvement over other tool.

The AI-Search system (MacDonald & Ciesielski, 2002) visualizes how to solve 8-puzzle problems. It supports six general search techniques, such as A* or branch-and-bound, and three heuristics. It supports step-by-step and "burst" modes of execution. Each mode has associated a different level of detail in the visualization. The authors report on a formal evaluation with similar results for the two groups of students, but in questions related to qualitative performance of search algorithms the group using AI-Search performed better.

Comparing Optimization Algorithms

A step forward in experimenting with optimization algorithms consists in comparing the outcomes produced by different algorithms with respect to optimality (consequently, we do not consider here the EVEGA system). This process makes explicit the nature of optimality. We know of four systems that support this kind of inquiry.

Benchmark tests are often used to evaluate the quality of products by a set of common criteria. The Algorithm Benchmark system was designed to compare the performance of various algorithms or to evaluate the behavior of an algorithm with different input instances (Chen, Wei, Huang & Lee, 2006). In fact, Algorithm Benchmark is a comprehensive automated assessment system with enhanced facilities regarding algorithm performance. The measures that Algorithm Benchmark supports are memory utilization, time complexity and the output of algorithms; the latter measure can be used to compare the results of alternative optimization algorithms for a problem. The authors illustrate the system capabilities with several examples, one of them consisting in comparing five suboptimal algorithms (i.e. heuristics) for the traveling salesman problem.

The GreedEx system (Velázquez-Iturbide, Debdi, Esteban-Sánchez & Pizarro, 2013) supports a didactic method summarized in Section 3. It allows experimenting with the optimality of candidate selection functions for six predefined problems (the activity selection problem and five knapsack problems). The user is given a specific set of selection functions for each problem and must experiment to determine which corresponding greedy algorithms are optimal or suboptimal. GreedEx supports flexible input of data, and visualizes the execution state of the current algorithm. For the sake of more flexible experimentation, the system provides several execution functions (and their corresponding way of data generation) with different degree of detail. The data gathered experimentally are stored, for their comparison,

in four tables with different levels of abstraction. In addition GreedEx supports several mundane learning activities, such as exporting information into graphical files. The system has been evaluated for usability and educational effectiveness, with statistically significant positive results, and has been used to identify and remove students' misconceptions.

The GreedExCol system (Velázquez-Iturbide, Paredes-Velasco et al., 2013) is a collaborative extension of GreedEx. It extends the first phase of individual experimentation with a second phase for discussion of the results within small groups. It has also been evaluated for usability, educational effectiveness and motivation, with statistically significant positive results for the two latter factors.

The OptimEx system (Velázquez-Iturbide, Martín-Torres & González-Rabanal, 2013) is a generalization of GreedEx, intended to experiment with any optimization algorithm. The system does not support the algorithm-specific features of GreedEx (e.g. visualizations), but provides statistical data resulting from comparing the results of different algorithms that solve the same problem. The system does not judge the accuracy of data, but demands the user to identify an optimal algorithm. Consequently, inconsistencies are detected and the user should later fix them (e.g. a suboptimal algorithm producing better outcomes than an optimal algorithm). OptimEx has been evaluated for usability and has been used to detect students' misconceptions on optimization.

Summary of Systems

We have reviewed a number of educational systems that support to some degree experimentation with optimization algorithms. They are summarized in Table 1, where each row contains features of a particular system and where each group of systems is separated by double edges from adjacent groups. Each cell may be in blank (if the system does not support the corresponding column feature or if we did not find any reference to it in the cited literature) or it may contain one or several abbreviations. The columns represent the different features selected:

- Column "input data" denotes how input data are entered, either by some form of edition (E), loading a file (L), randomly generating it (G) or it is present but hidden to the student (H).
- Column "checking" identifies what the system checks, either a problem (P) or a specific algorithm for the problem (A).
- Column "communication" refers to the kind of human-computer or human-human communication that the system supports, either a simple assessment of the student's answer (A), an explanation of the assessment (E) or a discussion among members of a team (D).
- Column "visualization" simply identifies whether the system visualizes the algorithm; other useful features of algorithm visualization are not considered here, e.g. textual explanations or stop-and-think questions (Naps et al., 2003).
- Column "algorithms" identifies if the system supports visualizations of predefined algorithms (P) or of user-constructed algorithms (U).
- Column "comparison" differentiates the kind of measures the system compares, either time (T), space (S) or the measure to optimize (O).
- Column "evaluation" shows if any evaluation of the system or the students was held, either anecdotal evaluation (A), system usability (U), educational effectiveness (E), students' motivation (Mo), or identification of students' misconceptions (Mi).

We may notice that many systems could be extended with features provided by other kinds of systems. In particular, systems for problem understanding, checking algorithm correctness, and comparing the optimality of different algorithms are complementary. For instance, Jutge.org could be extended with functions for comparison, or OptimEx could be extended with assessment functions. Note also that PILOT actually is a hybrid system with features for problem understanding, checking algorithm correctness and tutoring for algorithm understanding.

Some systems only support a set of predefined algorithms. Obviously, it would be desirable to extend them to support any algorithm. However, it is very difficult or even impossible to provide such universal support for some features. This is the case of generating understandable explanations of user's errors for any algorithm. Most systems that support user algorithms neither provide visualization functions. This is due to the difficulty of delivering useful, general visualizations (e.g. OptimEx) or to the fact that visualization is not a major concern for the system builders (e.g. Jutge. org). We should also note that systems supporting user visualizations are often at the expense of a substantial effort of users to learn how to build visualizations.

Classification of Systems

The systems presented so far can be analyzed from several points of view. Table 4 presents a classification of the systems according to the taxonomies by Laurillard (2012), Herron (1971) and Jonassen (2000).

According to Laurillard (2012), all the systems facilitate learning through practice. Consequently, we associate each system with one of the digital technologies she identifies. Systems aimed at understanding either problems or algorithms fall in the category of tutoring systems. Algorithm animation systems are a subclass of simulation systems. Finally, the systems which are open and allow the user to develop their own algorithms and experience with them in the form foreseen by the system can be considered microworlds, aimed at

Table 3. Comparison of features of educational systems for optimization algorithms

Group of Systems	System	Input Data	Check	Commun-ication	Visualization	Algorithms	Comparison	Evaluation
Understanding problems	AλgoVista	E	P		X	P/U		A
	PILOT	G	P/A	E	X	P		
Checking algorithm correctness	Jutge.org	H	P	A		U		
Understanding algorithms by tutoring	DIDAGRAPH	E/L/G	A	E	X	P/U		
	GRAPHs	E/L	A	E	X	P		
Understanding algorithms by visualization	DisViz	E			X	P		
	IAPPGA	E			X	P		A
	EVEGA	E/G			X	P/U	T	A
	GraphMagic	E/L			X	P/U		A/E
	VisualGraph	E/L/G			X	P/U		
	INTEGER	E			X	P		A/E
	AI-Search	?			X	P		A/U/E
Comparing algorithms	Algorithm Benchmark	L	P	A		U	T/S/O	
	GreedEx	E/L/G			X	P	O	U/E/Mi
	GreedExCol	E/L/G		D	X	P	O	U/E/Mo
	OptimEx	E/L/G		A		U	O	U/Mi

visualizing algorithms, assessing their correctness or comparing their relative optimality.

The taxonomy by Herron (1971) makes a sharp distinction between systems which only allow practicing with predefined algorithms and systems which are open. We interpret Herron's terms in the following way: the goal corresponds to the aim of the educational task, the materials are the algorithms under study and the input data used for practice, the method is the procedure to be used for accomplishing the educational task, and the answer corresponds to the outcome expected from the educational task.

Following this interpretation, tutoring systems working with predefined problems or algorithms only support a confirmation/verification task. The goal consists in understanding the working of the algorithms and the method consists in some form of tracing the algorithm execution. As a result,

the student either answers correctly to the posed questions or not. Structured inquiry is achieved by visualization or comparison systems using predefined algorithms. In the case of visualization systems, different goals can be stated. The inquiry method and some materials (e.g. input data) will vary for different goals, but the system provides the visualization and animation support necessary for the inquiry. In the case of comparison systems, the goal and the method are given but the students may apply them freely with their own input data. A good example is GreedEx (Velázquez-Iturbide, Debdi et al., 2013), where the authors of the system proposed a well-defined experimentation process but they did not even know in advance all the optimality results of the different selection functions implemented (Velázquez-Iturbide & Debdi, 2011). Finally, guided inquiry is supported by systems which allow the user to provide his/

Table 4. Classification of educational systems for optimization algorithms

Group of Systems	System	Learning Through...	Kind of Inquiry	Cognitive Tool
Understanding problems	AλgoVista	practice (tutoring, microworld)	Confirmation/ verification, guided	Microworld
	PILOT	practice (tutoring)	Confirmation/verification	
Checking algorithm correctness	Jutge.org	practice (microworld)	Guided	Microworld
Understanding algorithms by tutoring	DIDAGRAPH	practice (tutoring, simulation)	Confirmation/ verification, guided	Visualization
	GRAPHs	practice (tutoring)	Confirmation/verification	
Understanding algorithms by visualization	DisViz	practice (simulation)	Structured	
	IAPPGA	practice (simulation)	Structured	
	EVEGA	practice (simulation)	Structured, guided	Visualization
	GraphMagic	practice (simulation)	Structured, guided	Visualization
	VisualGraph	practice (simulation)	Structured, guided	Visualization
	INTEGER	practice (simulation)	Structured	
	AI-Search	practice (simulation)	Structured	
Comparing algorithms	Algorithm Benchmark	practice (microworld)	Guided	Microworld
	GreedEx	practice (simulation)	Structured	
	GreedExCol	practice (simulation), collaboration	Structured	
	OptimEx	practice (microworld)	Guided	Microworld

her own algorithms, where the goal consists in developing an algorithm without further guidance.

The point of view of Jonassen (200) is more demanding on the systems. Only those systems that allow the user to create his/her own algorithms are capable to support the creation of distinct knowledge from that embodied by the tool developer. The remaining systems fit the categories of either visualization tools or microworld tools. The latter category comprises assessment, visualization and comparison systems, as in the analysis with Laurillard's framework.

EDUCATIONAL EVALUATIONS

In this section we briefly describe different evaluations of students' motivation, students' difficulties, and students' misconceptions on learning optimization algorithms. Most of them were cited in the two previous sections. We discarded the description of anecdotal evidence given their lack of relevance, as well as evaluations that reported deficiencies or difficulties in their procedure. We have also omitted usability evaluation of systems given their lack of interest for the purpose of the chapter. Finally, we omitted evaluations which are subjective (e.g. students' satisfaction), given their risk of suffering the placebo or Hawthorne effects, and evaluations of educational effectiveness given their standard format.

Students' Motivation

The only evaluation of motivation we are aware of was conducted using the GreedExCol system (Velázquez-Iturbide, Paredes-Velasco et al., 2013). The instrument used to measure motivation was the EMSI questionnaire (Martín-Albo, Núñez and Navarro, 2009). The EMSI scale has 14 items grouped into the four dimensions of motivation. The evaluation did not detect an improvement in the global motivation of the experimental group over the control group. However, a statistically significant increase was measured for implicit motivation.

Students' Difficulties

We may highlight the findings reported by Ginat (see Section 3) and the findings with the assistance of the OptimEx system (see Section 4). They are summarized below.

Ginat (2007) has reported on several difficulties found in students trying to design non-trivial algorithms. He noticed that students often design an algorithm, and they get convinced about its correctness without having carried out comprehensive testing or reasoning. If somebody (typically, the instructor) points out a case for which the algorithm works wrongly, the student "patches" the algorithm. In general, the problem lies in the "hasty design" of an algorithm. However, as students insist in patching, they get involved in a cycle of instructor's notifications and "futile patches". Patching is a valuable strategy for problem solving under certain circumstances, but it does not work if the design of the algorithm is wrong.

Hasty designs most often come from one of the following reasons (Ginat, 2007):

- Association of some words in the problem statement to a particular, inadequate perspective.
- Consideration of local properties, rather than global ones.
- Oversimplification of the relevant properties to build an algorithm, not considering some hidden properties.
- Adoption of a common design-technique without a rigorous analysis of its adequacy, e.g. the greedy technique (Ginat, 2003).

- Premature adoption of a particular design pattern for a problem because it looks analogous to another problem in which this pattern was used.

Patches are introduced by the student into his/her algorithm when he/she is reported a new input case for which the algorithm does not give the desired outcome. Patching typically takes one of the two following forms (Ginat, 2007):

- A patch that solves the new case is added, separately from the previously solved cases, without changing the algorithm for the previous cases.
- Some local modification is made of the initial algorithm, which handles together both the previous cases and the new case.

Optimization Misconceptions

Danielsiek, Paul and Vahrenhold (2012) researched students' difficulties on different topics of algorithm and data structures, but they only report on the results on heaps and binary search trees, invariants, and dynamic programming. Their research methods included short tests and think-aloud interviews. In relation to our review, they report on the students' difficulties in mastering dynamic programming, and some misconceptions of the divide-and-conquer technique. In particular they hypothesized whether students conflated the divide-and-conquer and the dynamic programming techniques. However, no clear conclusion can be extracted from their investigations but the extremely difficulty of mastering dynamic programming.

Velázquez-Iturbide (2013) analyzed the reports of students solving in pairs a guided-discovery assignment on greedy algorithms using GreedEx. Apart from some difficulties, he detected that many students exhibited one or several of the three following misconceptions:

- **Inconsistent Reasoning:** Some groups were inconsistent in the interpretation of the results of their experimentation. For instance, some groups formulated proposals based on one single input data set while ignoring the results of other data sets, others discarded some selection functions without having found a counterexample for them, or even made different proposals in different parts of their report.

- **Additional Optimization Criterion:** In general, an optimization problem may have several optimal solutions for given input data and may be solved optimally by different algorithms. A number of pairs of students believed that only one optimal selection function was possible. Consequently, several groups restated the target function by incorporating an additional optimization criterion. The criterion, either maximization or minimization, which was not present in the original problem statement.

- **Dependence on Input Data:** An optimal selection function must give the best solution for any input data. Suboptimal selection functions may give an optimal value for some input data but they give a suboptimal value for other input data. Some groups thought that the optimal selection function could vary, depending on the specific input data, without making clear the criterion for selecting any selection function. Interestingly, this factor is always present with the previous one, but not the other way.

Once these misunderstanding were detected, an intervention was made to improve the didactics of greedy algorithms (Velázquez-Iturbide, 2013). The original didactical method, based on an experimental method and the GreedEx tool, was complemented with didactic materials and a modified teaching schedule. The teaching materials explicitly addressed the most problematic issues,

and the schedule was adapted to make room to the experimental method in the classroom (and not only in the laboratory). These interventions were made and refined in two consecutive academic years, resulting in a dramatic decrease in the percentage of the most severe misunderstandings.

A later study analyzed the reports that students elaborated using OptimEx to compare exact and approximate optimization algorithms (Velázquez-Iturbide, 2014). The analysis again revealed some of these difficulties and misunderstandings. On the one hand, students had problems in interpreting the outcomes of optimization algorithms displayed by OptimEx. Data collected often reveal that an algorithm is suboptimal when it is supposed to give an exact, optimal solution. On the other hand, students' explanation of their findings reveals a shallow understanding of optimality concepts. A problem lies in the use of an imprecise vocabulary to describe different situations. For instance, it is different to speak about an "optimal" algorithm that always yields the optimal outcome than to speak about which algorithm, among several ones, is "optimal" for a specific input data.

CONCLUSION

We have reviewed the CS research literature on the teaching and learning of optimization algorithms. In particular, three important issues for teaching optimization algorithms have been reviewed. Firstly, we have reviewed educational methods which partially or completely address optimization algorithms. Secondly, educational software systems have been reviewed and classified according to technical and educational criteria. Thirdly, evaluations involving students are presented, with an emphasis on difficulties and misunderstandings.

We may notice that the number of didactic methods specifically devoted to optimization algorithms is very small. However, according to some studies (Velázquez-Iturbide, 2013), students misunderstand some optimality concepts. Notice that there is not a widely accepted subject matter in computer science curricula where basic concepts of optimization could be integrated. Related concepts of discrete mathematics, such as combinatory or probability have been identified in the ACM curricular recommendations (ACM & IEEE Computer Society, 2013), concept inventories (Almstrum, Henderson, Harvey, Heeren, Marion, Riedesel et al., 2006), and prestigious algorithms textbooks that include preliminary concepts (Brassard and Bratley, 1996; Cormen et al., 2009). However, optimization concepts (e.g. maximization and minimization properties, or upper and lower bounds) are not addressed at all.

Systems that, at least partially address optimality are of a very varied nature. The systems that best support open inquiry can be characterized as microworlds, according to Laurillard or Jonassen. They allow students to develop their own algorithms and assess their optimality, either individually or collectively. It would be desirable to have them extended with additional features that facilitate or extend their educational use, e.g. visualization. Furthermore, new insights can be obtained by using the frameworks here used in unexplored directions.

The survey intends to consolidate current knowledge about the education of this class of problems and algorithms for researchers interested in computer science education. A potential use of the survey is to identify opportunities for future research. For instance, teaching methods for optimization algorithms conceived from non-practice approaches still are rare. We have also identified opportunities for designing novel educational systems, for instance by complementing the functions of different classes of systems. Finally, studies on students' difficulties and misconceptions give an opportunity to design new teaching methods and systems.

ACKNOWLEDGMENT

This work was supported by research grant TIN2011-29542-C02-01 of the Spanish Ministry of Economy and Competitiveness.

REFERENCES

ACM & IEEE Computer Society, The Joint Task Force on Computing Curricula. (2012). *Computer Science curricula 2013*. Retrieved February 23, 2014 from http://www.acm.org/education/CS2013-final-report.pdf

Almstrum, V. L., Henderson, P. B., Harvey, V. J., Heeren, C., Marion, W. A., & Riedesel, C. et al. (2006). Concept inventories in computer science for the topic discrete mathematics. *ACM SIGCSE Bulletin*, *38*(4), 132–145. doi:10.1145/1189136.1189182

Atchison, W. F., Schweppe, E. J., Viavant, W., Young, D. M., Conte, S. D., & Hamblen, J. W. et al.. (1968). Curriculum'68: Recommendations for academic programs in computer science. *Communications of the ACM*, *11*(3), 151–197. doi:10.1145/362929.362976

Baldwin, D. (1992). Using scientific experiments in early computer science laboratories. In *Proceedings of the 23rd SIGCSE Technical Symposium on Computer Science Education, SIGCSE'92* (pp. 102-106). New York, NY: ACM Press. doi:10.1145/134510.134532

Ben-Ari, M. (2001). Constructivism in computer science education. *Journal of Computers in Mathematics and Science Teaching*, *20*(1), 45–73.

Brassard, G., & Bratley, P. (1996). *Fundamentals of Algoritmics*. Hertfordshire, UK: Prentice-Hall.

Braught, G., Miller, C. S., & Reed, D. (2004). Core empirical concepts and skills for computer science. In *Proceedings of the 35th SIGCSE Technical Symposium on Computer Science Education, SIGCSE'04* (pp. 245-249). New York, NY: ACM Press. doi:10.1145/971300.971388

Bridgeman, S., Goodrich, M. T., Kobourov, S. G., & Tamassia, R. (2000). PILOT: An interactive tool for learning and grading. In *Proceedings of the 31st SIGCSE Technical Symposium on Computer Science Education, SIGCSE'00* (pp. 139-143). New York, NY: ACM Press. doi:10.1145/330908.331843

Chen, M.-Y., Wei, J.-D., Huang, J.-H., & Lee, D. T. (2006). Design and applications of an algorithm benchmark system in a computational problem solving environment. In *Proceedings of the 11th Annual Conference on Innovation and Technology in Computer Science Education, ITiCSE'06* (pp. 123-127). New York, NY: ACM Press. doi:10.1145/1140124.1140159

Clancy, M. (2004). Misconceptions and attitudes that interfere with learning to program. In S. Fincher & M. Petre (Eds.), *Computer Science Education Research* (pp. 85–100). London, UK: Routledge.

Coffey, J. W. (2013). Integrating theoretical and empirical computer science in a data structures course. In In *Proceedings of the 44th SIGCSE Technical Symposium on Computer Science Education, SIGCSE'13* (pp. 23-27). New York, NY: ACM Press. doi:10.1145/2445196.2445211

Cohen, L., Manion, L., & Morrison, K. (2001). *Research Methods in Education* (5th ed.). New York: Routledge.

Collberg, C., Kobourov, S. G., & Westbrook, S. (2004). AlgoVista: An algorithmic search tool in an educational setting. In *Proceedings of the 35th SIGCSE Technical Symposium on Computer Science Education, SIGCSE'04* (pp. 462-466). New York, NY: ACM Press. doi:10.1145/971300.971457

Cormen, T. H., Leiserson, C. E., Rivest, R. L., & Stein, C. (2009). *Introduction to Algorithms* (3rd ed.). Cambridge, MA: The MIT Press.

Dagdilelis, V., & Satratzemi, M. (1998). DIDAGRAPH: Software for teaching graph theory algorithms. In *Proceedings of the 3rd Annual Conference on Innovation and Technology in Computer Science Education, ITiCSE'98* (pp. 64-68). New York, NY: ACM Press. doi:10.1145/282991.283024

Danielsiek, H., Paul, W., & Vahrenhold, J. (2012). Detecting and understanding students' misconceptions related to algorithms and data structures. In *Proceedings of the 43rd SIGCSE Technical Symposium on Computer Science Education, SIGCSE'12* (pp. 21-26). New York, NY: ACM Press. doi:10.1145/2157136.2157148

Deci, E. L., & Ryan, R. M. (1985). *Intrinsic Motivation and Self-determination in Human Behavior*. New York, NY: Plenum Press. doi:10.1007/978-1-4899-2271-7

Denning, P. J. (2007). Computing as a natural science. *Communications of the ACM, 50*(7), 13–18. doi:10.1145/1272516.1272529

Denning, P. J., Comer, D. E., Gries, D., Mulder, M. C., Tucker, A. B., Turner, A. J., & Young, P. R. (1989). Computing as a discipline. *Communications of the ACM, 32*(1), 9–23. doi:10.1145/63238.63239

Forišek, M., & Steinová, M. (2012). Metaphors and analogies for teaching algorithms. In *Proceedings of the 43th SIGCSE Technical Symposium on Computer Science Education, SIGCSE'12* (pp. 15-20). New York, NY: ACM Press. doi:10.1145/2157136.2157147

Giménez, O., Petit, J., & Roura, S. (2012). Jutge. org: An educational programming judge. In *Proceedings of the 43th SIGCSE Technical Symposium on Computer Science Education, SIGCSE'12* (pp. 445-450). New York, NY: ACM Press.

Ginat, D. (2003). The greedy trap and learning from mistakes. In *Proceedings of the 34th SIGCSE Technical Symposium on Computer Science Education, SIGCSE'03* (pp. 11-15). New York, NY: ACM Press. doi:10.1145/611892.611920

Ginat, D. (2007). Hasty design, futile patching and the elaboration of rigor. In *Proceedings of the 38th SIGCSE Technical Symposium on Computer Science Education, SIGCSE'07* (pp. 161-165). New York, NY: ACM Press. doi:10.1145/1268784.1268832

Ginat, D. (2008). Learning from wrong and creative algorithm design. In *Proceedings of the 39th SIGCSE Technical Symposium on Computer Science Education, SIGCSE'08* (pp. 26-30). New York, NY: ACM Press. doi:10.1145/1352135.1352148

Haberman, B., Averbuch, H., & Ginat, D. (2005). Is it really an algorithm – The need for explicit discourse. In *Proceedings of the 10th Annual Conference on Innovation and Technology in Computer Science Education, ITiCSE'05* (pp. 74-78). New York, NY: ACM Press. doi:10.1145/1067445.1067469

Hansen, S., Tuinstra, K., Pisani, J., & McCann, L. I. (2003). Graph Magic: A visual graph package for students. *Computer Science Education, 13*(1), 53–66. doi:10.1076/csed.13.1.53.13541

Herron, M. (1971). The nature of scientific enquiry. *The School Review, 79*(2), 171–212. doi:10.1086/442968

Ihantola, P., Ahoniemi, T., Karavirta, V., & Seppälä, O. (2010). Review of recent systems for automatic assessment of programming assignments. In *Proceedings of the 10th Koli Calling International Conference on Computing Education Research, Koli Calling 2010* (pp. 86-93). New York, NY: ACM Press. doi:10.1145/1930464.1930480

Jonassen, D. H. (2000). *Computers as Mindtools for Schools* (2nd ed.). Upper Saddle River, NJ: Merrill.

Khuri, S., & Holzapfel, K. (2001). EVEGA: An educational visualization environment for graph algorithms. In *Proceedings of the 6th Annual Conference on Innovation and Technology in Computer Science Education, ITiCSE'01* (pp. 101-104). New York, NY: ACM Press. doi:10.1145/377435.377497

Kolikant, Y. B.-D. (2005). Students' alternative standards for correctness. In *Proceedings of the First International Workshop on Computing Education Research, ICER'05* (pp. 37-43). New York, NY: ACM Press.

Kommers, P. A. M., Jonassen, D. H., & Mayes, T. M. (Eds.). (1992). *Cognitive Tools for Learning*. Heidelberg, Germany: Springer-Velag. doi:10.1007/978-3-642-77222-1

Laurillard, D. (1987). The different forms of learning in psychology and education. In J. Richardson, M. Eysenck & D. Warren-Piper (Eds.), Students Learning (pp. 198-207). Buckingham, UK: Open University Press.

Laurillard, D. (2012). *Teaching as a Design Science*. New York, NY: Routledge.

Lazaridis, V., Samaras, N., & Zissopoulos, D. (2003). Visualization and teaching simplex algorithm. In *Proceedings of the 3rd IEEE International Conference on Advanced Learning Technologies, ICALT'03* (pp. 270-271). Athens, Greece: IEEE Computer Society Press. doi:10.1109/ICALT.2003.1215078

Lucas, J., Naps, T. L., & Roessling, G. (2003). VisualGraph - A graph class designed for both undergraduate students and educators, In *Proceedings of the 34th SIGCSE Technical Symposium on Computer Science Education, SIGCSE'03* (pp. 167-171). New York, NY: ACM Press. doi:10.1145/611892.611960

MacDonald, P., & Ciesielski, V. (2002). Design and evaluation of an algorithm animation of state space search methods. *Computer Science Education*, *12*(4), 301–324. doi:10.1076/csed.12.4.301.8622

Martín-Albo, J., Núñez, J. L., & Navarro, J. G. (2009). Validation of the Spanish version of the Situational Motivation Scale (EMSI) in the educational context. *The Spanish Journal of Psychology*, *12*(2), 799–807. doi:10.1017/S113874160000216X PMID:19899680

Matocha, J. (2002). Laboratory experiments in an algorithms course: technical writing and the scientific method. In *Proceedings of the 32nd ASEE/IEEE Frontiers in Education Conference, FIE'02* (pp. T1G 9-13). Champaign, IL: Stipes Publishing. doi:10.1109/FIE.2002.1157917

McCracken, D. D. (1989). Three "lab assignments" for an algorithms course. In *Proceedings of the 20th SIGCSE Technical Symposium on Computer Science Education, SIGCSE'89* (pp. 61-64). New York, NY: ACM Press.

Mehta, D., Kouri, T., & Polycarpou, I. (2012). Forming project groups while learning about matching and network flows in algorithms. In *Proceedings of the 17th Annual Conference on Innovation and Technology in Computer Science Education, ITiCSE'12* (pp. 40-45). New York, NY: ACM Press. doi:10.1145/2325296.2325310

Naps, T., Roessling, G., Almstrum, V., Dann, W., Fleischer, R., & Hundhausen, C. et al. (2003). Exploring the role of visualization and engagement in computer science education. *ACM SIGCSE Bulletin*, *35*(4), 131–152. doi:10.1145/782941.782998

Norman, D. (1983). Some observations on mental models. In D. Gentner & A. Stevens (Eds.), *Mental Models* (pp. 7–14). Hillsdale, NJ: Erlbaum.

Papamanthou, C., & Paparrizos, K. (2003). A visualization of the primal simplex algorithm for the assignment problem. In *Proceedings of the 8th Annual Conference on Innovation and Technology in Computer Science Education, ITiCSE'03* (p. 267). New York, NY: ACM Press. doi:10.1145/961511.961631

Prince, M. (2004). Does active learning work? A review of the research. *The Journal of Engineering Education*, *93*(3), 223–231. doi:10.1002/j.2168-9830.2004.tb00809.x

Ramani, K. V., & Rama Rao, T. P. (1994). A graphics based computer-aided learning package for integer programming: The branch and bound algorithm. *Computers & Education*, *23*(4), 261–268. doi:10.1016/0360-1315(94)90014-0

Reed, D., Miller, C. S., & Braught, G. (2000). Empirical investigation through the CS curriculum. In *Proceedings of the 31st SIGCSE Technical Symposium on Computer Science Education, SIGCSE'00* (pp. 202-206). New York, NY: ACM Press.

Ryan, R. M., & Deci, E. L. (2000a). Self-determination theory and the facilitation of intrinsic motivation, social development, and well-being. *The American Psychologist, 55*(1), 68–78. doi:10.1037/0003-066X.55.1.68 PMID:11392867

Ryan, R. M., & Deci, E. L. (2000b). Intrinsic and extrinsic motivations: Classic definitions and new directions. *Contemporary Educational Psychology, 25*(1), 54–67. doi:10.1006/ceps.1999.1020 PMID:10620381

Sahni, S. (2005). *Data Structures, Algorithms, and Applications in Java* (2nd ed.). Summit, NJ: Silicon Press.

Sánchez-Torrubia, M. G., Torres-Blanc, C., & Escribano-Blanco, M. A. (2010). GRAPHs: A learning environment for graph algorithm simulation primed for automatic fuzzy assessment. In *Proceedings of the 10th Koli Calling International Conference on Computing Education Research, Koli Calling 2010* (pp. 62-67). New York, NY: ACM Press. doi:10.1145/1930464.1930473

Sanders, I. (2002). Teaching empirical analysis of algorithms. In *Proceedings of the 33th SIGCSE Technical Symposium on Computer Science Education, SIGCSE 2002* (pp. 321-325). New York, NY: ACM Press.

Shaffer, C.A., Cooper, M.L., Alon, A.J.D., Akbar, M., Stewart, M., Ponce, S., & Edwards, S.H. (2010). Algorithm visualization: The state of the field. *ACM Transactions on Computing Education, 10*(3), article 9.

Shepard, T., Lamb, M., & Kelly, D. (2001). More testing should be taught. *Communications of the ACM, 44*(6), 103–108. doi:10.1145/376134.376180

Sherstov, A. A. (2003). Distributed visualization of graph algorithms. In *Proceedings of the 34th SIGCSE Technical Symposium on Computer Science Education, SIGCSE'03* (pp. 376-380). New York, NY: ACM Press. doi:10.1145/611892.612011

Tichy, W. F. (1998). Should computer scientists experiment more? *IEEE Computer, 31*(5), 32–40. doi:10.1109/2.675631

Velázquez-Iturbide, J.Á. (2013). An experimental method for the active learning of greedy algorithms. *ACM Transactions on Computing Education, 13*(4), article 18.

Velázquez-Iturbide, J. Á. (2014). *Una evaluación cualitativa de la comprensión de la optimalidad. Serie de Informes Técnicos DLSI1-URJC, 2014-03.* Madrid, Spain: Departamento de Lenguajes y Sistemas Informáticos I, Universidad Rey Juan Carlos.

Velázquez-Iturbide, J. Á., & Debdi, O. (2011). Experimentation with optimization problems in algorithm courses. In *Proceedings of the International Conference on Computer as a Tool, EUROCON'11.* Lisbon, Portugal: Universidade de Lisboa. doi:10.1109/EUROCON.2011.5929294

Velázquez-Iturbide, J. Á., Debdi, O., Esteban-Sánchez, N., & Pizarro, C. (2013). GreedEx: A visualization tool for experimentation and discovery learning of greedy algorithms. *IEEE Transactions on Learning Technologies, 6*(2), 130–143. doi:10.1109/TLT.2013.8

Velázquez-Iturbide, J. Á., Martín-Torres, R., & González-Rabanal, N. (2013). OptimEx: un sistema para la experimentación con algoritmos de optimización. In *Proceedings of SIIE13 XV International Symposium on Computers in Education* (pp. 30-35). Viseu, Portugal: Universidade de Viseu.

Velázquez-Iturbide, J. Á., Paredes-Velasco, M., & Debdi, D. (2013). GreedExCol: una herramienta educativa basada en CSCL para el aprendizaje de algoritmos voraces. In Proceedings of XV Simposio Internacional de Tecnologías de la Información y las Comunicaciones en la Educación (SINTICE 2013), Libro de Actas (pp. 96–103). Madrid, Spain: SCIE.

Velázquez-Iturbide, J. Á., Pareja-Flores, C., Debdi, O., & Paredes-Velasco, M. (2012). Interactive experimentation with algorithms. In S. Abramovich (Ed.), *Computers in Education* (Vol. 2, pp. 47–70). New York, NY: Nova Science.

Wu, M. (2005). Teaching graph algorithms using online Java package IAPPGA. *ACM SIGCSE Bulletin, 37*(4), 64–68. doi:10.1145/1113847.1113879

ADDITIONAL READING

Ala-Mutka, F. M. (2005). A survey of automated assessment approaches for programming assignments. *Computer Science Education, 15*(2), 83–102. doi:10.1080/08993400500150747

Algoviz (2009). *Algoviz.org - The algorithm visualization portal*. Retrieved February 23, 2014 from http://algoviz.org

Anderson, L. W., Krathwohl, D. R., Airasian, P. W., Cruikshank, K. A., Pintrich, P. R., Raths, J., & Wittrock, M. C. (2001). *A Taxonomy for Learning, Teaching and Assessing: A Revision of Bloom's Taxonomy of Educational Objectives*. New York, NY: Addison Wesley Longman.

Barrows, H. S. (1986). A taxonomy of problem-based learning methods. *Medical Education, 20*(6), 481–486. doi:10.1111/j.1365-2923.1986. tb01386.x PMID:3796328

Berque, D., Bogda, J., Fisher, B., Harrison, T., & Ibhn, N. (1994). The KLYDE workbench for studying experimental algorithm analysis. In *Proceedings of the 25th SIGCSE Technical Symposium on Computer Science Education, SIGCSE'94* (pp. 83-87). New York, NY: ACM Press. doi:10.1145/191029.191065

Berry, J., Dean, N., Fasel, P., Goldberg, M., Johnson, E., MacCuish, J., et al. (1995). LINK: A combinatorics and graph theory workbench for applications and research. Tech. Rep. 95-15. Piscataway, NJ: DIMACS.

Bird, R. S. (1980). Tabulation techniques for recursive programs. *ACM Computing Surveys, 12*(4), 403–417. doi:10.1145/356827.356831

Blum, M., & Kannan, S. (1995). Designing programs that check their work. *Journal of the Association for Computing Machinery, 42*(1), 269–291. doi:10.1145/200836.200880

Edwards, S.H. (2003). Improving student performance by evaluating how well students test their own programs. *ACM Journal of Educational Resources in Computing, 3*(3), article 1.

Esteban-Sánchez, N., Pizarro, C., & Velázquez-Iturbide, J. Á. (2014). Evaluation of a didactic method for the active learning of greedy algorithms. *IEEE Transactions on Education, 57*(2), 83–91. doi:10.1109/TE.2013.2275154

Fincher, S., & Petre, M. (Eds.). (2004). *Computer Science Education Research*. London, UK: Routledge Falmer.

Freisleben, B., & Roessling, G. (2002). ANIMAL: A system for supporting multiple roles in algorithm animation. *Journal of Visual Languages and Computing, 13*(3), 341–354. doi:10.1006/jvlc.2002.0239

Guay, F., Vallerand, R. J., & Blanchard, C. (2000). On the assessment of situational intrinsic and extrinsic motivation: The Situational Motivation Scale (SIMS). *Motivation and Emotion, 24*(3), 175–213. doi:10.1023/A:1005614228250

Johnsonbaugh, R., & Kalin, M. (1991). Graph generation software package. In *Proceedings of the 22nd SIGCSE Technical Symposium on Computer Science Education, SIGCSE'91* (pp. 151-154). New York, NY: ACM Press.

Jurado, F., Molina, A. I., Redondo, M. A., Ortega, M., Giemza, A., Bollen, L., & Hoppe, H. U. (2009). Learning to program with COALA, a distributed computer assisted environment. *Journal of Universal Computer Science, 15*(7), 1472–1485.

Kumar, A.N. (2005). Generation of problems, answers, grade, and feedback – Case study of a fully automated tutor. *ACM Journal of Educational Resources in Computing, 5*(3), article 3.

Mehlhorn, K., & Näher, S. (1995). LEDA: A platform for combinatorial and geometric computing. *Communications of the ACM, 38*(1), 96–102. doi:10.1145/204865.204889

Naps, T. L. (2005). JHAVÉ: Supporting algorithm visualization. *IEEE Computer Graphics and Applications, 25*(5), 49–55. doi:10.1109/MCG.2005.110 PMID:16209170

Stasko, J. T., Domingue, J., Brown, M. H., & Price, B. A. (Eds.). (1997). *Software Visualization*. Cambridge, MA: The MIT Press.

Velázquez-Iturbide, J. Á. (2013). Using textbook illustrations to extract design principles for algorithm visualizations. In W. Huang (ed.), Handbook of Human Centric Visualization (pp. 227-249). New York, NY: Springer Science+Business Media. doi:10.1007/978-1-4614-7485-2_9

Wing, J. M. (2006). Computational thinking. *Communications of the ACM, 49*(3), 33–35. doi:10.1145/1118178.1118215

KEY TERMS AND DEFINITIONS

Algorithm Assessment: Check of the adequacy of an algorithm with respect to one or several properties, typically correctness, efficiency or optimality. When the performance of several algorithms is compared, we speak about benchmarking.

Algorithm Visualization: Graphical representation of the main features of an algorithm, without a direct relation to its implementation. Dynamic algorithm visualization is called algorithm animation.

Experimentation: Practical activity where an entity is studied by gathering and analyzing data of its behavior. Ideally, experimentation should be based on the scientific method.

Microworld: Learning system designed for exploration, experimentation and discovery in a given domain. The user is free to create his/her own experiences, subject to the constraints and rules embodied in the system.

Misconceptions: Mental models constructed by a learner in an attempt to understand an entity which are incompatible with the conceptual models transmitted by the instructor about the entity.

Motivation: Motivation is a central issue in human behavior, in particular in learning, since it is at the core of biological, cognitive, and social regulation processes. It can be intrinsic, when it responds to the personal interests of the individual, or extrinsic, when it responds to external influences.

Optimality: Property of optimization algorithms regarding whether their outcomes are the maximal (for maximization problems) or the minimal (for minimization problems).

Optimization Problem: Combinatorial problem whose solution must optimize a given measure, either a maximization or a minimization one.

Section 2
Teaching Strategies

Chapter 5
Massive Open Online Course Management:
Learning Science and Engineering through Peer-Reviewed Projects

Ana M. Pessoa
Polytechnic Institute of Porto, Portugal

Luis Coelho
Polytechnic Institute of Porto, Portugal

Ruben Fernandes
Polytechnic Institute of Porto, Portugal

ABSTRACT

Massive Open Online Courses (MOOC) are gaining prominence in transversal teaching-learning strategies. However, there are many issues still debated, namely assessment, recognized largely as a cornerstone in Education. The large number of students involved requires a redefinition of strategies that often use approaches based on tasks or challenging projects. In these conditions and due to this approach, assessment is made through peer-reviewed assignments and quizzes online. The peer-reviewed assignments are often based upon sample answers or topics, which guide the student in the task of evaluating peers. This chapter analyzes the grading and evaluation in MOOCs, especially in science and engineering courses, within the context of education and grading methodologies and discusses possible perspectives to pursue grading quality in massive e-learning courses.

1 INTRODUCTION

Education, if taken as the 'training' or 'upbringing' of offspring, is transversal in many animal species. Wolf packs involve all their members in the care of pups, including in playing with them. These playing habits include chases and 'toys' such as bones or the skins of dead animal. The pups 'kill' the toys and carry them around, raising the possibility of the play being a practice of future adult actions. However, Humanity has

DOI: 10.4018/978-1-4666-7304-5.ch005

integrated education in a formal manner that is unique. From an early beginning of preservation of knowledge and skills in Pre-History (Akinnaso, 1992), to a formal declaration in the Human Rights, Education (article 26, Human Rights Declaration, United Nations, 2009) evolved as society itself changed, adjusting not only to the needs but also to the values (ethical, economical or even artistic) of the people that commanded decisions on the affairs of everyday living.

Though educational methods have been subject of evaluation and critique from the moment that writing become available, the massification of public educational systems, in the 19th Century, made it an academic subject and both a governmental and private concern (Stray, 2001). From the Industrial Revolution to present day, few controversies have stood as perennial as the 'proper educational system' to be officially adopted, including age limit and if school attendance should be mandatory. In recent years, the explosion of new multimedia platforms offering a plethora of Massive Open On-line Courses (MOOC) added new questions to an already mined subject: are these new options as qualified as the more orthodox courses in developing competences? And if so, how can we determine the extent of their quality?

In this chapter, these and other questions are addressed, through analysis of the available data and review of published studies of the subject. The importance of MOOC is increasing by the second, literally, and, according to its more fervent defenders, it may become a substitute for formal higher education in the long run. Therefore, reflexion on its organic is significant for all areas that intertwine human society, since education is pervasive to culture, customs and living, the basis of what give us identity.

1.1 Education and Mass Education

Pedagogy became a social controversy with the advent of mass education, especially with the massification of higher education. The educa-tional methods had been focused in preparing ruling elites and soon it became clear that there was a socio-economic context that voided much of former assumptions. Thus, systematization of teaching/learning techniques became slowly a mark in most countries, and the compulsory nature of school became practically universal. Exception has been made, until now, to higher education. Though one of the purposes of universal education is the maintenance of civilization, nowadays of present technological substance, the respect for adult human autonomy forbade higher education from becoming compulsory. As consequence, adult autonomy prevents higher education from being provided in free manner by governments in general. Most countries assume that the students should pay for higher education and a small amount of scholarships, usually offered by benefactors or institutions, permit exceptional individuals to attend universities, otherwise economically out of their reach.

This poses a question, not easily answered: if the significance of higher education is undisputed in national economies and social stability, why is it so largely left to the whims of familiar and individual economies?

The point of MOOC is that such question is outdated in many ways. Higher education is now available for free, without boundaries of age, money, status or nationality. The effects of such paradigmatic change might have in social and economic areas are yet to be seen, as these new learning platforms are still starting to impact individuals. However, it is clear that a new revolution of educational systems and, therefore, a revolution in social values is starting in the coziness of homes around the globe.

It should be noted that MOOCs are not the first attempt of massive tertiary education but they have several differences, one of them with particular social appeal, namely that the most reputed universities of the world have provided for free many of their courses in MOOC form. To have you name in a certificate associated to a specific college is a motivation that has sprung massive adhesion to MOOCs, and the platforms are not indifferent to this, as they publicize it emphatically. With the widespread of Internet access, the potential is for billions of individuals not only increase their educational status and knowledge but also their capacity to intervene in pedagogical and academic archetypes. This is a potential increase that tends to human infinite.

1.2 The Advent of MOOCS

E-learning in general and MOOCs in particular are not the first attempt of distance learning. In the 19th Century, correspondence courses, namely on civil services areas of expertise, were promoted at a friendly knock in the door (Clark, 1906). Until the end of two first decades of 20th Century, millions of persons enrolled in these courses sold by professional salesmen, though the completion rate was residual (Kett, 1994). The advent of radio broadcast brought the possibility of indiscriminate diffusion of education and by 1922 universities started to broadcast lectures on their own radios. The perspectives were clear from the beginning as journalists wrote "Will the classroom be abolished and the child of the future be stuffed with facts as he sits at home or even as he walks about the streets with his portable receiving-set in his pocket?" (Bliven, 1924). However, the problem of success as measured by completion of the courses continued. Moreover, issues regarding quality in the evaluation increased, as fraud was nearly undetectable.

Though never completely abandoned, universities tried new approaches to distance or e-learning in the eighties, especially in collaboration with television networks. The advent of internet led to the first experiences on MOOC, using instructional videos and in 2003, four million Chinese were presented with courses via web as educational platform for business degrees. The term MOOC itself was first designated in 2008, as David Cornier and Bryan Alexander, respectively from the University

of Prince Edward Island and National Institute for Technology in Liberal education, reacted to a new course of the National Research Council. For the first time thousands of online students received tuition for free and some of the educational tools MOOCs came to be known, such as threaded discussions and internet meetings, also made their premiere. Two categories were clear. There were those that defended MOOC as an online interactive learning platform that could substantiate free basic education worldwide and those that were more inclined to prioritize higher education from reputed institutions through MOOCs.

1.3 Questions Regarding Quality

Assessment, evaluation and grading are considered indispensable in Education, though opinions may divide regarding the object and concern of the assessment. The next section will take a deeper analysis of these but it is sufficient to note that the quality of the evaluation was a controversial aspect of MOOCs since the earlier stages. Furthermore, the controversy and discussion regarding it have not diminished with their expansion and popularity, rather it has become more inflated. The Internet, the exact vehicle that supports MOOCs, is filled with complains, accusations and empirical blogged "thesis" regarding the poorness of MOOCs quality, being their evaluation methods the forefront of the sustenance for their case. A degree stands for something, a common belief and a status declaration even. When the ground it stands shakes, the educational system behind may crumble and the fact is that the quality of these new multimedia platforms can stand tall only if they pass the test of grading with reliability.

These questions have urgency to be answered since the last year (2013) saw the first appearance of the first MOOCs-for-credit by Udacity and of the first entirely MOOC-based Master's Degree, offered by the joint forces and expertise of Udacity, AT&T and the Georgia Institute of Technology. Higher education is reaching everyone, not completely free, but at bargain prices and people are flocking in. If these degrees are to be the basis of economies and development, then it must be assured that they are sound in the terms that education has been provided in the academic institutions. Moreover, methodologies in areas such as programming, information technology or mathematics differ from those of arts and/or humanities. Therefore, and taking Coursera as an example, since arts and humanities courses represent just a quarter of the MOOCs offer, the majority of the students and of the available degrees are basing their educational quality in evaluation forms that might not be as adequate as the classic. Yet, it is impossible to evaluate tens of thousands of students in the classic form, as the human response of teachers can never be given in useful time. The challenge is presented and the solution must come, either through classic analysis or creative proposal. And it must come soon.

2 GRADING AS PART OF LEARNING PROCESS

A *grade*, in the context of Education, stands to be both a level of academic development as well as an individual state of achievement in a particular subject. Grading, logically, designates the act of allocating a grade to someone. It is implicit the notion of quality in the act of grading as well as of the value it carries for the student. Though some might dispute grading and grading methods in Education, when one discusses the effects it should bear in the individual academic and personal development, the goal of quality itself as an outcome of both Education and grading seems without controversy. Nevertheless, quality is not only an enduring aspect in Education but also a social dependent characteristic. Through the ages, educational quality could mean memorization, arithmetic capacity or personal skills. What stands out from the three former examples is how much different are the methods to assess the degree of

individual achievement or "educational quality" in each situation. As result, the history of grading methodology not only encompasses the evolution of pedagogy but of social needs and technological skills.

2.1 Grading and Grading Methodologies

Education become of widespread access from the Industrial Revolution onwards. With this came the change of a solid paradigm: that the payment of a teacher, usually as a tutor, would be dependent of the 'quantity' of students and not of the quality of 'mentorship' that had reigned as accepted educational coordinate. William Farish, a tutor in the University of Cambridge on late 18th Century, played a key role in this transition (Stray, 2001). Farish considered that he would profit (literally) if he could assess the educational evolution of his students in a swift and systematic manner. The systematization swiftly focused in 'test-passing' as normative to evaluate the degree of achievement in the educational system.

Testing and written testing particularly become the standard until recently. The almost universal adhesion to this grading methodology can be explained by two factors: (1) it is a democratic method, which treats every student in an equal manner when facing evaluation; and (2) it simplifies the work of a teacher, whether the class is twenty or two hundred students. The detractors contend that: (1) every individual is unique and democratic methods based on equality are inherently unjust; and (2) teachers should not be lazy, but mentors.

It is not the purpose of this chapter to debate the pertinence of the written test methodology. There is yet to be presented a grading or evaluation method that is pristine in principle and flawless in execution. However, it is not an idle exercise to analyze its merits and faults and the specific quality it enhances in individual academic achievement, as one synthesizes the grading and evaluation methods in general and in MOOCs in particular.

Written tests in Education tend to be standardized in order to ensure equal, as in *inter pares*, evaluation. The format, the difficulty and even the extent of contents are fixed and the students have information regarding these aspects prior to the application of the test. The time and place for the evaluation through a written test is also fixed and available to the examinee. Depending on the purpose of the test, they can evaluate many capacities, such as memorization of facts, logic reasoning, and mathematic problem-solving or even linguistic competences. In defense of the standardized written tests one should consider some of their advantages: (1) both the test and correction criterion are equal for all the examinees, which provides a clear platform to distinguish quality; (2) The versatility of written test permits to evaluate different skills and acquired knowledge in an unbiased manner; (3) It is an adaptable means of evaluation, since you can adjust length, difficulty or type of question according with context or purpose; (4) It allows massive and swift evaluation.

Regarding point number (2), it should be noted that, although the final form of the written test may vary to infinity, the basic format is well established and forms the corner-stone to both the versatility and capacity of adaptation to a given context of a written test. The formats may include multiple-choice quizzes, alternate response, short answer, essay, completion type, or mathematical questions.

Whatever the form or style, grading can be seen not only as the measurable result of the educational process but as an instructional tool as well. Though tests (and written tests in particular) are the normative and general rule regarding the final evaluation and the attribution of a specific grade, they can be used in formative evaluation, or assessment, as well. In formative evaluation the feedback obtained through the results of the tests "enables students to restructure their understanding/skills and build more powerful ideas and capabilities" (Nicol & MacFarlane-Dick, 2005).

2.2 Online Grading Methods

MOOCs are massive e-learning platforms. Being massive, the number of students in a course can be on the order of tens of thousands. Being on line, the validity of grading is disputed. Both imply that, if MOOCs desire to be a learning platform with prestige on solid ground, the evaluation methods need to be feasible for classes of unimaginable magnitude in presential lectures and credible when live vigilance of teachers is absent in evaluation periods. Though there are no absolute rules, the most common methods used to evaluate and grade the students in MOOCs are multiple-choice quizzes and peer-reviewed assignments. The methods have merits and problems and are the main source to student disagreement of the evaluation process, particularly in the case of peer-reviewed evaluation.

Peer-reviewed evaluation is a process of grading where the evaluators of any student are the other peer students of the course, though the evaluation should be based on teacher's guidelines. This method was not invented specifically for MOOCs but meets its requirements for evaluation feasibility of large classes, as it frees teachers from the grading task. One should not, however, dismiss interesting pedagogical aspects of this grading method, just because it is a useful tool to liberate the teacher from the evaluation responsibility. By imposing the grading task on students, they can acquire new insight of the course's material and improve their own subsequent work. Moreover, by assuming the grading task, the students became more aware of the details of grading and grading process, developing critical thinking, which in turn will allow more quality in future assignments.

Peer-reviewed seemed the natural choice in massive open-learning courses for evaluating skills and competences unable to be tested through quizzes, for example. A superficial reading from

Table 1. Main benefits of self and peer assessment (adapted from Falchikov,2005)

A. Skill Development	B. Personal Development
Ability to actively collaborate Development of judging skills Supports lifelong learning	Enhances autonomy Enhances accountability Develops the ability to get involved
C. Learning Experience	**D. Emotional**
Promotes learning exchange Encourages reflection on personal role and collaboration Better understanding of assessment procedures Enhances learning by observing peers work	Brings increased confidence Can reduce stress

blogs and forums, though, spots immediately that one of peer-reviewed problems is enhanced in MOOCs: the agreement of grades is high (in this case comparing those assigned by students and those teachers would give). Bias, not to mention complete absence of understanding of the criteria and requirements provided to guide the evaluation, are common complains. Moreover, and this complain is in accordance with Saddler and Good's (2006) findings, peer reviewers tend to undergraduate. Even the resource to average the grade allocated from a sample of peer reviewers has not eradicated the problem.

From the teacher's point of view several issues arise when dealing with a PA. The first is that the students will need to have training on evaluation their peers and this will represent an additional pedagogical challenge (with all effort made on preparing and providing detailed and optimized materials and classes).

However, from an empirical point of view, some areas of knowledge seem more pervasive to this problem than others. The more creative and subjective the matter, the more complains. In science and engineering, the construction of criteria and peer-reviewing appear to be more consensual.

To close this section we present on Table 1 the main benefits of self and peer assessment for students.

3 LEARNING SCIENCE AND ENGINEERING IN MOOCS: ASSESSMENT METHODOLOGIES

Science and Engineering present specific educational idiosyncrasies, which led to the development of particular pedagogical tools. The study of scientific subjects implies a transversal sense of how experiment, mathematics and philosophy relate in the development of science and technology (Mathews, 1994) which result in methodological approaches such as problem-based learning (PBL) (US National Research Council, 2000), process-oriented guided inquiry learning (POGIL), and peer-led team learning (PLTL) (Eberlein et al., 2008). The concept relies in learning within context, experience and case studies, which implies adequate assessment. Therefore, science and engineering assessment are a challenging task, with many debatable topics and issues. Science and engineering assessment in MOOCs takes the debate to new levels of controversy.

Nevertheless, there are two common problems that affect the assessment of many MOOCs that are reduced in science and engineering courses. The first problem is related with the language, since most courses are mainly provided in English language and many students are non-native speakers. While their comprehension skills might be sufficient to follow the course's lectures and materials, their writing and expression skills are often limited which can be a serious handicap during evaluation. In science and engineering topics, expertise is acquired usually dealing with numbers, equations and algorithms. In programming courses the exercises are aimed to show proficiency in a programming language, which is independent from the culture or communication language and is based on well-defined rules and structures. Hence the communication problem is in this case minimized. A second problem comes from the intrinsic subjective nature of human thought. Again, science and engineering main objectives are usually directed to obtaining a tangible solution and hence the judging ambiguity is highly reduced.

3.1 Automatic Assessment

The assessment of students in such MOOCs, namely in programming courses, can be done automatically when the concepts and their evaluation are completely deterministic (e.g. declaration of two variables and make a sum, creating methods in a class, etc.).

This approach requires nearly no staff for evaluation and the results can be promptly showed to the student (Mora, 2012). The process can be focus on the automatic parsing and interpretation of the code or on the execution of the code followed by an evaluation of the outputs according with the algorithm's desired behavior (automatic evaluation). In any case, an evaluation mechanism must be available and integrated with the learning platform. During the learning process the students can be invited to test some of their ideas on free on-line coding web sites such as the ones in codepad.com or writecodeonline.com. The preparation of the questions asked is of special care as is necessary to ensure that the possible answers are completely objective and unique (not subject to any deviation resulting from the creativity of those who are being evaluated). The time required to develop good questions is also not so short and often require an experienced teacher who is able to understand student's reasoning and exploit their

most common flaws. The correct answer should not be obvious neither too simple to devise. For complex questions a successive division can be made, in a work breakdown approach, until a set of questions with unique objective answers is obtained, one for each question. From the student perspective the answers to each question can independently bring information and be useful for evaluation. However, as a part of the learning process, the students can also be asked to develop and follow the inverse route that the teacher has previously made. By other words, the student can be asked and guided to integrate several answers to find and devise the answers for bigger and more complex problems. The automatic assessment approach is thus invested with a double advantage, first it provides a fully automated approach to the assessment and second it allows an assessment by atomic concepts, being objective and human error proof.

3.2 Structured Grading and Training to Evaluate

When the evaluation is focused on a creative process or on questions with less restricted domains then automatic evaluation becomes a complex task with many unanswered questions. The computer programming domain easily falls into this category because, despite all the well-defined rules, the development of a particular algorithm or to devise the required steps to tackle a given problem can always subject to personal interpretation and vary from person to person, even assuring that the output of the system is correct. In fact, most computer programming courses include not only teaching a programming language but also many related topics covering the processes associated with the implementation of a software mechanism intended to be effective, robust and fast. Therefore topics such as algorithms, best coding practices, modularity, class models and data, testing, etc. can be included and often are. In the presence of the product of a creative exercise we should opt for an evaluation performed by humans who, unlike machines, are able to easily make a judgment in the presence of subjective principles.

When thousands of students are expected to participate, it's impractical and often infeasible to have a staff that can, in an acceptable time frame, evaluate all the submitted answers and provide detailed feedback. For this case and by the reasons given in section 1.3, we have identified peer assessment (PA) as a solution with great potential that is already being used in several MOOCs (for example in coursera.com, edx.org, udacity.com, miriadax.net). PA is widely accepted and has three main advantages: 1. Enables the existence of large classes where the assessment is focused on creative processes; 2. Offers students an interactive experience as they receive contextualized and focused feedback from their peers (which represent one of the advantages of learning in the classroom) (Hearst et al., 2000; Schon 1985); 3. While observing the work of others, students are confronted with distinct approaches and viewpoints of the same problem (Dannels & Martin, 2008). PA can also represent a quality mark since according to some authors (Mora, 2012; Kulkarni et al., 2013) the rigor put in the work is higher when it is intended to be rated by peers. A major reason for this is the fear of not being understood or properly evaluated by peers who have similar fears and expectations.

Hence in a MOOC with PA the students must learn the main study topics and additionally must also learn how to correctly assess their peers work. This means extra work for the teacher also since it must focus not only on the classes' topics but also on the careful presentation of the assessment procedures and rules. Students may also have the perception that the teachers responsibilities are being passed to their own which is not a correct view of the MOOC system.

We will now focus on the self-assessment workflow. First, to develop a peer assessment problem, we must start to define how many feedbacks a response must receive and how many responses a given student must assess. This is necessary in order to build a functional PA system that collects sufficient feedback from peers and is able to provide results that are statistically meaningful. To guarantee that everything works as planed it is necessary to motivate students to engage in the PA process by showing them the big advantages of such process. Several advantages have already been above mentioned but on the students learning experience perspective we can always refer that (1) the enhanced learning by observing the others mistakes and successful approaches and (2) the encouragement to develop better answers since they are intended to be shared with peers are two paramount and very strong motivations arguments for the students to join the assessment campaign. Nevertheless some students may refuse to participate in the assessment process due to lack of time or simply because they don't feel comfortable with it. Since PA is understood as part of the learning process and it is necessary to structurally support the correct operation of the MOOC, one possibility would be to make PA engagement mandatory. Another possibility would be to apply a grading penalty (less than 20%) to those who refuse to participate and evaluate their peers' work.

Then we must define and make public all due dates for the response and the following peers' evaluation. In an integrated approach, we must create the question and the rubric that should be both provided to the students simultaneously. This is important because: (1) when the evaluation rules are known and well understood the students can improve their work by directing their efforts to the staff's quality patterns; and (2) the existence of a rubric increases evaluation agreement among peers. The rubric can be designed to be holistic or analytic (Airasian, 2000, 2001) but in either case specific performance criteria and observable indicators must be identified as an initial step to development. Holistic rubrics can be better for experienced evaluators and creative tasks but, in this case, an analytical version, which has a much more refined definition of grading intervals, can be a better option since unexperienced raters are involved and a much better feedback can be provided (Mertler, 2001). This type of rubric can also be adapted to an automatic feedback system to simplify the process.

In order to understand what criteria are most valued by computer programming teachers we have gathered 23 grading rubrics, obtained from the web, from different universities around the globe (8 from US, 3 from Brasil, 7 from Europe, 2 from Canada, 1 from China and 2 from Australia). We have evaluated how frequently a given criteria is considered in the assessment grid and in what manner it affects the final classification in terms of relative weight. The obtained results are shown in Figure 1 where we can observe the 12 most relevant criteria. "Requirements and Specifications"

is the most frequent and rated criteria followed by "Documentation and Comments" and "Assignment Specifications" in terms of frequency. This set of 3 criteria represent, on average, 90% of the final grade with the later using only around 5% of the total. These results are somehow expected since fulfilling the software/application requirements and providing good documentation are the basis to build a solid solution for anyone that is collaborating in software development and needs to share the developed code.

Using the above described criteria we started to develop a rubric using the frequency and weight parameters as a support for our criterion mix. There is a wide coverage of rubric development strategies in scientific literature. Using the guidelines in Airasian, (2000, 2001), Mertler, (2001), Montgomery (2001), Nitko & Brookhart (2010),

Figure 1. List of rubric's criteria sorted by average classification weight (slashed bars and bottom axis) along with absolute frequency (solid bars and top axis) based on a set of computer programming assessment rubrics

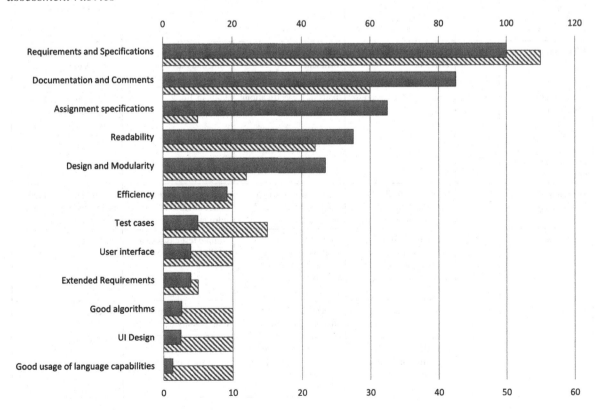

Tombari & Borich (1999) and Mertler (2001) we proposed in Table 2 a rubric for programming exercises. In this table the main highlights are: short list of criteria (which simplifies the understanding of the list and allows a faster identification of the most adequate classification), weighted criteria (allows to give more value to the most important topics); even number of levels for each criterion (the grader will be always forced to decide if a middle level answer show be rated above or below the water line); objective grading for levels (easy to understand); complete and objective descriptors for every rubric cell (reduces ambiguity and improves agreement between graders). The rubric

Table 2. Grading rubric for programming exercises

Criteria	Weight (%)	Excellent (100%)	Adequate (75%)	Poor (50%)	Not met (20%)
Requirements and Specifications	50%	No errors, program always works correctly and meets the all the specifications.	Minor details of the program specification are violated, program functions incorrectly for some inputs.	Significant details of the specification are not fulfilled. Program often exhibits incorrect behavior.	Program only functions correctly in very limited cases or not at all.
Documentation and Comments	20%	Documentation is well written and clearly explains how the code is structured, what is accomplishing and how.	The documentation consists of embedded comments and some simple header documentation that are useful to understand the code.	Simple comments embedded in the code with some simple header comments separating routines.	No documentation or the documentation is composed by simple comments embedded in the code that don't help the reader to understand the code.
Readability Covers indentation, whitespace, variable names and organization.	20%	No errors, code is clean, very understandable, and well organized.	Minor issues.	At least one major issue.	Major problems with more than 1 readability subcategories.
Efficiency	10%	The code is extremely efficient	The code is fairly efficient	Code is unnecessarily long and based on a brute force approach.	Code is huge and appears to be patched together.
Assignment Specifications Covers time, date, delivery format, file names, package, pipeline, etc.	(5%)	All specifications are met	Fails in 1 specifications	Fails in 1 or 2 specifications	Fails more than 2 specifications
Design and Modularity	(5%)	Solution is well structured and is easy to scale and maintain	Correctly structured but hard to scale and maintain.	Solution organization is not obvious but it is correct.	Solution organization is not obvious and it is not correct.
Test Cases	(10%)	Advanced and extensive test cases covering all algorithms user interaction possibilities.	Some advanced test cases covering an extended set of possibilities.	Simple test cases that explore the basic use of the code.	No test cases.
Extra Credit	(10%)	Programs that usefully extend the requirements, use a particularly good algorithm and cover special language capabilities.	At least 2 of: Programs that usefully extend the requirements; use a particularly good algorithm; cover lang. capabilities.	At least 1 of: Programs that usefully extend the requirements; use a particularly good algorithm; cover lang. capabilities	No extra credit

was also designed in a way that any assessment process for a given answer should take around 10 minutes (and no longer than 15 minutes) on average to conclude.

After the due date of submission the PA process starts. Students may have little exposure to different forms of assessment and so they may lack the necessary skills to correctly deal with their peer's work. So the PA should be based on a process identical to "calibrated peer assessment" (Carlson & Berry, 2003) where students, before starting to evaluate their peers work, must engage in a calibration stage to ensure they are able to correctly understand and apply a rubric to a given answer. Here, students evaluate a set of previously staff graded answers that contain some notes about why and how the rubric was used in specific situations. The student submits his grade and if it is not consistent with the staff grade then another staff graded answer is provided. After a set of calibration evaluations are performed (5 is recommended) or when both student and staff grades are similar then the student is considered to be prepared to evaluate their peers work. A pre-defined number of randomly selected and anonymously-presented answers from the peers are assigned to a student that should provide the related grades within a given time framework or before a due date. A staff graded answer can be included in the assigned set without the student knowledge. This gives a grading reference and will allow providing improvement feedback to the student. Each answer should be rated by an odd number of students, in a minimum number of three, whose results are then combined in equal proportion for calculating the final grade. If the student didn't perform well during calibration then a weighted average can be used in order to adjust his contribution in proportion to the students' ability to rate their peers. For baseline reference purposes, in addition to the staff rated answer, we can also ask the student to do his self-assessment. This will allow alerting to deviations from the average peer graded result. So when the

self-assessment differs greatly from a consistent evaluation by the peers one has the possibility to detect distinct perceptions on the taught topics, on the evaluation rules, on the form of expression or it can simply be indeed an overrated student performance. When such problems are detected the staff can always interfere and help to provide a correct assessment. This can be done either by including a new staff classification or by providing a corrective feedback to the grading student, always after discarding the first incorrect evaluation. From the student as evaluator perspective it is also possible to provide feedback since a staff rated answer is always present in the assign set of answers. Hence, when the student evaluates the staff rated answer within a given error threshold from the reference then a positive feedback can be given (for example in the form of a message). On the contrary, if there is a significant deviation from the staff grade, a negative feedback should be provided. After the peer-assessment due date the final assessment results are presented to the students along with the reviewers comments.

The described process is depicted in figure 2 where we can observe the process start, with the "question and rubric" being provided by the course staff, on top left. The process is presented in different colors to distinguish between the staff and student roles. The process can end immediately after its beginning, with the student opting out with participating in PA, or can fallow through all steps and terminate with the grades being provided to everyone.

3.3 Cheating Countermeasures

Among educators, one of the major concerns with assessment is cheating. In the case of MOOCs, that provide an on-line environment where students are completely anonymous and come from several countries with distinct cultures, this can be a serious threat to course quality and recognition. In fact Coursera has already reported several cases of plagiarism. This threat is especially

Figure 2. Peer assessment pipeline

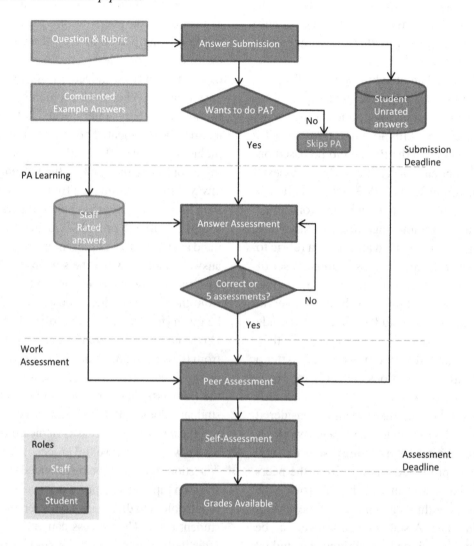

important when students are increasingly taking MOOCs for academic credit and not only for personal fulfillment and enrichment. Examples of on-line cheating can be obtaining information directly from on-line sources (e.g. Wikipedia) (Underwood & Szabo, 2003), repeating the assessments or obtaining answers from colleagues among others (Rowe, 2004). To minimize these problems counter measures can be developed for three cheating contexts (Cizek, 1999, 2003): (a) exchanging information with others, (b) use of forbidden materials and (c) counteracting or disrupting the process.

Since distinct cultures have different perspectives about plagiarism it is suggested, as a prevention measure, to provide, in the beginning of the course, clear and concise information about what is considered to be plagiarism, why it is not allowed and what are the consequences for those who do not respect the assessment rules. Furthermore, it is also recommended to discuss what levels of collaboration are acceptable because most MOOC platforms also provide information exchange system (e.g. forums). For a more proactive attitude other measures can be adopted such as providing a limited time for evaluation, providing a limited number of submissions or increasing the number of test forms either by changing questions sequence as well as changing the sequence for multiple option answers. More recently Coursera provided a paid proctoring system where a human has access to the student webcam and validates his identity and observes all the actions during the assessment period.

In the special case of programing exercises it is also possible to use software similarity tools (Schleimer et al, 2013) to automatically detect possible plagiarism occurrences.

3.4 Challenges in Computer Programming MOOCs

When learning computer programming the students are asked to develop programs or project by themselves in a context where they can have access to many information sources, an extended development period and the possibility to test their code, nevertheless they still sometimes fail to obtain a successful result. In many cases this is due to an erroneous belief that the code is working. Situations like (1) the code compiles, (2) the staff provided test case leads to a correct result or (3) the code has run once are, among others, often perceived by students as a sign that they have obtained a correct answer for the problem. Teachers report that it is frequent to find students saying "I can understand the solution after I see it but I'm not able to develop it on my own.". This shows that teaching a programming language is not only explaining the intricacies of keywords and function but must also include the delivery of methodologies for understanding how a given situation can be translated to code instructions, how to create a logical sequence that encompasses all the possibilities in order to create a robust solution and also, during and after code development, how to minimize bug occurrence, how to create effective test cases and how to proceed in order to efficiently detect, localize and correct coding errors. In typical room classes a part of the de-

bugging skills is passed during student/teacher interaction which is not the case in MOOCs and thus brings additional challenges when developing such a course.

For on-line computer programming exercises, in particular for basic level, it is important to promote a test driven development practice. The students should be encouraged to always think in test cases while or even before developing code. The test cases should be appropriate to small pieces of code and during development lots of coding/testing can be done. When learning the basis of programming this approach has several advantages: (1) is an easy methodology for students to understand; (2) builds confidence since it breaks down a big objective into smaller and objectives; (3) promotes a higher attention to requirements and their refinement; and (4) is scalable to greater dimension problems.

Since on-line MOOC platforms often provide a sandbox for computer programming courses where students can test their developments it is interesting to provide a pool of test cases for each exercises. Additionally, students can propose and contribute with more test cases to extend the pool.

The classical teaching approach is highly focused on output correctness and students are not encouraged to thoroughly test their code. A test driven methodology requires a different behavior that must be encouraged by teachers in order to induce a cultural change. Hence, as a part of the assessment, the student can also be rewarded by test case validity and completeness.

4 FUTURE RESEARCH DIRECTIONS

MOOCs are still in an early age and many questions are still arising. Teaching methodologies are being adapted as well as assessment approaches to this new massive scale teaching/learning paradigm. While teaching materials can often be reused and extended from e-learning courses, the evaluation techniques must be seriously rethinked in order to tackle the overwhelming number of involved students. The main challenges now are on how to continuously improve assessment by introducing fast and effective grading methodologies while providing and maintaining the trust in the education system.

Formal aspects are also of concern. With the explosion of course offerings in the last few years one of the sensitive points is course accreditation. Individual schools can pursue and develop mechanisms for quality monitoring and assurance but it is important to find internationally accepted rules for such mechanism. This a challenging subject since agreements and increased cooperation between worldwide education organizations are required in order to develop fast and simple accreditation procedures. Another problem that need to be tackled is student identification during assessment when formal credit is earned. Again this requires a higher integration of global communities for the development identification systems as well as a comparable credit system.

5 CONCLUSION

MOOC are changing the way Education is organized and not before long, Higher Education will look very different than it does today. The core functions of institutions (knowledge creation, teaching, testing, and credentialing) must quickly adapt to this emerging paradigm. In this chapter we have started by providing a comprehensive overview of MOOC history. We have highlighted the main advantages of this kind of courses and have explained how they are creating a revolution on the education map. The most important challenges have also been covered bearing in mind the quality and social recognition along with the related institution's prestige. We have covered the paramount evaluation issues. We have started by showing how grading is important for the learning process and how these can be put to work on-line. Then we have made the bridge to MOOCs and we

have shown that science and engineering courses are highly suitable to this teaching/learning system. In particular (1) science and engineering are based in logical, avoiding the subjective nature of assessment in other MOOCs and (2) the language issues, which may be a major problem in most MOOCs for non-english speaking students are minimized in because proficiency is acquired through number, mathematics and algorithms, a universal language.

With respect to evaluation we have outlined the most popular assessment methodologies. Automatic grading is the most desirable system in programming courses due to the possibility of objective evaluation of outputs or inputs. When the questions are too complex then division can be made accordingly and assessment can made through this set of questions. Automation of process and objective evaluation are two advantages. However for creative processes (such as computer programming) we have shown that evaluation relies predominantly in peer-reviewed assessment (PA). For this we have presented a detailed explanation for an assessment pipeline. For each step we have shown what the main threats are and have presented state-of-the-art practices, always from a science and engineering perspective and giving a special attention to computer programming cases. Key points are (1) the motivation of student to engage in PA as a part of the learning process; (2) the inclusion of a penalty to those refusing to evaluate their peers work; (3) the integrated development of questions and rubrics considering previous peers answers.

To simplify the assessment process we have shown the importance of a clear and concise rubric and have proposed a comprehensive set of criteria based on the analysis of twenty-three world-gathered grading rubrics. Specific performance criteria and observable indicators are the first step of developing the correcting rubrics. Evidences showed that "Requirements and Specifications" are the most frequent and rated criteria. In particular, a set of three criteria ("Requirements and

Specifications", "Documentation and Comments" and "Assignment Specifications") represent, on average, 90% of the final grade. The rubric for programming exercises main properties, based in the above criteria, are: short list of criteria; weighted criteria; even number of levels for each criterion; objective grading for levels; complete and objective descriptors for every rubric cell. To adjust the rubric to specific cases we have also proposed a set of optional criteria. Then, to reinforce unbiased quality evaluation, we have showed how PA must be preceded by a calibration stage and a posterior self-assessment phase. The results of the calibration stage can then be used to further adjust the assessment of the peers of the student in a more objective manner.

Still with quality in mind we have covered the main issues related with cheating in on-line courses as students are increasingly taking MOOCs for academic credit. Examples of suggested implementable countermeasures are: clearer information prior to the course, limited time for evaluation and number of submissions, increased number of test forms and even a paid proctoring system. Regarding programming exercises, software similarity tools that can automatically detect possible plagiarism are available and can be used. Finally we have presented some open challenges for the development of better structured MOOCs in science and engineering. Especially in programming areas we can include topics or methodologies such as learning to translate situation to code instructions, creating robust solutions through logical sequences, minimizing bug occurrences, effective tests, and procedures in code errors detection. We have also shown that test driven methodologies in programming courses should be encouraged in order to induce pedagogical change from output correctness to thorough code testing.

As final remarks we can consider that PA is an efficient and effective methodology to monitor students' progress in MOOCs and that the additional staff effort placed on the development of the PA structure is largely compensated by the reduction in assessment workload. In the end, the student will have for sure an enhanced learning experience. And that is still an undisputed sign of educational achievement.

REFERENCES

Airasian, P. W. (2000). *Assessment in the classroom: A concise approach* (2nd ed.). Boston: McGraw-Hill.

Airasian, P. W. (2001). *Classroom assessment: Concepts and applications* (4th ed.). Boston: McGraw-Hill.

Akinnaso, F. N. (1992). Schooling, Language and Knowledge in Literate and Nonliterate Societies. *Comparative Studies in Society and History*, *34*(1), 68–109. doi:10.1017/S0010417500017448

Bliven, B. (1924, June). Article. *The Century Illustrated Monthly Magazine*, *108*, 148.

Carlson, P. A., & Berry, F. C. (2003). Calibrated peer review™ and assessing learning outcomes. In *Proceedings of the 33rd Annual Frontiers in Education Conference*. Piscataway, NJ: IEEE Digital Library doi:10.1109/FIE.2003.1264740

Cizek, G. J. (1999). *Cheating on tests: How to do it, detect it, and prevent it*. Mahwah, NJ: Lawrence Erlbaum.

Cizek, G. J. (2003). *Detecting and preventing classroom cheating: Promoting integrity in assessment*. Thousand Oaks, CA: Corwin Press.

Clark, J. (1906). The correspondence school—Its relation to technical education and some of its results. *Science*, *24*(611), 327–334. doi:10.1126/science.24.611.327 PMID:17772791

Dannels, D. P., & Martin, K. N. (2008). Critiquing critiques a genre analysis of feedback across novice to expert design studios. *Journal of Business and Technical Communication*, *22*(2), 135–159. doi:10.1177/1050651907311923

Eberlein, T., Kampmeier, J., Minderhout, V., Moog, R. S., Platt, T., Varma-Nelson, P., & White, H. (2008). Pedagogies of engagement in science: A comparison of PBL, POGIL, and PLTL. *Biochemistry and Molecular Biology Education, 36*(4), 262–273. doi:10.1002/bmb.20204 PMID:19381266

Falchikov, N. (2005). *Improving assessment through student involvement: Practical solutions for aiding learning in higher and further education*. London: Routledge Falmer.

Hearst, M., Kukich, K., Hirschman, L., Breck, E., Light, M., & Burge, J. et al. (2000). The debate on automated essay grading. *Intelligent Systems, 45*(2), 123–129.

Kett, J. (1994). *Pursuit of Knowledge Under Difficulties: From Self-Improvement to Adult Education in America, 1750-1990*. Stanford, CA: Stanford University Press.

Kulkarni, C., Wei, K. P., Le, H., Chia, D., Papadopoulos, K., & Cheng, J. et al. (2013). Peer and self-assessment in massive online classes. *ACM Transactions on Computer-Human Interaction, 20*(6), 33. doi:10.1145/2505057

Matthews, M. R. (1994). *Science teaching: The role of history and philosophy of science*. New York: Routledge.

Mertler, C. A. (2001). Designing scoring rubrics for your classroom. *Practical Assessment, Research & Evaluation, 7*(25).

Montgomery, K. (2001). *Authentic assessment: A guide for elementary teachers*. New York: Longman.

Mora, M. C., Sancho-Bru, J. L., Iserte, J. L., & Sánchez, F. T. (2012). An e-assessment approach for evaluation in engineering overcrowded groups. *Computers & Education, 59*(2), 732–740. doi:10.1016/j.compedu.2012.03.011

Nicol, D., & MacFarlane-Dick, D. (2004). *Rethinking Formative Assessment in HE: a theoretical model and seven principles of good feedback practice*. Quality Assurance Agency for Higher Education.

Nitko, A. J., & Brookhart, S. M. (2010). *Educational Assessment of Students*. Englewood Cliffs, NJ: Pearson.

Rowe, N. C. (2004). Cheating in online student assessment: Beyond plagiarism. *Online Journal of Distance Learning Administration, 7*(2).

Sadler, P., & Good, E. (2006). The impact of self- and peer-grading on student learning. *Educational Assessment, 11*(1), 1–31. doi:10.1207/s15326977ea1101_1

Schleimer, S., Wilkerson, D., & Aiken, A. (2003). Winnowing: local algorithms for document fingerprinting. In *Proceedings of the 2003 ACM SIGMOD Int. Conf. on Management of Data*. ACM doi:10.1145/872757.872770

Schn. Donald A & RIBA Building Industry Trust (1985). The design studio: An exploration of its traditions and potentials. London: Royal Institute of British Architects.

Stray, C. (2001). The shift from oral to written examination: Cambridge and Oxford. *Assessment in Education: Principles, Policy & Practice, 8*(1), 33–50. doi:10.1080/09695940120033243

Tombari, M., & Borich, G. (1999). *Authentic assessment in the classroom: Applications and practice*. Upper Saddle River, NJ: Merrill.

Underwood, J., & Szabo, A. (2003). Academic offences and e-learning: Individual propensities in cheating. *British Journal of Educational Technology, 34*(4), 467–477. doi:10.1111/1467-8535.00343

United Nations (2009). *Universal declaration of human rights*. Author.

US National Research Council and Committee on Developments in the Science of Learning with additional material from the Committee on Learning Research and Educational Practice. (2000). How People Learn: Brain, Mind, Experience, and School (2nd ed.). Washington, DC: National Academy Press.

KEY TERMS AND DEFINITIONS

Computer Programming: Is a process by which a given computational problem is translated into am executable program.

Educational Paradigms: Represent sets of ideas and theories about how the teaching/learning process should be developed.

Engineering Education: Is the area of education related with engineering principles and its professional practice.

Grading: Represents, in the chapter's context, the process of classifying student's performance according to a given set of pre-defined qualities and rules.

MOOC: Is the abbreviation for Massive Open Online Courses. These courses are offered to an unlimited number of participants under a web based teaching/learning environment.

Peer-Revision: Is a process by which a given work is reviewed by the author's peers.

Rubric: In academic terminology, is a set of criteria and/or rules, often related with the learning objectives, which is used for defining standard performance ratings.

Chapter 6
Using Simulation Games in Teaching Formal Methods for Software Development

Štefan Korečko
Technical University of Košice, Slovakia

Ján Sorád
Technical University of Košice, Slovakia

ABSTRACT

Because of the current trend of massification of higher education, motivation of students is a serious issue, especially in courses closely related to mathematics. The ones that undoubtedly belong to this group are courses dealing with formal methods for software development, such as Z notation, B-Method, or VDM. The chapter shows how a customized simulation game can be used to bring a domain typical for utilization of formal methods, the railway domain, to students and thus motivate them to learn these sophisticated ways of software development. By means of two examples, it demonstrates that such a tool, despite its limited scope, can be used to teach a variety of concepts related to formal methods. It also discusses related approaches to teaching formal methods, describes the customized game and its application in teaching, and evaluates experience with the application.

INTRODUCTION

We live in the era of massification of higher education. We encounter not only highly motivated and interested students but also average ones, where didactic methods, usually used on lower types of schools become relevant. All kinds of subjects in university curricula are affected by this situation but maybe the most suffering ones are those closely related to the field of mathematics. And formal methods courses definitely belong to this group.

Formal methods (FM) are rigorous mathematically based techniques for the specification, analysis, development and verification of software and hardware. Rigorous means that a formal method provides a formal language with unambiguously defined syntax and semantics and mathematically based means that some mathematical apparatus (formal logic, set theory, etc.) is used to define the

DOI: 10.4018/978-1-4666-7304-5.ch006

language. But as Cerone, Roggenbach, Schlingloff, Schneider and Shaikh (2013) note, a language is not enough to constitute a formal method. To call it a method, procedures that allow doing something with specifications written in the language have to be present, too. An example of a well-known FM are regular expressions (Cerone et al., 2013): Syntax of its language can be specified by a context-free grammar. For the semantics there are several ways how to define it, for example by specifying corresponding sets of words or constructing a finite automaton that recognizes words satisfying given expression. A procedure can, for example, be a replacement of every word that satisfies given expression by another word. There are many ways how to classify FM and one, especially interesting from the educational point of view, is a taxonomy based on automation of their procedures and on how easy it is to use them. This taxonomy distinguishes between lightweight and heavyweight formal methods. Lightweight formal methods usually do not require deep expertise. The heavyweight ones are more complex, less automatic, but also more finely grained and powerful (Almeida, Frade, Pinto, & de Sousa, 2011). We can say that for a lightweight FM it is enough to learn its language and know what button to hit in corresponding software tool to do this or that. Often it is not even necessary to learn formal semantics of its language, an explanation in a natural language is sufficient. The aforementioned regular expressions are a lightweight FM. To use them for a text search or replacement in a text editor one just has to read few lines in the editor user's manual, write an expression to an appropriate text field and press a button next to it. On the other hand, significant examples of heavyweight FM are those involving theorem proving as a method of software correctness verification. In principle, the theorem proving cannot be fully automated because underlying theories are usually not decidable. So, to prove assertions about a system a human assistance is often required and to be able to assist one has to possess knowledge about the

syntax and formal semantics of the language of given FM and operation of its prover. This means a lot of effort but as Harrison (2008) points out, theorem proving brings substantial benefits over other, highly automated, verification methods (e.g. model checking). Provided that properties of a system are correctly specified, its formal verification can ensure that the properties will hold in any state of the system. In an ideal world all software should be like this – 100% verified before its delivery to users. But in reality we use to get faulty software, be it games, operating systems or firmware, and faults are fixed afterwards by means of updates.

As university teachers we sometimes experience resistance from students when a new language or method is introduced, even if it is a widely used one. And position of formal methods courses in software engineering curricula is much worse. Not only are FM too close to the unpopular math but there are not many companies using them in practice. And, especially in the case of the heavyweight ones, we can find them only in specific application areas where their use and cost are justified (Almeida et al., 2011). Of course, we would like to see more widespread utilization of FM and we hope to achieve it by introducing as much students as possible to the art of their application. A big obstacle here is an elective status of many FM courses. So, the essential question is how to motivate students to take FM courses and to stay in them. It is critical to properly choose an application area on which the use of FM will be demonstrated and for which the students will develop something using formal methods. An area where a software fault is able to cause too much damage or loss of lives before any update can be applied. In addition, it should be an area where formal methods have already been successfully applied. According to the comprehensive survey (Woodcock, Larsen, Bicarregui, & Fitzgerald, 2009) and its recent update (Fitzgerald, Bicarregui, Larsen, & Woodcock, 2013) the most of FM industrial success stories can be found in the areas of transportation, finance and defense. What these areas have in common is that they are "physically" out of reach when teaching formal methods. But we have to make them available to students in a believable and funny way. To do this we propose to take existing (simulation) games and modify them in order to allow communication with formally developed software. The games will provide virtual representations of the areas with devices controlled by the software developed using FM. This chapter presents one concrete implementation of the proposal and its use in an undergraduate formal methods course at the home institution of the authors. The implementation offers a virtual railway domain, provided by a modified simulation game called Train Director (http://www.backerstreet.com/traindir) and a proxy application, which communicates with Train Director (TD) and allows to load a control module that controls devices (signals and switches) in a scenario simulated in TD. The control module is a Java application, which should, but not have to, be developed by formal methods.

The rest of the chapter is organized as follows. The next section deals with existing approaches to teaching formal methods. The third one is dedicated to the implementation of the proposal itself. It describes important choices the authors made and their reasons, tools that have been modified and developed and use of the implementation in education, including two examples. The fourth section presents other developments of the proposal and ideas for future work. The fifth one deals with the work related to this and the final section concludes with an evaluation of gained experience and cost of developed solutions.

BACKGROUND

The importance of teaching formal methods properly is evident from a number of specialized workshops and meetings, held in association with significant FM conferences and symposia,

exclusively or partially dedicated to the FM education. Examples of these are "Teaching Formal Methods" meetings from 2004, 2006 and 2009 or "Fun with Formal Methods" workshop from 2013. And problems related to recruitment to and retention on FM courses is one of the main topics of these events. The reasons of these problems are similar to our situation: To make computer science and software engineering study more accessible FM courses are becoming elective (Reed, & Sinclair, 2004) and it is hard to motivate present-day, practically oriented, students to deal with FM (Larsen, Fitzgerald, & Riddle, 2009), especially considering that FM are used in industry in the most developed countries only (Cristiá, 2006).

A proper choice of examples and their relation to practice is regarded as important by Reed and Sinclair (2004), Larsen, et al. (2009), Liu, Takahashi, Hayashi and Nakayama (2009), Cerone et al. (2013) and many others. Reed and Sinclair (2004) and Liu et al. (2009) advocate for such choice of examples that will clearly show benefits of formal methods, i.e. show what can be achieved by using FM but not by other approaches. Larsen, et al. (2009) agree and present two undergraduate introductory courses, taught at universities in Denmark and UK, where important concepts are illustrated by examples derived from industrial case studies. In the courses presented they focus on lightweight formal methods, or a lightweight use of formal methods with greater possibilities, but they also mention other courses, which deal with a "heavier" stuff like formal verification. Teaching heavyweight FM is the topic of Feinerer and Gernot (2009), who review four tools with respect to their suitability for teaching formal software verification by theorem proving. They state that despite the tools for formal software verification didn't reach the automation level of model checkers used in hardware verification, they have become automated enough to be used more often in the industry. This is supported by the evaluation results in their paper.

In (Cristiá, 2006) the situation in teaching FM in Argentina is described. Its author especially deals with the reasons why to teach formal methods in a country without any industry that uses them and, together with Feinerer and Gernot (2009), shares our belief that FM should be used more often in the industry and that this can be achieved via properly educated students. While virtually all educators stress out an importance of good tool support, Liu et al. (2009) suggest handwriting formal specifications as the best way to learn syntax and semantics of given formal language.

Regarding our proposal, it is important to mention the work of Balz and Goedicke (2010), who implemented an idea similar to it in several aspects. They had took a game-oriented visual simulation environment called Greenfoot (http://www.greenfoot.org/) and added a small framework to it, which allows to embed formally specified software into an application developed and simulated in Greenfoot. The framework supports one formal method, state machines, and these machines are written in annotated Java, similarly to the rest of applications for Greenfoot. In addition, Balz and Goedicke (2010) provide a tool that is able to transform the embedded machines to more abstract models that can be analyzed and verified in the UPPAAL tool (http://www.uppaal.org/).

It should be also noted that introducing games and gaming concepts into higher education is not uncommon nowadays. The Greenfoot tool, mentioned above is one example of this. Its primary role is to teach Java programming to high school students and undergraduates by letting them to develop simple 2D graphical programs like simulations or games. There is even a journal dedicated to the topic of educating in funny ways – the "Transactions on Edutainment", issued as a part of the Springer LNCS series.

RAILWAY SIMULATION IN FORMAL METHODS COURSE

In our effort to increase attractiveness of a formal methods course and to clearly demonstrate importance of FM to students we modified the Train Director game to be a virtual application area for control software developed by FM. The section explains why we implemented our proposal in this way (1st subsection), how the modified game and related proxy application operate (2nd subsection) and how they can be used in teaching process (3rd subsection). The 4th subsection presents concrete examples of control software, developed in a formal method called B-Method. The examples demonstrate that the limited scope of the game is not an obstacle in teaching various aspects of formal methods. The final, fifth, subsection discusses usability of our implementation for other formal methods and other approaches to software engineering.

In this section we use the *italics font* when referring to tools that create the virtual application area and the Arial Narrow font for names, methods (operations), variables and other parts of control modules and code in the language of B-Method.

Reasons and Choices

The first choice we made is that of the railway domain. As it was mentioned earlier, the domain, which virtual representation we would like to create should have a history of successful formal methods application. To have a desired motivational effect it also has to be a domain almost every student has experience with and where automated systems in control of human lives or valuable assets already exist. And students should be able to easily imagine being jeopardized by failures of these systems. According to recent surveys (Woodcock et al., 2009; Fitzgerald et al., 2013) FM have been most successfully used in the areas of finance, defense and transportation with transportation being the largest one.

In finance, FM have been applied to various areas, such as transaction processing and electronic cash systems. But these situations are usually not life-threatening and our real-life experience teaches us that when something accidentally goes wrong with our finances, we report it to our bank, which usually solves the case in our favor.

The military is without any doubt a good domain for FM application. There are also some really scary stories of computer systems malfunction related to it. For example, on June 3, 1980 U.S. early warning systems had detected multiple incoming Soviet nuclear ballistic missiles and preparations for retaliation started. Fortunately, it was classified as a false alarm. Subsequent investigation identified a faulty computed chip as the cause of the incident. In favor of this domain is also the fact that utilization of formal methods is mandatory for certain classes of military software (e.g. UK Defense Standard 00-55 issue 2). But we are no more living in the cold war, the military service is not mandatory in most countries and young people usually see military systems as something distant, encountered only in computer games and during air shows or military parades.

Transportation domain is a huge one, containing various means of individual and public transport and we can even include space exploration here. The space exploration is an ideal area for FM: software in space probes should be correct as it is difficult if not impossible to fix it. And formal methods have already been used here, for example the SPIN model checker in the development of the Cassini probe or Mars exploration rovers (Woodcock et al., 2009). In addition, it is the "home" of one of the most legendary stories of software failure, often used by formal methods propagators – the crash of the Ariane 5 rocket in 1996, caused by a program that unsuccessfully tried to convert a 64-bit floating point number to a 16-bit signed integer. But most of the Earth's inhabitants are not worried about failures of space vehicles – maybe with the exception of cases when some of them fall on their heads.

In air transport there are standards for airborne software that involve formal methods, such as DO-178C/ED-12C. And FM are really used here, too. For example, Airbus used the SCADE Suite from Esterel Technologies (http://www.esterel-technologies.com/) for the development of most of the A380 and A400M critical on-board software (Woodcock et al., 2009). There are many automated systems in airplanes, the term "autopilot" is known for decades. But trained personnel are always present on board, so the perception of threat from computer systems is not that significant. The same is true for flight dispatching. And, in fact, not that much people travel by airplanes.

On the contrary, almost everyone is involved in the road transport. Computer systems are routinely used in cars and signaling on crossroads is automated. Nevertheless, there is always a person controlling a vehicle. Autonomous vehicles already exist but are not used by public. Malfunctioning signaling definitely presents a threat but signals are usually used in urban areas with limited speed, so if there are consequences they are usually not lethal and affect relatively small number of people. In addition, car accidents are quite common and cars are designed with this in mind.

Finally, we got to the domain of our choice, to the railway, which we consider the most suitable one and there are reasons to it. The first is its status of a widely used mean of public transportation almost everyone has an experience with. This is also true for the road transport, but what is specific is that fully automated, driverless, trains already exist and are used by public. It is no wonder: trains are bounded to rails, therefore their behavior is easier to define and control than in the case of road vehicles. Driverless trains operate daily on Line 14 of the Paris metro, CDGVAL Charles de Gaulle airport shuttle rail service or Line 9 of the Barcelona metro. And safety-critical parts of control software for these trains and related equipment, like signaling or platform screen doors, have been developed by B-Method (Abrial, 1996), a heavyweight formal method for verified software development. An evidence of this can be found in (Lecomte et al., 2007), (Lecomte, 2009), (Abrial, 2007), (Boulanger, 2012) or in the surveys mentioned above. Size and mass of trains is in general much bigger than of the road vehicles, therefore they are less controllable. This, together with limitation of their movement because of rails, results in much more significant possible consequences of accidents than in the case of road vehicles. From teacher's point of view an attractive feature of the domain is an ease in which various naturally looking situations can be created: every track layout is a special situation of its own and we can consider different purposes of individual trains, stations or tracks, priority of the trains and so on. It is just necessary to find a game that allows us to build and simulate such layouts.

Fortunately, there are several candidates. In (Korečko, Sorád, & Sobota, 2011) we published results of the search for such game. Two hot candidates were considered – Open Rails (http://www.openrails.org/) and Train Director. Both fulfilled our basic criteria: they allow to build and simulate railway scenarios with working signals and switches, in both it is possible to have more than one train in the simulation and they are open source. There are also big differences between the two. The Train Director focuses on the operation of centralized traffic control. Therefore it provides only schematic 2D representation of the track layout and operation of trains is simplified. On the other hand, Open Rails is a successor of the Microsoft Train Simulator, so it provides nice 3D graphics and sophisticated train models. In 2011 we opted for Train Director because of its relative simplicity and temporal unavailability of the Open Rails source code. Later we also started with modification of the Open Rails, but this is still under development. A question related to this choice is why we didn't implement a new game but modified an existing one. First, we believe that modifying an existing game requires less effort. Second, this way we can use scenarios already developed by others. And there is also a chance

that community around the game will help in propagation of formal methods.

At first glance it seems that there is a controversy in our choices: We are trying to improve formal methods education but the tools we offer work with Java applications. And Java is a general purpose programming language, not a formal method or language. But Java is also a language which is supported by code generators of many formal methods tools for software development. It is also a very popular programming language and most software engineering students encounter it during their study. Paradoxically, the formal method we use, the B-Method, doesn't support code generation to Java, but we developed our own compiler called BKPI compiler (Korečko, & Dancák, 2011), which is based on the French software jBTools (Voisinet, Tatibouet, & Hammad, 2002).

Some may argue that it will be better for our tools to work directly with formal specifications and not only with applications (in Java) generated from them. But we disagree, because the purpose of the tools is to create a virtual application area for formally developed software and not to make its development too simple for students.

Train Director and TS2JavaConn

The virtual railway environment is provided by two tools: a modified version of the game Train Director and a newly developed TS2JavaConn, implemented in Java. TS2JavaConn is the proxy application that provides communication between the game and control modules.

Train Director

The *Train Director* (*TD*) is a centralized traffic control simulator. In TD a player can create a railway scenario and simulate it. The scenario consists of a schematic track layout (Figure 1) and a train schedule, which has a form of a text file. The player's goal during the simulation is to throw

Figure 1. Modified Train Director during simulation

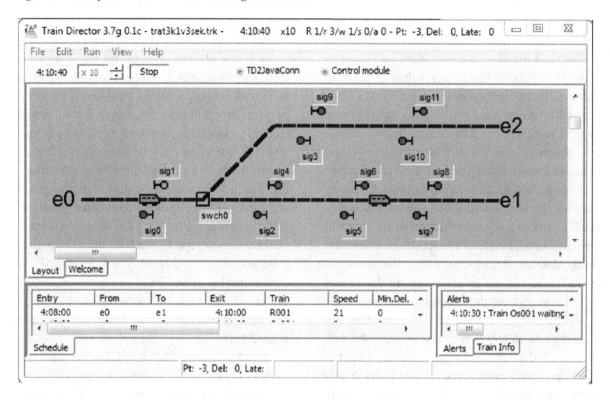

switches and clear signals in such a way that the trains will follow the schedule. The game changes some of the signals automatically and prevents collisions. One of the features that persuaded us to choose it is a presence of a simple server interface for external control. While changes in its user interface are almost invisible, internally a lot of code has been modified in order to adjust the game for our purposes. We disabled the internal logic and implemented train collisions. We also added a possibility to name signals and switches and to show the names in the user interface. This was necessary, because without the names it will be impossible to refer to individual signals and switches from the control modules. The build-in server interface was changed, too. The original version worked with messages containing coordinates of mouse clicks, the new one sends and receives detailed information about events and commands and their parameters.

The modified Train Director communicates with TS2JavaConn by means of messages sent via a TCP connection. TD is able to send *request messages* and *informational messages*. A *request message* is sent to TS2JavaConn every time a train stops before a red signal (*requestGreen* message), wants to enter a track layout (*requestDepartureEntry*) or departure from a station (*requestDepartureStation*). These messages also contain data necessary for a corresponding control module. The data include a name of corresponding signal, entry point or station, name of the train and names of stations the train should visit according to the schedule. An entry point is a named end of a track, where trains can enter or leave the layout. When and where a train enters and should leave the layout is specified in the schedule of the scenario. A station is just a named track section. Whether and for how long a train stops at the station is defined in the schedule, too. *Informational messages* include *sectionLeave*, which is sent to TS2Java-Conn when a train leaves current track section and *sectionEnter*, sent when it enters a new one. In the real railway a track can be arbitrarily divided into sections. In Train Director we simplified it in such a way that a track section always starts and ends at some signal, switch or entry point. Train Director also receives messages. These messages are commands from TS2JavaConn to, for example, start or stop a simulation or to change states of signals or switches.

Figure 1 shows the modified TD during a simulation of a scenario with a simple layout. The layout has three entry points (*e0, e1, e2*), one switch (*swch0*) and twelve signals (*sig0* to *sig11*). The track sections are named by elements on their ends, from left to right. If there are two signals at the same place (e.g. *sig0* and *sig1* in Figure 1) then the one guarding given section is used for naming. So, for Figure 1 we have *e0_sig0*, *sig1_swch0, swch0_sig2, swch0_sig3* and so on.

TS2JavaConn

The development of the second tool, *TS2JavaConn* (Figure 2), was necessary because Train Director is a C++ application and control modules are in Java. The second reason was that we intend to use it with other railway simulators as well.

The *control modules* are Java applications. Every module has to contain one *"main" class*, which provides interface for communication with the railway scenario it controls (via TS2JavaConn). This interface consists of methods called when the messages are received from Train Director and enquiry methods used to retrieve information about states of track devices from the control module. The enquiry methods are called before the commands changing states of signals or switches are sent to Train Director. Another mandatory part of every module is a *configuration file*, which defines how the methods of the module are mapped to messages from and to Train Director, what are their names, parameters and return values. A wide range of op-

tions is available: for input and output parameters we can use primitive types, like integer or boolean, enumerated sets or mappings. The methods can be non-parametric, where corresponding message parameters are parts of their names or parametric, where they are usual parameters. For example, in a control module for the scenario depicted in Figure 1 we need twelve methods, i.e. reqGreen_sig0 to reqGreen_sig11, to respond to the *requestGreen* messages for signals in a non-parametric version, but only one method, reqGreen(sig), in a parametric one. Examples of both versions are given in the "Examples for B-Method Course" section. It is also possible to read values of control module variables directly and not via the enquiry methods. Number of additional classes and libraries in control modules is not limited, so the modules can be really sophisticated and complex applications. A question may be asked why we bother with the non-parametric representation, but our practical experience shows that more complicated data representation, necessary for the parametric one, can make fully automated verification (proofs) impossible even for the simplest scenarios.

TS2JavaConn provides a GUI where a user can load a control module (first button in the toolbar in Figure 2) unload the module (2nd button) open a tab with a control module generator (3rd button), reset the connection with TD (4th button) or control the simulation in TD (round buttons). The "Element state" part of the "Overview" tab lists all track elements in the simulated scenario and indicates their state in TD (the column with the title "S" in Figure 2) and in the control module (the column with the title "M"). The "Logger" part records communication between TD and the control module. The module generator can create the configuration file and control module specification (without bodies of methods or operations) in Java and in languages of formal methods B-Method and Perfect Developer. For Java and B-Method both parametric and non-parametric versions are supported.

Figure 2. TS2JavaConn during simulation

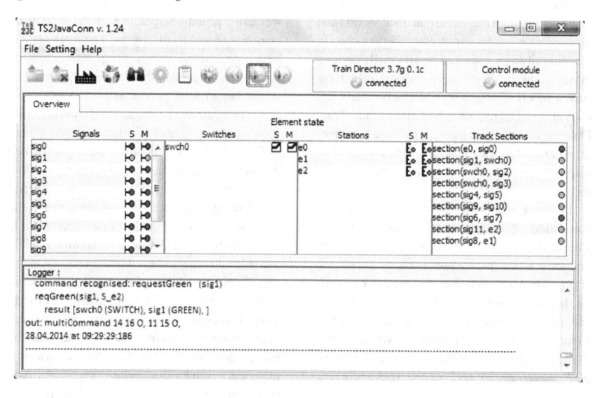

Communication Process

In addition to showing the user interface of the tools, Figure 1 and Figure 2 also capture an actual communication between Train Director and TS2JavaConn with a control module loaded. The tools are shown exactly after the moment when a request for clearing the signal *sig1* is received from the train *Os001*. As we can see in the "Logger" part, TS2JavaConn responds by calling parametric method reqGreen with parameters sig1 and S_e2 from the connected control module. The method changes the values of variables that represent *sig1* and *swch0*. Position of the switch is changed because the destination of *Os001* is the entry point *e2*. This is indicated by the value of the second parameter of reqGreen, the S_e2. After the execution of reqGreen is finished, TS2JavaConn reads values of module variables by calling corresponding enquiry methods and sends modified ones

to the simulator, using so-called *multiCommand* message. The simulator reacts by setting *sig1* to green and changing the position of *swch0*.

One may wonder why we use the value S_e2 and not e2 for the entry point *e2*. This is because entry points have two meanings; they can be treated as signals or as stations. They are seen as signals when a train enters the layout: the train can enter only after the corresponding entry point is set to green. And they are regarded as stations when they define destinations of trains. The prefix "S_" indicates the station role. The concrete form of the prefix can be set in the configuration file.

Simplifications

Of course, the virtual railway, as represented by the tools, is considerably simplified when compared to the real one. The most significant simplifications are:

1. **Unrealistic Train Operation:** In Train Director the parameters as length or weight of trains are not considered, so a train fits any section and can stop immediately.

2. **Absolute Reliability of Trains and Track Devices:** Trains never disobey signals and signals and switches always operate according to orders given.

3. **Absolute Reliability of Communication Links:** Provided that both tools are initialized properly, all messages are delivered correctly, without any (simulated) loss or corruption of data.

4. **Sequential Processing of Requests:** The communication between Train Director and TS2JavaConn described above is always executed as one atomic operation. So, if two requests, say *A* and *B*, occur immediately one after the other then *B* is processed only after the results of *A* (i.e. changes in the corresponding control module) manifest in simulated scenario.

It is possible to remove all the simplifications. For example, the reliability can be lowered by introducing randomness to the operation of trains, switches and signals and to the communication between the game and control modules. But for now, we do not intend to do this. At least not for the Train Director. Because even as it is, it provides enough challenges for reliable software development within the scope of an undergraduate FM course.

Utilization in Teaching

The tools, the modified Train Director and TS2JavaConn, can be used during both lectures and practices. A good place to introduce Train Director is a lecture about typical application areas for (heavyweight) formal methods. In this way we can easily show why software correctness is critical there and motivate students to deal with the game before introducing a concrete

formal method. The second benefit is important, because, as our experience shows, if the tools and the method are introduced too close to each other, some students tend to focus more on the tools. On lectures dedicated to a concrete formal method the tools can be used for examples demonstrating various aspects of the method (two such examples for B-Method are shown in the next subsection). The advantage here is time saved because it is not needed to explain context of each example. On the other hand, we do not recommend showing only examples prepared with the tools. Otherwise students can get an impression that formal methods are all about the railway.

While the use of the tools on lectures is beneficial, the best place for them is on practices, where students are given assignments to develop a dependable control module for a railway scenario. The corresponding teaching process usually looks as follows:

1. **Scenario Creation:** A teacher creates a new scenario or modifies an existing one in Train Director. He should be aware that not all types of track devices can be used, only simple red/green signals and two-way switches.

2. **Scenario Analysis:** The scenario is presented to a student with a task to develop a controller for it. The student analyzes the scenario by "playing" with it in Train Director. Both original and modified versions of Train Director can be used for this task. If the modified Train Director is disconnected from TS2JavaConn, switches and signals can be operated manually.

3. **Control Module Development:** After getting familiar with the scenario the student develops the control module itself, using given formal method and tools available for it. The student should start with data representation of elements from the scenario (i.e. track sections, switches, signals, stations, trains) and formalization of safety require-

ments, continue with writing operations (methods), verification and refinement tasks and finish with code generation. Provided that his FM is supported, the student can use the module generator of TS2JavaConn to create the configuration file and an empty main component of the module. The teacher assists during the development, if necessary.

4. **Simulation:** The student loads compiled module into TS2JavaConn and simulates corresponding scenario with the module in control. The teacher can provide alternative schedules for the scenario to find out whether the module is really correct.

As it can be seen from the process, our tools really act as a virtual domain and nothing more (except for the module generator). They are intensively used in phases 1, 2 and 4 but during the development itself the student relies on the standard tools available for given formal method. This fulfills our intention to emulate real development process as close as possible.

Examples for B-Method Course

This subsection presents two examples, two control modules, specified in the language of B-Method, which highlight different features of this formal method. The first module, intended for an introductory lecture, is very simple and concentrates on basic capabilities of B-Method and formalization of safety requirements. The second one is composed from several components, including parametric ones, and uses different data representation as the first one. One of its purposes is to show reusability in B-Method. The first module uses nonparametric operations (methods), the second uses parametric ones.

B-Method

B-Method (B) (Abrial, 1996) is a state based model-oriented heavyweight formal method

for software development. Its strength lies in a well-defined development process, which allows specifying a software system as a collection of components, called B-machines, and refining such an abstract specification to a concrete one. The concrete specification can be automatically translated to a general purpose programming language. An internal consistency of the abstract specification and correctness of each refinement step are verified by proving a set of predicates, called proof obligations (PObs). All components in B are written in its own B-language, a combination of the Zermelo-Fraenkel set theory and the Guarded Command Language (Dijkstra, 1976). There is an industrial-strength software tool Atelier B (http://www.atelierb.eu/), which supports the whole development process, including proving and code generation to C and ADA. Proofs in Atelier B can be done in fully automatic or human-assisted (interactive) mode. Another useful tool for B-Method is ProB (Leuschel, & Butler, 2003). It allows to animate and model check specifications written in B-language. By animation we mean running or simulation of formal specification, despite the fact that it contains unimplementable features like nondeterminism and non-termination. The B-machine is a component consisting of several clauses:

```
MACHINE M(p)
CONSTRAINTS C
SETS St
CONSTANTS k
PROPERTIES Bh
VARIABLES v
DEFINITIONS D
INVARIANT I
ASSERTIONS A
INITIALISATION T
OPERATIONS
y<--op(x) = PRE P THEN S END
```

The most important are MACHINE clause with a name M of the machine and a list p of its formal parameters, the VARIABLES (or CONCRETE_VARI-ABLES) containing a list v of state variables, IN-VARIANT with properties I of the state variables, INITIALISATION with an operation T that establishes an initial state of the machine and OPERATIONS that contains its operations. We say that the machine is internally consistent if I holds in each of its states. St is a list of deferred and enumerated sets. They represent new types. Constants of the machine are listed in k and a predicate Bh defines properties of St and k. D is a list of macro definitions and A is a list of lemmas used to simplify proof of the PObs. Only the MACHINE clause is mandatory.

Every operation has a header and a body. The header includes its name (op) and optional input and output parameters (x, y). The body is written in the Generalized Substitution Language (GSL), a part of the B-language. GSL contains several constructs, or "commands", called generalized substitutions (GS). They include:

- x := e. Assignment of a value of expression e to variable x.
- S1 ; S2. Sequential composition: do GS S1 then GS S2.
- S1 ∥ S2. Parallel composition: do S1 and S2 at once.
- PRE E THEN S1 END. Preconditioning. It executes S1 if E holds. Otherwise it doesn't terminate.
- IF E THEN S1 ELSE S2 END. Conditional statement: if E holds, do S1, otherwise do S2. In B this is not a basic GS but a combination of two other GS.

The list is not complete; GS that are not used in examples below are excluded. The formal semantics of GSL is defined by the weakest precondition calculus (Dijkstra, 1976). Standardly, the body has the form of PRE GS, however if P is TRUE then it consists only of S ("PRE P" is replaced by "BEGIN").

The PObs for B-machine assert that T always establishes an initial state in which I holds and that for each operation op it holds that if op is executed from a state satisfying I and P then it always terminates in a state satisfying I.

The development process of B is a verified stepwise refinement, where an abstract specification, consisting of B-machines (MM), is modified in one or more steps into an implementable one and correctness of each step is proved. There are two additional components used during the process – Refinement (RR) and Implementation (II). Structures of MM, RR and II are similar, but there are some differences. For example GS ";" and loops are not allowed in MM and "∥" and PRE are not allowed in II. A RR or II can refine only one MM or RR but one MM or RR can be refined by more RR or II . To refine means to modify data or operations. Interfaces (i.e. parameters and operation headers) of a refining and a refined component have to be the same. Invariant of RR or II defines not only properties of its variables but also a relation between its variables and variables of the component it refines. Proof obligations of RR and II are similar to those of MM, but take into account operations and variables of the components they refine.

In II we have to use CONCRETE_VARIABLES clause instead of VARIABLES. Concrete means implementable and therefore not all types are allowed. We can also use the CONCRETE_VARI-ABLES clause in MM and RR. Then variables listed in this clause remain the same in all subsequent refinements and we do not need to list them again.

As it was mentioned above, a specification in B usually consists of more than one component. To access contents of one component from another one several composition mechanisms can be used. For example, SEES and USES allow different level of read-only access, INCLUDES allows to call operations of accessed component in the accessing one and IMPORTS has the same meaning as INCLUDES, but for implementations. These mechanisms are usually defined right after the CONSTRAINTS or REFINES clause.

Figure 3. Track layout from example 1 with names of sections and signals

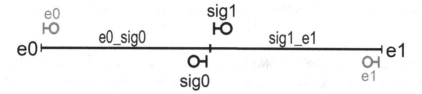

Example 1: For One Lecture

This introductory example is a control module for a very simple scenario (Figure 3) with two signals (*sig0, sig1*), two entry points (*e0, e1*) and two sections (*e0_sig0, sig1_e1*). The specification of the module consists of two components – the B-machine trat1k and its refinement, the implementation trat1k_i.

The machine trat1k is shown in Figure 4. To simplify the matter as much as possible its variables (clause CONCRETE_VARIABLES) match the track devices. Types of the variables are defined in the first three lines of the INVARIANT clause and they are enumerated sets, listed in the SETS clause. The operator "&" is conjunction, "or" is disjunction and ":" means "belongs to". The last three lines of the INVARIANT are safety conditions, formalized from safety requirements on the module. The INITIALISATION sets all signals to red and all sections to free. Entry points are treated as signals only. There are 16 nonparametric operations. The first four are enquiry operations, which return values of corresponding variables. It is also possible to have getSec operations, returning occupation status of sections, but they are not mandatory as the occupation of sections is not used on the Train Director side. The next two are to respond to the *requestDepartureEntry* messages from Train Director and the two after them to the *requestGreen* messages. The next four respond to the *sectionEnter* messages and the last four to the *sectionLeave* messages. The capital letter "N" means "eNtry point" and "I" means "sIgnal". We have two sections but there are four operations in

each of the last two groups. This is to be able to treat an entry or leave from each side differently (albeit it is not necessary in this case).

The implementation trat1k_i is not shown because it is nearly identical to the machine trat1k. It just doesn't contain clauses CONCRETE_VARIABLES and INVARIANT and "||" is replaced by ";". After translation of trat1k_i to Java a class trat1k is created with methods named exactly as operations in trat1k (and trat1k_i). This class is then loaded in TS2JavaConn as a control module for the scenario from Figure 3.

The example is very suitable for explaining how safety requirements can be formalized into the invariant. Here we have two safety requirements:

1. *Only one of the signals guarding a section can be green.* This is formalized to the condition "e0=red or sig0=red" for *e0_sig0* and to "e1=red or sig1=red" for *sig1_e1*.

2. *A signal guarding a section can be green only if the section is free.* This is formalized to the condition "(e0=red & sig0=red) or e0_sig0=free" for *e0_sig0* and to "(sig1=red & e1=red) or sig1_e1=free" for *sig1_e1*.

Thanks to the trivial data representation it is easy to connect informal requirements to corresponding logical assertions (conditions).

An example like this also provides an ideal opportunity to show what FM like B can do and what they cannot do. Actually, the only extra thing B can do is to verify (prove) that the conditions we wrote in the INVARIANT clause hold in every possible state of given system. This is very valu-

Figure 4. Source code of B-machine trat1k

```
MACHINE trat1k                              OPERATIONS
SETS
  PROP_SIGNAL={green, red};                 ss <-- getSig_sig1 = BEGIN ss:=sig1 END;
  PROP_SWITCH={switched, none};             ss <-- getSig_sig0 = BEGIN ss:=sig0 END;
  PROP_SECTION={free,occup}                 ss <-- getSig_e0 = BEGIN ss:=e0 END;
                                            ss <-- getSig_e1 = BEGIN ss:=e1 END;
CONCRETE_VARIABLES
  e0, e1, /*entry points*/                  reqGreen_e0 =IF sig0 = red & e0_sig0= free THEN e0:=green END;
  sig1, sig0, /*signals*/                   reqGreen_e1 = IF sig1 = red & sig1_e1 = free  THEN  e1:=green END;
  e0_sig0, sig1_e1 /*track sections*/
                                            reqGreen_sig0 = IF e0 = red & e0_sig0 = free THEN sig0:=green END;
INVARIANT                                   reqGreen_sig1 = IF e1=red & sig1_e1= free THEN sig1:=green   END;
  e0:PROP_SIGNAL & e1:PROP_SIGNAL &
  sig1:PROP_SIGNAL & sig0:PROP_SIGNAL &     enterNI_e0_sig0 = BEGIN e0_sig0:=occup || e0:=red || sig0:=red END;
  e0_sig0:PROP_SECTION & sig1_e1:PROP_SECTION   enterIN_sig1_e1 = BEGIN sig1_e1:=occup || sig1:=red || e1:=red END;
  &                                         enterNI_e1_sig1 = BEGIN sig1_e1:=occup || sig1:=red || e1:=red END;
  (e0=red or sig0=red) & (e1=red or sig1=red) &   enterIN_sig0_e0 = BEGIN e0_sig0:=occup || e0:=red || sig0:=red END;
  ((e0=red  & sig0=red) or e0_sig0=free) &
  ((sig1=red &  e1=red) or sig1_e1=free)    leaveNI_e0_sig0 = BEGIN e0_sig0:=free END;
                                            leaveIN_sig1_e1 = BEGIN sig1_e1:=free END;
INITIALISATION                              leaveNI_e1_sig1 = BEGIN sig1_e1:=free END;
  e0:=red || e1:=red || sig1:=red || sig0:=red ||   leaveIN_sig0_e0 = BEGIN e0_sig0:=free END
  e0_sig0:= free || sig1_e1:= free          END
```

able but it is not enough to guarantee correctness, because there is no way B-Method can verify that the conditions in the INVARIANT are correct. As Bowen and Hinchey (2006) note: "If the organization has not built the right system (validation), no amount of building the system right (verification) can overcome that error." For example, the aforementioned software of the crashed Ariane 5 rocket was functioning perfectly, in accordance with corresponding requirements. But these requirements were wrong (Le Lann, 1997). In fact, they were wrong because they were taken, together with the software itself, from the previous version of the rocket, Ariane 4. Back to our example, we can easily modify the safety requirements and operations in such a way the module will be fully verified but nevertheless causes an accident. Another thing B cannot guarantee is correctness of the interface. We can show that if we interchange bodies of the operations in trat1k, excluding the first four ones, its invariant will still hold.

Example 2: Introducing Advanced Concepts

The second module controls the scenario already shown in Figure 1. It is possible to define a module for this scenario in the exactly same way as the previous one, but here we would like to introduce more advanced concepts of B-Method. Its primary purpose is to show how to use compositional mechanisms to design a control module with reusable components. It also uses the DEFINITIONS clause and a separate file with definitions to make specifications more readable while using primitive data types. Operations are parametric and data representation no more corresponds exactly to the devices in the scenario. Some variables have mappings as types. Verification of this module requires small amount of interactive proving.

The layout of the scenario is divided into four parts (Figure 5 c). Each part is controlled by a separate machine. There are three CntrlSimpleTrack machines and one Cntrl3WayTrack machine. To distinguish between the three machines they are named – trN, trS and trD. All are included in one "main" machine, Controller3way3secTr. States of the devices are represented as values 0 and 1, but meaningful aliases are assigned to them in definitions in a separate file values.def (Figure 6a). This file is then linked to each component of the module. The operator "==" means "rewrites to". Composition of the module is shown in Figure 5 d), where ellipses are B-machines and rectangles are implementations.

The machine CntrlSimpleTrack and its implementation CntrlSimpleTrack_i represent a controller for a straight track of arbitrary length (measured in sections). Layout of the track with data representation of its elements is shown in Figure 5 b) and specification of the machine in Figure 6 b). The operator "-->" means total function, "=>" is implication, "*" is Cartesian product, "{x}" is a set consisting of an element x, "!" is "for all", "x..y" is an integer interval from x to y and "f(x)" is a value of a function f in x. All three variables are in fact arrays of the length length, storing values 0 and 1. All operations are parametric. The first three are enquiry operations; next two react to requests for green signals the sixth to entering a section and the last one to leaving a section. The capital letter "R" means that the corresponding operation deals with signals for trains heading from left to right, "L" for trains in opposite direction.

The control module for the part with switch (Figure 5 a) is specified in the machine Cntrl3WayTrack (Figure 7) and its implementation Cntrl3WayTrack_i. The style of these specifications is similar to the previous example, with three exceptions. First, all three sections are represented as one "logical" section by the variable swSec. Second, the operation reqGreenN has a parameter dir to determine how the position of the switch should be changed. Third, there is only one operation for section entering (enter3w) and one for leaving (leave3wAll) and leave3wAll should be called only when a train leaves the entire part.

All is put together in the machine Controller3way3secTr (Figure 8) and its implementation Controller3way3secTr_i. This machine includes the previous machines for individual parts and defines sets to represent track devices in the entire layout. The entry points are present in both SIGNALS and STATIONS, in the latter with the prefix "S_". The value "NE" represents an undefined station. Additional definitions are added to assign alternative, more meaningful names, to variables from included machines. The variables of Controller3way3secTr map names of track devices to indices of arrays in included CntrlSimpleTrack machines. The first three operations are enquiry operations returning status of signals, sections and switches. The operation responding to *reqest-DepartureEntry* and *requestGreen* messages is reqGreen with two parameters, sg and st. The first one is a name of a signal or an entry point, the second is the destination of given train. The second parameter is used to set the switch. The operation enter responds to entering a section, no matter from which direction. For the *sectionLeave* messages we need two operations, one for each direction. This is because of the specific nature of leave3wAll from Cntrl3WayTrack.

To make proving easier a PROPERTIES clause that repeats definition of sets from SETS can be added to Controller3way3secTr. The content of these two clauses will be the same. Only ";" will be replaced by "&". There are no alternative names for track sections sig1_swch0, swch0_sig2, swch0_sig3 in the DEFINITIONS clause. Instead of them we refer directly to variable swSec from Cntrl3WayTrack.

In addition to the utilization of composition mechanisms and reusable components the example also shows that sometimes an approach unnatural at first sight has to be used to achieve effective performance from tools of given FM (the Atelier B's prover in this case). Namely, one can easily see that abstract variables of the machine Controller3way3secTr are in fact constants. So,

Figure 5. Track layout from example 2 with names of sections, switches and signals (a-c): whole layout (c), component with switch (a) and straight track component (b). Composition of B specification components of corresponding control module (d)

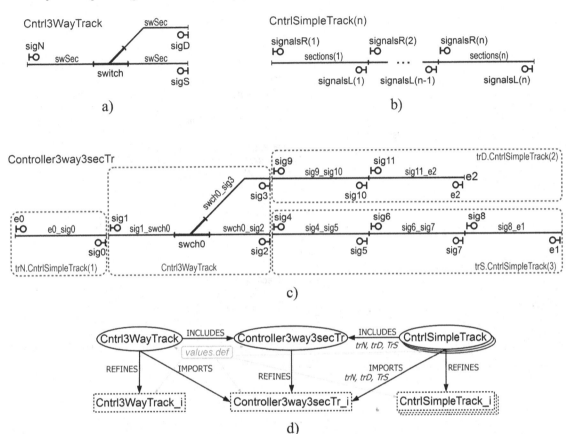

c)

d)

the ABSTRACT_CONSTANTS clause will be more appropriate for them. But, if we define them as constants then their properties (8th to 12th line in the INVARIANT clause) will require a use of the interactive prover. To be sure that they remain constant we can repeat the content of the INITIALI-SATION clause in INVARIANT with "||" replaced by "&". Adjusting specifications to tools is not that uncommon in the world of FM, Feinerer and Gernot (2009) report a similar experience with Perfect Developer.

This and the previous example primarily aim at verification and not that much at refinement and abstraction (which is, for example, in contrary to (Larsen et al., 2009)). However, it is possible to explore refinement and abstraction more, especially with reusable components. For example, the component Cntrl3WayTrack has a potential for data refinement: on the most abstract level (B-Machine) we can represent sections exactly as in corresponding track layout (i.e. 3 sections) and then refine it to one "logical" section and thus reduce memory requirements.

Another common feature of both modules is that they always allow access to only one section. A negative consequence of this is that deadlocks can occur when trains from opposite directions meet on the same straight track. They will not collide but they cannot move anymore. But nothing prevents us to build more sophisticated, deadlock-

Figure 6. Source code of definitions file values.def (a) and B-machine CntrlSimpleTrack (b)

```
DEFINITIONS  red==0; green==1;diverg==0; straight==1;free==0; occup==1
```

(a)

```
MACHINE CntrlSimpleTrack(length)           OPERATIONS
CONSTRAINTS length:NAT & length>0          res<--getSignalR(no) = PRE no:1..length THEN res:=signalsR(no) END;
DEFINITIONS "values.def"                    res<--getSignalL(no) = PRE no:1..length THEN res:=signalsL(no) END;
                                            res<--getSection(no) = PRE no:1..length THEN res:=sections(no) END;
CONCRETE_VARIABLES sections, signalsR, signalsL
INVARIANT                                   reqGreenR(sigNo)= PRE sigNo:1..length THEN
 sections : (1..length)-->(0..1) &           IF signalsL(sigNo)=red & sections(sigNo)=free THEN
 signalsR : (1..length)-->(0..1) &              signalsR(sigNo):=green END
 signalsL : (1..length)-->(0..1)            END;
 &
 !xx.((xx:(1..length)) =>
     ((signalsR(xx)=red) or (signalsL(xx)=red)))    reqGreenL(sigNo)= PRE sigNo:1..length THEN
 &                                           IF signalsR(sigNo)=red & sections(sigNo)=free THEN
 !xx.((xx:(1..length)) =>                        signalsL(sigNo):= green  END
     ((signalsR(xx)=red & signalsL(xx)=red)   END;
      or sections(xx)=free))
                                            enterSec(secNo)= PRE secNo:1..length THEN
INITIALISATION                               sections(secNo):=occup ||
 sections := (1..length)*{free} ||           signalsR(secNo):=red || signalsL(secNo):=red
 signalsR := (1..length)*{red}  ||          END;
 signalsL := (1..length)*{red}
                                            leaveSec(secNo)= PRE secNo:1..length THEN sections(secNo):=free END
                                            END
```

(b)

free modules. This opens new possibilities, such as an introduction of recursive functions and loops to components with array-like variables (e.g. CntrlSimpleTrack).

Beyond B-Method

Because of the maturity of its tools and a reputation of an industrially used FM, the B-Method is our primary choice when developing control modules. But thanks to the configurable interface and the fact that modules connect on the Java application level the TS2JavaConn and modified Train Director can be used with ones developed by other formal methods as well. To demonstrate it we developed control modules with three other formal methods, which offer Java code generator – the Vienna Development Method (VDM), namely

its object-oriented version VDM++ (Fitzgerald, Larsen, Mukherjee, Plat, & Verhoef, 2005), the language Perfect (Crocker, 2004) and Event-B (Abrial, 2010). For VDM++ the build-in compiler of VDM++ Toolkit (http://www.vdmtools. jp) was used to generate Java code. Similarly, the code from specification in Perfect was generated from its tool Escher Verification Studio (http:// www.eschertech.com/products/). There are two Java code generators for Event-B and its software platform Rodin (http://www.event-b.org) and we used EB2J (http://eb2all.loria.fr). All these modules use primitive types for message parameters and non-parametric operations (methods). The Java code generated from Escher Verification Studio and VDM++ Toolkit worked without modifications; in the EB2J case it was necessary to add an explicit constructor. Creation of an empty

Figure 7. Source code of B-machine Cntrl3WayTrack

```
MACHINE Cntrl3WayTrack
DEFINITIONS "values.def"
CONCRETE_VARIABLES
 sigN, sigS, sigD, swSec, switch

INVARIANT
 sigN:0..1 & sigS:0..1 & sigD:0..1 & swSec:0..1 &
 switch:0..1 &
 (sigN=green => (sigD=red & sigS=red)) &
 (sigD=green => (sigN=red & sigS=red)) &
 (sigS=green => (sigD=red & sigN=red)) &
 (sigN=green => swSec=free) &
 (sigD=green => (swSec=free & switch=diverg)) &
 (sigS=green => (swSec=free & switch=straight))

INITIALISATION
 sigN:=red || sigS:=red || sigD:=red || swSec:=free ||
 switch := straight

OPERATIONS

res<--getSigN = BEGIN res:=sigN END;
res<--getSigS = BEGIN res:=sigS END;

res<--getSigD = BEGIN res:=sigD END;
res<--getSwitch=BEGIN res:=switch END;
res<--get3wSec =BEGIN res:=swSec END;

reqGreenN(dir)= PRE dir:0..1 THEN
 IF sigS=red & sigD=red & swSec=free
 THEN sigN:=green || switch:=dir END
END;

reqGreenD=
 IF sigN=red & sigS=red & swSec=free
 THEN sigD:=green || switch:=diverg END;

reqGreenS=
 IF sigN=red & sigD=red & swSec=free
 THEN sigS:=green || switch:=straight END;

enter3w= BEGIN
 sigN:=red || sigS:=red || sigD:=red || swSec:=occup END;

leave3wAll = BEGIN swSec:=free END
END
```

nonparametric module in the language Perfect is supported by TS2JavaConn.

Of course, there is no need to use formal methods at all when developing the control modules; they can be programmed in Java only. In this way the tools can be used to teach testing or writing programs annotated with Java Modeling Language (www.jmlspecs.org/) specifications. The tools can be also suitable for introducing high school students or pupils into programming, maybe even with a gentle introduction to safety issues.

FUTURE DEVELOPMENT

There are several ways in which we intend to further develop the ideas and results presented in this chapter. The first one is to successfully finish modifications of the Open Rails (OR) train simulator to provide functionality at least similar to the modified Train Director. Being 3D simulator with sophisticated model of train operation, OR offers much more possibilities of what to

control and how to control than Train Director. For example, we can allow a control module to take charge of not only track equipment but also the trains. In OR trains do not stop instantly before signals but obey laws of physics, so we can incorporate parameters such as distance from a signal and speed and weight of trains into the modules. OR is compatible with Microsoft Train Simulator (MSTS), therefore routes designed for MSTS can be used in OR and there are many of them, realistically capturing railways from all over the world. This means a lot of material for control module creation. OR also offers a multiplayer mode. It will be interesting to see how successful the control modules are when trains are operated by unpredictable human players.

Another way in which the "railway control" idea can be explored is to go physical. Namely, to use digitally controlled model railway instead of the simulated one. To possess such an installation can be interesting for promotional purposes. Formally developed control modules can be also

Figure 8. Source code of B-machine Controller3way3secTr

```
MACHINE Controller3way3secTr
INCLUDES   trN.CntrlSimpleTrack(1), trD.CntrlSimpleTrack(2),
              trS.CntrlSimpleTrack(3), Cntrl3WayTrack
SETS
  SIGNALS = {e0,sig0,sig1,sig2,sig3,sig4,...,e1,sig9,...,e2};
  SWITCHES = {swch0};
  SECTIONS = {e0_sig0,sig1_swch0,swch0_sig2,...,,sig11_e2};
  STATIONS = {NE,S_e0,S_e1,S_e2}

DEFINITIONS "values.def";
  E0  == trN.signalsR(1); Sig0   == trN.signalsL(1);
  E0_sig0 == trN.sections(1);
  Sig1 == sigN; Sig2 == sigS; Sig3   == sigD; Swch0   == switch;
  ...
  Sig9   == trD.signalsR(1);     Sig11  == trD.signalsR(2);
  Sig10 == trD.signalsL(1);      E2 == trD.signalsL(2);
  Sig9_sig10 == trD.sections(1); Sig11_e2 == trD.sections(2)

ABSTRACT_VARIABLES
  trNSigR, trNSigL, trNSec, trSSigR, trSSigL, trSSec,
  trDSigR, trDSigL, trDSec

INVARIANT
  trNSigR:SIGNALS>+>{1} & trNSigL:SIGNALS>+>{1} &
  trNSec:SECTIONS>+>{1} &
  trSSigR:SIGNALS>+>(1..3) & trSSigL:SIGNALS>+>(1..3) &
  trSSec:SECTIONS>+>(1..3) &
  trDSigR:SIGNALS>+>(1..2) & trDSigL:SIGNALS>+>(1..2) &
  trDSec:SECTIONS>+>(1..2)
  &
  dom(trNSigR) V dom(trNSigL) V {sig1, sig2, sig3} V dom(trSSigR) V
  dom(trSSigL) V dom(trDSigR) V dom(trDSigL) = SIGNALS
  &
  dom(trNSec)V {sig1_swch0, swch0_sig2, swch0_sig3} V
  dom(trSSec)  V dom(trDSec) = SECTIONS ///(mpPr2)
  &
  (E0=red or Sig0=red) & ((E0=red & Sig0=red) or E0_sig0=free)
  &
  (Sig1=green => (Sig3=red & Sig2=red)) &
  (Sig3=green => (Sig1=red & Sig2=red)) &
  (Sig2=green => (Sig3=red & Sig1=red)) &
  (Sig1=green => swSec=free) &
  (Sig3=green => (swSec=free & Swch0=diverg)) &
  (Sig2=green => (swSec=free & Swch0=straight))
  & ... &
  (Sig9=red or Sig10=red) &  (Sig11=red or E2=red) &
  ((Sig9=red & Sig10=red) or Sig9_sig10=free) &
  ((Sig11=red & E2=red) or Sig11_e2=free)
```

```
INITIALISATION
  trNSigR:={e0|->1} || trNSigL:={sig0|->1} || trNSec:={e0_sig0|->1} ||
  ...
  trDSigR:={sig9|->1, sig11|->2} || trDSigL:={sig10|->1, e2|->2} ||
  trDSec:={sig9_sig10|->1, sig11_e2|->2}

OPERATIONS

res <-- getSig(sg) = PRE sg:SIGNALS THEN
  IF sg:dom(trNSigR) THEN res:=trN.signalsR(trNSigR(sg))
  ELSIF sg:dom(trNSigL) THEN res:=trN.signalsL(trNSigL(sg))
  ELSIF sg:dom(trSSigR) THEN res:=trS.signalsR(trSSigR(sg))
  ELSIF sg:dom(trSSigL) THEN res:=trS.signalsL(trSSigL(sg))
  ELSIF sg:dom(trDSigR) THEN res:=trD.signalsR(trDSigR(sg))
  ELSIF sg:dom(trDSigL) THEN res:=trD.signalsL(trDSigL(sg))
  ELSIF sg=sig1 THEN res:=sigN
  ELSIF sg=sig2 THEN res:=sigS
  ELSE  res:=sigD END //sg=sig3
END;

res <-- getSec(sc) = ...
res <-- getSwch(sw) = PRE sw:SWITCHES THEN res:=switch
END;

reqGreen(sg, st) = PRE sg:SIGNALS & st:STATIONS THEN
  IF sg:dom(trNSigR) THEN ok<--trN.reqGreenR(trNSigR(sg))
  ELSIF sg:dom(trNSigL) THEN ok<--trN.reqGreenL(trNSigL(sg))
  ELSIF sg:dom(trSSigR) THEN ok<--trS.reqGreenR(trSSigR(sg))
  ELSIF sg:dom(trSSigL) THEN ok<--trS.reqGreenL(trSSigL(sg))
  ELSIF sg:dom(trDSigR) THEN ok<--trD.reqGreenR(trDSigR(sg))
  ELSIF sg:dom(trDSigL) THEN ok<--trD.reqGreenL(trDSigL(sg))
  ELSIF sg=sig1 THEN
    IF st=S_e2 THEN ok<--reqGreenN(diverg)
    ELSE ok<--reqGreenN(straight) END
  ELSIF sg=sig2 THEN ok<--reqGreenS
  ELSIF sg=sig3 THEN ok<--reqGreenD
END;

enter(sc) = PRE sc:SECTIONS THEN
  IF sc:dom(trNSec) THEN trN.enterSec(trNSec(sc))
  ELSIF sc:dom(trSSec) THEN trS.enterSec(trSSec(sc))
  ELSIF sc:dom(trDSec) THEN trD.enterSec(trDSec(sc))
  ELSE enter3w END
END;

leaveR(sc) = ... ;
leaveL(sc) = ...
END
```

used in automated systems based on hardware platforms like Arduino or Intel Galileo.

We also intend to utilize the competitive nature of human beings to propagate formal methods. On the basis of our experiences with Train Director we are developing an online platform, connected to social networks, which will be able to host various simulators, representing various domains, and control modules for scenarios simulated in them. Users of the platform will have the option to prepare (challenging) scenarios or control modules for them.

Scenes or games created for existing gaming and visualization engines can be also used as virtual application areas for formally developed software. We would like to continue in our experiments with the Unity engine (https://unity3d.com/), which can be used for free and offer scripting in C#, the language supported by several formal methods tools. We already made a visualization of the Boiler case study from (Abrial, 1996) and modified several existing scenes to be able to host control modules.

Other areas worth exploration include population of agent systems by formally developed agents or entering a gaming competition, such as the StarCraft AI Competition, with a verified bot.

RELATED WORK

The perception of problems with formal methods education here is similar to opinions of other educators and researchers, but the solution offered differs. We follow the same basic idea as Larsen et al. (2009) that FM should be demonstrated on examples derived from industrial practice, but contrary to them we focus on one domain and provide tools that create virtual representation of the domain. While the approach we have used is strongly tool-oriented, it can be used in accordance with Liu et al. (2009), who prefer handwriting formal specifications, at least when learning the language of given method: Specifications of simple control modules, like the one from Example 1, can be written by hand on the basis of experimentation with corresponding scenario in Train Director within one practice. Our approach also follows principles of teaching formal methods, defined by Cerone et al. (2013). Most notably, it allows to focus on one formal method (principle 1) with industrial-strength tool support (principles 3 and 5) and provides a stable platform for lab classes (principle 6). Moreover, we picked up

the railway domain, which is familiar to students from everyday life and Java as the target language because students usually know it well from other courses (principle 7). And the approach stimulates not only exploration of syntax and semantics of the formal method taught but also of associated procedures of formal verification and refinement (principle 8). Finally, playing with trains is fun (principle 10).

The work most similar to ours is (Balz, & Goedicke, 2010), where the game-oriented visual simulation environment Greenfoot (http://www.greenfoot.org/), intended for teaching object orientation with Java, has been enhanced by a small framework that allows to embed state machines into an application developed and simulated in Greenfoot. It is based on an idea similar to ours, namely to adapt existing simulation and visualization tool for "hosting" programs developed by formal methods. On the other hand, they fix the formal method (automata) but not the domain and the tools they provide work in opposite direction: from concrete models (in Greenfoot) to abstract ones (in UPPAAL). It is, however, possible that further development of the experiments with gaming and visualization engines mentioned in the previous section will lead to a framework similar to that of Balz and Goedicke (2010).

Creation of the tools described here was also inspired by existing solutions for graphical animation and visualization of formally specified systems. There are two such tools for Event-B, available as plug-ins for the Rodin platform. The first is Brama (http://www.brama.fr/), which allows to make custom visualizations by connecting a specification in Event-B with Adobe Flash animation. The connection between specification and animation is defined by a gluing code, written in ActionScript. Brama has been successfully used in industrial projects, for example in the development of a commuter rail platform screen door controller (Lecomte, Servat, & Pouzancre, 2007). The second one is B-Motion Studio (Ladenberger, Bendisposto, & Leuschel, 2009), which tries to be simpler than Brama: animations are composed from pictures and the gluing code is written in B-language. These solutions differ from ours in the fact that visualizations have to be created from scratch but do not have limited domain, they connect with formally developed software on the specification and not implementation level and are limited to one formal method. Their primary purpose is also different: they are intended for presentation of formal specifications to customers and domain experts in an understandable way. Another solution with such purpose is the APEX framework (Silva, Ribeiro, Fernandes, Campos, Harrison, 2010). It connects OpenSimulator (http://opensimulator.org/), a multi-user 3D application server for creation and running of 3D virtual environments, with CPN Tools (http://cpntools.org/). CPN Tools is an editor, simulator and analyzer for Coloured Petri nets (CPN). Despite using a different kind of formal method (CPN) it is similar to ours in utilizing an existing tool (OpenSimulator) to create virtual environments with devices managed by formally developed controllers (here by CPNs). There are also similarities in architecture: CPN Tools and OpenSimulator communicate using TCP/IP via a special communication/execution component, just like Train Director or Open Rails communicate with a control module via TS2JavaConn.

CONCLUSION

After two years of using the modified Train Director and TS2JavaConn in our formal methods course we can consider its deployment as a success. When compared to previous years we have seen students more engaged and even students that didn't score very well in other theoretical computer science-based courses managed to accomplish assignments that incorporated the tools without significant problems. One may say that it's not a big deal when everything we get at the end is to watch a simulation, but after coping with such "strange"

things like specifying invariants, refinements and conducting proofs students deserve the reward to see the result of their work performing in a believable way. The "believable way" is the key term here. Limited application program interfaces of existing formal methods tools and the time required to perform the "strange" things make it impossible for students to develop within a FM course systems comparable in size and functionality to those they already developed on other courses. And to develop some oversimplified "caricatures" of such systems is hardly motivating and satisfying. The control modules shown here look simple and primitive when compared with source codes of contemporary information systems. But they are something "special", not an "ordinary" software and deliver exactly what is asked from them, so the simplicity is not perceived as inappropriate.

The practical use of the tools wasn't without problems. During the first year the need to write specifications of control modules and modify configuration files manually was reported as the greatest setback by students. As a reaction to this we implemented the control module generator to TS2JavaConn. Some students also complained that the process of compilation and running of control modules is somehow complicated. That they have to generate Java code first then compile it and load the compiled module in TS2JavaConn. But it was our intention not to make this a one click task. The reason was to force the students to stay on the formal methods side as long as possible and to run only a finished and verified module with corresponding scenario. And not, as during ordinary software development, run the executable program after every minor change in the code.

Another question is the cost of the implementation. Considering the time required for modification of Train Director and development of TS2JavaConn it could be cheaper to develop a new game from scratch. But TS2JavaConn works also with Open Rails and its core is reused in the prototype of the online platform mentioned above. Preparation of various scenarios for Train Director is very cheap; the ones used in the examples above can be created within few minutes. On the other hand, to prepare a scene for a gaming or visualization engine, useable as a virtual application area, requires significantly more time. But here we can "employ" students of another course that deals with 3d graphics or virtual reality, who can prepare such scenes as their assignments.

The tools and examples presented in this chapter can be downloaded from https://kega2012.fm.kpi.fei.tuke.sk/.

ACKNOWLEDGMENT

This work has been supported by KEGA grant project No. 050TUKE-4/2012: "Application of Virtual Reality Technologies in Teaching Formal Methods". The authors would like to thank Ján Genči for his suggestions on some titles for the Additional Reading section.

REFERENCES

Abrial, J. R. (1996). *The B-Book: Assigning Programs to Meanings*. Cambridge, UK: Cambridge University Press. doi:10.1017/CBO9780511624162

Abrial, J. R. (2007). Formal methods: Theory becoming practice. *Journal of Universal Computer Science, 13*(5), 619–628.

Abrial, J. R. (2010). *Modeling in Event-B: System and Software Engineering*. Cambridge, UK: Cambridge University Press. doi:10.1017/CBO9781139195881

Almeida, J. B., Frade, M. J., Pinto, J. S., & de Sousa, S. M. (2011). *Rigorous Software Development. An Introduction to Program Verification*. London: Springer-Verlag. doi:10.1007/978-0-85729-018-2

Balz, M., & Goedicke, M. (2010). Teaching Programming with Formal Models in Greenfoot. In *Proceedings of the 2nd International Conference on Computer Supported Education* (pp. 309-316). Valencia: INSTICC Press.

Boulanger, J. L. (Ed.). (2012). *Formal Methods: Industrial Use from Model to the Code*. London: ISTE – John Wiley & Sons.

Bowen, J. P., & Hinchey, M. G. (2006). Ten Commandments of Formal Methods ... Ten Years Later. *IEEE Computer, 39*(1), 40–48. doi:10.1109/MC.2006.35

Cerone, A., Roggenbach, M., & Schlingloff, H., Schneider, & G. Shaikh, S. (2013). Teaching Formal Methods for Software Engineering – Ten Principles. In *Proceedings of Fun With Formal Methods, Workshop affiliated with the 25th Int. Conf. on Computer Aided Verification*. Saint Petersburg: Academic Press.

Cristiá, M. (2006). Teaching formal methods in a third world country: what, why and how. In *Proceedings of the conference on Teaching Formal Methods 2006*. London: BCS London Office.

Crocker, D. (2004). Safe Object-Oriented Software: The Verified Design-By-Contract Paradigm In *Proceedings of the Twelfth Safety-critical Systems Symposium* (pp. 19-41) London: Springer-Verlag.

Dijkstra, E. W. (1976). *A Discipline of Programming*. Englewood Cliffs, NJ: Prentice Hall.

Feinerer, I., & Gernot, S. (2009). Comparison of tools for teaching formal software verification. *Formal Aspects of Computing, 21*(3), 293–301. doi:10.1007/s00165-008-0084-5

Fitzgerald, J., Bicarregui, J., Larsen, P. G., & Woodcock, J. (2013). Industrial Deployment of Formal Methods: Trends and Challenges. In A. Romanovsky & M. Thomas (Eds.), *Industrial Deployment of System Engineering Methods* (pp. 123–143). Berlin: Springer-Verlag. doi:10.1007/978-3-642-33170-1_10

Fitzgerald, J., Larsen, P. G., Mukherjee, P., Plat, N., & Verhoef, M. (2005). *Validated Designs for Object-oriented Systems*. New York: Springer.

Harrison, J. (2008). *Theorem Proving for Verification. Computer Aided Verification, LNCS* (Vol. 5123, pp. 11–18). Berlin: Springer-Verlag. doi:10.1007/978-3-540-70545-1_4

Korečko, Š., & Dancák, M. (2011). Some Aspects of BKPI B Language Compiler Design. *Egyptian Computer Science Journal, 35*(3), 33–43.

Korečko, Š., Sorád, J., & Sobota, B. (2011). An External Control for Railway Traffic Simulation, In *Proceedings of the Second International Conference on Computer Modelling and Simulation* (pp. 68-75). Brno University of Technology.

Ladenberger, L., Bendisposto, J., & Leuschel, M. (2009). Visualising Event-B Models with B-Motion Studio *Proceedings of Formal Methods for Industrial Critical Systems, 5825*, 202–204. doi:10.1007/978-3-642-04570-7_17

Larsen, P. G., Fitzgerald, J., & Riddle, S. (2009). Practice-oriented courses in formal methods using VDM++. *Formal Aspects of Computing, 21*(3), 245–257. doi:10.1007/s00165-008-0068-5

Le Lann, G. (1997). An Analysis of the Ariane 5 Flight 501 Failure - A System Engineering Perspective. In *Proceedings of the 1997 International Workshop on Engineering of Computer-Based Systems*. IEEE. doi:10.1109/ECBS.1997.581900

Lecomte, T. (2009). Applying a Formal Method in Industry: A 15-Year Trajectory. *Proceedings of Formal Methods for Industrial Critical Systems, 5825,* 26–34. doi:10.1007/978-3-642-04570-7_3

Lecomte, T., Servat, T., & Pouzancre, G. (2007). Formal Methods in Safety-Critical Railway Systems. In *Proceedings of 10th Brasilian Symposium on Formal Methods*. Ouro Preto.

Leuschel, M., & Butler, M. (2003). ProB: A model checker for B. In *Proceedings of FME 2003: Formal Methods,* (LNCS), (vol. 2805, pp. 855–874). Berlin: Springer-Verlag. doi:10.1007/978-3-540-45236-2_46

Liu, S., Takahashi, K., Hayashi, T., & Nakayama, T. (2009). Teaching Formal Methods in the context of Software Engineering. *ACM SIGCSE Bulletin, 41*(2), 17–23. doi:10.1145/1595453.1595457

Reed, J. N., & Sinclair, J. E. (2004). Motivating study of Formal Methods in the classroom. In C. N. Dean & R. T. Boute (Eds.), *TFM 2004 (LNCS),* (Vol. 3294, pp. 32–46). Berlin: Springer-Verlag. doi:10.1007/978-3-540-30472-2_3

Silva, J. L., Ribeiro, Ó. R., Fernandes, J. M., Campos, J. C., & Harrison, M. D. (2010). The APEX Framework: Prototyping of Ubiquitous Environments Based on Petri Nets. In *Human-Centred Software Engineering (LNCS),* (Vol. 6409, pp. 6–21). Berlin: Springer-Verlag. doi:10.1007/978-3-642-16488-0_2

Voisinet, J. C., Tatibouet, B., & Hammad, A. (2002). jBTools: An experimental platform for the formal B method. *Proceedings of PPPJ, 2,* 137–140.

Woodcock, J., Larsen, P. G., Bicarregui, J., & Fitzgerald, J. (2009). Formal methods: Practice and experience. *ACM Computing Surveys, 41*(4), 19:1-19:36.

ADDITIONAL READING

Berger, F., & Muller, W. (2012). Towards an Open Source Game Engine for Teaching and Research. In *Transactions on Edutainment VIII, LNCS* (Vol. 7220, pp. 68–76). Berlin, Heidelberg: Springer-Verlag. doi:10.1007/978-3-642-31439-1_7

Bicarregui, J., Hoare, C. A. R., & Woodcock, J. (2006, June). The verified software repository: A step towards the verifying compiler. *Formal Aspects of Computing, 18*(2), 143–151. doi:10.1007/s00165-005-0079-4

Bjorner, D. (2001). On teaching software engineering based on formal techniques - thoughts about and plans for - a different software engineering text book. *Journal of Universal Computer Science, 7*(8), 641–667.

Boerger, E. (2003). Teaching ASMs to practice-oriented students with limited mathematical background. [Oxford Brookes University.]. *Proceedings of Teaching Formal Methods, 2003,* 5–12.

Brakman, H., Driessen, V., Kavuma, J., Bijvank, L. N., & Vermolen, S. (2006). Supporting Formal Method Teaching with Real-Life Protocols. In *Formal Methods in the Teaching Lab – A Workshop at the Formal Methods 2006 Symposium* (pp. 59–67).

Burgess, C. J. (1995). *The role of Formal Methods in Software Engineering education and industry.* UK: University of Bristol.

Cai, Y., & Goei, S. L. (Eds.). (2014). *Simulations, Serious Games and Their Applications.* Springer Science+Business Media Singapore. doi:10.1007/978-981-4560-32-0_1

Catano, N., & Rueda, C. (2009). Teaching Formal Methods for the Unconquered Territory. In *Proceedings of Teaching Formal Methods 2009, LNCS* (Vol. 5846, pp. 2–19). Berlin, Heidelberg: Springer-Verlag. doi:10.1007/978-3-642-04912-5_2

Forišek, M., & Steinová, M. (2013). *Explaining Algorithms Using Metaphors.* Springer. doi:10.1007/978-1-4471-5019-0

Freitas, S., & Liarokapis, F. (2011). Serious Games: A New Paradigm for Education? In *Serious Games and Edutainment Applications.* London: Springer-Verlag. doi:10.1007/978-1-4471-2161-9_2

Gibson, J. P. (2008). Formal methods-never too young to start. In Z. Istenes (Ed.), *Proceedings of Formal Methods in Computer Science Education* (pp. 151–160). Budapest.

Gibson, J. P. (2008). Weaving a Formal Methods Education with Problem-Based Learning. In *Proceedings of the Third International Symposium ISoLA 2008, CCIS vol. 17* (pp. 460-472). Berlin – Heidelberg: Springer-Verlag. doi:10.1007/978-3-540-88479-8_32

Gibson, J. P., & Méry, D. (1998). Teaching formal methods: lessons to learn. In *Proceedings of the 2nd Irish conference on Formal Methods* (pp. 56-68).

Glass, R. L. (2004). The mystery of formal methods disuse. *Communications of the ACM, 47*(8), 15–17. doi:10.1145/1012037.1012052

Heitmeyer, C. (1998). On the need for practical Formal Methods. In *Formal Techniques in Real-Time and Fault-Tolerant Systems, LNCS* (Vol. 1486, pp. 18–26). Berlin, Heidelberg: Springer-Verlag. doi:10.1007/BFb0055332

Ishikawa, F., Taguchi, T., Yoshioka, N., & Honiden, S. (2009). What Top-Level Software Engineers Tackle after Learning Formal Methods: Experiences from the Top SE Project. In *Proceedings of Teaching Formal Methods 2009, LNCS* (Vol. 5846, pp. 57–71). Berlin, Heidelberg: Springer-Verlag. doi:10.1007/978-3-642-04912-5_5

Jaspan, C., Keeling, M., Maccherone, L., Zenarosa, G. L., & Shaw, M. (2009). Software Mythbusters Explore Formal Methods. *IEEE Software*, *26*(6), 60–63. doi:10.1109/MS.2009.188

Malan, D., & Leitner, H. (2007). Scratch for budding computer scientists. *ACM SIGCSE Bulletin*, *39*(1), 223–227. doi:10.1145/1227504.1227388

Moller, F., & O'Reilly, L. Formal Methods for First Years. In *Proceedings of Fun With Formal Methods, Workshop affiliated with the 25th Int. Conf. on Computer Aided Verification*. Saint Petersburg.

Morrison, B. B., & DiSalvo, B. (2014). Khan academy gamifies computer science. In *Proceedings of the 45th ACM technical symposium on Computer science education* (pp. 39-44). ACM. doi:10.1145/2538862.2538946

Race, P. (1998). Teaching: Creating a Thirst for learning? In S. Brown, S. Armstrong, & G. Thompson (Eds.), *Motivating Students* (pp. 47–57). London: Kogan Page.

Spies, K., & Schatz, B. (2006). A Playful Approach to Formal Models — A field report on teaching modeling fundamentals at middle school. In *Formal Methods in the Teaching Lab – A Workshop at the Formal Methods 2006 Symposium* (pp. 45–52).

Trow, M. (1973). *Problems in the Transition from Elite to Mass Higher Education*. Berkeley, California: Carnegie Commission on Higher Education.

Whitton, N. (2010). *Learning with Digital Games. A Practical Guide to Engaging Students in Higher Education*. New York: Routledge.

Woolsey, K. (2008). Where is the New Learning. In R. N. Katz (Ed.), *The Tower and the Cloud: Higher Education in the Age of Cloud Computing* (pp. 212–218). Educase.

KEY TERMS AND DEFINITIONS

Control Module: A program controlling some device or devices (e.g. signals and switches in a track layout). It is a reactive system, that is it reacts to external events such as requests from trains (definition specific to this chapter).

Formal Language: A language with unambiguously defined syntax and semantics. The semantics is defined using some mathematical apparatus.

Formal Method: Mathematically based technique for specification, analysis, development and verification of computer systems. Consists of a formal language and procedures that allow to perform desired tasks with specifications written in the language.

Formal Specification: A description of a (hardware or software) system in a formal language.

Formal Verification: A process of using some mathematical apparatus to prove that a system has corresponding formally specified properties.

Railway Scenario: A scenario for a railway simulation game, consisting of a track layout and a schedule for trains that operate on the layout (definition specific to this chapter).

Refinement: A transformation from an abstract specification of a system to a concrete, executable one.

Track Device: A signal, a switch or a track section in a track layout (definition specific to this chapter).

Chapter 7
An Effective Way to Teach Language Processing Courses

Maria João Varanda Pereira
Instituto Politécnico de Bragança, Portugal

Nuno Oliveira
Universidade do Minho, Portugal

Daniela da Cruz
Universidade do Minho, Portugal

Pedro Rangel Henriques
Universidade do Minho, Portugal

ABSTRACT

All of us that teach Language Processing topics are aware that a great part of the students face big difficulties and a lack of motivation inherent to the concept abstraction level and to the technical capacities required to implement efficient processors. In order to overcome this problem, a starting point is to identify the main concepts involved in Language Processing subject and to consider that a person learns when he/she is involved in a process. The authors argue that motivation is a crucial factor to engage students in the course work, and it is highly dependent on the languages used to work on during the course. Therefore, they discuss the characteristics that a language should have to be a motivating case study. The authors think that LP teachers should be very careful in their choices and be astute in the way they explore the underlying grammars along the course evolution.

1. INTRODUCTION

Learning was, is and will be difficult. The student has to interpret and understand the information he got, and then he has to assimilate the new information merging it with his previous knowledge to generate new knowledge.

However teaching is becoming more and more difficult as new student generations are no more prepared to absorb information during traditional classes.

Both statements are true in general, but they are particularly significant in domains that require a high capability for abstraction and for method-

DOI: 10.4018/978-1-4666-7304-5.ch007

ological analysis and synthesis. This is the case of Computer Science (CS), in general, and of Language Processing (LP) in particular.

As we will show in the sequel, many other authors, researching and teaching in LP domain, have recognized the difficulties faced by both students and teachers. To overcome these difficulties, which frequently lead to the failure and dissatisfaction of all the participants in the learning activity, and keeping in mind that higher education should focus on improving students' problem solving and communication skills, three main approaches can be identified:

- Exploring different teaching methodologies;
- Choosing motivating and adequate languages to illustrate concepts and to create project proposals;
- Resorting to specific tools tailored to support the development of grammars and language processors in classroom context.

As previously introduced in (Varanda Pereira, Oliveira, Cruz, & Henriques, 2013), our focus is the second approach. Considering that *a person just learns when he is involved in a process*, we argue that motivation is a crucial factor to engage students in the course work allowing them to achieve the required knowledge acquisition. In this chapter, we show that motivation is highly dependent on the languages used to work on during the course. We will discuss the characteristics that a language should have to be a motivating case study. LP teachers should choose carefully the sample languages used to explore the underlying grammars along the knowledge transfer process.

Li (2006) states that most topics in a compiler course are quite theoretical and the algorithms covered are more complex than those in other courses. Usually the course content contributes to the lack of student's motivation, giving rise to the student's fail and to the teacher frustration. To improve teaching and learning, there are some effective approaches such as *concept map-*

ping, *problem solving*, *problem-based learning*, *case studies*, *workshop tutorials* and *eLearning*. In particular Problem-based Learning enables students to establish a relation between abstract knowledge and real problems in their learning. It can increase their interest in the course, their motivation to learn science, make them more active in learning, and improve their problem solving skills and lifelong learning skills. Problem-based Learning is a student-centered teaching approach; however, it was shown (Li, 2006) that the approach gets better results when enrolling students that are not at the first year.

Project-based Learning is another relevant approach to teach compilers. Although similar, Project-based and Problem-based Learning are distinct approaches. In Problem based, the teacher prepares and proposes specific problems (usually focused in a specific course topic, and smaller in size and complexity than a project) and the students work on each one, over a given period of time, to find solutions to the problems; after that, the teacher provides feedback to the students. In Project-based Learning the students, more than solve a specific problem, have to control completely the project; usually the project covers more than one topic and run over a larger period of time.

Islam and Khan (2005) also agree with the complexity of the compiler course and consequently with the students difficulties in this subject. They propose an approach based on templates. Since the automatic construction of compilers is a systematic process, the main idea is to give students templates to produce compilers. The students just have to fill the parts necessary to implement the syntax and the semantics of the language.

Some other authors deal with the problem choosing carefully the language they use for the illustration of concepts or for exercises/projects, as we describe below.

Henry has published a paper (Henry, 2005) about the use of Domain Specific Languages for teaching compilers. He says that building a compiler for a domain specific language can engage students more than traditional compiler course projects. In this chapter we uphold and recommend a similar idea. In the cited paper, Henry proposes the use of a new programming language GPL (Game Programming Language). GPL and the tools provided can be used to create exercises or projects that keep the students motivated because they can define, compile and test video games.

Years ago, Aiken introduced in (Aiken, 1996) the Cool Project that was based in an academic programming language used to teach compiler construction topics. Cool (Classroom Object-Oriented Language) is the name for both a small programming language and its processor. Two years later, a language called Jason (Just Another Simple Original Notation) was created by Siegfried (1998). It is a small language based in ALGOL that is used just for academic purposes. Although small, it contains all the important concepts of procedural programming languages that allow the students to extrapolate how to design larger-scale compilers.

Adams and Trefftz (2004) propose the use of XML to teach compiler principles. They argue that XML processing or Programming Language processing are quite similar tasks, and that a compiler course can be a good place in a Computer Science curriculum to introduce at the same time the main concepts associated to both domains. According to that proposal, the students develop their own grammar and test their project using the tool XMLlint. The authors also describe their experience following that approach.

Some other authors, for instance Mernik and Demaille, handle the problem resorting to adequate supporting tools. For that purpose, some compiler construction tools were developed to be used in classrooms.

In this trend, one of the most significant examples is the work of Mernik and Zummer (2003) on LISA system. Using LISA it is possible to use a friendly interface to process Attribute Grammars and generate Compilers (lexical, syntactic and semantic components can be exercised solely or in a whole); useful visualizations are available for each compiler development/execution phase. These visualizations are the key point of LISA; they help students to understand easily the process or the internal structures involved in each phase.

VisualLISA, (Oliveira, Henriques, Cruz, & Varanda Pereira, 2009; Oliveira et al., 2010), is a visual interface for LISA, as depicted in Figure 1. Users can pick up, from the left-hand side dock (see Figure 1), grammar icons and build up attributed productions with the associated evaluation rules and contextual conditions. To assure legibility and cope with scalability, the visual environment is completely modular and production oriented---this is, each window corresponds to a production (grammar derivation rule), and more than one production window can be created to allow for the separate definition of different attribute evaluation rules. VisualLISA is strongly recommended to be used in the context of Language Processing Courses due to the natural way an attribute grammar can be *drawn* after it is imagined. After drawing a new grammar, VisualLISA editor generates a readable textual LISA description, for further processing, and also generates an intermediate XML representation (called XAGRA) also very easy to read and understand. For more details, please look at http://www3.di.uminho.pt/~gepl/VisualLISA/.

Other example of this tool-based teaching approach can be seen in (Demaille, Levillain, & Perrot, 2008), where the authors introduce a complete compiler project based on Andrew Apple's Tiger language and on his famous book Modern Compiler Implementation (Apple, & Ginsburg, 2004; Apple, & Palsberg, 2002). They augmented Tiger language and chose C++ as the implementation language. Considering a compiler as a long pipe composed of several modules, the project is divided in several steps, and students are requested to implement one or two modules. In particular the authors have invested efforts in tools to help students develop and improve their compiler.

Figure 1. VisualLISA editor

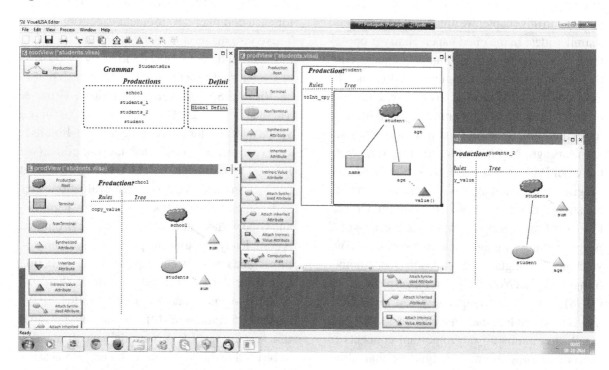

Barrón-Estrada, Cabada, Cabada and García (2010) combine theoretical and practical topics of the course using diverse modern technologies such as mobile learning, web-based learning as well as adaptive or intelligent learning. They develop a software tool that allows to create learning material for the compiler course to be executed in different learning environments.

Our proposal differs from the others in the sense that we do not create a special language to support our teaching activities. Instead we systematize how to take profit of the toy languages chosen to introduce different topics and evolve from a concept to the next concept in a smooth and challenging way in order to keep students interested and engaged.

The chapter will be organized as follows. Section 2 presents a Concept Map that describes the main topics that should be taught in an introductory Language Processing course, and identifies the requirements that a student must satisfy for achieving the course goals. As a consequence, Section

3 discusses the difficulties felt by students when attending a LP course. Then Section 4 introduces our proposal to overcome the difficulties, and defines the characteristics of an adequate language that is, on one hand, motivating, and, on the other hand, that enables to progress incrementally the teaching activity. To illustrate our proposal, in Section 5 we introduce five case studies that will allow us to discuss teaching matters from lexical to syntactic and semantic concerns. The paper ends in Section 6 with a synthesis of our contribution.

2. BUILDING A LP COURSE

In this section we define the subjects that should be taught in an introductory, one semester, Language Processing course (also called many times, a Compiler course) that is supposed to appear in the second or third year of a university degree on Computer Science or Software Engineering.

Before identifying the concepts that should be introduced by the teacher and understood by the apprentices, it is mandatory to define the learning objectives.

Learning Objectives

At the end of the course unit the student is expected to be able to work with techniques and tools for formal specification of programming languages and automatic construction of language processors.

More than that, the student should understand the language processing tasks—the main approaches and strategies available for language analysis and translation—as well as the associated algorithms and data structures.

Course Contents

Now we can list the main topics that must be included in the contents of any LP course:

- **Languages and Programming Languages:** Concept, formal definition, syntax versus semantics, general purpose (GPL) versus domain specific languages (DSL); examples; Language Design.
- **Formal Specification of Languages using Regular Expressions (RE).**
- **Formal Specification of Languages using Grammars (Gr):** Symbols or tokens of an alphabet, derivation rule or production, derivation tree, abstract syntax tree, contextual condition, attribute evaluation, etc...
- **Language Processors:** Objectives, requirements and tasks; automatic generation tools (*Lexer*, *Parser* and *Compiler Generators*).
- **Lexical Analysis using Regular Expressions and Reactive Automata:** Dealing with symbols (names and values).
- **Syntactic Analysis using Context-Free Grammars (CFG) and Parsers:**

  ○ Top-Down Parsing, TD (Recursive-Descendant, and LL(1));
  ○ Bottom-Up Parsing, BU (LR(0), LR(1), SLR(1), LALR(1)).
- **Semantic Analysis using Translation Grammars (TG) and Syntax Directed Translation (SDT):** Evaluating and sharing symbol-values, static semantic validation, and code generation using hash-tables and other global variables.
- **Semantic Analysis using Attribute Grammars (AG) and Semantic Directed Translation (SemDT):** Attribute evaluation, static semantic validation, and code generation using Abstract Syntax Trees and Tree Traversals.

Part of these topics—those concerned with languages, grammars, and processing approaches—is more theoretical and will be introduced resorting to formal definitions and algorithms, while the other part—concerned with the implementation of language processors and their automatic generation— is more practical and can be supported by the development of exercises and projects, either manually from the scratch or resorting to tools.

Examples of problems that can be the subject of the above mentioned projects are: text filters; compiler for small or medium size programming languages; or translators for domain specific languages.

Topics to Learn in an LP Course: A Concept Map

From the course content, presented above, we can infer the main concepts that characterize that area (knowledge domain):

PL: Programming Language
GPL: General Purpose Language
DSL: Domain Specific Languages
RE: Regular Expression
Gr: Grammar; Terminal and Non-Terminal Symbols, Start-symbol, Productions

Figure 2. A concept map describing the LP knowledge domain

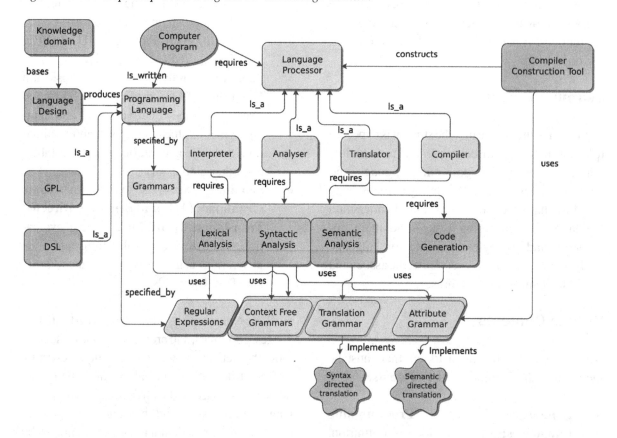

CFG: Context Free Grammar

TG: Translation Grammar

AG: Attribute Grammar.

LA: Lexical Analysis

SynA: Syntactic Analysis (or Parsing))

SemA: Semantic Analysis

CG: Code Generation

SDT: Syntax Directed Translation;

SemDT: Semantic Directed Translation

LP: Language Processor; Interpreter, Analyzer, Compiler, Translator

LPG: Language Processor Generator or CG – Compiler Generator.

To formalize that knowledge (whose items were listed above), that a student is supposed to acquire in order to achieve the course objectives, we built a Concept Map, or an ontology, describing the *Language Processing Domain*, as shown in

Student Skills Required to Learn LP

From the Concept Map introduced in the previous subsection, we can identify the minimum programming skills that a student should have to understand the basic definitions and learn the topics involved in a Language Processing course. They are

- Knowledge about the basics of computer programming, at least in a imperative (procedural) programming language;
- Knowledge about the basic iterative and recursive algorithms;
- Knowledge about standard data structures (properties and operations) like *lists, sets, trees, graphs, tables (matrix)* and *hash-tables*.

3. DIFFICULTIES FACED BY STUDENTS

When we deal with first year students attending introductory programming courses we know that we need several months to teach a programming language like C, C++ or Java. This happens because students have usually difficulties to interpret the problem statement, to analyze it, to translate what they want to do into an algorithm or a sequence of basic commands or operations. Besides the high level of abstraction required by those tasks, another difficulty arise from the fact that there are several ways to describe the same task in an algorithmic or programming language and the beginner needs to choose the more convenient one. Moreover, to code an algorithm, the student must pay careful attention to all lexical, syntactic and semantic details of the programming language. There are a high amount of functions and methods spread out along a big set libraries or classes that they have to use in an appropriate way. Moreover the students have usually lots of difficulties in algorithm understanding and they cannot see clearly the relation between the problem and the implementation of the program that is supposed to solve it. There are also data structures that are complex to define and to use.

These are the skills that are at least required for following successfully a Language Processing (LP) course.

As remembered before, in LP courses the objective is to teach language/grammar theory and principles as well as compiler construction techniques. For that, we must focus in presenting lexical, syntactic and semantic techniques. These techniques are complex and the students must understand the abstract concepts involved in the problem domain and be able to map them into the program domain concepts. In practice we have observed that students have difficulties in defining regular expressions since they have a strong expressive power using short specifications. Also the next steps are not easy. *Parsing* or *attribute*

evaluation algorithms, *bottom-up* and *top-down processes* are subjects difficult to teach and difficult to understand.

There are lots of students that, when faced with such difficulties, give up. As students are not motivated---due to the fact that the application field is not interesting for most of them---they do not go deeply on studding and discontinue the course work.

4. OVERCOMING THE DIFFICULTIES: LANGUAGES TO SUPPORT LEARNING

We have identified the main concepts that must be taught in a Language Processing course (LPc), and the competences or abilities required to assure students success in such a course. We also identified the common struggles faced by LP learners.

In this section we introduce our proposal to overcome the negative factors that lead apprentices to fail.

We assume that the permanent search for new pedagogical methods and techniques, that can be used alone or combined with traditional approaches, is a duty of every teacher in the context of any course. Problem-based learning or Project-based learning are two examples, discussed in section 1.1, of new methods introduced to improve the students' engagement. Also the resort to eLearning instruments, like forums or collaborative work platforms, is another example of that principle.

Our group also advocates the use of Automatic Grading Systems (AGS). The authors are, for some years, deeply involved in the development of an AGS (Quimera), as can be seen in (Fonte et al., 2012, 2013, 2014). AGS in the context of the teaching/learning process are two fold tools. On one hand, they support teachers assessing in an effective and fair way students belonging to big classes where problem- or project-based learning was adopted; on the other hand, they stimulate students to proceed on, as they provide detailed and immediate feedback (after the completion of a given exercise).

We also recognize the relevant role of didactic tools to support LP teaching/learning as mentioned in the Introduction. *Grammar Editors, Compiler Generators, Visualizers and Animators* (that enable to follow the generation or compilation processes) are important examples of tools that shall be adopted to ease the students' task and to help them in understanding the basic concepts.

However our goal is to devise a strategy to improve students' motivation as the safest way to get them involved in the course activities helping them to learn with success LP concepts, methods, techniques and tools. With that in mind, we advocate the use of specially tailored languages that will be employed: (i) to illustrate concepts introduced in theoretical classes; (ii) to create exercises to solve in practical classes; and (iii) to elaborate project proposals for student's homework.

Based on many years of teaching experience, we believe that this is the most effective approach to overcome the mentioned difficulties, ending up with high ratio students-approved/attendants. In the last ten or fifteen years, considering medium sized classes with an average number of 150 students, we measured that around 50% of the attendants are assessed (this is, 50% of the class students complete all the assessment duties) and that around 90% of them are approved.

On one hand, we argue that those languages shall be small and simple. Small is measured in terms of the underlying grammar; a language is said small if the number of non-terminal and terminal symbols is small, as well as the number of grammar productions (or derivation rules). Simple is a twofold characteristic: the objects described by the language shall not be sophisticated and must be familiar for most of the students; and the tasks involved in the required processing shall be natural and not too complex for understanding or implementing. More than that, we believe that those languages shall possess an incremental character. This is, it shall be possible and straightforward to extend gradually the core language (the language initially proposed) in order to cover more objects in the language domain, or to add requirements concerning the processor output.

On the other hand, we argue that the chosen support languages shall be defined over special domains, instead of being programming languages. Usually domain specific languages use keywords (literal terminals) that are strongly related with domain concepts which makes easier the relation between program and problem domains. These domains must be instinctive for the apprentices; this is, well defined and closed to their common knowledge. In such context, the programs that students are supposed to develop, instead of being traditional compilers, will be *translators*—that, for a given input text, produce an output text in a different language—or *generic processors*—that extract data from the source text and compute information to be outputted.

Summing up, we propose the choice of appealing, small and simple Domain Specific Languages (DSLs), by opposition to the recourse of General Purpose programming Languages (GPLs).

The main idea is to start explaining a specific domain and then use a DSL already created or create a new one. The advantage of this approach is based on the fact that everyone knows what kind of things will be expressed by the program written with this DSL and the teacher can concentrate his efforts in explaining how to specify the language using a grammar or how to build a language processor using a compiler construction tool. The students can train the specification of lexical and syntactic parts and they have no problem to understand the semantic rules they have to define because the map between the program and the problem domain is more intuitive. The teachers can tune each DSL example in order to include more or less complexity depending on the course objectives. They can incrementally add features to the new language and show how to overcome each difficulty.

The approach here recommended consists in choosing one friendly domain and a simple processing task and then write the grammar for the intended DSL and develop the respective processor. This step will cover the basic lexical, syntactic and semantic concepts. To teach more complex concepts or methods, or to discuss alternative strategies and techniques, the grammar shall evolve covering more domain components or performing more processing tasks. After this stage, other similar and equivalent DSLs shall be used to reinforce all the ideas so far presented.

Concerning project proposals, it is crucial that the language domain is attractive for the students and the project statement is opened enough to give room for their creativity, regarding both the language definition and the processing requirements.

5. ILLUSTRATING THE PROPOSAL: EXAMPLES

In this section we present some language examples to instantiate the approach proposed in the previous section. The examples introduce similar languages than can be used as alternatives to teach grammars (definition and variants, lexical and syntactic issues, static and dynamic semantic aspects of language processing).

Any of these languages are appropriate for an incremental approach enabling the teacher to start with a short and simple problem statement. Then at a first stage, the teacher can ask the students to write the grammar (CFG and RE for terminals) and build by hand some derivation trees. Then he can elaborate the statement covering more concepts in problem domain in order to extend the grammar. After dealing with the basic lexical and syntactic topics, the teacher can enrich the problem statement adding now some requirements for the desired output leading to the introduction of semantic actions, writing the correspondent translation grammar (or, if it is the course objective, to the introduction of attributes, evaluation and translation rules and the correspondent attribute grammar). The requirements can be

successively incremented with semantic constraints to introduce validation in semantic actions and error handling (or to introduce contextual conditions in attribute grammars).

These steps shall be complemented with practical exercises supported by generating tools.

1st Example: Book Index

The first example is concerned with book indexes. The main idea is to define a book title and for each page a set of topics that can be found in that page. So, the concepts involved in this domain are: book, page, title and special term (topic).

Writing grammars according to the domain description requires that the domain concepts and the relations between such concepts are well understood. A good starting exercise is to outline an ontology (a conceptual map) where the relations between the several domain concepts are expressed. Notice that this approach is feasible due to the domain size and consequently, this happens because the domain is a specific one. Once the domain is studied and internalized, writing the grammar is much about giving a concrete shape to the relations among the domain concepts. This shape defines the syntax of the language.

The graph shown in Figure 3 defines the ontology for this case-study.

For each book, a title and one or more pages can be specified; and for each page one or more topics can be associated. The concrete context free grammar is shown in Listing 1.

The grammar allows for specifying the syntax of the language. The source program written in this language is divided in two parts: a header and a body (Lines). The header has a reserved word (INDEX) and the title of the book. The body is composed of one or more lines and each line defines the set of topics for one page. The page is defined as a number and a topic is defined as a String. A sentence of the grammar is expressed below to show a concrete and correct source text as seen in Listing 2.

Figure 3. Book index ontology

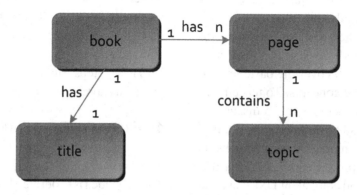

Listing 1.

```
p1:       Book     →  Head Lines '.'
p2:       Head     →  INDEX Title
p3:       Title    →  String
p4,p5:    Lines    →  Line | Lines ';' Line
p5:       Line     →  Page '=' Topics
p6:       Page     →  num
p7,p8:    Topics   →  Topic |Topics ',' Topic
p9:       Topic    →  String
```

Listing 2.

```
INDEX "Sample Book 1"
1 = t1,t2,t3;
2 = t1,t4,t2,t5;
3 = t4,t3,t2,t6.
```

Although the grammar is very simple this exercise allows for proposing different tasks to the students that are not so simple. Some examples of output requirements that can be formulated in this context are:

- 1st level tasks (use only atomic global variables, no need to store intermediate values, and simple semantic actions):
  - Compute the total number of pages
  - Compute the total number of different terms (or topics)

- 2nd level tasks (require intermediate and complex data structures and more elaborated semantic actions):
  - Verify that there are not repeated pages
- 3rd level tasks (require still more complex data structures to store intermediate values and more sophisticated semantic actions):
- Generate an output with the desired Book Index following the structure in Listing 3:

To perform these tasks the student need to associate appropriated semantic actions to each

Listing 3.

```
Index
t1: 1, 2.
t2: 1, 2, 3.
t3: 1, 3.
t4: 2, 3.
```

grammar production in order to update the counters (1st level tasks), to directly produce an output (1st level tasks) or to save the information in an intermediate structure. Working over that structure it is possible to count distinct topics (2nd level tasks) and to produce an output that shows the information in a different order and format (the Index produced in the 3rd level task).

2nd Example Shopping List

The second example is also a very simple one that has a short statement and small domain, but that exhibits some complexity typical of *list languages* like the programming language Lisp. It is also a common sense domain that does not require a long explanation but that is prone to involve the students.

Consider that someone wants a very simple language to describe his/her shopping list, which can be composed of one item, or more items. Items have just a product name and they can appear isolated or grouped. Each group represents a sublist of products that belong to the same category.

This domain can be described by the ontology depicted in Figure 4.

Notice that the idea is to create sub-lists of items inside the global shopping list but each such sub-list follows exactly the same syntax of a shopping list.

The concrete context free grammar that derives from the description above is the shown in Listing 4:

This grammar is strongly recursive and must be carefully explained to the students. One of the best ways to do this is to present a valid sentence of the grammar and ask the students to construct

Figure 4. Shopping list onntology

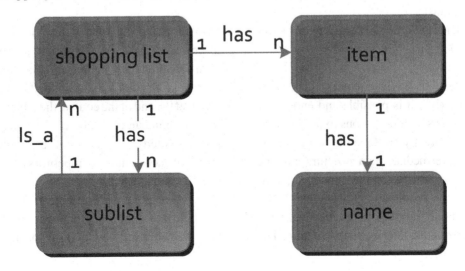

Listing 4.

```
p1,p2:    ShoppingList    → Item | '(' SubList ')'
p3:       SubList         → ShoppingList OtherS
p4,p5:    OtherS          → | ',' SubList
p6:       Item            → Name
p7:       Name            → String
```

Listing 5.

```
(rice, (wine, beer, water), paper, (showergel, soap))
```

the derivation tree. In this case, it must be clear that the grammar allows to specify lists composed of items or lists separated by ','. Each item has a name that is a `String`.

A sentence of the grammar is expressed below to show a concrete and correct source text in Listing 5:

Some examples of output requirements that can be formulated in this context are:

- 1st level tasks:
  - ○ Compute the total number of items
  - ○ Compute the maximum list length
- 2nd level tasks:
  - ○ Verify that there are no repeated items
- 3rd level tasks:
  - ○ Generate a dot file to draw a hierarchical structure of items

In the 1st level tasks, the counters can be computed "on the fly"; it is possible and enough to associate simple semantic actions to productions p2 and p6 to directly produce the result. In the 2nd level, an intermediate data structure must be filled during the parsing (by the semantic actions associated to the productions); at the end (after parsing the input file), the items repeated shall be removed from that intermediate structure. The

task at the 3rd level uses that intermediate structure to collect the information needed to generate the output file.

Notice that the three difficulty levels correspond, like in the previous example, to the complexity of the data structures and of the semantic actions that are required to produce the desired output. We believe that the successful achievement of the tasks in one level will motivate students to improve their code and proceed to the next phase, learning more about the construction of language processors.

3rd Example: Orienteering Paths Planner

Foot Orienteering is a widely developed sport in Portugal. Basically, an athlete receives a map with a marked path; in that path there are signaled control points that must be visited in the required order; at the end of the course, the athletes return to the start point and are scored according to control points visited and also according with the time spent. In each contest, competitors are divided by age classes; a different path is given to each age class (corresponding to different difficulty levels).

In order to help the organization of competition, we propose a new DSL to specify the list of

Figure 5. Orienteering paths planner ontology

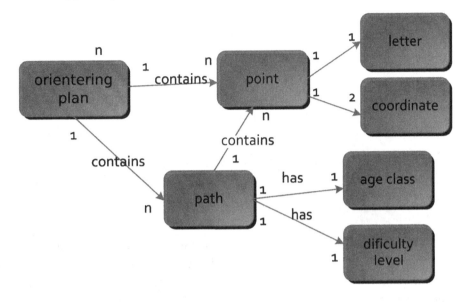

paths (each path will be, therefore, a list of control points), so that the distance can be calculated and the course be visualized. The domain for this problem is described by the ontology depicted in Figure 5.

The required language should start by identifying all the control points of a given area where the competition takes place. Each point will be identified with an acronym and its Cartesian coordinates.

Also, the language should enable us to define each path, indicating its difficulty level (soft, medium or hard), age class, and list of points (described by acronyms). The order in the list establishes the visiting order.

OPPL was the language created based on the domain defined above. Its concrete context free grammar is shown in Listing 6.

This grammar allows for clearly separating the point specifications from the path specifications. A list of (one or more) points and a list of (one or more) paths are the main parts of the grammar. Each point has a letter and a pair of numbers (that define its coordinates). Each path has a level (implemented as an enumerated variable), an age (represented as the *greater than* '>' character and

Listing 6.

```
p1:        OPPL    → POINTS Points PATHS Paths
p2,p3:     Points  → Point | Points Point
p4:        Point   → letter '(' num ',' num ')'
p5,p6:     Paths   → Path | Paths Path
p7:        Path    → Level Age '(' List ')'
p8:        Age     → '(' '>' num ')'
p9,p10:    List    → List ',' letter | letter
p11:       Level   → SOFT | MEDIUM | HARD
```

Listing 7.

```
POINTS
A(3,5)
B(4,2)
C(5,5)
D(9,9)
E(5,15)
PATHS
SOFT   (>10) (A,B,C)
MEDIUM (>20) (A,C,B,D)
HARD   (>20) (A,E,C,D,B)
```

a number) and a list of point identifiers (denoted as letters).

A sentence of the grammar is expressed below to show a concrete and correct source text (Listing 7).

Some examples of output requirements that can be formulated in this context:

- 1st level tasks (require simple global variables and simple semantic actions):
  ◦ Compute the total number of points
  ◦ Compute the total number of paths
  ◦ Compute the number of points in each path
- 2nd level tasks (concerning intermediate data structures, nothing special is needed but the semantic actions should be more elaborated):
  ◦ Compute the length of a path
- 3rd level tasks (as in the previous examples, these tasks require complex intermediate data structures to store the data collected from the input text in order to build the output code):
  ◦ Generate dot code to visualize the paths

This example allows the teacher to convince students how easy it is to solve an apparently complex (but really interesting) problem, when following its structural definition. This is, when adding the semantic actions to the appropriate syntactic rules.

In this case, both 1st and 2nd level tasks can be performed updating the counters and printing the results directly in each production. As happens with the other examples, the 3rd level task needs an intermediate structure; such structure allows for collecting the necessary information during parsing, which is then used to produce the output.

It is possible to add more productions to the grammar in order to cope with the athlete information. In this case new symbols must be created representing names, numbers, time spent, scores for each athlete, etc. More exercises can be proposed taking profit of this new information; so, new output results can be required, like athletes ranking, partial scores, historical results, and so on.

4th Example: Lavanda

Let's, then, introduce a domain to work with (and within). Informally, let's think of a big launderette company that has several distributed facilities (collecting points) and a central building where the launder is made. The workflow on this company is as follows: each collecting point is responsible of receiving laundry bags from several clients, sending them to the central building in a daily basis.

The bags are dispatched to the central building with an ordering note that identifies the collecting point, the date and describes the content of a set of bags.

Going deeply, each bag is identified by a unique identification number, and the name of the client owning it. The content of each bag is separated in one or more items. Each item is a quantified set of laundry of the same type, that is, with the same basic characteristics, for an easier distribution at washing time. The collecting point's workers should always typify the laundry according to a class, a kind of tinge and a raw-material. The class is either body cloth or household linen; the tinge is either white or colored and finally, the raw-material is one of cotton, wool or fiber.

Once in the central building, the ordering notes are processed for several reasons: enter the notes' information into a database, calculate the number of bags received, produce statistics about the type of cloth received, and define the value that each client must pay and so on. Doing such processing by hand is risky because humans are easily error-prone. Therefore, an automatic and systematic way of processing the information in the notes is desirable. A reasonable way of achieving this is to use the computer to do the job. In this context, the design of a computer language to describe the contents of an ordering note supported on a formal grammar is the way to go.

Lavanda is the Domain Specific Language defined in the context of the domain described rigorously by the ontology in Figure 6.

The main purpose for design this language is to develop a tool that automatically creates the ordering notes that the collecting points of the launderette company daily send to the central building.

The Context Free Grammar that formalizes the syntax of the language Lavanda, according to the ontology drawn, is shown in Listing 8.

This grammar represents the information concerned with one order. Each order is defined by a header and a set of bags. Each bag has a number, a client identification and a set of items. Each item is defined by a type and a quantity.

A valid sentence written according to that grammar is presented in Listing 9.

Some examples of output requirements that can be formulated in this context.

- 1st level tasks (once again this tasks can be solved using just atomic global variables and simple semantic actions):
  - Compute the total of bags in the order

Figure 6. Lavanda ontology

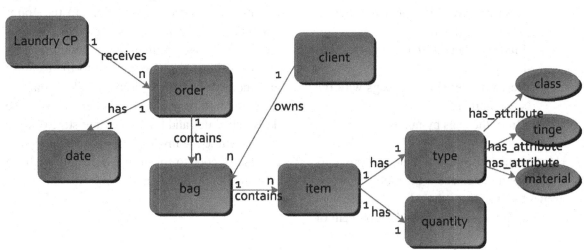

Listing 8.

```
p1:           Order       → Header Bags
p2:           Header      → DAY date CP IdCP
p3,p4:        Bags        → Bag | Bags ';' Bag
p5:           Bag         → BAG num CLI IdCli ':' '(' Items ')'
p6,p7:        Items       → Item | Items ',' Item
p8:           Item        → Type Quantity
p9:           Type        → Class '-' Tinge '-' Material
p10:          IdCP        → id
p11:          IdCli       → id
p12:          Quantity    → num
p13,14:       Class       → BODY | HOUSE
p15,16:       Tinge       → WHITE | COLOR
p17,18,19:    Material    → COTTON | WOOL | FIBER
```

Listing 9.

```
DAY 2013-03-20 CP Lidl
BAG 1 CLI ClientA:
(BODY-COLOR-COTTON 1, HOUSE-COLOR-COTTON 2)
BAG 2 CLI ClientB:
(BODY-WHITE-FIBRE 10)
```

- ◦ Compute the total of items in the class body clothes
- ◦ Compute the total of items delivered by each client
- 2nd level tasks (the tasks in this group require the use of complex data structures to store intermediate values and more complex semantic actions):
  - ◦ Find the client with the biggest number of white items
  - ◦ Verify if there are two bags with the same number
  - ◦ Order the bags by number

This example is longer than the previous ones and has a statement a bit more complex, but allows the teacher to show how a convenient structural definition enables the development of simple semantic actions to perform sophisticated transformations.

In this case, only two levels of tasks are proposed: a 1st level including tasks that are solved using direct translation and a 2nd level where the results must be computed after parsing. It is also possible to add more productions to the grammar in order to cope with some other concepts like prices, washing times and scheduling. This allows adding more complexity to the exercise and more tasks can be proposed like: compute the amount to be paid by each client, consult the daily scheduler and the processing state of each bag, generate the invoices for each client, generate HTML code to construct a Web page with the information involved, and so on.

5th Example: Genea

The last example shows how in a completely different domain (but still common sense one) we can define a language with characteristics similar to the previous examples. We believe that students can be engaged in the exercises proposed around this subject.

Let's, then, introduce another domain to work with (and within). A research organization devoted to demography and history has a complex application that constructs genealogical trees from simple specifications of families and offers a lot of statistics, computations and relation-based information.

Family records consist of the basic part of each family which is the parents and their children. As it is obvious, dates play an important role in history, therefore born, death and wedding dates are important in this domain.

All persons are identified with their first name, but only the parents (a father or a mother) have

their family names (as before marrying). Children hire their family name from the father. In contrast with the parents, children must have their gender defined.

Although small and very well defined, this domain is full of common-sense restrictions and relations that need to be respected. The most important ones concern chronological order, and age related issues.

Regarding this simple domain, described by the conceptual map (or ontology) shown in Figure 7, the researchers decided to build a language capable of specifying each family.

This conceptual map has a novelty concerned with the use of the relation 'is_a' between two concepts: `father is_a person`, `mother is_a person` and `child is_a person`. This taxonomic relation has some influence when deriving the grammar, as it will be shown below.

Genea was the language defined based on this domain. The concrete context free grammar is the

Figure 7. Genea ontology

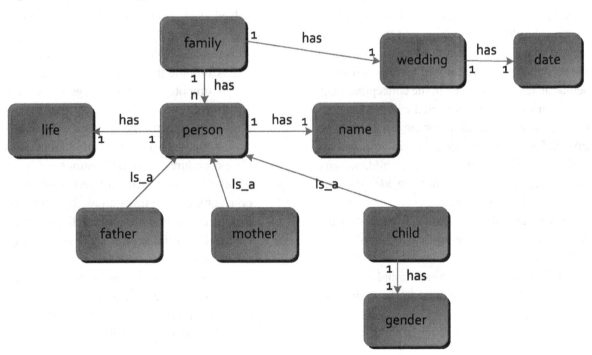

Listing 10.

```
p1:       Genea      → Families
p2,p3:    Families   → Family | Families ';' Family
p4:       Family     → Parents WED Wedding CHILDREN Children
p5:       Parents    → Parent Parent
p6:       Parent     → Type ':' Name Name Life
p7,p8:    Children   → & | Children Child
p9:       Child      → Gender Name Life
p10:      Life       → '(' Born '-' Death ')'
p11,12:   Type       → FATHER | MOTHER
p13,14:   Gender     → MALE | FEMALE
p15:      Born       → date
p16,17:   Death      → date | '?'
p18:      Wedding    → date
p19:      Name       → id
```

following (notice that the empty string symbol is denoted by &) (Listing 10).

This grammar doesn't strictly follow the conceptual map, because its final design depends on the actual context in which the language will be used and depends also on the inspiration of each designer. In the grammar it is possible to define exactly the number of parents (that should be necessarily 2). The restriction that one of the parents should be a father and the other one should be a mother was not taken into account in the syntactical level; it will be imposed at the semantic level. Moreover, in the conceptual map, name and life are associated with Person concept but in the grammar they were repeated in two productions, one that is concerned with parents and another that is concerned with child, because the concept Person was not considered useful as a symbol of the grammar.

A sentence of the grammar is expressed below to show a concrete and correct source text (Listing 11).

In the following list, some examples are presented of requests formulated in the context of this exercise.

- 1st level tasks (use only atomic variables and simple semantic actions):
  - Compute the number of children in each family, total and separated by gender
  - Compute the total of families in the description
- 2nd level tasks (these tasks can also be solved with atomic variables but require more elaborated semantic actions and the storage of intermediate values):
  - Compute the average age at death
  - Compute the mother's age at the first birth (average)
  - Concatenate the mother's surname with the father's surname so that children hire both family names
- 3rd level tasks (here the difference is mainly conceptual; these tasks allow the introduction of contextual conditions that must be checked to validate the semantics of the source text):
  - Verify for each family that the death date is greater than the birth date
  - verify for each family that the wedding date lies within the birth and

Listing 11.

```
FATHER: Herman Einstein (1847.08.30 - 1902.10.10)
MOTHER: Pauline Koch (1858.02.08 - 1920.02.20)
WED 1876.08.08
CHILDREN
MALE Albert (1879.03.14 - 1955.04.18)
FEMALE Maja (1881.11.18 - 1951.06.25) ;
FATHER: Albert Einstein (1879.03.14 - 1955.04.18)
MOTHER: Mileva Maric (1875.12.19 - 1948.08.04)
WED 1903.01.06
CHILDREN
MALE Hans (1904.5.14 - 1973.07.26)
MALE Eduard (1910.07.28 - 1965.10.25)
```

death interval with respect to both parents

- 4th level tasks (require more complex intermediate data structures to store the extracted data in order to produce the desired output code):
  - Generate dot specifications in order to visualize the family tree
  - Generate an SQL statement to insert each child in a database with all the respective info (including child's surname)

Lots of interesting exercises can be proposed in the context of this language. Four sets of tasks are presented here with an incremental level of complexity.

This example is appropriate to motivate students because on one hand it deals with common sense concepts, and on the other hand enables the generation of a real database from a high-level source description, validating the input data. It can also be easily extended with more syntactic rules and more semantic actions.

6. CONCLUSION

Teaching Language Processing courses (or Compilers) for more than twenty years, the authors have a solid knowledge about the topics that must be introduced, and they are aware of the difficulties such topics rise on the students. They also know well how these difficulties are in general heavy to be overcome due to the pupils' lack of motivation to study grammar theory or compiler classic subjects. Looking every year to improve the academic indicators (like the ratios *approved/ assessed* or *assessed/attendants*) of the teaching success associated to those courses, the authors found a way they are systematically following each year. They strongly believe that the approach introduced and discussed along this chapter---the choice and adoption of appropriate Domain Specific Languages to motivate apprentices---is promising.

The use of DSLs in teaching methodologies allows choosing a knowledge domain appropriated to the students. When students are aware of the domain, its main concepts and relations, it is much easier to explain and discuss the processing of a language in that domain. In this sense, the efforts made to explain a subject like language processing do not dependent any more on the complexity of GPL grammars.

The usual grammar size of DSLs is more appropriate for teaching when compared with GPLs. Smaller grammars allow the students to understand better the concepts involved. Moreover, Domain Specific Languages can be easily changed, adapted or incremented depending on the complexity of the example that the teacher desires to show and discuss with students.

Working within these small and common sense domains we can hope that the students quickly and easily guess the processing results expected for the given source text samples. This allows to easily test the language processor developed and decide whether it is well implemented or contains errors that must be fixed.

Our proposal differs from the others in the sense that we do not create a special language to support our teaching activities. Instead we present the characteristics that a language, and its grammar, should exhibit to be helpful. Besides that, we systematize how to take profit of the toy languages chosen to introduce different topics and evolve from a concept to the next concept, in a smooth and challenging way in order to keep students interested and engaged.

We have been applying this approach the last ten years at Universidade do Minho and Politécnico de Bragança. The results obtained are encouraging. The average percentage of successful students (when doing all practical exercises and the theoretical exam) is 85%. This means that students, who decide to attend the classes and do the practical exercises, become motivated and involved enough to also study the underlying theory, attaining the minimum requirements to be approved. Unfortunately if we consider the percentage of students who register in the course and those who actually do all the assessment work demanded, we obtain every year a smaller figure (around 60%). This, however, happens in all the other courses of the same academic year.

REFERENCES

Adams, D., & Trefftz, C. (2004). Using XML in a compiler course. *ACM SigCSE Bulletin*, 36(3), 4–6. doi:10.1145/1026487.1008001

Aiken, A. (1996). *Cool: A portable project for teaching compiler construction*. SigPLan.

Appel, A., & Ginsburg, M. (2004). *Modern Compiler Implementation in C*. Cambridge University Press.

Appel, A., & Palsberg, J. (2002). *Modern Compiler Implementation in Java*. Cambridge University Press. doi:10.1017/CBO9780511811432

Barrón-Estrada, M. Cabada, Ra., Cabada, Ro., & Garcia, C. (2010). A hybrid learning compiler course, Lecture Notes in Computer Science, 6248, 229–238.

Demaille, A., Levillain, R., & Perrot, B. (2008). A set of tools to teach compiler construction. *ACM SIGCSE*, 40(3), 68–72. doi:10.1145/1597849.1384291

Fonte, D., Cruz, D., Gançarski, A., & Henriques, P. (2013). A Flexible Dynamic System for Automatic Grading of Programming Exercises, OASIC. SLATE.2013 *Symposium on Languages, Applications and Technologies*, 29, 129-144.

Fonte, D., Vilas Boas, I., Oliveira, N., Cruz, D., Gançarski, A., & Henriques, P. (2014). Partial Correctness and Continuous Integration in Computer Supported Education. In *Proceedings of CSEdu'2014: 6th International Conference on Computer Supported Education*. CSEdu.

Fonte, D., Vilas Boas, I., Cruz, D., Gançarski, A., & Henriques, P. (2012). Program Analysis and Evaluation using Quimera. In *Proceedings of ICEIS'2012 --- 14th International Conference on Enterprise Information Systems*, (pp. 209-219). ICEIS.

Henry, T. (2005). Teaching compiler construction using a domain specific language. *ACM SIGCSE*, *37*(1), 7–11. doi:10.1145/1047124.1047364

Islam, Md., & Khan, M. (2005). *Teaching compiler development to undergraduates using a template based approach*. Center for research on Bangla language processing (CRBLP), Brac University.

Li, Z. (2006, November). Exploring effective approaches in teaching principles of compiler. *The China Papers*.

Mernik, M., & Zumer, V. (2003). An educational tool for teaching compiler construction. *IEEE Transactions on Education, 46*(1), 61–68. doi:10.1109/TE.2002.808277

Oliveira, N., Henriques, P., Cruz, D., & Varanda Pereira, M. (2009). VisualLISA: Visual Programming Environment for Attribute Grammars Specification. In *Proceedings of the International Multiconference on Computer Science and Information Technology -- 2nd Workshop on Advances in Programming Languages (WAPL'2009),* (pp. 689-696). WAPL.

Oliveira, N., Varanda Pereira, M., Henriques, P., Cruz, D., & Cramer, B. (2010). VisualLISA: A Visual Environment to Develop Attribute Grammars. *Related Technologies and Applications, 7*(2), 266–289.

Siegfried, R. (1998). The Jason programming language, an aid in teaching compiler construction. In *Proceedings of ESCCC-98*. ESCCC.

Varanda Pereira, M., Oliveira, N., Cruz, D., & Henriques, P. (2013). Choosing Grammars to support Language Processing Course, OASIcs. SLATE.2013 *Symposium on Languages, Applications and Technologies, 29,* 155-169.

KEY TERMS AND DEFINITIONS

CFG (Context Free Grammar): Is a grammar that only defines the syntax of a language. A CFG is a four tuple composed of a set of Terminal symbols (T) that belong to the language Vocabulary, a set of Non-terminal symbols (N) that are abstractions of sub-sentences with special meaning, a set of Derivation Rules or grammar Production (P) that define how each Non-terminal symbols is expanded into other Non-terminal or Terminal Symbols, and the grammar Axiom or Start-symbol (S) that is the Non-terminal from which all valid sentences must derive. This is, a sequence of Terminal symbols in T is a valid sentence of the language defined by a given CFG if and only if that sequence derives from S applying the grammar Derivation Rules in P.

DSL (Domain Specific Language): Is a kind of Formal Language defined to be used in a restrict domain for a special purpose.

GPL (General Purpose Language): Is a kind of Formal Programming Language created to be used to instruct computers to solve problems in general domains (not only in a specific one). For instance, a problem in the area of Physics can be solved using the same GPL as another problem in the area of Natural Language Translation or Accounts.

Grammar: Is a formalism to define rigorously the syntactic and the semantic rules of a Language. The Sender that needs to write a sentence in that language must follow the grammar rules to create a valid sentence, and the Receiver must also follow the same grammar to interpret it, this is, to extract the sentence's meaning.

Language Processing: Is the analysis and translation (or transformation) of sentences of a given language. This process is compulsory so that the computer can understand (extract the meaning) the sentences written and provided by the Programmer in order to execute them, this is, to perform the actions described by the processed sentences.

Language Processing Course: Is a set of lectures where the students learn theoretical concepts and pratical aspects about programming languages formalization and implementation. The first topic is concerned with the rigorous design and specification of languages, and the second topic is concerned with methods and techniques to interpret (process) those languages using a computer. Usually these courses also teach how to construct automatically the referred language processors based on the formal specification of the language. The practical work proposed make the students capable of building concrete processors.

Language Processor: Is a computer program, a software tool (as, for instance, a Compiler or an Interpreter) aimed at processing the sentences of a given Language. Given a sentence (the so-called input or source-text), a Language Processor must analyze it to check if it is valid according to the grammar rules, and to extract its meaning; after that analysis phase (composed of three layers; lexical analysis, syntactic analysis and semantic analysis), if no errors are found, the Language Processor transforms the input into the desired output (maybe a target-text or a value).

Language: A set of sentences, being a sentence a sequence of symbols that belong to a given alphabet or vocabulary. Symbols are combined according to a set of syntactic and semantic rules. Each sentence has a meaning, and Languages are used to communicate transporting messages from a Sender to a Receiver. Natural Languages (NL) are used when both Sender and Receiver are Human Beings and Programming Languages (PL) are used to control machines, i.e., the Receiver is a machine (for instance, a Computer). PL are Formal Languages because syntactic and semantic rules are defined rigorously prior to their first use.

Ontology: An ontology formally represents knowledge as a set of concepts (general concepts or classes, and occurrences of the concepts, or instances) within a domain, and the relationships among those concepts (hierarchical or taxonomic relations, and non-taxonomic relations). It can be used to reason about that domain described through the definition of its objects their properties and relations.

TG (Translation Grammar): Is a CFG extended with Semantic Actions to define also the semantics of the underlying language. Semantic Actions are pieces of code that are attached to each Production in P (the set of the CFG Derivation Rules) to describe the semantic constraints that must be observed by the symbols in a concrete sentence and also to define how the sentences must be transformed or processed.

Chapter 8
A Sports Science Approach to Computer Programming Education

M. Costa Neves
SportTools – Technology for Sport Company, Portugal

M. Ramires
SportTools – Technology for Sport Company, Portugal

J. Carvalho
Polytechnic Institute of Setúbal, Portugal

M. Piteira
Polytechnic Institute of Setúbal, Portugal

J. Santos
Polytechnic Institute of Setúbal, Portugal

N. Folgôa
Polytechnic Institute of Setúbal, Portugal

M. Boavida
Polytechnic Institute of Setúbal, Portugal

ABSTRACT

Learning computer programming is for most of the new students a difficult task. Besides the computer language learning of the syntax and all the aspects related with the compiler or the IDE environment, programming also has its artistic counterpart, where the individual personality is indissociable of the way he programs. Therefore, the main difficulties identified in students are closely related with aspects of their personality: self-confidence, resiliency, creativity, and autonomy. The sports science approach emerged naturally as all the authors were involved in high performance training for several years. The personality characteristics one needs to develop in students are similar to elite sports athletes in order to cope with the stress associated with their activity. In this chapter, the authors present a case study that took place at the Polytechnic Institute of Setubal with 28 students with different backgrounds and a workload of 8 hours per day.

DOI: 10.4018/978-1-4666-7304-5.ch008

INTRODUCTION

As a starting point, it's important to state that the study presented here was not originally considered by our team or by the external elements involved, as research work or something that would have its outcome as a report or other type of academic production.

By consequence, this work was not preceded by any type of profound literature or review or by an extended overview of the area. The foundation of this experiment is based in a truly multidisciplinary team, composed by academics that are working in education related fields, by elements involved in lecturing computer programming, psychologists, academics from the social sciences, experts in sport's neuropsychology, athletes, coaches, performance analysts and as experts in sport's technology. This team was not created with the purpose of developing this study or this experiment, this group is working together for more than 10 years in elite sports.

The experimental gathering toke place because of a simple challenge:

"We believe that part of the difficulties we face when teaching computer programming are not related with the difficulty of the subject or the quality of the educational materials available to the students.

Computer programming, like its mental counterpart, deal with the necessity of taking risks, be able to learn from the mistakes, to be resilient, and above all to take decisions.

This type of difficulties is the same we face when teaching (training) athletes to be prepared to compete in elite sports. In most cases, the technical aspects of the sport are not the main cause for a young athlete to not succeed or to achieve performance levels clearly above their capacities.

In sport, mostly in Sailing but also in Tennis and Boccia (Paralympic Sport), we have deal with exactly the same type of problems, which are mostly related with anxiety management and the capacity to clearly define objectives that are simultaneously tangible and challenging.

Can we coach our students and apply strategies that lead to more autonomy in the learning process, to promote their confidence and the capacity to take risks in the decision process? Can we do it the same way we promote self-esteem and anxiety control in our athletes?

And in the other way around, can we define performance goals (skills or capacities) that makes the student to be aware of their evolution, a crucial aspect to improve resilience, self-confidence? And can we define performance objectives in functional terms, objectives that may exceed the boundaries of a specific class or one particular part of the program?"

That was the challenge that put the team working together in a very unusual environment. The athletes were computer programming students. Technical, tactical or physical training, were replaced by different aspects of programming, in our case web programming, database management and server-side programming.

The approach remains the same, precise goal definition, motivational videos, anxiety control and some form of personalized mental training, based on initial personality assessment.

Finally, we maintained the same terminology used in sport's training, namely the microcycle based approach, used in almost all sports. Initially, because all of us were acquainted with this type of terminology, and later because we wanted to reflect the idea that we were training our students to develop their programming skills rather than teaching a programming language.

The terminology helped us to be provocative and to generate some type of curiosity and arousal attention in our students from day 1, when we presented the training schedule and stated the reason we were doing it and the way we will do it.

The Reason: "For Those That Believe That We Always Need a Reason"

The idea of using periodized training methodology concepts, in the planning of a computer programming course, came because of the experience in early courses where we developed several experiments related with the identification of personality aspects that could be related with the performance of the student.

Among the students with lower results it was possible to identify a pattern that was essentially related with the fear to fail, the lack of self-confidence and low resiliency.

Those related with sport and sport training, know that these are the type of problems that every coach has to deal when preparing young athletes to compete at a higher level. The main problem, besides the technical or physical aspects of the athlete, is to make him, or her, understand the training process as a path to achieve new skills and to be better prepared to perform.

Performance goals, not only results, are the key to overcome all fears, because unlike the results from a competition, performance goals are personal and only based on ourselves.

In order to apply this approach to two modules of the course, database management systems and web programming technologies, we used a standard sports periodization method with the definition of a "competitive phase" and a "preparation phase".

The main idea was that during the competitive phase students wouldn't have any type of technical support from the teachers. The competitive phase was materialized by the development of a project where all the support they had from the teacher was related with concepts, ideas, motivation, but no coding related issues.

During the preparation phase, none of the work developed in the classes, exercises or assignments, were taken into account in students assessment.

The complete absence of assessment at the preparation phase was a key element in order to challenge the student sense of autonomy.

The definition of the objectives to be achieved, presented as performance goals that could be clearly measured and understood, was not based in the programming mechanisms that were present in the course, but in terms of the systems the students should be able to develop in the last stage of the course.

The objectives, in most cases, exceeded the boundaries of a specific type of module and were presented as something that could be achieved as a combination of the skills acquired in different modules. As in sport, we stated the importance of a specific type of training not as a local objective but as a way to achieve a broader objective, something more related with the evolution of the athlete as a whole.

In this case we presented programming objectives as the capacity to develop a system similar to other systems already used by the students every day, like a reservation website, photo management website or even their timetable website.

The Way: "For Those That Didn't Noticed That the Happiness Is the Way"

The study was conducted in a Technological Specialization Course, a course that is very particular in its structure, with a heavy workload and with almost all the student work developed in the class lab. The amount of time the students are in class and working with the same group of teachers, more than 100 hours per module, was very well suited for the type of approach that we planned.

The Web Programming Module focused 3 main themes:

- **HTML:** All the main elements of html5.
- **CSS:** Cascading style sheets, focus on positioning.

- **Javascript:** Interaction and DOM manipulation.

The Database Management Systems Module, focused on:

- **ER Model:** Entity relationship model and the relational model.
- **SQL:** The sql language (ddl and dml).
- **PHP:** The php language.

All the "training" was planned with a goal in mind: being capable of developing a specific project (individual theme projects suggested by the students, in groups of 2) in the form of a database backed up website with authentication and different user roles or privileges. Besides its technical conformity, each project must be presented as a product. Each product should have a specific target and design that complies with the identified target.

The different course's modules were treated as different training aspects, and as in sport, with notion that is not possible to improve conditioning in several areas at one time. We used the microcycle terminology to identify 7 to 9 days training periods with a very specific skill associated with each learning microcycle. Web Programming and Database Management microcycles were planned together in order to avoid an overload of information (or should we say overtraining?).

Each microcycle was defined with a clear objective of what the student should be capable of doing after that training period. The objective was defined in terms of the type of system or application the student should be able to develop after that phase. Those phases were presented and discussed with the students.

The idea of discussing their evolution in terms of the functionalities of the systems they were able to develop was also a motivating factor because all of them could understand the type of system they will be able to develop in a few weeks.

We must say that probably this type of course, and this course in particular, was the best possible solution to try this approach. We had the opportunity to adapt the schedule of the course and to have the two modules that were part of the experiment almost side by side and taking 90% of the time of the course in the first 2 months. Finally, we had the chance to have a third module, the final project, schedule to the end of the course. The idea was to analyze the impact that this approach could have in the short-term (2 months) and in the long-term (7 months), with the same teachers (coaches) involved in the final class of the course.

This course took place from November 2011 until July 2012, with 28 students and with 2 teachers working simultaneously. The idea of having two teachers working together in the classroom was a key factor for the success of the experiment, and was quite similar to the way a sport's technical teams work.

BACKGROUND

This experimental approach appeals to several background experiences in different areas such as Programming Education, Learning Technologies, Sports Training Methodology and Sports Psychology. This background makes a brief insight into the applied concepts that we used in our approach.

Programming Education

Programming is an important expertise for computer science students and is a subject that involves skills in algorithm design, program writing, syntax comprehension as well as program logic and abstract power (Jenkins, 2002).

Programming is a hierarchical skill where students acquire a basic skill before advance to the next level. For example, students need to learn the basic syntax and then the semantic, structure and style, gradually. However, during the class, the teacher will continue teaching without waiting for student to fully understand a given topic, usually because of the courses time constrains and also because of the student's different levels of knowledge and learning ability.

Programming is a process that translate an algorithm into a programming language code. For many students the hardest task of programming is not this translation, but the interpretation of the problem requirements specification and its translation into an algorithm.

So, to program, students need to develop several skills such as, problem interpretation, algorithms design, algorithms translation into program code and writing code with the correct syntax and structure (Morgado & Barbosa, 2013a).

Generally, programming subject is offered level by level; beginner classes take place during the first semester, intermediate classes in the second and third semester and advance class in subsequent semester. Students who failed to get approval in one level will have to repeat this level, only those who have obtained approval follow to the next level. Unfortunately, for some students even though they have been approved, they still have a lack of confidence in programming. When they took the next course, they will face a problem where they need to learn a new thing as well as improving their previous programming skills.

The programming language used at teaching introductory programming courses is also a problem. Generally, the aim of the programming course is to teach student on how to program. Programming language is just a way used to achieve that aim. However, most programming languages used for teaching are not actually designed for teaching but instead for the programming industry. Therefore, it is possible that is not the appropriate language for teaching programming (Rahmat et al., 2011).

Most students believe that programming is a difficult subject to understand and achieve a good level. This view is passed to new students and thus gives the impression that this subject is the hardest subject. In this context, many research works have been conducted to study the main

difficulties and proposed solutions to solve this problem (Morgado et al., 2013b)

For instance, research works aims to identify teaching topics in the first year and the level of comprehension felt by students in order to identify and apply strategies to help students to learn the most difficult concepts. Piteira and Costa (2013), conducted some studies to identify the perceived difficulties in programming concepts, situated learning, learning context and contents.

Others studies are being performed in order to propose solutions to overcame some of the problems in program learning. These studies proposed different approaches based on tools to support program learning (Piteira & Costa, 2013; Denning & McGettrick, 2005; Milne & Rowe, 2002).

Sports Science Concepts

In recent years numerous sports scientists and several high level coaches considered the structured training programs according the principles of periodization, one of the principal aspects that bring many benefits for the training process. (Rowbottom, 2000; Castelo et al., 1999; Afonso & Pinheiro, 2011)

According to several authors, periodization is described as planned long-term variation of the volume and intensity of training to prevent overtraining and promote optimal performance during the period of time where runs the most important competition of the season. In this context, the training volume is the amount of work performed per exercise, per day or per month and the intensity is the relation between work and time (Wathen et. al., 2008; Afonso & Pinheiro, 2011; Koprivica, 2012).

To enable coaches and athletes to work with a long-term plan it is important to use manageable units that incorporate short-term and middle-term goals. In these sense the systematic organization of the training is structured in microcycles, mesocycles and macrocycles (Rowbottom, 2000).

A macrocycle refers to an annual plan (or four years plan in the Olympic case) developed regarding the better performance in the most important competition of the cycle. The macrocycle is subdivided in several mesocycles.

The mesocylce is usually a training block with 2-6 weeks long and refers to a specific training purpose that could be organized by general preparation, specific preparation, competition and transition (before start a new plan). Each mesocycle have several microcycles.

A microcycle is a shorter period of time (usually one week) where a group of training sessions is organized according the macrocycles and mesocycle main goals regarding quantity, quality and the nature of the training stimulus (Zahradník, 2012).

Psychological Approach

The high-level sport competition it's related with the increasing of the athletes anxiety levels. The high anxiety levels have directly influence in the sports performance.

The anxiety is an unpleasant emotional state of fear or apprehension that can appear in the presence of recognizable threat or even in the absence of danger. This emotional state is marked by a disproportionate reaction facing the real danger intensity.

Chambless et al. (2000), describes a large number of somatic and cognitive symptoms that are related with anxiety. The somatic symptoms such as: tremor, muscle stiffness, restlessness, hyperventilation, sweating, palpitations, etc., can also appear combined with several cognitive signals like: apprehension and psychic restlessness, hyper vigilance and distractibility, loss of concentration and insomnia.

The described signals can be related with some temporary events (state anxiety) or can be a permanent way of reacting (trait anxiety) (Spielberger, 1985).

The internal and external pressure, in most athletes, is caused by the obligation of winning to satisfying our society that promote the success and punish the loss. Thus, the athletes are trying to reach their own goals but also the other person's goals (coach, parents, friends, club, among others) which can put the athlete under pressure and affect their sports performance.

According to Martens et al. (1990) the origin of the anxiety causes before a competition are the uncertainty and the conferred result importance. One of the main uncertainty sources could be the coach figure when he tries to motivate their athletes but he isn't succeeded and leaving them insecure, causing anxiety.

The coach extreme behavior (absent or extremely stringent), the injustice or the lack of game knowledge could have a negative interference in athletes behavior. The behavior interference can also be made by parents, family or even team mates.

The atmosphere inside the team can also have a positive or negative influence, helping to build strong friendship bounds or otherwise to produce conflicts among athletes (Donohue, 2007).

The sports performance can also be influenced by self-efficacy that refers to self-belief about the capabilities to complete tasks and reach goals (Bandura, 1997, 2003).

Some studies reveal that athletes with positive self-efficacy of their sport capabilities can decrease the anxiety levels during the competition. Thus, self-confident athletes had less anxiety levels than others who doubt of their capabilities (Duda et al., 1995). Assuming that anxiety and self-efficacy influence each other, this two aspects should be worked together to promote other psychological skills such as: motivation, concentration, confidence and resilience. Therefore, were designed plans and established goals in order to promote and develop these psychological skills.

According with Latham and Locke (2007), one goal is something that one person try to reach, is the target of a defined action.

The Goals Definition is one of the most popular motivational techniques to increase sport performance and productivity (Weinberg & Gould, 2003; Martens et al., 1990). Thus, one goal can be defined based on the result, on the performance or even in the process.

The "result goal" is measured according to the competition result, so this objective depends not only on the individual effort, but also the skill / ability to compete against an opponent.

The "performance goal" is focused in reach a certain performance level, that is independent of other competitors and it's measured by comparing with previous performances.

The "process goals" are related with the tasks that the athlete should complete during the sport performance so that can be the best possible.

The definition of these three types of goals it's important because they can play an important role in athlete changing behaviors. The "result goal" can help in the motivation management and the "performance and process goals" are less dependent on the opponent, therefore are more accurate and adjustable (Weinberg & Gould, 2003).

The goals definition may directly influence the athletes performance in four different ways: focus their attention in specific tasks, increasing the effort and intensity of the action, while making them more persistent over the failure and allows them to develop new strategies for problem solving and learning (Weinberg & Gould, 2003).

Martin and Gill (1991) tried to explain the relation between goals defined by athletes and their anxiety, motivation, confidence and resilience levels. The athletes that define "result goals" tend to produce unrealistic expectations that can lead them to low levels of confidence and increase anxiety, thus negatively affecting performance. However the "performance goals" are easiest manageable and could help the athlete to produce realistic expectations and consequently achieving optimized motivation, concentration, confidence, resilience and anxiety levels.

Weinberg and Gould (2003), in order to promote a positively performance influence, defined a set of principles that must incorporate the goal definition:

1. Define specific goals;
2. Define difficult but realistic goals;
3. Define long-term goals in conjunction with short-term objectives;
4. Define performance goals, outcome and process;
5. Define goals for competition and training;
6. Develop strategies to achieve those goals;
7. Consider the personality of the athlete;
8. Develop commitment to the goal set;
9. Provide ways of evaluating goals and their feedback's.

The self-efficacy and anxiety impact can directly influence the athletes performance. Thus, the goals definition have a major importance in the training process and relate the several components of the training such as strategic, tactical, physical and psychological skills with relevant impact in the perception of self-efficacy and anxiety control.

The programming education and the sports training have the same fundamental principles, the skills acquisition through learning methods. The learning ability is an individual intrinsic skill and can be developed by several types of action that promote cognitive and motor activity and also affective processes. The described concepts are intimately connected in the sports field and we also believe that they can be related inside the classroom environment.

COMPUTER PROGRAMMING: THE COACH AND THE TEACHER

For many years some of us were simultaneously teachers and coaches, but in different fields. We were teachers at the University, mainly from the computer science but also from the social sciences, and coaches at an elite level in several sports, from sailing and athletics to adapted sports.

During those years, until this "challenge" took place, we never questioned why did we used the both terms so distinctively. It was clear that we were teaching our students and coaching our athletes and the boundaries were clear and well defined.

We believe that this boundaries were only or essentially epistemological. The objective was the same in both cases, to create top level performers!

This led us to some questions. "What are the main differences between these two contexts? What's the difference between our behavior as leaders and what's the difference between the ones that we teach or coach?"

Teaching Sport and Coaching Computer Programming

We tried to identify the main differences we had in this two contexts, in respect to our students or athletes and in respect to ourselves and our behavior in the process.

Our students and athletes were approximately the same age, around 20's, the typical age that most students enter University or these pre-university courses. The 20's are also the age that most athletes reach an elite level.

The main differences between our students and our athletes is based in expectations about the way the training process will help, according to the long-term objectives, to fulfill their goals and the way they can clearly state their objectives. The performance goals are planned to be obtained along the process.

- **Long-Term Goals:** Most of our athletes have a clear definition of their long-term goals, the objectives they dream about in 3 to 5 years. Most of them dream about entering the National team, win championships at a National or International level, or to be at the Olympics. Our students assume that finishing their courses will open doors

and will give them new professional opportunities. The great majority of our students don't have a "dream goal" in mind, and passion is the fuel needed when adversity strikes.

- **Performance Goals:** Every coach knows that performance will change over time, not only because of the training plan that defines performance peaks at specific moments, but also because of a large number of factors that contribute to the capacity of an athlete be at his top level. Because of these fluctuations in performance it's always important to define short-term references that may be used not only to evaluate performance but also to give a motivating signal that something is improving, that the overall plan is being executed. The definition of these performance goals must be completely understood by the athlete in order to divert attention from results, something that is clearly outside the capacity of the athlete or the coach to control. It's important that we can "see" that we are performing better, we need to find a way to measure the evolution without relying in results that clearly depends not only in the performance of our athletes but also in the performance of their opponent. In different sports this performance goals may be defined as the capacity to finish a distance, the time to achieve an objective, the number of specific technical or tactical elements to be performed, but never the result. Measuring only by result can lead us to take the lack of performance of our opponent as an outstanding improvement in our performance. It's difficult to define and present this type of performance goals when teaching computer programming, we tried to do that in our approach. Define performance goals in this case is to state that the next 3 or 4 classes will lead us to a level that will enable us to do, or develop, something new.But, the objective should not be stated only in local terms, the objective should be presented in terms of the new type of functionality that the students should be able to develop after this "training" period. The definition of performance goals in short-terms, that should be identified or related with an expected outcome, closely resembles the microcycle approach used in sports training.

- **Performance Evaluation:** Most of our athletes are perfectly aware of their performance level in the different aspects of their training and in respect to the different skills required to perform at an elite level in their sports. This self-awareness is crucial in order to discuss the type and intensity of the work to be developed and to define (negotiate) short-term objectives, or performance goals.The performance evaluation is scheduled and discussed between the coach and the athlete and is perfectly defined, not only in the technical details and particularities, but also in terms of the expected overall performance outcome.We don't really know if our students have this type of perception. That the local evaluation of their knowledge (the technical details of a specific theme), made by them or by their teachers, its only part of a process to achieve a more broader outcome, the capacity to design, develop and create something, in this case a computer system or solution.Sometimes it seems that the local evaluation is the only perceived outcome. In Sport, this would mean that we could have an athlete developing some sort of strength training (weight lifting) with the sole objective of lifting more weight, instead of knowing that the reason behind that specific part of the training was gaining velocity, or other type of objective directly related with their long-term goal of

being a better athlete and be more competitive in their sport.

- **The Head Coach, and The Technical Team:** Finally, our athletes have a technical team lead by a head coach that works toward an unified objective. We could say that a class may be similar to a team in team sports, but in that case the situation is the same. The team as a objective in common, and technical team works, sometimes with a personalized plan for each athlete towards that same objective.In this particular point, our students have clearly a less personalized type of training. If we think of our students as individual athletes we have to say, in that case, the coach and the elements responsible for the mental and physical training, the physiologist, the physiotherapist and the rest of the team are working together and adapting their intervention according to the type of work developed by their peers. If we think of our students as part of a team, a football team for instance, we have that strange feeling that we are developing exactly the same type of training for all the players. The striker, the midfielder and even the goal keeper are preparing themselves exactly the same way.Eventually it's important to find a way to teach our students that, more important than reach an average level, in all aspects of their student life, is to excel in a few of them.

It was easy to identify differences between our students and our athletes, just by looking at them or more precisely, just by speaking and discussing ideas with them. And probably that's the starting point, we have no doubt that we spend clearly more time speaking with our athletes than with our students!

And this could be the starting point to the required self-analysis. When we identified the differences between our athletes and our students, we noticed that those differences have nothing to do with the complexity or the difficulty to perform their tasks.

The differences are also based in ourselves. Can we identify the differences in our behavior when teaching or when coaching, besides the fact already stated that we communicate less and by consequence that we barely know our students?

As a starting point we could take the words of Carol Ann Tomlinson (2011) in their multidimensional characterization of a coach:

- Great Coaches know their sport
- Great Coaches develop player's skills
- Great Coaches are great motivators
- Great Coaches are team builders

It's interesting to notice that when we think about sport, these topics don't cause any question, in fact for most of us that is the way we see a coach. And from a coach perspective, all this aspects are indissociable along with technical and tactical aspects of the training process.

How and why do we behave differently as coaches and as teachers, having in mind that the goal is the same: to produce top level performers. Lets follow the different dimensions stated by Carol Ann Tomlinson (2011).

- **Knowing our Sport:** When we say that a coach knows his sport, it's not just a question of knowing the technical aspects, the rules governing their sport or who are the top players. The coach has to know the real challenges posed to his players, the type of stress they will face during the competition and the best way to protect and prepare the athlete for the real world. How to speak, how to dress, how to behave according to the protocol, how to deal with the media, just to name a few. When we teach we assume we don't need to be so fully knowledgeable about our "sport". Most of us don't have the time or the opportunity to learn about the real challenges posed to our young computer athletes. We focus on the technical aspects of the area and we don't have a clear perspective about the outside competition. We follow our area like an adept or sports fan follow their athletes.

- **Developing Player Skills:** The development of the player skills is essentially the result of studying the player, understand his limitations and identify the best possible evolution in their performance. It's a natural thing to do in sport, because we all know that the differences between athletes lead us to the necessity to identify different approaches or different paths for them to evolve and to compete at a top level. It's not difficult to do the same with our students, but isn't natural. We know that some of them have a natural talent for design, are very good in math or are passionate for some particular type of system or application. Anyway, most of the courses will not enable the development or the refinement of a particular type of skill, the traditional course structure, specially if don't possess any type of alternate paths, tends to promote the students that perform well in the different areas instead of identify and focus on the talented skill.

- **Being a Motivator:** Every coach likes the idea of "not being" a motivator. The best motivation we can have is just win or better that to have a clear perspective that our performance is increasing at the right pace. When we were perfect, but the others were just better, or when there are doubts about it, being a motivator is part of the job. We can all be motivators in every aspect of our lives, but being a motivator requires that the people that are listening us, believes in us. We need to know the ones we want to motivate, and we need to spend some time understanding and sometimes discussing the reasons behind the failure.

- **Being a Team Builder:** First we need to assume that we want that our students and our athletes behave like a team. We would like that they don't see their success only as an individual effort. In sport, and not only in team sports, we normally want our athletes to help each other and to surpass their obstacles with the help from each other. In the classroom it's more difficult to share the idea that we would like them to help each other in order to have better results. Because helping each other is usually quoted as cheating, as copying each other's work.

As a fact we behave quite differently as coaches and as teachers but probably the main difference was not stated by Tomlinson (2011). We normally have a profound knowledge about our athletes. We study their performance and plan their training according to all the information we have about them. This type of work is highly personalized. We may reduce the intensity, the frequency or produce changes in the training plan because of personal, familiar or medical reasons, or to adapt their effort according to other aspects of their lives like their academic studies.

We don't have this knowledge about our students, and this reduces our ability to personalize the type of work we can do with each student. And we don't have any type of additional information about their environment or other aspects of their lives.

Computer Programming: Developing a Training Plan

The training schedule, for the initial modules of this course (Web Programing and Database Management) was defined two weeks before the course starts. During 2 months, the only classes the students had were this two and once a week another class focused on algorithms and the basic programming mechanisms.

With a daily workload of 8 hours per day, the task was comparable to a pre-season training camp with the students (and teachers) working together from 9h00 AM until 6h00 PM. Besides de schedule definition we defined a number of long term goals we would like to address and discuss with the students, even before the first session.

Most of these goals were related with the topics we previously defined as being the most relevant differences in our experience as coaches and teachers:

- The definition of long-term goals (almost one year long)
- The definition of a performance measure
- The definition of short-term performance goals (usually 1 week)
- The technical team (the presence of multiple coaches or specialists)

We assume that in this experience we would try to behave the same way we do when coaching our athletes, namely, being more knowledgeable about our students, their motivations and interests. As coaches, we have to study these students and understand their strengths and weaknesses in order to adapt or personalize the training plan to each one of them.

Besides that, we want them to behave like a team, helping each other to surpass the problems and difficulties. That aspect, because of the final evaluation, was clearly the one that resembled more difficult to implement.

In the next section we'll describe the results obtained and strategies we adopted to achieve each one of these goals, but before the first contact with the students there were more aspects to plan and schedule.

Probably the problem that represented the biggest challenge was the performance measurement and the definition of performance goals in terms that could be fully understood by our students. Based not only on the terminology but inspired

Figure 1. Preparation phase plan with web programming themes

Preparation phase				
Microcycle 1	Microcycle 2	Microcycle 3	Microcycle 4	Microcycle 5
Web Architecture, Protocols Html and hypermedia	Structure (html)	Style (css+html)	Interactivity (javascricpt+css+html)	Integration with the server-side modules (join database microcycle 4)
(8 hours)	(20 hours)	(20 hours)	(30 hours)	(40 hours)

IS TU CS TU TU TU TU TU TU TU TU CS TU TU TU TU TU TU TU TU TU CS TU TU TU TU TU TU TU TU TU TU TU CS CS TU TU TU TU TU TU TU TU TU TU TU TU TU TU CS CS CS

IS — Initial Session
TU — Training Unit
CS — Control Session

by the concept underlying the periodization, we redefined the courses in terms of microcycles.

Each microcycle represents a stage of evolution, a stage that we wanted to be fully understandable for the student. So, we define each microcycle precisely, in terms of the type of system the students should be able to develop in that stage. It was not an abstract phase, all the schedule was defined prior of its start, something like, after November 22, the students should be able to develop a system with a set of functionalities.

By the end of each microcycle a small project was proposed for development, being able to do it was a signal that performance was achieved.

A microcycle ranged from 16 to 24 hours, and the last 4 hours (approximately 20% of the microcycle duration) was devoted to develop the project associated with that microcycle (these projects were designated as microcycle control points).

Each microcycle was composed of 2 hours blocks, meaning that each microcycle was normally composed by 5 of these blocks. Each block represented a specific feature considered relevant within the objective to be achieved in that microcycle, and accordingly to the underlying concept, each block was a training session.

Each training session has a specific goal, stated in the beginning of the session, and presented not only in terms of the expected result (2 hours after) but also in terms of the outcome that should be observed in respect to the objectives defined in the microcycle. Each training session had a small

exercise or set of exercises to be developed in the last part of the session.

Explains the relevance of each 2 hours block of a class and the objective of that particular training session. It was a lot easier than it seems. Figure 2 shows part of the training plan with the Web Programming training sessions in yellow and the Database training sessions in blue. The final phase of one database microcycle is visible in the afternoon of the fourth day (thursday), identified as MS-control (Microcycle Control).

This work was developed for the Web Programming and Database management classes, and that gave complexity to the process. We had to measure the intensity of each microcycle in order to avoid overtraining. The way we planned this load balance, the difficulty level and overall effort was once again borrowed from sports training.

We wanted to have a light start, with a load increase by the end of the first microcycle, alternating peaks between the two classes (similar to different types of training) and we placed the worst part near the last microcycle. The last one, in each class, should be very light in order to enable some rest, to give them time to discuss solutions and to prepare them for the competition.

With the entire schedule defined we noticed that in sport we have an external competition and here we had to deal with the fact of being both coaches and judges. The model we planned is based in trust, working as a team, sharing objectives and strategies to achieve those goals. Continuous

Figure 2. Part of training plan weekly presented to the students
It is an interesting exercise to do.

9h00 11h00	3	M2-FormsCTL	M2_JS2_[DOM_F]	PHP5	M3_HTML_POS		
11h00 13h00	4	M2-JS[DOM_F]	M2_JS2_DomCTL	PHP-controlo	M3_CSS_POS		
14h00 16h00	7	9	M2-CTL	MS-controlo	MER2,1		
16h00 18h00	8	10	M2_CTL	MS-controlo	SQL2.1		

evaluation, grading or any sort of formal evaluation will ruin this approach, so the solution was to simulate an external competition (or evaluation).

We clearly separate the class schedule in two periods: training and competition. The competition phase took less than 2 weeks.

During the training phase we (coaches) worked together with the students in order to achieve the best performance level we can. We don't perform any type of evaluation neither produce notes or information that could help in the final grading.

During the preparation phase, the development of a project proposed by each team of two, there was available help from the coaches, but they could and should help each other in their projects. At the competition phase, or the final (and unique) evaluation, they only had help at the presentation (almost daily) of the developed work.

A final presentation was scheduled in a large conference room, with public audience and recorded on video (we liked the idea of the additional competition stress).

Which sport has his own characteristics and every athlete has to develop his own psychological strategy to deal with all typical situations from his sport.

Every sport has several basic skills to achieve a optimal psychological functioning. These psychological skills, integrated in most of training plans and we can find them in all succeed athletes. These basic skills are: anxiety control, concentration, self-confidence and self-efficacy.

An psychological training plan should identify, analyze and develop cognitive and psychological abilities which are directly related with sports performance.

Working these kind of capabilities is associated to the idea of the psychological skills can be learned, acquired and improved in the same way than physical and technical skills.

The psychological training phases in elite athletes are: strategical competition plan, psychological skills evaluation, goals definition and intervention strategies, psychological skills training, pre-competition, competition and after competition.

There is not an optimal technique to develop the psychological basic skills from elite athletes, because the training it depends from several factor such as: the defined goals, the available range of time, the athlete individual characteristics, etc., and the theorical guideline from the intervention psychologist.

TPSI-6: A Team of Programming Athletes

TPSI was the Portuguese Acronym for the name of the course, Information Systems Programming and Technologies, being the number a reference to 6th edition. Some of us had already been involved with this course that was created to simultaneously give access to the University (with several equivalences) and to prepare the students that didn't want to continue their studies to have a technical certification.

After six editions it was clear for us that most of the students already knew the structure and the type classes they will attend. An additional difficulty to the implementation of a different approach. From the beginning we knew that the first day was crucial in the definition of three main elements:

- Leadership
- Goal definition
- Trust

We presented ourselves and gave a general overview of the two modules and we also presented the schedule and our microcycle approach. Then, we went to see the public presentations of the final project courses from computer science, in one of the school's conference rooms.

The next day we revealed the reason for seeing the presentations in the conference room and stated our objectives:

- We want them to be able to present a final project (the third and final class of the course) in that same conference room.
- We will teach them, not only the technicalities of the process, but also the other competences needed to speak in front of an audience.
- We expect that their final projects will have the same type of quality that they saw in those computer science final projects.

We defined our long term goals and that was the best way to invite them to define their own goals. On the other side, the 2 hour's training sessions and the microcycle structure were easily understood by the students.

The sports terminology was also a way to state the difference of this approach and an ice breaker in terms of our relation with the students.

It took us less than a week, to have our students to fully understand this model and to adopt the sports metaphor in a daily basis. In the classroom, we had the training sessions and the control sessions, a simple way to implement a very basic performance measurement mechanism.

Eventually, it took a bit longer for them to believe that any type of evaluation, other than the performance analysis, would be developed in the preparation phase. On the other hand we started the analyzing process of our students in terms of their objectives and their psychological profile.

In terms of performance the results were clearly above our expectations, but its important to notice that when reaching the hardest phase of the plan, the 4th / 5th microcycle (5 weeks), they were staying in school 2 or 3 hours after the end of the classes. We must say that the same was happening with us, due to the necessity to adapt some of the materials and the original schedule.

Near the end of the preparation phase we noticed the pre-competitive anxiety and we spent some time, during the training sessions, explaining how to reduce anxiety through breath control.

When we approached the end of our classes, we had fully identified the characteristics of our students. Therefore, we had the opportunity to help them to define the type of project (propose) for the competition phase.

We also knew witch of our students planned to continue their studies and those that wanted to start working when finishing the course.

Finally, the training came to an end, and the competition started. During the competition they presented the state of their work on a daily basis, and we focused a bit more in their social abilities, in terms of presentation and public speaking.

Six months later we reunite to the third and final module of the course. This final module was essentially the final project of the course, the one that from the beginning was promised to have is final presentation in the same conference room where we took them in the first day.

During the initial 2 months period (the Web Programming and Database Management Systems classes) and later, in the final project, we developed a number of activities that were clearly complementary to computer programming. Posture, anxiety control, public speaking and media training were part of a side project that we believe could help them to develop socially and to promote their self-esteem. Those are competencies that are relevant not only professionally but also in our social life.

We decided to develop this activities because we do this type of work with our athletes and with ourselves, and we used the same type of tools and the same methodology we use with our top athletes. We spent some time recording presentations, simulating interviews and part of these materials were available for them to see and to discuss. We used TMS - Training Management System, a tool that provide us the opportunity to annotate video and to share notes between our students over the web. The TMS is used as a media training tool for athletes but also for different types of public figures that need to be constantly coached because of their exposure. We also had the opportunity to have this type of remote coaching available to our students, the same way we use it with our top athletes.

The results were excellent and were visible in the way students approached their final public presentations.

Solutions and Recommendations

Every different experience provides us an opportunity to learn not only about the experience in itself, but also about ourselves and the way we react to new challenges. The idea of using our training experience to adopt a different approach, in this course, was essentially a challenge and an opportunity to address some mental issues that we believed were essentially the same we face in sports training.

We started focusing our attention in the behavior of our students and ended analyzing our own behavior in terms of the capacity to explain the real life importance of the things we teach.

Motivation was crucial and particularly relevant in the less prepared students. Goal definition and goal negotiation (between students and teachers) was an effective way to manage the motivation level.

We brought two main rules from this experience to our regular teaching activity:

- Keep grading in its place, don't mix it as if it was part of the learning processHelping our students to be at their top level should be understood by them as our mission, we are partners in the learning process. And then evaluation it's a necessity to reward the effort.But the grading or the evaluation process, it's the consequence, not the reason. Now we always explain the course or class objectives without speaking about evaluation. Because evaluation its not an objective
- Explain the why before the how

At the beginning it was a real challenge to explain with a real world examples the relevance of a lesson. But it really makes the difference to explain first why its important, why it's present in the real world systems that we use, and then how to create something with it.Most of our courses have bottom-up approach that makes it difficult for the students to understand or to identify the relevance of the subject.

We liked the experience, coaching our students was very rewarding but probably the most effective part of it was that in order to coach them we had to know them first.

FUTURE RESEARCH DIRECTIONS

Probably part of the emerging trends are already under our eyes, used by different groups of students and eventually not seen as new model or a new paradigm. If they are allowed, part of our students will assist a computer programming class the same way they behave in the other aspects of their lives, using a messaging application to change notes and with an increasing tendency to google instead of ask.

Slides are better seen in the computer screen than in the projected image and the presence in the classroom, if optional, it's evaluated as an investment. More than a problem this is an opportunity for the teacher's role to evolve and to be more similar to an "education manager". In some of our courses we give to our students a perfectly defined schedule of the themes and solutions that will be addressed in each class. It's not just a matter of organization but also for them to have the opportunity to choose which ones to attend. Being able to choose, to adapt the learning path to the characteristics and objectives of the student, gives us new opportunities towards a more personalized learning.

The Personalization of the learning experience is something that we would like to see being discussed in more detail and that we believe that will be very interesting in terms of research opportunities.

CONCLUSION

The idea of a sports training methodology applied to the programming education revealed an interesting approach for teacher and students that want to work as a team, share goals and plan each "season" in order to acquire skills that provide an efficacy increase and higher performance.

The course schedule, based on goals definition was interesting and was very accepted by the students. We noticed higher motivation levels, bigger resilience and consequently, a bigger capacity to achieve goals.

We decided to draw our conclusions of this experiment from the premises and questions we posed in the beginning of the chapter:

- Can we coach our students, and apply strategies that lead to more autonomy in the learning process to promote their confidence, and the capacity to take risks in the decision process? Can we do it the same way we promote self-esteem and anxiety control in our athletes?

Our students performed very well and had an unusual awareness about their weaknesses regarding the task or the theme they were studying. The main reason, in our opinion was the clear definition of the long term goals, the definition of what we want to achieve and the multiple possible ways to achieve the desired result. The result here was understood as a practical or technical capacity to design, implement and put to work a specific type of system or solution. Being able to foreseen the new skills we were developing and anticipating the added value that they represent, was a natural way to improve self-esteem. Anxiety was treated separately and outside the technical aspects of the learning process. The idea of using media training and anxiety control techniques to improve the way the students speak in public was very important and gave a physical component and more personal dimension to the process.

- Can we define performance goals that make the student to be aware of their evolution, a crucial aspect to improve resiliency and self-confidence? And can we define performance objectives in functional terms, outside the boundaries of a specific class or one particular part of the program?

That's probably one of the more interesting outcomes of the experiment. We were able to clearly defined very short-term performance goals and that was one of the biggest challenges in the initial planning. The definition of these objectives, that we want to achieve in "2 hours" were very important for the students to focus their attention and to manage time and effort. But having these short-time goals was also very useful, in the teacher's perspective, adapting what was really important to be told, facing the level or the background of each student. It's almost like defining the destination, suggest a way to arrive there but leaving to path to achieve it as a personal decision for the student. Once again, it's important to express this short term objectives not only in its details but also as the added capacity to develop new things.

- How and why do we behave differently as coaches and as teachers, having in mind that the goal is the same: to produce top level performers?

We behave differently because our roles are not as similar as it seems. It's true that in both cases we're trying to produce top level performers, but it's not clear for all the participants which goals are we have in common. Our commitment to our group, or our team, is based on trust and on the knowledge we have from each other, and there are big differences in that respect among two contexts.

Being more knowledgeable about our students, understanding their personal goals and characteristics is probably the best way to close the gap between these two worlds.

A final word about the outcome of this project in a personal perspective. Probably this experience was one of the most challenging tasks that we had, as teachers. In spite of the elite sport's approach, we are specially proud of the results we achieved with the less prepared "athletes". We managed to create a form of specialization within the class that gave opportunity for several "narrow skilled" students to really excel in their focus area.

It's really important to find a way that within a class we could define several paths for different students with different characteristics to succeed, to be top level in different ways.

And we have to say it ... It was Fun!

REFERENCES

Afonso, R., & Pinheiro, V., (2011). *Modelos de periodização convencionais e contemporâneos.* Retrieved from http://www.efdeportes.com

Bandura, A. (1997). *Self Efficacy: The exercise of control.* New York: WH Freeman and Co.

Bandura, A., & Locke, E. (2003). Negative self-efficacy and goal effects revisited. *The Journal of Applied Psychology, 88*(1), 87–99. doi:10.1037/0021-9010.88.1.87 PMID:12675397

Bobrovnik, V.I. (2014). Structure and logical organization of current studies in track and field sports. *Pedagogics, Psychology, Medical-Biological Problems of Physical Training and Sports, 3,* 3-18.

Castelo, J., Barreto, H., Alves, F., Mil-Homens, P., Carvalho, J., & Vieira, J. (1999). *Metodologia do treino desportivo.* Lisboa: Faculdade de Motricidade Humana - Serviço de edições.

Chambless, D. L., Beck, A. T., Gracely, E. J., & Grisham, J. R. (2000). Relationship of cognitions to fear of somatic symptoms: A test of the cognitive theory of panic. *Depression and Anxiety, 11*(1), 1–9. doi:10.1002/(SICI)1520-6394(2000)11:1<1::AID-DA1>3.0.CO;2-X PMID:10723629

Denning, P. J., & McGettrick, A. (2005). Recentering computer science. *Communications of the ACM, 48*(11), 15–19. doi:10.1145/1096000.1096018

Derkach, V. N., & Yedinak, G. A. (2014). On the question of periodization training content and Paralympic athletes with disorders of the musculoskeletal system in the light of the general theory of sports training. *Pedagogics, Psychology, Medical-Biological Problems of Physical Training and Sports, 5*.

Donohue, B., Miller, A., Crammer, L., Cross, C., & Covassin, T. (2007). A standardized method of assessing sport specific problems in the relationships of athletes with their coaches, teammates, family, and peers. *Journal of Sport Behavior*.

Duda, J., Chi, L., Newton, M.L., Walling, M.D., & Catley, D. (1995). Task and ego orientation and intrinsic motivation in sport. *Journal of Sport Psychology, 26*, 40–63.

Jenkins, T. (2002). On the difficulty of learning to program. In *Proceedings of the 3rd Annual Conference of the LTSN Centre for Information and Computer Sciences (vol. 4*, pp. 53-58). LTSN.

Koprivica, V. (2012). Block Periodization - A Breakthrough or a misconception. *Sport Logica, 8*(2), 93–99.

Lister, R., Adams, E., Fitzgerald, S., Fone, W., Hamer, J., Lindholm, M., … Thomas, L. (2004) A multi-national study of reading and tracking skills in novice programmers. *ACM SIGCSE Bulletin, 36*(4).

Martens, R., Vealley, S., & Burton, D. (1990). *Competitive anxiety in sport*. Champaign, IL: Human Kinetic.

Martin, J. J., & Gill, D. L. (1991). *The relationships among competitive orientation, sport-confidence, self-efficacy, anxiety, and performance*. Academic Press.

McWhorter, W. (2008). *The Effectiveness of Using Lego Mindstorms Robotics Activities to Influence Self-Regulated Learning in a University Introductory Computer Programming Course*. (Doctoral Dissertation). University of North Texas.

Milne, I., & Rowe, G. (2002). Difficulties in Learning and Teaching Programming – Views of Students and Tutors. *Journal of Education and Information Technologies, 7*(1), 55–66. doi:10.1023/A:1015362608943

Morgado, C., & Barbosa, F. (2013a). A Structured Approach to Problem Solving in CS1/2. *International Journal of Advanced Computer Science, 7*(3), 355–362.

Morgado, C., Sampaio, B., & Barbosa, F. (2013b). Building collaborative quizzes. In *Proceedings of the 13th Koli Calling International Conference on Computing Education Research* (Koli Calling '13). ACM.

Mow, I. T. (2008). *Issues and Difficulties in Teaching Novice Computer Programming. Innovative Techniques in Instruction Technology, E-learning, E-assessment, and Education* (pp. 199–204). Springer Netherlands. doi:10.1007/978-1-4020-8739-4_36

Piteira, M., & Costa, C. (2013). Learning Computer Programming - Study of difficulties in learning programming. In *Proceedings of the ISDOC 2013 International Conference on Information Systems and Design of Communication* (pp. 75-80). Lisboa, Portugal: ACM. doi:10.1145/2503859.2503871

Rahmat, M., Shahrani, S., Latih, R., Yatim, N. F. M., Zainal, N. F. A., & Rahman, R. A. (2011). Major problems in basic programming that influence student performance. *Journal Procedia – Social and Behavioral Sciences, 59*, 287-296.

Rowbottom, D. J. (2000). Periodization of Training. Philadelphia: Lippincott Williams & Wilkins.

Spielberger, C. D. (1985). Assessment of state and trait anxiety: Conceptual and methodological issues. *Southern Psychologist, 2*(4), 6–16.

Tomlinson, C. A. (2011). One to Grow On / Every Teacher a Coach. In *Coaching* (pp. 92–93). The New Leadership Skill.

Wathen, D., Baechle, T. R., & Earle, R. W. (2008). Periodization. In Human kinetics (3rd ed.). National Strength & Conditioning Association.

Weinberg, R. S., & Gould, D. (2003). *Fundations of sport and exercise Psychology*. Champaingn, IL: Human Kinectics.

Winslow, L. E. (1996). Programming Pedagogy – A psychological overview. *ACM SIGCSE Bulletin*, *28*(3), 17–22. doi:10.1145/234867.234872

Zahradník, D., & Korvas, P. (2012). *The Introduction into Sports Training*. Brno: Masaryk University.

KEY TERMS AND DEFINITIONS

Anxiety: Unpleasant emotional state of fear or apprehension that can appear in the presence of recognizable threat or even in the absence of danger.

Computer Programming: Process that translate an algorithm into a programming language code.

Periodization: Planned long-term variation of the volume and intensity of training to prevent overtraining and promote optimal performance during the period of time where runs the most important competition of the season.

Self-Efficacy: Self-belief about the capabilities to complete tasks and reach goals.

TMS: Training Management System, a tool that manage a media library that enable to annotate video and to share notes between several users, usually used by athletes and public figures for media and mental training.

TPSI-6: TPSI was the Portuguese Acronym for the name of the course, Information Systems Programming and Technologies, being the number a reference to 6th edition.

Section 3
Frameworks and Tools

Chapter 9
Ensemble:
An Innovative Approach to Practice Computer Programming

Ricardo Queirós
Polytecnic Institute of Porto, Portugal & University of Porto, Portugal

José Paulo Leal
CRACS & INESC-Porto LA, Faculty of Sciences, University of Porto, Porto, Portugal

ABSTRACT

Currently, the teaching-learning process in domains, such as computer programming, is characterized by an extensive curricula and a high enrolment of students. This poses a great workload for faculty and teaching assistants responsible for the creation, delivery, and assessment of student exercises. The main goal of this chapter is to foster practice-based learning in complex domains. This objective is attained with an e-learning framework—called Ensemble—as a conceptual tool to organize and facilitate technical interoperability among services. The Ensemble framework is used on a specific domain: computer programming. Content issues are tacked with a standard format to describe programming exercises as learning objects. Communication is achieved with the extension of existing specifications for the interoperation with several systems typically found in an e-learning environment. In order to evaluate the acceptability of the proposed solution, an Ensemble instance was validated on a classroom experiment with encouraging results.

INTRODUCTION

For someone to acquire, improve or even maintain a complex skill it is necessary to practice it on a regular basis (Gross, 2005), (Eckerdal, 2009). The amount of practice required depends on the nature of the activity and on each individual. How well an individual improves with practice is directly related with its inherent capabilities, its previous know-how about the domain and the type of feedback that is available for improvement. If feedback is either non-existent or inappropriate, then the practice tends to be ineffective or even detrimental to learning.

An apt example of a complex skill is music. Learning music requires discipline and persever-

DOI: 10.4018/978-1-4666-7304-5.ch009

Figure 1. Noteflight application

ance while acquiring the concept of reading scores, practising an instrument or playing with a group. In order to enhance these skills and motivate young students, instructors use e-learning, mainly in introductory courses, to make the learning of music more appealing. One good example is the NoteFlight[1] web application (Figure 1), a tool designed to teach music by creating, viewing, printing and hearing music notation. The tool was recently integrated[2] with Moodle, a popular LMS. This integration enables instructors to create assignments (e.g. giving students a partial composition to be completed), to manually grade the student submissions and to give them feedback promptly.

Besides music, there are other areas where evaluation is a key component in practice such as management, health sciences, electronics. Playing business games in management courses, or simulating a human patient in life sciences courses, or simulating an electronic circuit in electronics courses are examples of learning processes that require the use of special authoring, rendering and assessment tools. These tools should be integrated in instructional environments in order to provide a better learning experience. However,

these tools would be too specific to incorporate in an e-learning platform. Even if they could be provided as pluggable components, the burden of maintaining them would be prohibitive to institutions with few courses in those domains.

The motivation for this work comes from yet another domain with complex evaluation: computer programming. Introductory programming courses are generally regarded as difficult and often have high failure and dropout rates (Ala-Mutka, 2005), (O'Kelly, 2006), (Robins, 2003). Researchers pointed out several causes for these rates (Esteves, 2010). The most consensual are: teaching methods based on lectures about programming language syntaxes, subject complexity (learning how to program means to integrate knowledge of a wide variety of conceptual domains such as computer science and mathematics while developing expertise in problem understanding, problem-solving, unit testing and others) and student's motivation (the public image of a "programmer" as a socially inadequate "nerd" and the reputation of programming courses as being extremely difficult affects negatively the motivation of the students).

Many educators claim that "learning through practice" is by far the best way to learn computer programming and to engage novice students (Gross, 2005), (Eckerdal, 2009). Practice in this area boils down to solving programming exercises. Nevertheless, solving exercises is only effective if students receive an assessment on their work. An exercise solved wrong will consolidate a false belief, and without feedback many students will not be able to overcome their difficulties.

A number of learning tools and environments have been built to assist both teachers and students in introductory programming courses.

Rongas, Kaarna, and Kalviainen (Rongas, 2004) established a classification for these tools dividing them into four categories: 1) integrated development interfaces, 2) visualization tools, 3) virtual learning environments, and 4) systems for submitting, managing, and testing exercises. To the best of the author's knowledge, no e-learning environment described in the literature integrates all these facets (Verdu, 2011), (Gomes, 2007), (Esteves, 2010).

For instance, an evaluator should be able to participate in learning scenarios where teachers can create exercises, store them in a repository and reference them in a LMS and students solve the exercises in integrated development environments and submit to evaluators who delivers an evaluation report back to students.

Several systems (Somyajit, 2008), (Verdu, 2011), (Xavier, 2011), (Guerreiro, 2008) try to address this issue allowing the integration of automatic assessment tools with course management systems but these approaches rely on ad hoc solutions or proprietary plug-ins rather on widely accepted international specifications for content description and communication among systems.

In this paper we present a proposal for an e-learning framework called the Ensemble E-Learning Framework (EeF). The EeF is a conceptual tool to organize a network of e-learning systems and services based on content and communications specifications. The EeF is the basis for the design and implementation of Ensemble instances as realizations of the framework. In this work we present the specialization of the Ensemble framework for a specific domain: the computer programming learning domain. In order to validate the instance, we use the Ensemble instance in a Polytechnic School and we present the main results.

The structure of the chapter is as follows. The second section presents a brief background on the topics of e-learning standards and systems. The third and fourth section details the Ensemble framework specialization for the computer programming domain. The next section validates the use of an Ensemble instance in classroom. We conclude the chapter with the presentation of the main contributes of this work and a brief discussion of future research.

BACKGROUND

The Ensemble framework recommends the use of several types of e-learning systems, as well of several international e-learning specifications. Thus, a detailed study was made to identify the most prominent and mature e-learning systems and specifications.

E-Learning Systems

The evolution of eLearning can be summarized by the transition of the early monolithic systems developed for specific learning domains to the new systems that can invoke specialized services and be plugged in any eLearning environments. These types of systems evolved from Content Management Systems (CMS). The CMS was introduced in the mid-1990s mostly by the online publishing industry. This type of system can be defined as a data repository that also includes tools for authoring, aggregating and sequencing content in order to simplify the creation, administration and access to online content (Nichani, 2009). The content is organized in small self-contained pieces of information to improve reusability at the content component level. These content components when used in the learning domain are called "learning objects" (LO) and the systems that manage them are called Learning Content Management Systems (LCMS) (Leal & Queirós, 2010). LO are context independent, transportable and reusable pieces of instruction that are digitally managed and delivered (Rehac, 2003). There are other definitions for Learning Objects (LO). Rehak & Mason (Rehac, 2003) define a learning object as: "a digitized entity which can be used, reused or referenced during technology supported learning".

Nowadays services play a crucial role in learning processes. These services can be easily recombined in different learning processes to assist on the teaching-learning process. This chapter focuses on learning processes within domains with complex evaluation such as computer programming learning. In this domain there are several candidates to offer services such as those referred by Rongas, Kaarna, and Kalviainen (Rongas, 2004), namely: LMSs, LORs and ASs.

In the LMS side, an interoperability comparative study (Leal, 2012) was conducted to select an LMS on which to base the development of e-learning systems integrating heterogeneous components. Two LMSs vendors were chosen (Moodle and Blackboard) and their interoperability features were analysed by splitting in two facets (learning content management and academic management) reflecting the broad classes of systems of a typical LMS operational environment.

In the LOR side, an interoperability study (Queirós, 2013) was conducted on the existing repository software distinguishing two categories of repositories - digital libraries and learning objects repositories. It also focused on the distinction between the actual repositories and the software used to implement them, highlighting the differences in their interoperability features.

Finally, a survey (Queirós, 2012) was made on ASs for programming exercises focusing on their interoperability features. The survey gathered information on the interoperability features of the existent ASs and compared them regarding a set of predefined criteria such as content specification and interoperation standards with other tools.

E-Learning Standards

In the eLearning context, standards are generally developed for the purposes of ensuring interoperability and reusability in systems and of the content and meta-data they manage. In this context, several organizations (IEEE, AICC, IMS, ADL) have been developed standards and specifications regarding the creation of standards, specifications, guidelines, best practices on the description and use of eLearning content. In the last decade practitioners of eLearning started valuing more the interchange of course content and learners' information, which led to the definition of new standards. These standards are generally developed to ensure interoperability and reusability in content and communication. In this context, several organizations (IMS, IEEE, ADL, ISO/IEC) have developed specifications and standards (Friesen, 2005). These specifications define, among many others, standards related to learning objects (Rehak and Mason, 2003), such as packaging them, describing their content, organizing them in modules and courses and communicating with other eLearning systems.

Packaging is crucial to store eLearning material and reuse it in different systems. The most widely used content packaging format is the IMS Content Packaging. An IMS CP learning object assembles resources and meta-data into a distribution medium, typically an archive in zip format, with its content described in a manifest file in the root level. The manifest file - named imsmanifest.xml - adheres to the IMS CP schema and contains several sections such as Metadata to describe the package as a whole and Resources to refer to resources (files) needed for the manifest and metadata describing these resources.

The metadata included in the manifest uses another standard - the IEEE Learning Object Metadata. The IEEE LOM is a data model used to describe a learning object. The model is organized in several categories that cover general data, such as title and description, technical data such as object sizes, types and durations, educational characteristics and intellectual property rights, among many others. These categories are very comprehensive and cover many facets of a LO. However, LOM was designed for general LO and does not to meet the requirements of specialized domains, such as the automatic evaluation of programming exercises. For instance, there is no way to assert the role of specific resources, such as test cases or solutions. Fortunately, IMS CP was designed to be straightforward to extend through the creation of application profiles.

The term Application Profile generally refers to "the adaptation, constraint, and/or augmentation of a metadata scheme to suit the needs of a particular community". A well know eLearning application profile is SCORM that extends IMS CP with more sophisticated sequencing and Contents-to-LMS communication.

The IMS GLC is also responsible for another application profile, the Question & Test Interoperability specification. QTI describes a data model for questions and test data and, since version 2.0, extends the LOM with its own meta-data vocabulary. QTI was designed for questions with a set of pre-defined answers, such as multiple choice, multiple response, fill-in-the-blanks and short text questions. Although long text answers could be used to write the program's source code, there is no way to specify how it should be compiled and executed, which test data should be used and how it should be graded. For these reasons we consider that QTI is not adequate for automatic evaluation of programming exercises, although it may be supported for sake of compatibility with some LMS. Recently, IMS Global Learning Consortium proposed the IMS Common Cartridge that adds support for several standards (e.g. IEEE

LOM, IMS CP, IMS QTI, IMS Authorization Web Service) and its main goal is to shape the future regarding the organization and distribution of digital learning content.

The standardization of the learning content it is not enough to ensure interoperability, which is a major user concern with the existing systems (Leal and Queirós, 2010). In the last few years there have been initiatives (Holden, 2004) to adapt Service Oriented Architectures (SOA) to eLearning. These initiatives, commonly named eLearning frameworks, had the same goal: to provide flexible learning environments for learners worldwide. While eLearning frameworks are general approaches for eLearning system integration, several organizations proposed service oriented approaches specifically targeted to the LMS (IMS Digital Repository Interoperability – IMS DRI) and Repositories (IMS LTI).

The IMS DRI specification provides a functional architecture and a reference model for repository interoperability composed by a set of recommendations for common repository functions, namely the submission, search and download of LOs. It recommends the use of web services to expose the repository functions based on the Simple Object Access Protocol (SOAP) protocol, defined by W3C. Despite the SOAP recommendation, other web service interfaces could be used, such as, Representational State Transfer (REST) (Fielding, 2005).

A common interoperability standard that is increasingly supported by major LMS vendors is the IMS Learning Tools Interoperability (IMS LTI) specification. It provides a uniform standards-based extension point in LMS allowing remote tools and content to be integrated into LMSs. The main goal of the LTI is to standardize the process for building links between learning tools and the LMS. The IMS launched also a subset of the full LTI v1.0 specification called IMS Basic LTI. This subset exposes a unidirectional link between the LMS and the application. For instance, there is no provision for accessing run-time services in the LMS and only one security policy is supported.

THE ENSEMBLE FRAMEWORK INSTANCE

This chapter presents a specialization of the Ensemble framework (Queirós & Leal, 2013) for a new domain - computer programming. The presentation includes the overall architecture of the Ensemble instance followed by the description of the data and the integration models. The data model relies on the PExIL specification - an interoperability language for describing programming exercises - included as a LAO resource in an IMS CC package as recommended by the Ensemble specification. The integration model detailed how systems and services of this Ensemble instance are connected through the extension of the recommended specifications of the EeF. The integration model includes the creation of a new service for the communication with the AS based on the Evaluate service genre and the extension of the IMS DRI and LTI specifications for the integration of LOR and LMS, respectively. Then, a workflow of a network based on this Ensemble instance was presented showing how systems and services interact.

Finally, a selection of tools adjusted to the models was presented. This process was straightforward evidencing the interoperability features of the framework. Three of these systems and services that integrate this network were created from scratch, more precisely, the crimsonHex repository, the BabeLO converter and the Petcha Teaching Assistant. The acceptability of this Ensemble instance is validated in next chapter through an experiment in a pedagogical environment.

Architecture

This section presents the overall architecture of a network of e-learning systems and services participating in the automatic evaluation of programming exercises. The architecture (Figure 2) is composed by the following components:

- Teaching Assistant (TA) to interface the users with the network and to mediate the communication among all components;
- Integrated Development Environment (IDE) to code the exercises;
- Assessment System (AS) to evaluate exercises of students;
- Learning Objects Repository (LOR) to store and retrieve exercises;
- Learning Management System (LMS) to present the exercises to students;
- Conversion System (CS) to convert exercises formats.

Data Model

The concept of Learning Object (LO) is fundamental for producing, sharing and reusing content in e-Learning (Friesen, 2005). In essence a LO is a container with educational material and metadata describing it. Since most LOs just present content to students they contain documents in presentation formats such as HTML and PDF, and metadata describing these documents using LOM (or other metadata format). When a LO includes exercises to be automatically evaluated by an e-learning system, it must contain a document with a formal description for each exercise. The QTI specification is an example of a standard for this kind of definitions that is supported by several e-learning systems. However, QTI was designed for questions with predefined answers and cannot be used for complex evaluation domains such as the programming exercise evaluation (Leal & Queirós, 2009). In particular, the programming exercise domain requires interdependent resources (e.g. test cases, solution programs, exercise description) usually processed by different services in the programming exercise life-cycle. This kind

Figure 2. Overall architecture of the ensemble instance

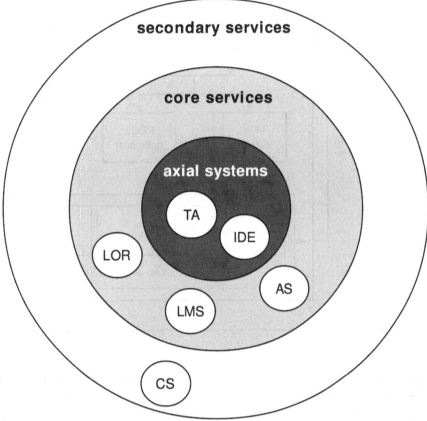

of data cannot be characterized as metadata as they are data effectively needed for evaluation.

The data model of the Ensemble instance extends the IMS CC specification for describing programming exercises. This extension is achieved by adding a new LAO resource in the CC package (Figure 3) as recommended by the Ensemble specification.

A LAO resource contains an XML descriptor that serves as the entry point for the target system. The descriptor file is not intended to be displayed within the target system. Rather, it is intended to be processed by the target system upon import of the cartridge. The descriptor file (pexil.xml) is associated with a LAO by means of a file element. It includes references for two XML documents: pexildefinition.xml and pexilmanifest.xml. The former describes all data needed for the generation of the evaluation resources. The latter is a manifest with references for all the evaluation resources generated. These resources - called associated content resources - comprise the exercise description, tests and feedback files and the solution program.

Integration Model

The integration model depicted in Figure 4 relies on communication standards recommended by the Ensemble specification. This network model abstracts specific systems and focuses on system types. For instance, it is possible to use in this network any repository as long it supports the IMS CC specification to formalize the description

Figure 3. Programming exercise as a IMS CC package

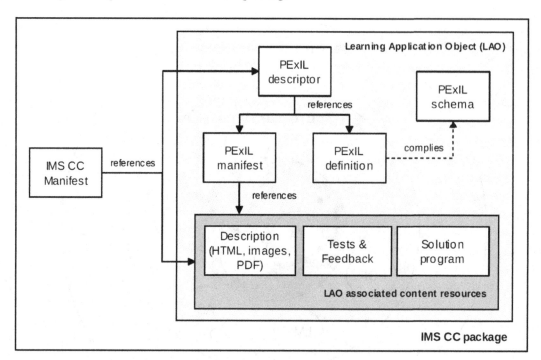

of programming exercises and it implements the IMS DRI specification for communication with other services.

The previous subsections report on the efforts made to integrate the systems and services of an Ensemble instance for the computer programming domain. These efforts included the creation and extension of communication specifications such as:

- The extension of the IMS DRI specification for the integration of LOR;
- The extension of the IMS LTI specification for the integration of LMS;
- The creation of an evaluation service for the communication with the AS.

For each specification the interface definition and response bindings were presented. This subsection summarizes all the interactions among systems and services based on these specifications and represented in the UML sequence diagram depicted in Figure 5.

The workflow presented in Figure 5 starts by the selection of an LTI activity by the student. This activity was previously configured by the teacher by selecting a collection of exercises. After selection, the LMS launches the TA through the Launch function of the LTI specification passing the user and course parameters. In order to present the programming exercises to the student the TA forwards the search to the LOR using the Search DRI function with the given collection URL. Meanwhile the TA gets from the AS the evaluation capabilities for later evaluation using the ListCapabilities function. In general each student is able to make several submissions for the same exercise and an activity may include several exercises. Each evaluation starts with an Evaluate request from the TA to the AS, sending a program and referring an exercise and a programming language. The AS retrieves the LO from the repository to have access to test cases, special correctors and other metadata. The AS responds with a ticket and an evaluation report, if the evaluation

Figure 4. Network component diagram

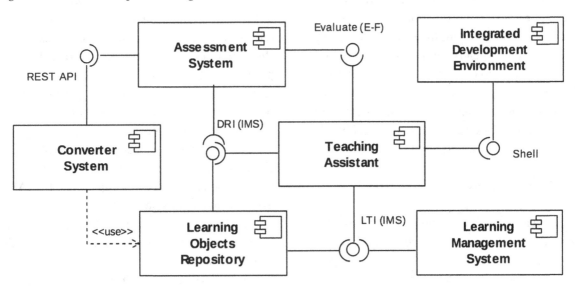

Figure 5. Sequence diagram of the Ensemble instance

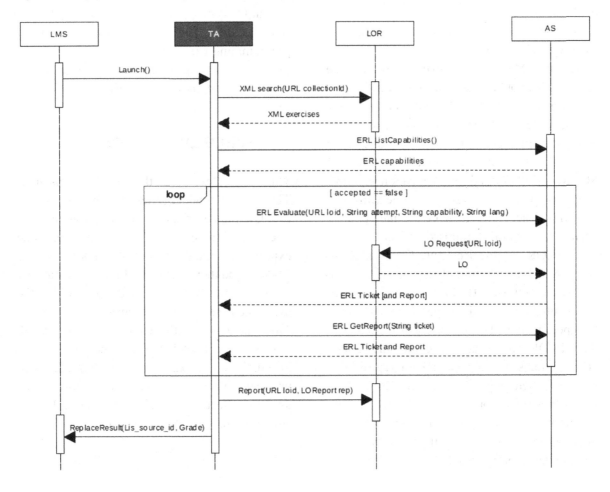

is completed within a certain time frame. The TA may retrieve the evaluation report using the GetReport function with the ticket as argument. When the student ends the session, the TA sends an usage report to the LOR using the DRI report function and a grade back to the LMS using the LTI replaceResult function. This latter feature is not yet implemented due to the missing Full LTI support by the most important LMS.

Tools Selection

The data and integration model of this Ensemble instance relies on content and communication standards as recommended by the Ensemble specification. These interoperability effort abstracts specific systems and focus on system types. This approach has facilitated the selection of tools for deployment purposes.

The next paragraphs discuss the selection of each type of system or service.

On the LMS side the choice fell on Moodle since it is a popular and open source LMS, arguably the most popular LMS nowadays (Davis, 2009), (Cole, 2007). This LMS has made efforts to support interoperability with other e-learning systems at two levels: content (e.g. IMS CP, SCORM, IMS CC) and communication (e.g. IMS LTI). Also successfully tests were made with Sakai LMS on this network evidencing the interoperable characteristics of the proposed approach.

The LOR system selected was CrimsonHex - a software for the creation of repositories of programming exercises. The exercises are described as learning objects and complying with the IMS CC specification. The repository also adheres to the IMS DRI specification to communicate with other systems. Other software for repositories were analysed (e.g. Flori, HarvestRoad Hive, IntraLibrary) but none of them met the domain requirements for the content and communication interoperability and most of them follow a commercial development model.

The AS system selected was Mooshak (Leal & Silva, 2003). Mooshak is an open source system for managing programming contests on the Web including automatic judging of submitted programs. This was the logical choice after the survey made to 15 assessment systems. One of the most important reasons for its selection was the support of web services.

The IDE system selected was Visual Studio Express for C\# assignments. Successful tests were made also with the Eclipse IDE for JAVA assignments on this network.

The TA system selected was Petcha (Queirós & Leal, 2012). Petcha has a two-fold goal: to coordinate the systems and services of this network and to interface with users, both teachers and students. Given the specificity of this role no other similar systems were found.

The CS system selected was BabeLO (Queirós & Leal, 2013). This system converts formats of programming exercises among systems. At the time of writing this dissertation no other system was found with these characteristics.

ENSEMBLE EVALUATION

This chapter evaluates the Ensemble instance. The Nielsen's model (Nielsen, 1994) is used to evaluate the acceptability of Petcha as the user interface of the network. For this evaluation an experiment was conducted with undergraduate students and their teachers. This chapter starts by presenting the evaluation model followed in the experiment based on the heuristics of Nielsen. Then, the design of the experiment is described. The description includes the methodology followed, the educational context and infrastructure where the experiment occurs and the instruments used to collect the data. Finally, the evaluation results are presented and analysed.

Evaluation Model

According to Nielsen (Nielsen, 1994) the acceptability of a system is defined as the combination of social and practical acceptability. The former determines the success/failure of the system, since the more the system is socially acceptable the greater is the number of people using it. The latter relates factors such as usefulness, cost, reliability and interoperability with existing systems. An adaptation to the Nielsen's model (Nielsen, 1994) is depicted in Figure 6.

The *usefulness* factor relates the utility and usability offered by the system. Utility is the capacity of the system to achieve a desired goal. As the system perform more tasks, more utility he has. Usability is defined by Nielsen as a qualitative attribute that estimates how easy is to use an user interface. He mentions five characteristics involved in the concept of usability: *ease of learning* - the system should be easy to learn so that the user can start doing some work with the system; *efficiency* - the system should be efficient to use, so after the user learns the system, a high level of productivity is possible; *memorability* - the system should be easy to remember so that the casual

user is able to return to the system after a period without using it, without requiring to learn it all over again; *errors* - the system should prevent the user from committing errors as should deal with them gracefully and minimizing the chance of occurring catastrophic errors; *satisfaction* - the system should be pleasant to use so that users become subjectively satisfied when using. The *cost factor* was not considered since Petcha is a free (and open source) software. The *reliability* is the ability of a system or component to perform its required functions under stated conditions for a specified period of time. *Interoperability* is the ability of two or more systems or components to exchange information and to use the information that has been exchanged.

This chapter presents an acceptability evaluation on an Ensemble network for the computer programming domain. To carry out this evaluation an experiment was conducted in a higher education school. This evaluation focuses on three facets: usefulness, reliability and interoperability.

For the usefulness facet, a questionnaire based on the Nielsen's heuristics was filled in by students in the end of that experiment. On one hand, the results showed that the aesthetic

Figure 6. System acceptability
Adapted from Nielsen

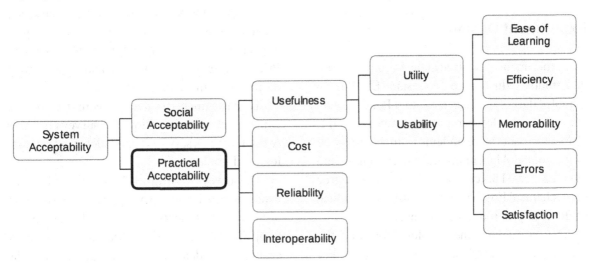

was the heuristic with higher values of satisfaction. The respondents claim that the minimalist design is one of the strongest points of Petcha (the front-end of the Ensemble network). On the other hand, the results reveal deficiencies in three areas: flexibility, freedom and documentation. In the flexibility heuristic, the respondents felt difficulties in personalize the user interface and speed up the execution of frequent actions (e.g. definition of short-cuts). The freedom heuristic was another area where students were not satisfied since Petcha does not allow, for instance, the undo/redo of actions. Finally, students complained of the unavailability of supporting documentation while using Petcha.

In the reliability facet students stated difficulties in understanding error messages and teachers complained about the lack of intuitiveness in the creation of exercises.

For the interoperability facet, the communication between pairs of systems was analysed during the experiment by comparing the expected values with the real values (those obtained through service logs). The results show that the proposed e-learning framework is useful in practice. The figures collected during the experiment are within reasonable bound from the expected values. These results show that the network is stable enough to handle a significant number of students, and exercises and can be used in a classroom setting.

Experiment Design

The experiment took place at the Escola Superior de Estudos Industriais e de Gestão (ESEIG) - a school of the Polytechnic Institute of Porto - during the months of October and November of 2011. The participants were students from the first-year of the course Algorithms and Programming and their teachers. This course is offered to the degree in Mechanical Engineering and aims to introduce students to programming concepts.

The experiment methodology followed the experimental research method (Oncu, 2011). For this purpose experimental and control groups (two classes from the same course) were settled. The first class (the experimental group) had 21 students and the second class (the control group) had 19 students.

Students of both groups have similar characteristics such as the gender and previous background. For instance, the gender in both groups were well distributed, respectively 62% and 57% of females in both groups.

The conditions of the experiment were also equal for both classes (e.g. syllabus, teaching times, teacher, labs, technical means).

Although it could be assumed that the population of the classes were almost randomly formed, strictly the experiment should be called a *quasi-experiment*. A completely randomised design was not possible due to operational reasons. Based on this type of design, a *static group comparison design* (Borg, 1971) was followed where students of class A used Ensemble (the experimental group) and students of class B did not use it (the control group).

The course has an average enrolment of 40 students per year divided in two classes. The course is organized in two lectures of one hour each and one lab session of 4 hours per week. The experiment occurred in 6 lab sessions. In each lab session both groups (a total of 40 students) had 3 exercises to solve. In the experimental group the teacher only intervenes to solve operational issues related to the use of Ensemble and does not give any feedback to students regarding the exercises. Prior to the experiment, teacher and students were prepared for the experiment.

The instruments used for collecting data on the experiment were the following: surveys (session & final survey), service logs, students' attendance logs and grades.

The surveys were fulfilled and collected on-line using Google Forms[3]. Two types of surveys were presented to students: session and final survey (Appendix 1). The former was filled in by both groups of students after each lab session. The questionnaire[4] includes questions on the number of solved exercises and the feedback impact. It had an average of 38 responses per session (the equivalent to 95% of the total of students). The latter was presented to the experimental group at the end of the experiment. The questionnaire includes questions on the Petcha usefulness and reliability. The final survey was completed by all the students from the experimental group.

The *service logs* were used to attest the accuracy of the experimental group questionnaires responses. The data collected in the surveys of the experimental class was checked against the logs of Petcha and other systems in the network. An average discrepancy of 4.6% between these two sets of values was found.

The *student attendance* and *student outcomes* (programming module and semester grades) were collected through the Academic Management System used at ESEIG. The data was exported to a spreadsheet to simplify the data processing.

Results and Discussion

In this section the Ensemble network is evaluated based on three Nielsen heuristics: usefulness, reliability and interoperability.

Usefulness

Usefulness combines the utility and usability of a system. Utility is the capacity of the system to achieve a desired goal. Usability is defined by Nielsen as a qualitative attribute that estimates how easy is to use an user interface.

Petcha was evaluated according to the Nielsen's model using a heuristic evaluation methodology. A heuristic evaluation is an inspection method for computer software that helps to identify usability problems in the user interface (UI) design. Jakob Nielsen's heuristics (Appendix 2) are arguably the most used usability heuristics for user interface design. Based on these heuristics a questionnaire (with 41 questions was designed in Google Forms.

The aim of the questionnaire is to identify usability problems in the UI design of Petcha. Two profiles of users answered this questionnaire in the end of the experiment: 21 students (experimental group) and 4 teachers (although only one was the teacher of the students that participated in the experiment).

Figure 7 shows the results obtained grouped by the Nielsen's heuristics. The data collected are shown in graphs. In the chart graphs the heuristics are sorted in ascending order of user satisfaction.

The results highlight deficiencies in three areas: Flexibility, User control and freedom, Help and documentation.

In regard to the flexibility of the system, respondents considered that the system do not allow the personalization of the interface as shown in Figure 8, more precisely, the activation/deactivation of certain functions and the configuration of the screens. The possibility of use of accelerator keys to speed up the interaction with the TA is also a handicap of Petcha.

The User control and freedom is the second worst facet (Figure 9). Most of the complaints focused on the inability to cancel or roll back mistakes made to a previous and safe state.

The Help and documentation is another heuristic with negative values as shown in Figure 10. The respondents state that is difficult to find help and documentation in Petcha.

The respondents reveal that the error messages are sometimes unclear and inadequate in Petcha. The respondents also state that the documentation is scarce and is hard to find it.

The final classification of Petcha is shown in Figure 11.

One can conclude that the majority of students classified Petcha as a good tool according to the parameters evaluated.

Regarding the teacher profile, Figure 12 shows the results obtained.

The results are similar to those of students. In one hand the aesthetic factor was the one with higher values of satisfaction. The respondents considered that the information contained on

Figure 7. Results of each heuristic in the student's profile

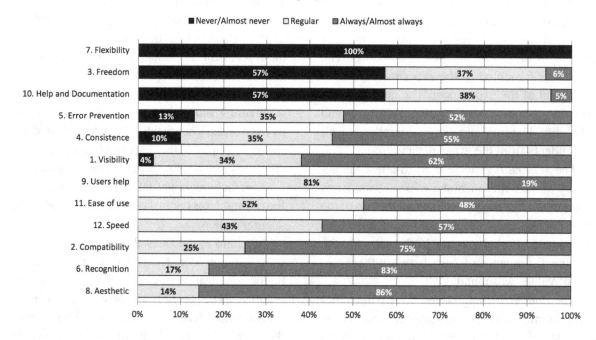

Figure 8. Evaluation of Petcha's flexibility

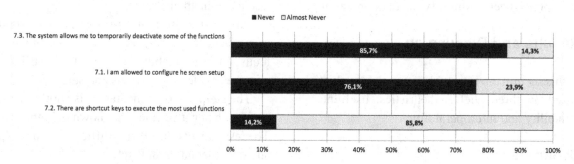

Figure 9. Evaluation of Petcha's freedom

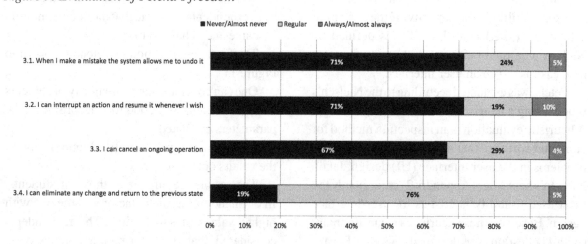

Figure 10. Results of each heuristic in the student profile

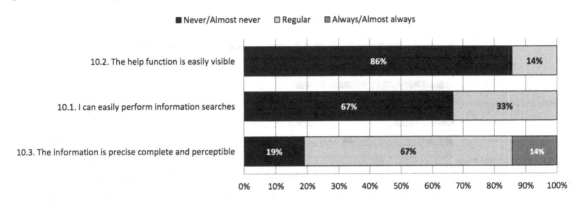

Figure 11. Classification of Pectha by students

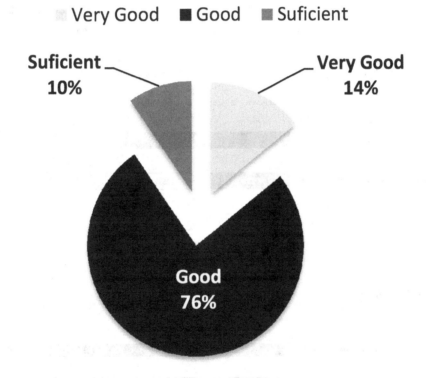

the screen is only what is needed and the system is aesthetically pleasing on the factors: color, brightness, etc. In the other hand the flexibility, freedom and documentation heuristics had some of the lowest values. However another heuristic had a low value: the Ease of Use. Figure 13 shows the results associated to this heuristic.

Reliability

The reliability of a system is the ability of a system or component to perform its required functions under stated conditions for a specified period of time.

In the final survey a reliability section was added in order to check on what tasks students

Figure 12. Results of each heuristic in the teacher profile

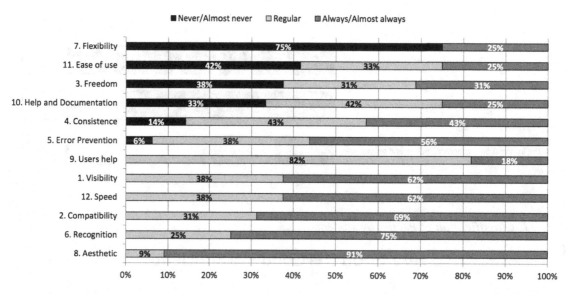

Figure 13. Results of the Ease of Use heuristic in the teacher profile

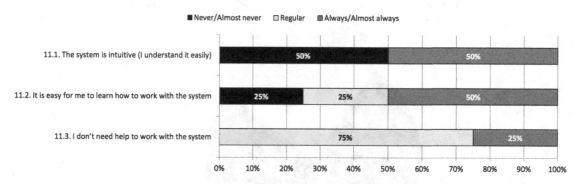

Figure 14. Reliability of Petcha

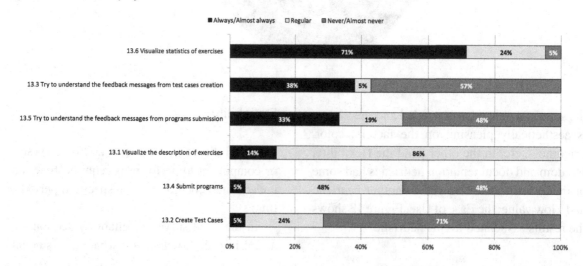

and teachers had the difficulties. Figure14 shows the results of the survey in this facet.

Students reported difficulties in understanding error messages related to programs submission. Some users have left comments and suggestions, and the following were the most common:

- The message wording should be more friendly;
- The feedback should be more complete;
- The help system is insufficient for novice users;
- The exercise statistics should be more complete (e.g. time to solve, students rankings).

The comments and suggestions of the teachers were the following:

- The creation of exercises is not intuitive;
- The evaluation based on test cases should be more flexible in the comparison between the outputs generated by the student solution with the accepted outputs;

```
\end{itemize}
```

Interoperability

In the design of the experiment a network was deployed based on the Ensemble instance previously. This network is composed by several systems and services that need to interoperate to achieve a common goal. In this subsection the interoperability of this network is validated. Table 1 summarizes the communication between pairs of systems. These results were gathered from 6 lab sessions. In each session a class of 21 students had 3 exercises to solve. Based on these figures were computed the following expected values: the expected number of accesses to the system that is given by multiplying the number of students with the number of assignments (21 * 6 = 126); and the expected number of accesses to the exercises by all the students that is given by multiplying the number of students with the number of assignments and with the number of exercises by assignment (21 * 6 * 3 = 378).

The first line of the table indicates that the system worked well since only nine extra sessions were used. These extra values were mainly due to the accidental closing of the application by students.

The number of exercises requested by the TA (Petcha) measures the number of times that students got an exercise statement from the repository. This action triggers an automatic request from Petcha to the repository. From the collected data it can be observed that not all exercises were actually read by all the students. There are two possible justifications: either the students did not have time to read all the available statements or some students may have given up after reading the exercise title. In any event students did not report any difficulty in accessing to problems

The third line of Table 1 is the number of exercises that students tried to solve. It is assumed that a student tried to solve an exercise when (s) he ran locally a set of tests to validate the code. The real number is less than the expected and less than the number of exercise statement accesses. Most likely some students read an exercise statement, but did not have time to code a solution, or run the tests, or simply given up on solving it.

The number of submissions is the number of requests for evaluation received by the AS. On average each student made approximately two submissions per exercise.

The number of exercises requests reflects the need of the AS to obtained the full LO from to repository given its reference. Since the AS has a cache mechanism the expected and real values are identical thus showing that the AS cache feature is working as expected and is accelerating the evaluation process.

The number of exercises in which the students got feedback should be similar to those of the

Table 1. Statistical data on interoperability of the network components

Observation Point	Expected	Real
# accesses to the system (LMS to TA)	126	135
# exercises requested to the repository (TA to LOR)	378	345
# exercises that students try to solve (TA to IDE)	378	342
# submissions (TA to AS)	378	819
# exercises requested to the repository (AS to LOR)	18	18
# exercises in which the students got feedback (AS to TA)	378	810

number of submissions. Since they are almost identical (a difference of 9) one can conclude that the communication among the two systems (TA and AS) works well.

CONCLUSION

Learning complex skills is hard. Introductory programming courses are generally regarded as difficult and often have high failure and dropout rates (Ala-Mutka, 2005), (O'Kelly, 2006), (Robins, 2003). Many educators claim that "learning through practice" is by far the best way to learn computer programming and to engage novice students (Gross, 2005), (Eckerdal, 2009). Practice in this area boils down to solving programming exercises. Nevertheless, solving exercises is only effective if students receive an assessment on their work. Assessing the work of students and providing individualised feedback to all students is time-consuming for teachers and frequently involves a time delay. The existent tools and specifications prove to be insufficient in complex evaluation domains where there is a greater need to practice (Rongas, 2004).

This work proposes an e-learning framework - called Ensemble - that acts as a conceptual tool in the definition and deployment of e-leaning networks using complex evaluation. The framework relies on interoperability standards and specifications, thus several studies and surveys were conducted to select the most relevant for the

framework. Based on this framework a network of systems and services was created and deployed for a specific domain - the computer programming domain. Content issues are tacked with a standard format to describe programming exercises as learning objects. Communication issues are addressed with the development or adaptation of systems and services for managing the life-cycle of exercises, namely their authoring, storage, conversion and assessment.

The framework instance was deployed for use in practical classes of undergraduate programming courses. The experience gained using Petcha (the pivot component) in this context and the experiments designed to assess the impact of this tool were also presented in this dissertation. These experiments showed an increase on exercises solving, attendance and grades when Petcha replaced a human Teaching Assistant (TA). However, these results show also that the automatic feedback provided by Petcha is less effective than that of a human TA. There is clearly room for improving automatic feedback in Petcha, although it can be argued that automated feedback is still a remedy for situations where a human TA is not available.

Contributions

The main contribution of this work is a conceptual model - the Ensemble framework - for the definition and deployment of e-learning networks using complex evaluation. The architectural model of this framework relies on central components (called axial systems) replicated for each teacher and student machines. One of these central components assumes a pivot role orchestrating all the communications within a single deployment of an Ensemble instance. Since it is distributed over each network user, this approach prevents any single-point-of-failure issues that might occur. This pivot component communicates locally with other axial systems and remotely with core and secondary services representing a distinctive feature regarding other e-learning frameworks.

Part of this main contribution is the specialization of the framework for a specific domain - the computer programming domain. This framework instance comprises several systems and services and their integration poses interoperability issues at two levels: content and communication. The content interoperability relies on the definition of an interoperability language for programming exercises called PExIL. The communication among systems and services was supported by the extension of existing specifications (e.g. IMS DRI, IMS LTI) and the creation of new ones (e.g. Evaluate service).

Other important contribution is the systematic study on the state of the art regarding e-learning systems and standards. This comprehensive study focuses on several surveys presented in the state of the art that were instrumental to chose the better e-learning systems and standards for the Ensemble framework. This contribution may prove helpful to other researchers studying the interoperability of e-learning systems.

The remaining contributions are related with the design and implementation of components that comprises the Ensemble network for the computer programming domain. These components are the crimsonHex repository (including a plug-in for accessing crimsonHex based repositories from Moodle), the Petcha teaching assistant and the BabeLO exercises converter. All these components are open source and can be downloaded from the following URL: http://ensemble.dcc.fc.up.pt.

Opportunities for Future Work

The motivation for this research was drawn from the computer programming domain. However, it was always kept in mind that the proposed concepts and tools could be used in other domains. The main opportunity for future research comes from extending this framework to other domains and requirements. Nevertheless, the evaluation of Ensemble and the validation of the thesis highlighted a number of issues that must be resolved in the computer programming instance of Ensemble.

Framework Validation

The main challenge resulting from this research is to apply the framework to other domains. Although the research hypothesis were in general validated, the framework as such is not yet validated since it was only applied to a single domain. One interesting domain is serious games applied to management courses where students develop their skills using simulation. Business simulation games improve the strategic thinking and decision making skills of students in several areas (e.g. finances, logistics, and production). Through these simulations students compete among them as they would in a real world companies. A business simulation service fulfils a role similar to that of the assessment systems in programming exercises and it also requires a repository containing specialized LO describing simulations. Thus, this specific domain poses challenges not only in the development of the network TA, but also in the refinement of the framework specifications and services (e.g. repository, assessment system) to meet the new evaluation domains requirements.

Framework Extension

The current version of the framework focuses mainly on exercise authoring, exchange and evaluation. Other kinds of data and services should be added to improve the practice-based environments supported by Ensemble, both in the computer programming domain and in new domains.

- **Plagiarism Checker:** This component can be added to the framework to avoid plagiarism and ensure good scholarly practices. This tool is transversal to several areas and is therefore a good candidate to integrate the Ensemble framework;
- **Sequencing Component:** Sequencing of exercises is another topic that can be explored in the future and it is closely related with pedagogical issues during the construction of a learning scenario. Several standards appeared in recent years trying to cope this topic but fail due its complexity for e-Learning systems to implement. One research path is to deliver exercises to students dynamically according with their profiles, knowledge evolution and course goals. An intended addition is a sequencing and adaptation tool to guide the student through a collection of expository and evaluation resources. The network pivot component will report the exercise assessment to this new tool that will use it to propose the appropriate content or exercise to the student;
- **E-Portfolio:** This is a special type of a repository where a collection of electronic evidence is assembled and managed by a user. They are distinct from LMSs since they are user-centric rather than course-centric. The integration of such tool in the Ensemble framework can be achieved at content or communication level through data (e.g. LeapA specification) or tools integration (e.g. IMS LTI specification);
- **Standards and Specifications:** Support for other LO package specifications (e.g. SCORM objects and for MathJax for displaying math expressions in the description of exercises.

Ensemble Instance Improvements

The computer programming instance of Ensemble is currently being used in the practical classes of undergraduate programming courses at ESEIG and will continue to be used in the next academic year. Several improvements are planned for immediate implementation based on the suggestions of teachers and students after the experiment. These improvements focus on Petcha - the visible system of the network, and include:

- **User Interface:** Make the GUI more intuitive and flexible;
- **Evaluation Reports:** Improve the visualization of the evaluation reports using new formats (e.g. PDF);
- **Statistics:** Improve statistical data on student activity (e.g. time to solve, rankings);
- **Help:** Extend the documentation to guide users;

In general, the improvements presented previously are minor issues that should be easily fixed for the next version of the Ensemble instance. There is also a collection of new features that would improve automatic assessment but that will require a major redesign of the AS.

- **Feedback:** Improve the feedback mechanism based on, for instance, the use of static analysis over the students' code. Existing work in this area (Nielson, 1999) can be used to improve the feedback given to students after submission.
- **New Evaluation Models:** A programming problem definition must have an unambiguous evaluation model. Typically a program from a student is assessed by the evaluator as a single program. Another approach is the student code be included within a set of programs from different learners for competitive evaluation. A third approach is where several programs from

different learners are evaluated simultaneously interacting with a central component (an "oracle") also in a competitive fashion. For instance, in the Tic Tac Toe game the student's program plays the game against the oracle;

- **Other Types of Languages:** The current evaluator can be configured for any programming language with a command line interface and processing standard input/output. There are computer languages that are not strictly programming but are regularly used in computer science courses such as query languages (e.g. SQL), modelling languages (e.g. UML) and user interfaces (e.g. HTML). In most cases these languages can be evaluated statically by comparing the submitted source code with the solution.

REFERENCES

Aguirre, S., Salvachua, J., Quemada, J., Fumero, A., & Tapiador, A. (2006). Joint degrees in e-learning systems: A web services approach. In *Proceedings of the 2nd IEEE International Conference on Collaborative Computing: Networking, Applications and Worksharing*. IEEE. Retrieved from http://jungla.dit.upm.es/ saguirre/publications/CollaborateCom20061:pdf

Al-Khalifa, H. S., & Davis, H. C. (2006). The evolution of metadata from standards to semantics in e-learning applications. In *Proceedings of Hypertext*, (pp. 69-72). Retrieved from http://doi.acm.org/10.1145/1149941.1149956

Al-Smadi, C. M. (2010). Soa-based architecture for a generic and flexible e-assessment system. In Proceedings of Education Engineering (EDUCON). IEEE.

Ala-Mutka, K. (2005). A survey of automated assessment approaches for programming assignments. *Journal of Computer Science Education, 15*(2), 83–102. doi:10.1080/08993400500150747

Alario, C., & Wilson, S. (2010). Comparison of the main alternatives to the integration of external tools in different platforms. In Proceedings of ICERI 2010. IATED.

Apostolopoulos, T. K., & Kefala, A. S. (2003). An e-learning service management architecture. In Proceedings of ICALT (pp. 140-144). ICALT.

Aroyo, L., & Dolog, P., jan Houben, G., Kravcik, M., Naeve, A., Nilsson, M., & Wild, F. (2006). Interoperability in personalized adaptive learning. *Journal of Educational Technology & Society, 9*(2), 4-18. Retrieved from http://www.ifets.info/journals/92=2:pdf

Barker, P., & Campbell, L. M. (2010). Metadata for learning materials: an overview of existing standards and current developments. *Technology, Instruction, Cognition and Learning, 7*(3-4), 225-243. Retrieved from http://www.icbl.hw.ac.uk/publicationFiles/2010/TICLMetadata/TICL-paper.MetadataForEducationpostref:pdf

Barret, H. (2010). *Electronic portfolios in stem - what is an electronic portfolio*. Retrieved from http://www.scribd.com/doc/40206175/E-Portfolio-Definition

Barret, H. (n.d.). Categories of eportfolio tools (Tech. Rep.). JISC.

Benford, S., Burke, E., Foxley, E., Gutteridge, N., & Zin, A. (2011). Early experiences of computer-aided assessment and administration when teaching computer programming. *Research in Learning Technology, 1*(2). Retrieved from http://www.researchinlearningtechnology.net/index.php/rlt/article/view/9481

Bersin. (2009). *Learning management systems 2009: Executive summary*. Bersin & Associates.

Blumenstein, M., Green, S., Nguyen, A., & Muthukkumarasamy, V. (2004, June). An experimental analysis of game: A generic automated marking environment. *SIGCSE Bulletin, 36*(1), 67–71. doi:10.1145/1026487.1008016

Britain, L. O. S. (1998). *A Framework for Pedagogical Evaluation of Virtual Learning Environments* (Tech. Rep.). Retrieved from http://www.leeds.ac.uk/educol/documents/00001237.htm

Burguillo, J. C. (2010). Using game theory and competition-based learning to stimulate student motivation and performance. *Comput. Educ., 55*(2), 566-575. Retrieved from doi: 10.1016/j.compedu.2010.02.018

Casella, G., Costagliola, G., Ferrucci, F., Polese, G., & Scanniello, G. (2007). A scorm thin client architecture for e-learning systems based on web services. *International Journal of Distance Education Technologies, 5*(1), 19–36. doi:10.4018/jdet.2007010103

Chae, G. B., Chandra, S., Mann, V., & Nanda, M. G. (2004). Decentralized orchestration of composite web services. In *Proceedings of the 13th international world wide web conference on alternate track papers & posters,* (pp. 134-143). New York, NY: ACM. doi: 10.1145/1013367.1013390

Cheang, B., Kurnia, A., Lim, A., & Oon, W.-C. (2003, September). On automated grading of programming assignments in an academic institution. *Computers & Education, 4*(1), 121–131. doi:10.1016/S0360-1315(03)00030-7

Chloros, G., Zervas, P., & Sampson, D. G. (2010). Ask-lom-ap: A web-based tool for development and management of ieee lom application profiles. In Proceedings of ICALT, (pp. 138-142). ICALT. doi:10.1109/ICALT.2010.46

Cole, J., & Foster, H. (2007). *Using Moodle: Teaching with the Popular Open Source Course Management System* (2nd ed.). O'Reilly Media. Retrieved from http://www.amazon.com/exec/obidos/redirect?tag=citeulike07-20&path=ASIN/059652918X

Curbera, F., Duftler, M., Khalaf, R., Nagy, W., Mukhi, N., & Weerawarana, S. (2002). Unraveling the Web services web: an introduction to SOAP, WSDL, and UDDI. *IEEE Internet Computing, 6*(2), 86-93. doi: 10.1109/4236.991449

Dagger, D., O'Connor, A., Lawless, S., Walsh, E., & Wade, V. P. (2007). Service-Oriented E-Learning Platforms: From Monolithic Systems to Flexible Services. *IEEE Internet Computing, 11*(3), 28-35. Retrieved from http://ieeexplore.ieee.org/xpls/abs/all:jsp?arnumber=4196172

Daly, C. (1999, June). Roboprof and an introductory computer programming course. *SIGCSE Bulletin, 31*(3), 155–158. doi:10.1145/384267.305904

Davis, C. C. B., & Wagner, E. (2009). *The Evolution of the LMS: From Management to Learning - Deep Analysis of Trends Shaping the Future of eLearning* (Tech. Rep.). Sage Road Solutions, LLC. Retrieved from http://www.loc.gov/standards/mets/mets-schemadocs.html

Douce, C., Livingstone, D., & Orwell, J. (2005). Automatic test based assessment of programming: A review. *Journal of Educational Resources in Computing, 5*(3), 4, es. doi:10.1145/1163405.1163409

Eap, T. M., Hatala, M., & Richards, G. (2004). Digital repository interoperability: design, implementation and deployment of the ecl protocol and connecting middleware. In *Proceedings of the 13th international world wide web conference on alternate track papers & posters,* (pp. 376-377). New York, NY: Academic Press. doi: 10.1145/1013367.1013483

Eckerdal, A. (2009). *Novice programming students' learning of concepts and practice.* (Unpublished doctoral dissertation). Uppsala University, Uppsala, Sweden.

Eckerson, W. W. (1995). Three tier client/server architecture: Achieving scalability, performance, and efficiency in client server applications. *Open Information Systems, 10*(1).

Edwards, S. H., Borstler, J., Cassel, L. N., Hall, M. S., & Hollingsworth, J. (2008). Developing a common format for sharing programming assignments. *SIGCSE Bull., 40*(4), 167-182. doi:10.1145/1473195.1473240

Edwards, S. H., & Pugh, W. (2006, March). Toward a common automated grading platform. In *Proceedings of Birds-of-a-feather session at the 37th sigcse technical symposium on computer science education.* ACM.

Ellis, R. K. (2009). *Field guide to learning management systems.* ASTD Learning Circuits.

Engels, S., Lakshmanan, V., & Craig, M. (2007, March). Plagiarism detection using feature-based neural networks. *SIGCSE Bull., 39*(1), 34-38. http://doi.acm.org/10.1145/1227504.1227324

Erl, T. (2005). *Service-oriented architecture - Concepts, technology and design.* Upper Saddle River, NJ: Prentice Hall.

Esteves, M., Fonseca, B., Morgado, L., & Martins, P. (2010). *Improving teaching and learning of computer programming through the use of the Second Life virtual world. British Journal of Educational Technology.* doi:10.1111/j.1467-8535.2010.01056.x

Farance, F., & Tonkel, J. (1999). *Ltsa specification - Learning technology systems architecture, draft 5* (Tech. Rep.). IEEE. Retrieved from http://ltsc.ieee.org/wg1/files/ltsa05:pdf

Fay, E. (2010). Repository software comparison: Building digital library infrastructure at lse. *Ariadne, 64.* Retrieved from http://www.ariadne.ac.uk/issue64/fay/

Fernandez, J. L., Carrillo, J. M., Nicolas, J., Toval, A., & Carrion, M. I. (2011). Trends in e-learning standards. *International Journal of Computers and Applications, 353*(1), 49–54. Retrieved from http://www.ijcaonline.org/dedce/number1/dece008.pdf

Fielding, R., & Taylor, R. (2000). Principled design of the modern web architecture. In *Proceedings of 22nd International Conference on Software Engineering,* (pp. 407-416). Academic Press. doi:10.1145/337180.337228

Friesen, N. (2004a). *Metadata in practice (chap. Semantic and Syntactic Interoperability for Learning Object Metadata).* Chicago, IL: ALA Editions.

Friesen, N. (2004b). Editorial - a gentle introduction to technical elearning standards. *Canadian Journal of Learning and Technology, 30*(3). Retrieved from http://www.cjlt.ca/index.php/cjlt/article/view/136

Friesen, N. (2005). *Interoperability and learning objects: An overview of e-learning standardization. Interdisciplinary Journal of Knowledge and Learning Objects.*

Gomes, A., & Mendes, A. J. (2007). Learning to program - difficulties and solutions. In *Proceedings of the International Conference on Engineering Education.* Retrieved from http://icee2007.dei.uc.pt/proceedings/papers/411.pdf

Gray, L. (2008). Effective practice with e-portfolios: Supporting 21st century learning. *JISC.* Retrieved from http://www.jisc.ac.uk/media/documents/publications/effectivepracticeeportfolios.pdf

Gross, P., & Powers, K. (2005). Evaluating assessments of novice programming environments. In *Proceedings of the first international workshop on computing education research*, (pp. 99-110). New York, NY: ACM. Retrieved from http://doi.acm.org/10.1145/1089786.1089796

Guerreiro, P., & Georgouli, K. (2008, 01). Enhancing elementary programming courses using e-learning with a competitive attitude. *International Journal of Internet Education, 10*.

Gutierrez Rojas, I. A., Crespo Garcia, R. M., Pardo, A., & Delgado Kloos, C. (2009). Assessment interoperability using qti. In *Interactive conference on computer aided learning*. Retrieved from http://www.iicm.tugraz.at/CAF2009

Harasim, L. (2006). *A History of E-learning: Shift Happened*. doi: doi:10.1007/978-1-4020-3803-7

Harman, K., & Koohang, A. (2006). *Learning objects: Standards, metadata, repositories, and LCMS*. Santa Rosa, CA: Informing Science Press.

Higgins, C. A., Gray, G., Symeonidis, P., & Tsintsifas, A. (2005). Automated assessment and experiences of teaching programming. *Journal of Educational Resources in Computing, 5*(1). http://doi.acm.org/10.1145/1163405.1163410

Hoel, T., & Mason, J. (2011). Expanding the scope of metadata and the issue of quality. In *Proceedings of 19th international conference on computers in education*. Retrieved from http://hoel.nu/publications/ICCEworkshop paper Hoel Mason2011/final.pdf

Ihantola, P., Ahoniemi, T., Karavirta, V., & Seppala, O. (2010). Review of recent systems for automatic assessment of programming assignments. In *Proceedings of the 10th koli calling international conference on computing education research*, (pp. 86-93). New York, NY: ACM. Retrieved from http://doi.acm.org/10.1145/1930464.1930480

Jackson, D., & Usher, M. (1997). Grading student programming using assyst. In Proceedings of technical symposium on computer science education, (pp. 335 -339). ACM.

Jena, S. (2008). *Authoring and sharing of programming exercises*. (Unpublished master's thesis). San Jose State University. Retrieved from http://scholarworks.sjsu.edu/etdprojects=19

Jenkins, T. (2002). On the Difficulty of Learning to Program. In *Proceedings of 3rd annual conference of ltsn-ics*. Retrieved from http://www.ics.ltsn.ac.uk/pub/conf2002/tjenkins.pdf

Jerman-Blazic, B., & Klobucar, T. (2005). Privacy provision in e-learning standardized systems: Status and improvements. *Computer Standards & Interfaces, 27*(6), 561–578. doi:10.1016/j.csi.2004.09.006

Juedes, D. (2003). Experiences in web-based grading. In *Proceedings of 33rd ASEE/IEEE Frontiers in Education Conference*. IEEE. doi:10.1109/FIE.2003.1266003

Kati Clements, J. M. P., & Gras-Velazquez, A. (n.d.). Educational resources packaging standards scorm and ims common cartridge - The users point of view. In Proceedings of Search and exchange of e-learning materials. Academic Press.

Klenin, A. (2011). Common problem description format: Requirements. In *Proceedings of ACMICPC World Final CLIS (Competitive Learning Institute Symposium)*. ACMICPC.

Kumar, P., Samaddar, S., Samaddar, A., & Misra, A. (2010). Extending ieee ltsa e-learning framework in secured soa environment. In *Proceedings of 2nd international conference on education technology and computer (icetc)*. doi:10.1109/ICETC.2010.5529417

Kurilovas, E. (2012). European learning resource exchange: A platform for collaboration of researchers, policy makers, practitioners, and publishers to share digital learning resources and new e-learning practices. In P. O. P. A. Cakir (Ed.), Social development and high technology industries: Strategies and applications. IGI-Global. Retrieved from http://www.igi-global.com/chapter/social-development-high-technology-industries/58723

Lahtinen, E., Ala-Mutka, K., & Jarvinen, H.-M. (2005, June). A study of the difficulties of novice programmers. *SIGCSE Bull., 37*(3), 14-18. doi: 10.1145/1151954.1067453

Lawrence, A. W., Badre, A. M., & Stasko, J. T. (1994). Empirically evaluating the use of animations to teach algorithms. In *Proceedings of Visual Languages 1994 IEEE Symposium*, (pp. 48-54). IEEE. Retrieved from http://citeseerx.ist.psu.edu/viewdoc/download?doi=10.1.1.25.8514rep=rep1type=pdf

Leal, J. P., & Queirós, R. (2009), Defining Programming Problems as Learning Objects. In *Proceedings of International Conference on Computer Education and Instructional Technology*. Venice, Italy: Academic Press.

Leal, J. P., & Queirós, R. (2010). *From eLearning Systems to Specialised Services. In A New Learning Paradigm: Competition Supported by Technology.* Sello Editorial.

Leal, J. P., & Queirós, R. (2012). A Comparative Study on LMS Interoperability. In Virtual Learning Environments: Concepts, Methodologies, Tools and Applications (pp. 1613-1630). Hershey, PA: Information Science Reference. doi: doi:10.4018/978-1-4666-0011-9.ch804

Leal, J. P., & Silva, F. M. A. (2003). Mooshak: A web-based multi-site programming contest system. *Software, Practice & Experience, 33*(6), 567–581. doi:10.1002/spe.522

Levensaler, L., & Laurano, M. (2010). *Talent management systems 2010: Mar-ket realities, implementation experiences and solution provider profiles.* Bersin & Associates.

Liang, Y., Liu, Q., Xu, J., & Wang, D. (2009, Dec.). The recent development of automated programming assessment. In *Computational intelligence and software engineering*, (pp. 1-5). IEEE. Retrieved from http://ieeexplore.ieee.org/stamp/stamp.jsp?tp=arnumber=5365307

lok Lee, F., & Heyworth, R. (2000). *Problem complexity: A measure of problem difficulty in algebra by using computer.* Academic Press.

Luck, M., & Joy, M. (1999). A secure on-line submission system. In Software - practice and experience, (pp. 721-740). Academic Press.

Malita, L. (2009). E-portfolios in an educational and ocupational context. *Procedia: Social and Behavioral Sciences, 1*(1), 2312–2316. doi:10.1016/j.sbspro.2009.01.406

Malmi, L., Karavirta, V., Korhonen, A., & Nikander, J. (2005, September). Experiences on automatically assessed algorithm simulation exercises with different resubmission policies. *Journal of Educational Resources in Computing, 5*(3), 7, es. doi:10.1145/1163405.1163412

Mandal, A. K., Mandal, C., & Reade, C. M. P. (2006). Architecture of an automatic program evaluation system. *CSIE.* Retrieved from http://sit.iitkgp.ernet.in/chitta/pubs/CSIEAIT06-p152.pdf

Mandal, C. V. L. R. C. M. P., & Sinha. (2004). A web-based course management tool and web services. *Electronic Journal of E-Learning, 2.* http://doi.acm.org/10.1145/1163405.1163412

Markiewicz, M. E., & de Lucena, C. J. P. (2001, July). Object oriented framework development. *Crossroads, 7*(1), 3–9. doi:10.1145/372765.372771

Mason, R., & Rehak, D. (2003). Keeping the learning in learning objects. In A. Littlejohn (Ed.), *Reusing online resources: A sustainable approach to e-learning*, (pp. 20-34). London: Kogan Page. Retrieved from http://oro.open.ac.uk/800/

Massart, D. A. (2010). Taming the metadata beast: Ilox. *D-Lib Magazine*, *16*(1), 11–12. Retrieved from http://www.dlib.org/dlib/november10/massart/11massart.html

McCallum, S. H. (2006). A look at new information retrieval protocols: Sru, opensearch. In *World library and information congress*. Retrieved from http://archive.ifla.org/IV/ifla72/papers/102-McCallum-en.pdf

McGreal, R. (2008). A typology of learning object repositories (H. H. Adelsberger, Ed.). Academic Press.

Meier, W. (2002). Exist: An open source native xml database. In Web-services, and database systems, node 2002 web and database-related workshops, (pp. 169-183). Springer.

Mory, E. H. (2007). Feedback Research Revisited. In D. H. Jonassen (Ed.), *Handbook of research for educational communications and technology*. Association for Educational Communications and Technology.

Nielsen, J. (1994). *Usability engineering*. San Francisco, CA: Morgan Kaufmann Publishers. Retrieved from http://www.worldcat.org/search?qt=worldcatorgallq=0125184069

Nielson, F., Nielson, H. R., & Hankin, C. (1999). *Principles of program analysis*. Secaucus, NJ: Springer-Verlag New York, Inc. doi:10.1007/978-3-662-03811-6

O'Kelly, J., & Gibson, J. P. (2006, June). Robocode & problem based learning: A non-prescriptive approach to teaching programming. *SIGCSE Bulletin*, *38*(3), 217–221. doi:10.1145/1140123.1140182

Ochoa, X., & Duval, E. (2009). Quantitative analysis of learning object repositories. *AACE*. Retrieved from http://ieeexplore.ieee.org/lpdocs/epic03/wrapper.htm?arnumber=5184802

Ochoa, X., Klerkx, J., Vandeputte, B., & Duval, E. (2011). On the use of learning object metadata: The globe experience. In Ec-tel, (pp. 271-284). Academic Press.

Oliveira, L., & Moreira, F. (2010). Personal learning environments: Integration of web 2.0 applications and content management systems. In *Proceedings of 11th European conference on knowledge management*. Academic Press.

Oncu, C. H. S., & Cakir, H. (2011). Research in online learning environments: Priorities and methodologies. *Computers & Education*, *57*(1), 1098–1108. doi:10.1016/j.compedu.2010.12.009

Pantel, C. (n.d.). *A framework for comparing web-based learning environments*. (Unpublished master's thesis). School of Computing Science, Simon Fraser University, Canada.

Pisan, Y., Richards, D., Sloane, A., Koncek, H., & Mitchell, S. (2003). Submit! A web-based system for automatic program critiquing. *Proceedings of the Australasian Conference on Computing Education*, *20*(1), 59-68. Retrieved from http://dl.acm.org/citation.cfm?id=858403.858411

Queirós, R., & Leal, J. P. (2012). Programming Exercises Evaluation Systems - An Interoperability Survey. Academic Press.

Queirós, R., & Leal, J. P. (2012). PETCHA: A programming exercises teaching assistant. In *Proceedings of the 17th ACM annual conference on Innovation and technology in computer science education* (ITiCSE '12). ACM. Retrieved from http://doi.acm.org/10.1145/2325296.2325344

Queirós, R., & Leal, J. P. (2013). crimsonHex: A learning objects repository for programming exercises. *Software, Practice & Experience, 43*(1), 911–935. doi:10.1002/spe.2132

Queirós, R., & Leal, J. P. (2013). Making Programming Exercises Interoperable with PExIL. In J. Ramalho, A. Simões, & R. Queirós (Eds.), Innovations in XML Applications and Metadata Management: Advancing Technologies, (pp. 38-56). Hershey, PA: Information Science Reference. doi: doi:10.4018/978-1-4666-2669-0.ch003

Queirós, R., & Leal, J. P. (2013). BabeLO - An Extensible Converter of Programming Exercises Formats. *IEEE Transactions on Learning Technologies, 6*(1), 38–45. doi:10.1109/TLT.2012.21

Queirós, R., & Leal, J. P. (2013). *Ensemble - An E-Learning Framework, Special issue on Cloud Education Environments at the Journal of Universal Computer Science.* JUCS. doi:10.3217/jucs-018-11-1454

Reek, K. A. (1989, February). The try system -or-how to avoid testing student programs. *SIGCSE Bulletin, 2*(1), 112–116. doi:10.1145/65294.71198

Rehak, M. R. D. R. (2003). Keeping the learning in learning objects. In A. Littlejohn (Ed.), Reusing online resources: A sustainable approach to e-Learning, (pp. 22-30). Academic Press.

Reilly, W., Wolfe, R., & Smith, M. (2006, April). Mit's cwspace project: Packaging metadata for archiving educational content in dspace. *Int. J. Digit. Libr., 6*(2), 139-147. 10.1007/s00799-005-0131-2

Repository Software Survey. (2010). Repositories Support Project. In *Combining schematron with other xml schema languages* (Tech. Rep.). Academic Press.

Robins, A., Rountree, J., & Rountree, N. (2003). Learning and teaching programming: A review and discussion. *Computer Science Education, 1*(3), 137–172. doi:10.1076/csed.13.2.137.14200

Rodriguez, E., Sicilia, M. A., & Arroyo, S. (2006). Bridging the semantic gap in standards-based learning object repositories. In *Proceedings of the workshop on learning object repositories as digital libraries current challenges,* (pp. 478-483). Academic Press.

Rogers, S. A. (2003). Developing an institutional knowledge bank at ohio state university: From concept to action plan. *Portal Libraries and the Academy, 3*(1), 125-136. Retrieved from http://muse.jhu.edu/content/crossref/journals/portallibrariesandtheacademy=v003=3:1rogers:html

Romli, R., Sulaiman, S., & Zamli, K. (2010, June). Automatic programming assessment and test data generation a review on its approaches. In Proceedings of Information technology (ITSIM). Academic Press. doi:10.1109/ITSIM.2010.5561488

Rongas, T., Kaarna, A., & Kalviainen, H. (2004). Classiffication of computerized learning tools for introductory programming courses: Learning approach. In *Proceedings of ICALT*. IEEE Computer Society. Retrieved from http://dblp.uni-trier.de/db/conf/icalt/icalt2004.htmlRongasKK04

Saikkonen, R., Malmi, L., & Korhonen, A. (2001, June). Fully automatic assessment of programming exercises. *SIGCSE Bulletin, 33*(1), 133–136. doi:10.1145/507758.377666

Sampson, D. G., Zervas, P., & Chloros, G. (2012). *Supporting the process of developing and managing lom application profiles: The ask-lom-ap tool. IEEE Transactions on Learning Technologies.*

Schulte, C., & Bennedsen, J. (2006). What do teachers teach in introductory programming? In *Proceedings of the second international workshop on computing education research,* (pp. 17-28). New York, NY: ACM. Retrieved from http://doi.acm.org/10.1145/1151588.1151593

Siddiqui, A., Khan, M., & Akhtar, S. (2008, August). Supply chain simulator: A scenario-based educational tool to enhance student learning. *Comput. Educ., 51*(1), 252-261. 10.1016/j.compedu.2007.05.008

Simon, B., Massart, D., van Assche, F., Ternier, S., Duval, E., Brantner, S., & Miklos, Z. (2005). A simple query interface for interoperable learning repositories. In *Proceedings of the 1st workshop on interoperability of web-based educational systems*, (pp. 11-18). Academic Press.

Spacco, J., Hovemeyer, D., Pugh, W., Emad, F., Hollingsworth, J. K., & Padua-Perez, N. (2006, June). Experiences with marmoset: Designing and using an advanced submission and testing system for programming courses. *SIGCSE Bulletin, 38*(3), 13–17. doi:10.1145/1140123.1140131

Striewe, M., & Goedicke, M. (2010). Visualizing data structures in an e-learning system. In Csedu, 172-179.

Tang, C. M. P. C., & Yu, Y. T. (2010). A review of the strategies for output correctness determination in automated assessment of student programs. In Proceedings of global Chinese conference on computers in education. Academic Press.

Tang, Y. Y. T. P. C. K. C. M. (2009a). An approach towards automatic testing of student programs using token patterns. In *Proceedings of the 17th international conference on computers in education*. Academic Press.

Tang, Y. Y. T. P. C. K. C. M. (2009b). Automated systems for testing student programs: Practical issues and requirements. In *Proceedings of the international workshop on strategies for practical integration of emerging and contemporary technologies in assessment and learning*. Academic Press.

Tastle, W. A. J., & Shackleton, P. (2005). E-learning in higher education: The challenge, eort, and return of investment. *International Journal on E-Learning*.

Ternier, S. (2008). *Standards Based Interoperability for Searching in and Publishing to Learning Object Repositories* [Interoperabiliteit voor het publiceren en ontsluiten van leerobjecten in repositories met gebruik van standaarden]. (Doctoral dissertation). K.U.Leuven. Retrieved from https://lirias.kuleuven.be/handle/123456789/242045

Ternier, S., Massart, D., Totschnig, M., Klerkx, J., & Duval, E. (2010). The simple publishing interface (spi). *D-Lib Magazine, 1*(6), 9–10. Retrieved from http://www.dlib.org/dlib/september10/ternier/09ternier.html

Tremblay, G., Guérin, F., Pons, A., & Salah, A. (2008, March). Oto, a generic and extensible tool for marking programming assignments. *Softw. Pract. Exper., 38*(3), 307-333. doi: 10.1002/spe.v38:3

Trtteberg, H., & Aalberg, T. (2006). *JExercise: A specification-based and test-driven exercise support plugin for Eclipse*. Academic Press.

Truong, N. K. D. (2007). *A web-based programming environment for novice programmers* (Doctoral dissertation). Queensland University of Technology. Retrieved from http://eprints.qut.edu.au/16471/

Tsunakawa, T. (2010). *Pivotal approach for lexical translation*. (Unpublished doctoral dissertation). University of Tokyo, Tokyo, Japan.

Tzikopoulos, M. N. V. R. A. (2009). An overview of learning object repositories. In T. Halpin (Ed.), Selected readings on database technologies and applications. IGI Global.

Vansteenkiste, M., & Deci, E. L. (2003). Competitively contingent rewards and intrinsic motivation: Can losers remain motivated? *Motivation and Emotion, 2*(7), 273-299. 10.1023/A:1026259005264

Varlamis, I., & Apostolakis, I. (2006). The present and future of standards for e-learning technologies. *Interdisciplinary Journal of Knowledge and Learning Objects, 2*(1). Retrieved from http://www.ijello.org/Volume2/v2p059-076Varlamis.pdf

Verhoe, T. (2008). Programming task packages: Peach exchange format. *International Journal Olympiads In Informatics, 2*(1), 192–207.

Wang, F. L., & Wong, T.-L. (2008). Designing programming exercises with computer assisted instruction. In *Proceedings of the 1st international conference on hybrid learning and education*. Berlin: Springer-Verlag. Retrieved from doi:10.1007/978-3-540-85170-7_25

Ward, J. (2004). Unqualified dublin core usage in oai-pmh data providers. *OCLC Systems & Services, 20*(1), 40-47. 10.1108/10650750410527322

Wiedenbeck, S., Labelle, D., & Kain, V. N. R. (2004). Factors affecting course outcomes in introductory programming. In *Proceedings of 16th annual workshop of the psychology of programming interest group*, (pp. 97-109). Academic Press.

Wilson, S., Blinco, K., & Rehak, D. (2004, July). *Service-Oriented Frameworks: Modelling the infrastructure for the next generation of e-Learning Systems* (Tech. Rep.). JISC Report. Retrieved from http://www.jisc.ac.uk/uploadeddocuments=AltilabServiceOrientedFrameworks:pdf

Xavier, J., & Coelho, A. (2011, 14-16 November). 2011). Computer-based assessment system for e-learning applied to programming education. In Proceedings of ICERI201, (pp. 3738-3747). IATED.

KEY TERMS AND DEFINITIONS

E-Learning Framework: A service-orientated approach to the development and integration of computer systems in the sphere of learning and education. Usually these types of frameworks come in two level: abstract and concrete.

ENDNOTES

[1]   NoteFlight web site: http://www.noteflight.com

[2]   NoteFlight demo with Moodle integration: http://videos.noteflight.com/MoodleBasicLTI.mov

[3]   http://www.google.com/google-d-s/forms/

[4]   http://goo.gl/AlhsL

202

Chapter 10

Moodle–Based Tool to Improve Teaching and Learning of Relational Databases Design and SQL DML Queries

M. Antón-Rodríguez
University of Valladolid, Spain

F. J. Díaz-Pernas
University of Valladolid, Spain

M. A. Pérez-Juárez
University of Valladolid, Spain

M. Martínez-Zarzuela
University of Valladolid, Spain

M. I. Jiménez-Gómez
University of Valladolid, Spain

D. González-Ortega
University of Valladolid, Spain

ABSTRACT

The challenge to prepare the graduates for working in a constantly changing environment like software engineering requires an effective learning framework. This chapter presents a tool, integrated in the Moodle learning management system, that allows students to train the process of designing relational databases. The tool also allows them to practice with SQL queries that are executed over relational databases previously designed. This chapter also describes the result of a qualitative analysis of its use in an engineering course offered at the University of Valladolid and focused on the teaching of the Web applications development. The results of the refereed study reveal that the tool was found useful by both students and teachers to support the teaching and learning process of relational databases.

INTRODUCTION

Computer programming university courses are concerned with providing the students with not only theoretical knowledge but also with the required skills for achieving a more efficient programming, which is something required for working in software development (Sancho-Thomas et al., 2009). However, contrariwise programming learning requires, today students are playing an increasingly passive role in their own education; the rise of the dropout rate and the lowering in the grades show signs of it. In this sense, e-learning tries to promote a more active involvement of the

DOI: 10.4018/978-1-4666-7304-5.ch010

students in their own learning process. As Law et al. (2010) suggest, an e-learning environment makes easy and can improve the motivation for learning and self-efficacy. Furthermore, in order to strengthen learners' programming skills, they need to do a lot of practice. Hence, practical activities play an important role in the learning process (Thomas & Paine, 2000). Another reason of trying to combine mainstream education system (face-to-face classes) with new e-learning systems is that sometimes professors has to work with crowded lab classes, where paying due attention to each student is practically impossible. By doing so, the professor can better utilize his/her time as well as take advantage of the learning time outside of school hours, so the effective learning time increases and quality of teaching clearly improves, which can be key in computer programming learning.

Therefore, the objectives of this chapter are to present a Moodle-based tool that aims to support the teaching and learning process of a relational database design, as well as the teaching and learning process of SQL DML queries to be executed over a previously designed relational database. As well as to test the tool in a university academic environment in order to determine the usefulness of the tool in such a context for both students and teachers.

BACKGROUND

The relational database was born in 1970 when E.F. Codd, a researcher at IBM, wrote a paper outlining the process of defining such a database. Since then, relational databases have grown in popularity to become the standard (Sumathi & Esakkirajan, 2007) (Churcher, 2012).

Originally, databases were flat. This means that the information was stored in one long text file, called a tab delimited file. Each entry in the tab delimited file was separated by a special character, such as a vertical bar (|). Each entry contained multiple pieces of information (fields) about a particular object or person grouped together as a record. The text file made it difficult to search for specific information or to create reports that included only certain fields from each record. An example of the file created by a flat database could be the following (shown in Box 1).

With such a file, it would be necessary to search sequentially through the entire file to gather related information, such as Lname or salary. On the contrary, a relational database allows to easily find specific information as well as to sort information based on any field and to generate reports that contain only certain fields from each record. Relational databases use tables to store information. The standard fields and records are represented as columns (fields) and rows (records) in a table.

By using a relational database, information can be quickly compared because of the arrangement of data in columns. The relational database model takes advantage of this uniformity to build new tables out of required information from existing tables. This way, it takes advantage of the relationship of similar data to increase the speed and versatility of the database.

Relational databases are created and manipulated by using a special computer language, named the Structured Query Language (SQL), which is the standard for database interoperability. SQL is the foundation for all of the popular Database Management Systems (DBMS) available today, from Access to Oracle.

Box 1.

Lname, FName, Age, Salary|Page, Jane, 30, $3200|Doherty, Mark, 43, $4320|Murray, Peter, 34, $2715|Roland, Richard, 40, $2730

203

The keystone of the Relational Model are the relations, which are made up of attributes. A relation is a set of attributes with values for each attribute such that each attribute name must be unique, each attribute value must be a single value only and all values for a given attribute must be of the same data type (Churcher, 2012). Moreover no two tuples in a relation can be identical. And, finally, the order of attributes is insignificant, as well as the order of the tuples.

The design process of a relational database is based in the definition of a set of relations that are normalized in order to remove any anomalies found (Sumathi & Esakkirajan, 2007). Based on a normalized relational model, the database is implemented by creating a table for each normalized relation in a relational database management system. This task is accomplished by using a SQL DDL script. DDL is the Data Definition Language part of the SQL language that includes the statements used to define the database structure or schema. In fact, it is the standard for commands that define the different structures in a database. DDL statements create, modify, and remove database objects such as tables, indexes, and users. Common DDL statements are CREATE, ALTER, and DROP.

Normalization is a process in which relations are systematically examined looking for anomalies and, when detected, those anomalies are removed by splitting up the relation into two new, related, relations. Normalization is an important part of the relational database design process (Churcher, 2012). And often during normalization is when the database designers are made aware of how really the data are going to interact in the database.

Finding problems with the database structure at the stage of design is strongly preferred to finding problems further along in the implementation process because at this point it is fairly easy to make changes.

Normalization can also be thought of as a trade-off between data redundancy and performance (Churcher, 2012). Normalizing a relation reduces data redundancy but introduces the need for joins when all of the data is required by an application such as a report query which impacts on performance.

Thus normalization is a central issue in the teaching and learning process of relational databases as well as the SQL language for the creation of the database first and to implement the Create Retrieve Update Delete (CRUD) functionality after.

In order to support the teaching and learning process in a course focused on web applications development a search in order to find useful educational tools was made. The course was part of several engineering study programs offered by the University of Valladolid. In this course the students needed to design and implement a relational database to interact with a responsive web interface.

In which refers to the design and implementation of the relational database the priority was to use a tool that helped students to understand the steps of the normalization process as well as to train with the Data Manipulation Language (DML) part of the SQL language in order to build the CRUD functionality.

(Martínez-González & Duffing, 2007) performed a study comparing the database teaching-learning process in three European universities of different countries. They concluded the need of using the work groups and project based learning as they are techniques well-suited for database learning, and taking advantage of multimedia learning platforms for helping in the learning process. (Domínguez & Jaime, 2010) described an active method for database design learning through developing practical tasks (project-based learning). Via role playing, the students learned both sides of database design, client side and developer side. The use of a course management system was a great support given the huge number of documents produced. It was also useful for providing the description and scheduling of tasks, for identifying teams of teams, and for the communication needs. They analyzed aspects such as exam dropout rates, exam passing rates, exam marks, and class attendance. Results obtained using this active learning approach were clearly better than those using the traditional one. (Cheunga et al, 2003) performed an experience for evaluating the educational impact of multimedia learning methods in database designing. They proved that these tools provide an effective learning, although they are not usually as easy to use as they must be.

Although we figured out the need to use multimedia tools, better integrated in a course management system, together with an active learning method, the literature review did not not reveal the existence of any educational tool related with the relational database design and implementation process that strengthened the understanding of the steps of the normalization process and that allowed students to train with SQL DML in order to implement CRUD functionality queries.

Taking into account the findings in the literature review and that the University of Valladolid has adopted Moodle as the institutional e-learning platform, it was decided to develop a Moodle-based tool to support the teaching and learning of a relational database design process, as well as the specification of SQL DML queries to be executed over the relational database previously designed.

MAIN FOCUS OF THE CHAPTER

Using the Database-SQL Moodle-Based Tool

When using the Database-SQL Moodle-based tool, the starting point for work is a SQL DDL script. Based on a DDL SQL script provided by the teacher for the definition of a relational database, the educational tool will present the student a list of fields and a set of tables initially empty. Then, by means of a drag and drop system, the student will distribute the fields among the different tables

of the relational database showed to him initially empty. The student will then select the primary and foreign keys for the different tables, and will indicate the existing relationships between the tables and its type.

The system will then proceed to show the student the visual representation of the relational database defined by him or her with the fields allocated for each table, highlighting primary and foreign keys, and the relationships identified by the student between the tables.

Based on the relational database designed, the Database-SQL tool will propose the student to implement different SQL DML queries previously defined by the teacher.

The Database-SQL tool will then allow the student to execute the queries over the relational database so he can observe if the result is coherent with the question proposed. These results will be based on a SQL DML script inserted by the teacher to upload initial data into the tables of the relational database defined.

From the teacher viewpoint, the Database-SQL Moodle-based tool will allow him to insert a SQL DDL script to define the tables and attributes of the relational database, then to insert a SQL DML script to fill the tables of the relational database with initial data, and finally to define a set of questions so the student can practice with SQL DML queries oriented to implement the CRUD functionality over the relational database defined. Of course, the teacher will be also able to assess the work done by the students regarding both, the design of the relational database and the specification of the SQL DML queries to be executed over the relational database previously designed.

From the student viewpoint, the Database-SQL Moodle-based tool will allow him or her to define the structure of the tables of the relational database taking as a starting point an initial list of attributes and by means of a drag and drop system. The Database-SQL Moodle-based tool will also allow him to determine the primary and foreign keys for the different tables as well as the relationships between the tables. Later he will be able to execute SQL DML CRUD queries over the relational database designed.

So the aim of the Database-SQL Moodle-based tool is twofold from the point of view of the student: on one side to practice with the design of relational databases which involves focusing on a normalization process, and, on the other side, to practice with SQL DML queries for the implementation of CRUD functionality over relational databases.

How the Teacher Will Interact with the Database-SQL Moodle-Based Tool

When a teacher wants to use the Database-SQL Moodle-based tool, first step consists of adding an activity of Database – SQL interactive exercise type to a course (see Figure 1).

Once an activity of Database – SQL interactive exercise type is added to a course, a screen that allows to set different parameters is shown to the teacher (see Figure 2).

The parameters of the Database-SQL interactive exercise that can be set by the teacher are the following:

- **Maximun Number of Tables:** When the student chooses the number of tables that he thinks the relational database must have, he will not be able to exceed this number.

- **Maximun Number of Fields per Table:** When the student chooses the number of fields that he thinks each table of the relational database must have, he will not be able to exceed this number. When the student drags and drops fields into a table and reaches this maximum number, the tool will not allow him to add more fields.

- **Starting Date:** The student will not be able to start the exercise before this date.

- **Ending Date:** The student will not be able to work on the exercise after this date.

- **Feedback:** If this option is activated, the student will receive feedback about his work.

- **Number of Tries:** Number of times that the student is going to be able to receive

Figure 1. Adding a database-SQL interactive exercise to a Moodle course

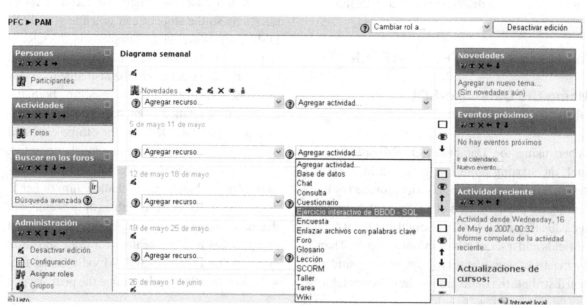

Figure 2. Setting the database-SQL interactive exercise parameters

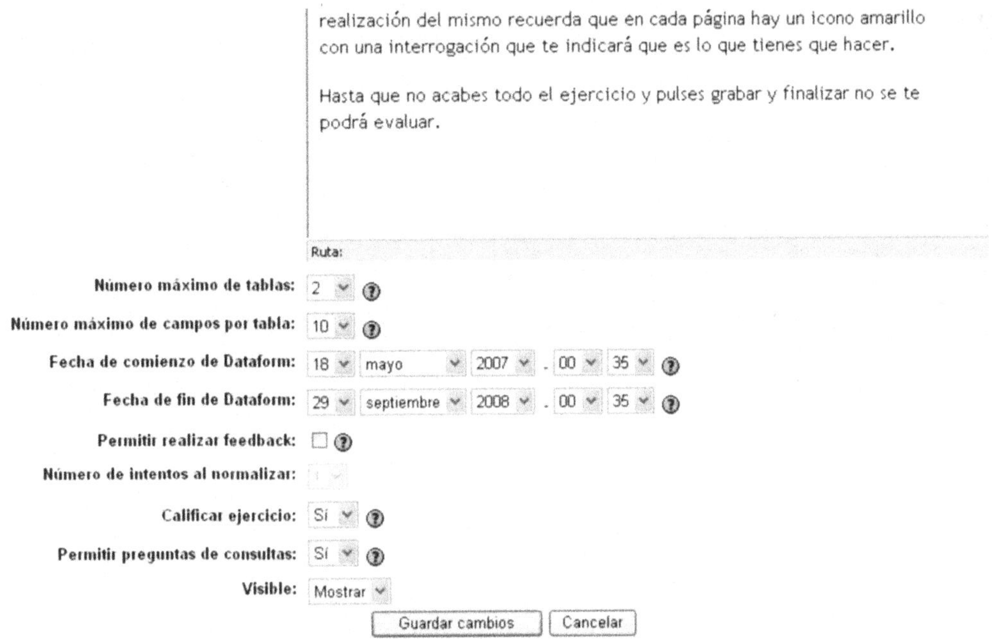

feedback and to use it in order to successfully complete the normalization process of the relational database design.

- **SQL DML CRUD Queries:** The teacher will be able to add questions related to the relational database which answer will consist in a SQL DML CRUD query to be executed over the relational database.
- **Grading:** The teacher will be allowed to grade the work of the student apart than to providing him or her with feedback related to his or her design of the relational database and to the SQL DML CRUD queries implemented.
- **Visibility:** It allows to initially show or hide the Database – SQL interactive exercise to the students.

Once the setting of the parameters is saved, the Database-SQL Moodle-based tool will allow the teacher to insert a SQL DDL script to create the relational database (see Figure 3).

At this step the Database-SQL Moodle-based tool offers the following possibilities:

Once the button with the label *Ejecutar script* (Executing script) is pressed, the script inserted for the creation of the database is executed. In case an error takes place, a feedback message is shown to the teacher containing relevant information (see Figure 4) and the teacher is sent back to the screen where the SQL DDL script for the creation of the relational database can be inserted. If, on the other side, the execution of the SQL DDL script is successful, the teacher is forwarded to a screen that shows the queries that have been executed for the creation of the relational database together with a success feedback message and a button with the label *Continuar* (Continue) that, if pressed, allows the teacher to proceed to the next step (see Figure 5).

The next step is to insert a SQL DML script to upload initial data into the relational database (see Figure 6).

Figure 3. Inserting a SQL DDL script to create the relational database

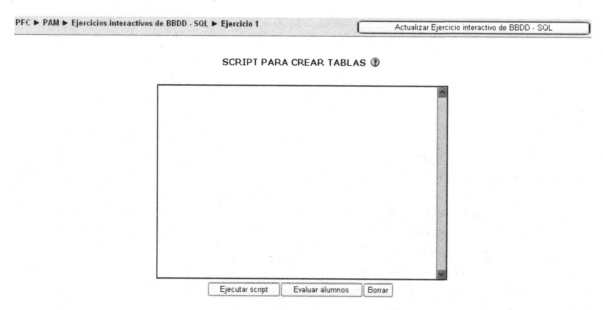

Figure 4. Error feedback message when the creation of the relational database with the SQL DDL script fails

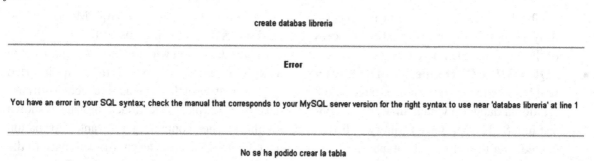

In this screen, when the button with the label *Ver campos BBDD* (View database fields) is pressed, the teacher is forwarded to another screen that shows a list of the fields that the student will have to use to design the different tables of the relational database. Obviously, these fields will be the ones defined by the teacher with the SQL DDL script inserted for the creation of the relational database. The primary key fields will appear marked with an "S". The column identified as *Dependencia* (Dependency) shows which field is the primary key for each field (see Figure 7).

If an error happens when the SQL DML script for the initial uploading of data into the database is executed, the teacher is sent back to the same screen. On the other side, if the execution of the SQL DML script for the initial uploading of data into the database is successful, the teacher is sent to a screen where he will be able to upload questions for the students related to SQL queries to be executed over the relational database. This screen also allows the teacher the possibility of uploading an image with the relational database design that will be shown to the student when he

Figure 5. Success feedback message when the creation of the relational database with the SQL DDL script is successful

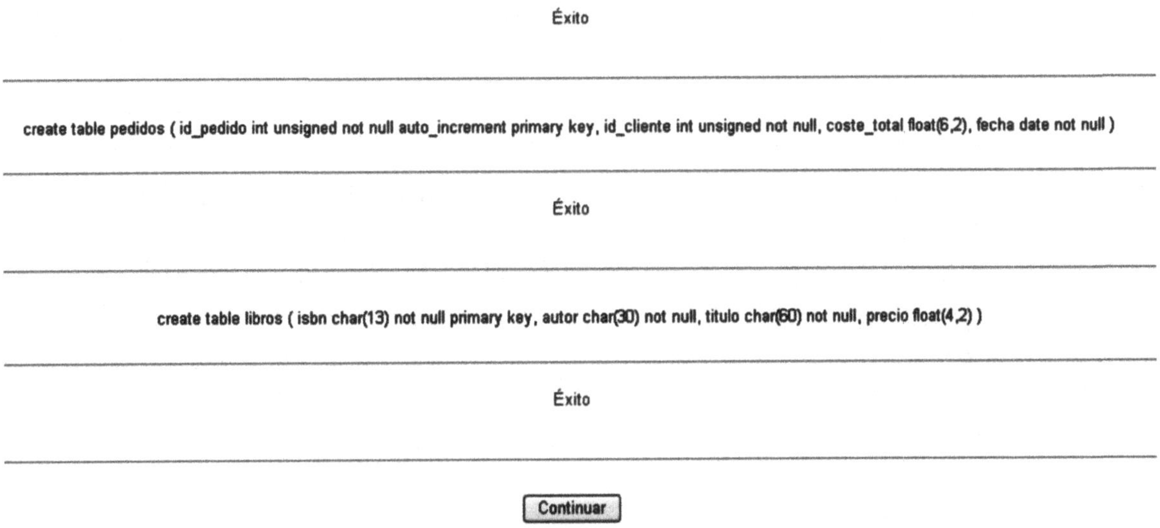

Éxito

_____

create table pedidos (id_pedido int unsigned not null auto_increment primary key, id_cliente int unsigned not null, coste_total float(6,2), fecha date not null)

_____

Éxito

_____

create table libros (isbn char(13) not null primary key, autor char(30) not null, titulo char(60) not null, precio float(4,2))

_____

Éxito

_____

[Continuar]

Figure 6. Inserting a SQL DDL script to upload initial data into the relational database

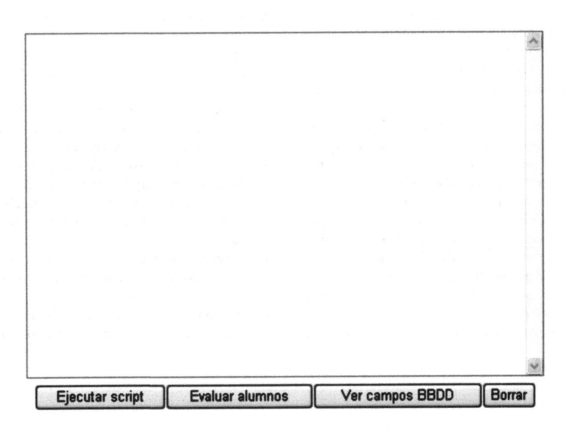

SCRIPT DE DATOS DE LAS TABLAS ⑦

[Ejecutar script] [Evaluar alumnos] [Ver campos BBDD] [Borrar]

Figure 7. List of fields for the tables of the relational database. Primary key fields are marked with an "S". The column Dependencia (Dependency) shows which is the primary key of which each field depends.

Orden	Nombre	Clave primaria	Clave foranea	Nombre clave	Dependencia
1	ID_CLIENTE	S		dataform_field_1	
2	FECHA			dataform_field_10	DATAFORM_FIELD_7
3	ISBN	S		dataform_field_11	
4	AUTOR			dataform_field_12	DATAFORM_FIELD_11
5	TITULO			dataform_field_13	DATAFORM_FIELD_11
6	PRECIO			dataform_field_14	DATAFORM_FIELD_11
7	NOMBRE			dataform_field_2	DATAFORM_FIELD_1
8	EMAIL			dataform_field_3	DATAFORM_FIELD_1
9	TELEFONO			dataform_field_4	DATAFORM_FIELD_1
10	DIRECCION			dataform_field_5	DATAFORM_FIELD_1
11	CIUDAD			dataform_field_6	DATAFORM_FIELD_1
12	ID_PEDIDO	S		dataform_field_7	
13	ID_CLIENTE			dataform_field_8	DATAFORM_FIELD_7
14	COSTE_TOTAL			dataform_field_9	DATAFORM_FIELD_7

has to answer the questions related to the SQL queries to be executed over the relational database (see Figure 8).

The button with the label *Borrar* (Delete) will allow the teacher to delete the inserted script and to start again.

The button with the label *Ver Preguntas* (View Questions) gives access to a screen where the list of questions already inserted is shown to the teacher. At this point, the teacher will be able to modify the content of a question – by pressing the button with the label *Actualizar preguntas* (Update questions) – or the delete a question – by pressing the button with the label *Borrar seleccionadas* (Delete questions) – (see Figure 9).

On the other side, the button with the label *Evaluar alumnos* (Evaluate students) allows the teacher to access to a page where he can see a list of the students of the course that will be able to take the exercise. For each student, the teacher can see the following information related to the execution of the exercise (see Figure 10):

- **Name and Picture:** In case the student has uploaded a picture to the Moodle platform in order to complete his profile.
- **Exercise Finished:** Indicates if the student has finalized the creation of the relational database, in which case, the teacher can start the evaluation of the task for that student.
- **Exercise Evaluated:** Indicates if the teacher has evaluated the work done by the student.
- **Evaluate Database:** If the student has ended the task, the teacher can start to eval-

Figure 8. Inserting questions for the students related with SQL queries to be executed over the relational database

INTRODUCIR PREGUNTAS ⑦

| Guardar pregunta | Ver preguntas | Evaluar alumnos | Ver campos BBDD | Borrar |

Subir imagen del esquema de la BBDD (16 Mb)

[Examinar...]

[Subir imagen de esquema BBDD]

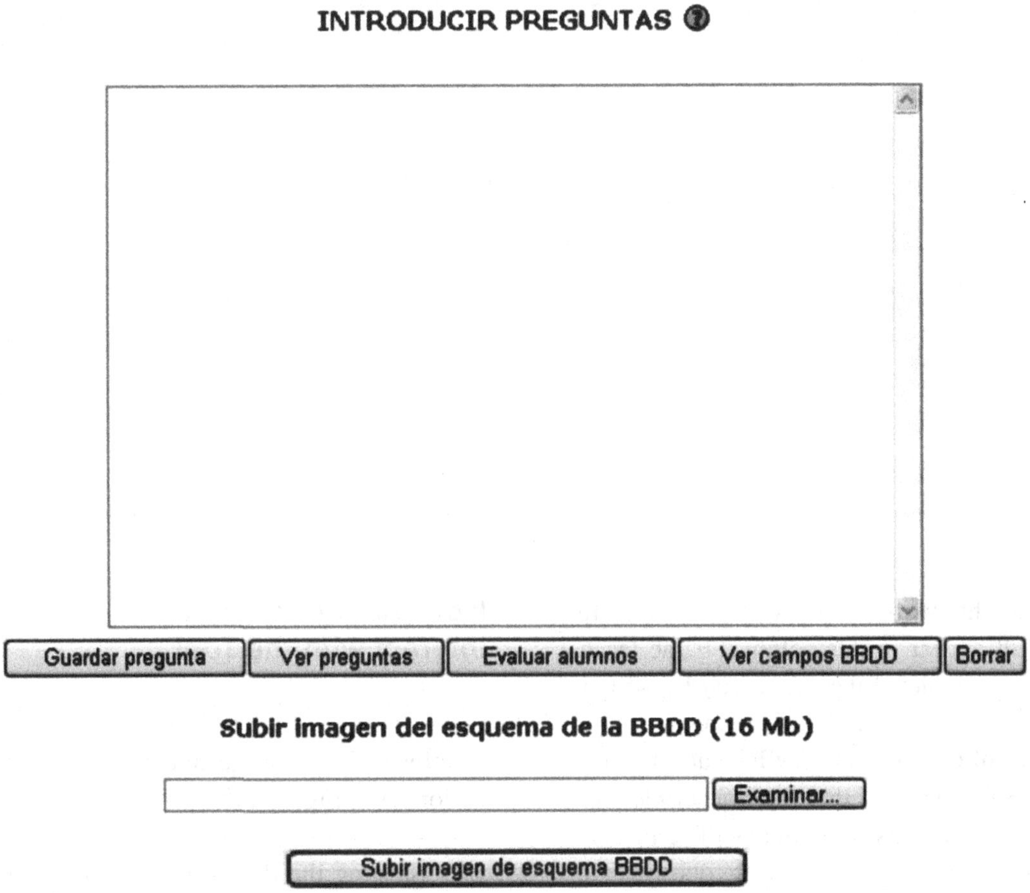

Figure 9. Updating or deleting questions for the students related with SQL queries to be executed over the relational database

Orden	Preguntas	Borrar
1	¿Cuántos clientes tienen un prefijo de su teléfono fijo que empieza por 983?	☐
2	¿Cómo se llaman los libros que ha sacado Rubén Pérez?	☐

[Actualizar preguntas] [Borrar seleccionadas] [Volver atrás]

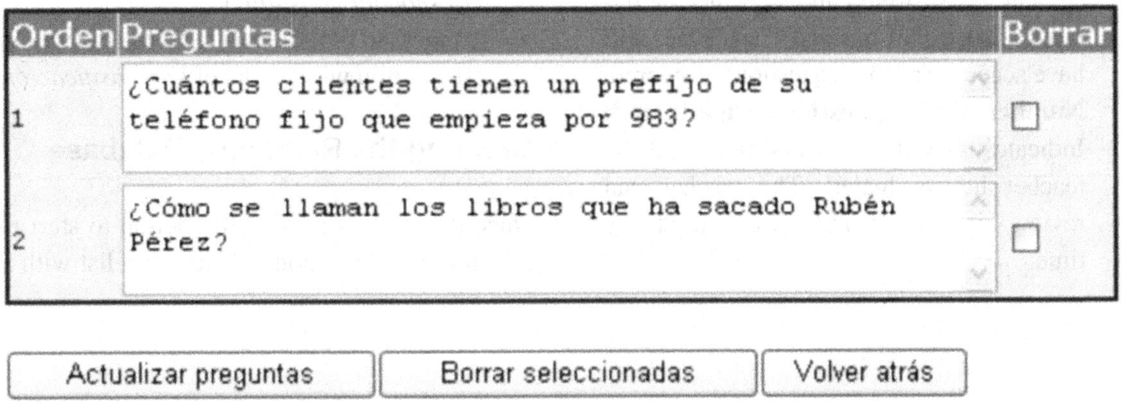

Figure 10. Summary of the information of the execution of tasks related to the creation of the relational database and to the SQL queries to be executed over the database done by the students

	Nombre y Apellidos	Ejer. finalizado	Nota	Ejer. evaluado	Evaluar BBDD	N. preguntas	N. preguntas contestadas	N. preguntas evaluadas
		no	0	no		0	0	0
		no	0	no		0	0	0
		no	0	no		0	0	0
		no	0	no		0	0	0
		no	0	no		0	0	0
		no	0	no		0	0	0
		no	0	no		0	0	0

uate his work by pressing the button that will appear in this column. If the teacher has completed the evaluation he will still be able to modify his assessment.

- **Number of Questions:** Indicates the number of questions that the teacher has made to the students. The value will be the same for each student because the questions formulated by the teacher are visible for every student.
- **Number of Questions Answered:** Indicates the number of questions that the student has answered and for which he has sent and saved the answer. The teacher will have access to the new questions answered.
- **Number of Questions Evaluated:** Indicates the number of questions that the teacher has evaluated. The teacher can review his grading and comments at any time.

How the Student Will Interact with the Tool

Once the student accesses the tool, he can read an informative message and has three alternative options (see Figure 11):

- Starting the design of the relational database (by pressing the button with the label *Comenzar diseño de BBDD*).
- Starting to answer the SQL queries (by pressing the button with the label *Responder consultas*).
- Access to the students ranking (by pressing the button with the label *Ver clasificación*).

Creating the Relational Database

Once the student presses the button to start the creation of the relational database, a list with all

Figure 11. Welcome page for students

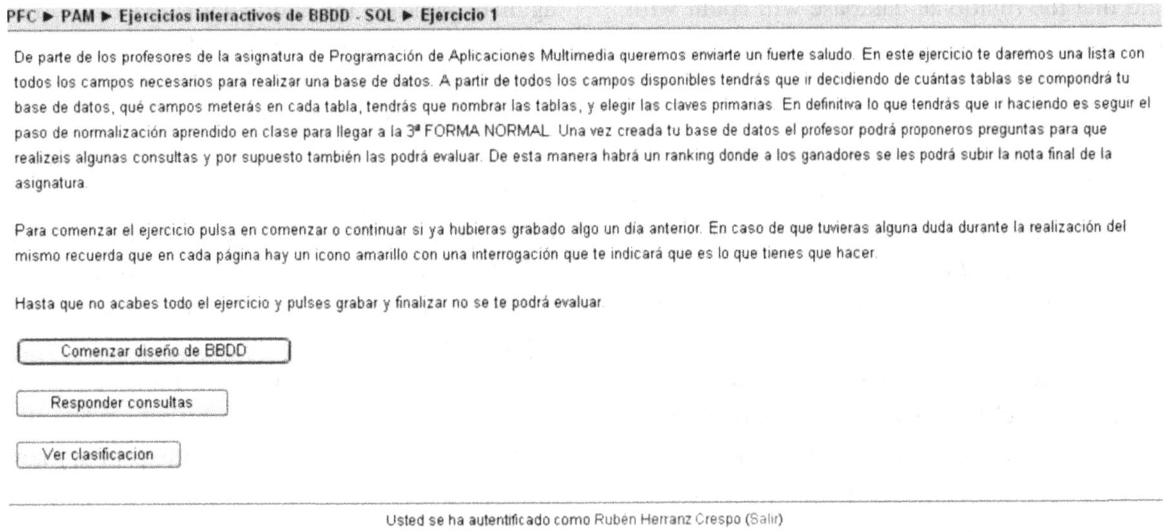

PFC ► PAM ► Ejercicios interactivos de BBDD - SQL ► Ejercicio 1

De parte de los profesores de la asignatura de Programación de Aplicaciones Multimedia queremos enviarte un fuerte saludo. En este ejercicio te daremos una lista con todos los campos necesarios para realizar una base de datos. A partir de todos los campos disponibles tendrás que ir decidiendo de cuántas tablas se compondrá tu base de datos, qué campos meterás en cada tabla, tendrás que nombrar las tablas, y elegir las claves primarias. En definitiva lo que tendrás que ir haciendo es seguir el paso de normalización aprendido en clase para llegar a la 3ª FORMA NORMAL. Una vez creada tu base de datos el profesor podrá proponeros preguntas para que realizeis algunas consultas y por supuesto también las podrá evaluar. De esta manera habrá un ranking donde a los ganadores se les podrá subir la nota final de la asignatura.

Para comenzar el ejercicio pulsa en comenzar o continuar si ya hubieras grabado algo un día anterior. En caso de que tuvieras alguna duda durante la realización del mismo recuerda que en cada página hay un icono amarillo con una interrogación que te indicará que es lo que tienes que hacer.

Hasta que no acabes todo el ejercicio y pulses grabar y finalizar no se te podrá evaluar.

| Comenzar diseño de BBDD |

| Responder consultas |

| Ver clasificación |

Usted se ha autentificado como Rubén Herranz Crespo (Salir)

the fields that he can use to create the relational database is shown. At the bottom of the screen, the student can introduce the number of tables that he thinks that the relational database may have taking into account the description of the problem and the list of fields proposed (see Figure 12).

He will then press the button with the label *Crear tablas y distribuir campos* (Create tables and distribute fields) in order to access to another screen where the list of fields will appear together with the number of tables that he selected. Initially these tables will be empty and will have no

Figure 12. List of fields that can be used for the creation of the database

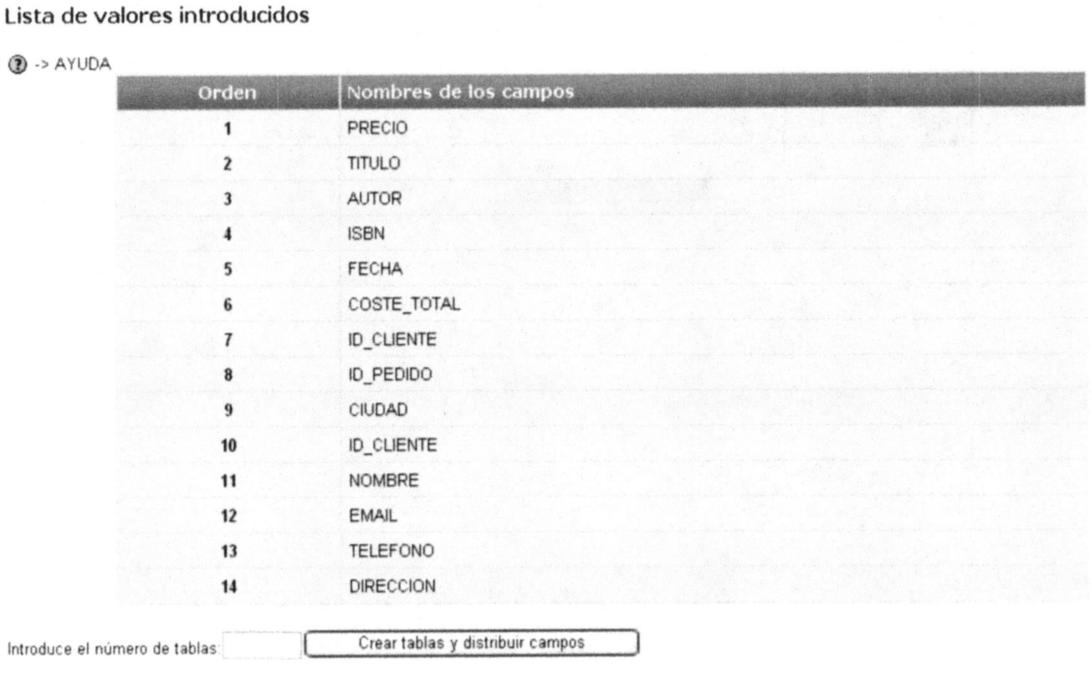

Lista de valores introducidos

② -> AYUDA

Orden	Nombres de los campos
1	PRECIO
2	TITULO
3	AUTOR
4	ISBN
5	FECHA
6	COSTE_TOTAL
7	ID_CLIENTE
8	ID_PEDIDO
9	CIUDAD
10	ID_CLIENTE
11	NOMBRE
12	EMAIL
13	TELEFONO
14	DIRECCION

Introduce el número de tablas: [   ] | Crear tablas y distribuir campos |

descriptive names. For example, if the student said that the relational database will count with four tables, he will access to a screen like the one shown in Figure 13.

At this point the student must choose a significant name for each table and insert it in the purple text field. Next he will have to distribute the fields shown in the list among the different tables by dragging and dropping each field into the adequate table. If during the process, when the student tries to drag and drop a field into a table and he is not allowed to, this means that the table has already reached the maximum possible number of fields established by the teacher when setting the initial parameters at the stage of creating the relational database exercise. The student will be also warned if he forgets to locate any of the fields

of the list. The student can also start the process again by pressing the button with the label *Volver a introducir número de tablas* (Enter number of tables again) if he thinks that the design he has reached is not normalized.

Once the student has distributed the fields among the different tables and reached a normalized design for the relational database he can save his work by pressing the button with the label *Guardar estructura de tablas y campos* (Save structure of tables and fields).

After saving his or her design, the student will be able to see it. He will also have to select the field that for each table must be the primary key and to decide if there are fields acting as foreign keys in any of the tables (see Figure 14).

Figure 13. Starting point for the design of the relational database

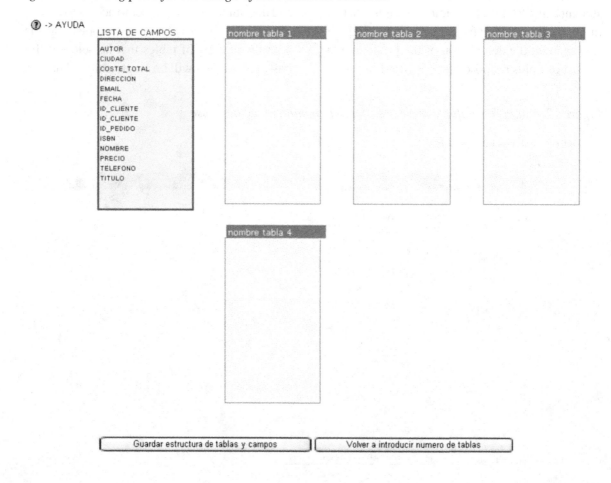

Figure 14. Initial design of the relational database

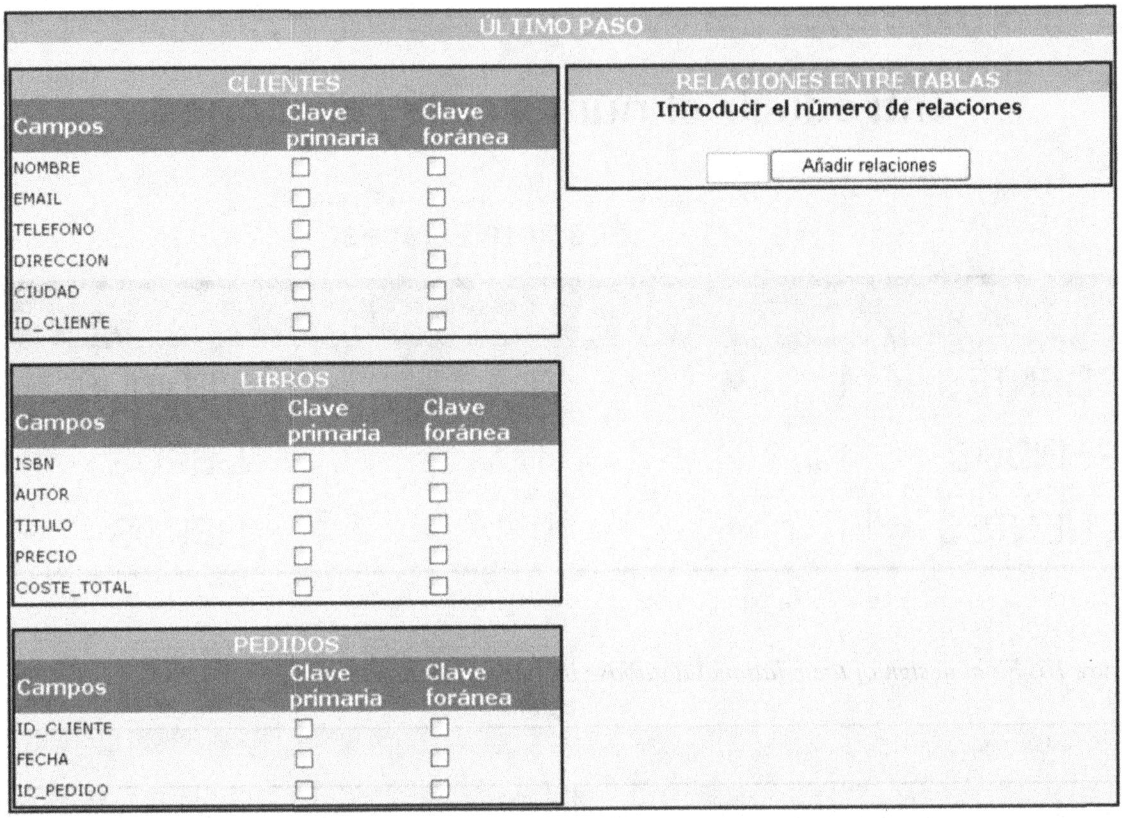

The student will also have to determine the number of relationships that exist between the tables. This task will be done by inserting a number in the adequate field and pressing the button with the label *Añadir relaciones* (Add relationships).

Immediately after the student will have to define each relationship by indicating the tables involved and the multiplicity in each end of the association or role that can be of different types: one-to-one, one-to-many or many-to-many (see Figure 15).

The student can now view his design including tables and relationships. And he also has the option to save it by pressing the button with the label *Guardar base de datos* (Save database) o to start again the exercise by pressing the button with the label *Comenzar de nuevo el ejercicio* (Start the exercise again) in case he thinks that

the design can be improved. The student must be aware that after saving his design the teacher will be able to access to it in order to make an evaluation (see Figure 16).

If when the teacher makes the initial setting of parameters he activates the possibility that the student gets feedback, it is at this point when the student will get this feedback. For example, the student will be reported if the fields that are primary keys have not been adequately selected (see Figure 17).

Another error about which the student will obtain feedback is in case he chooses adequate fields for primary keys but not every field is placed in the adequate table, which generates inadequate dependencies between fields (see Figure 17).

When the student receives feedback related to mistakes in his design, he can go back and make

Figure 15. Determining the characteristics of each relationship

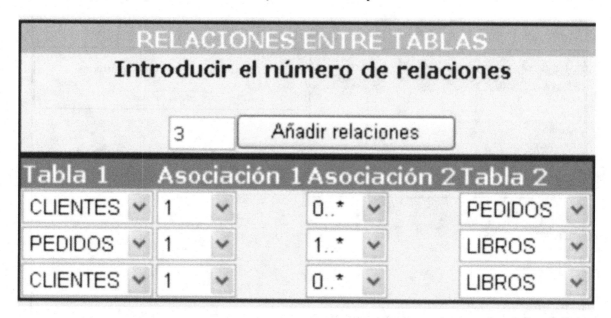

Figure 16. Final design of the relational database including relationships

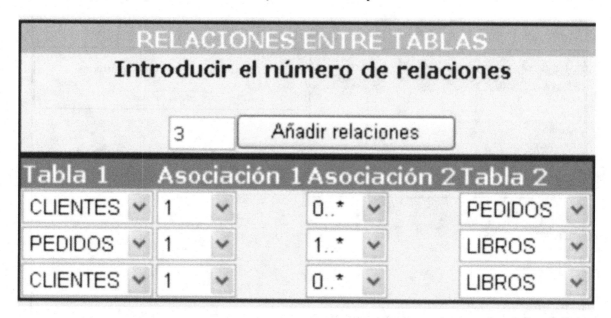

Figure 17. Feedback for the student related with the selection of the primary keys for the different tables of the relational database

> ## FEEDBACK
>
> El campo ISBN tiene que incluirse como clave primaria
> El campo ID_PEDIDO tiene que incluirse como clave primaria
> El campo ID_CLIENTE tiene que incluirse como clave primaria
>
> Volver atras

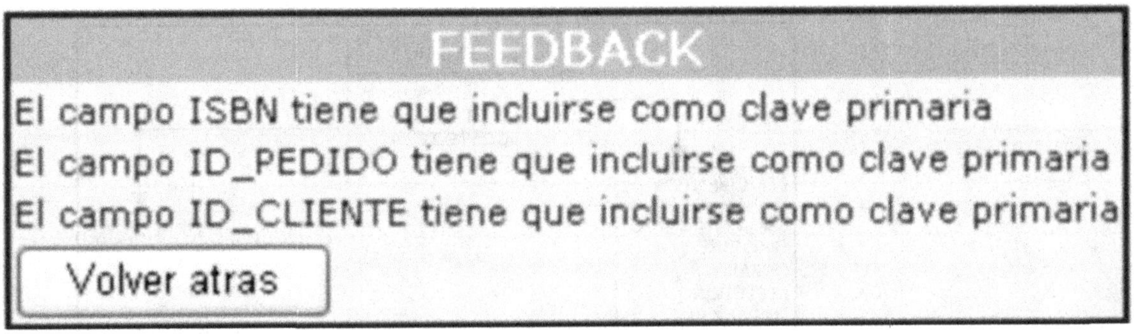

modifications in order to improve his design. On the other side, if everything is correct, the student will obtain a success feedback message.

Once the student has ended the creation of the database he can wait till the teacher evaluates his work, or else proceed with the questions related to SQL queries to be executed over the relational database designed.

Defining the SQL Queries to Be Executed over the Relational Database Created

If from the welcome page the student presses the button with the label *Responder consultas* he will be able to start answering the questions related with the definition of SQL queries to be executed over the relational database. The student will be shown the image with the design of the database previously uploaded by the teacher during the creation of the exercise together with a question related with an SQL query to be executed over the relational database (see Figure 19).

Before saving his answer the student can execute the query over the relational database by pressing the button with the label *Ejecutar consulta* (Execute query). This will help him to detect if there are mistakes in the query because he can check if the answer is related to the question (see Figure 20).

Once the student answers the first question he will proceed to the next one till he completes all the questions proposed by the teacher.

Assessment of the Teacher

The teacher can start the assessment of the work done by the student once he has ended the creation

Figure 18. Feedback for the student related with existing dependencies between fields in the different tables of the relational database

> ## FEEDBACK
>
> El campo COSTE_TOTAL no tiene como clave primaria a ISBN
> El campo FECHA no tiene como clave primaria a ID_CLIENTE
>
> Volver atras

Figure 19. Question for the student related with an SQL query to be executed over the relational database

Tenemos la siguiente BBDD:

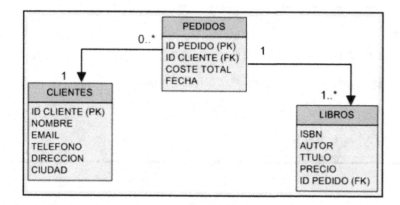

Consulta relacionada con la BBDD:

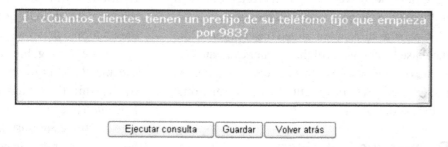

Figure 20. Executing the SQL query over the relational database

Consulta relacionada con la BBDD:

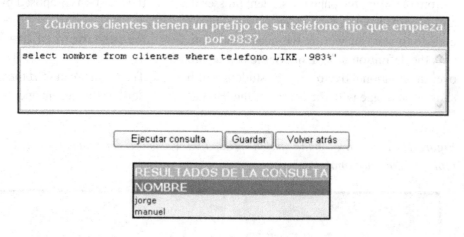

of the relational database or he has answered any of the questions related to SQL queries to be executed over the database. The teacher will know if he has tasks to be assessed because in such case the tool will give him the option to start his assessments (see Figure 21).

The teacher will be able to grade both type of tasks, on one side the design of the relational database made by the student (see Figure 22), and on the other side the SQL queries to be executed over the relational database (see Figure 23). The teacher will be also able to provide feedback to the students in both cases.

Results

As an open source software engineering project, the result of the present work is an application that meets all the requirements initially established. More specifically:

- It is designed as a module for the open source virtual e-learning platform Moodle that is the e-learning platform used by the University of Valladolid.
- It offers a friendly user interface for both students and teachers.
- It offers the possibility for the teachers to design exercises related to the normaliza-

tion of relational databases and to the students the possibility to do those exercises and to obtain feedback provided by the teacher once he has graded their work.

- It offers the possibility for the teachers to design exercises related to the implementation of SQL queries over the relational database designed and to the students the possibility to do those exercises and to obtain feedback provided by the teacher once he has graded their work.

The course for which the tool has been developed is a course focused on web applications development that was part of several engineering study programs offered by the University of Valladolid. The experiences were carried out during two academic courses, 2010-2011 and 2011-2012. Despite of the initial reluctance to use the tool at the laboratory, students finally started to use it on a regular basis in order to practice.

The students were encouraged to use the Database – SQL tool and then were invited to talk about their user experience, the benefits obtained, the problems found, the upgrades suggested, etc., in a Moodle forum.

The great majority of the students, more than 75%, considered the use of that the use of such a tool was very positive to improve the teaching

Figure 21. Assessing the work of the student

Nombre y Apellidos	Ejer. finalizado	Nota	Ejer. evaluado	Evaluar BBDD	N. preguntas	N. preguntas contestadas	N. preguntas evaluadas	Evaluar respuestas
	si	0	no	Evaluar	2	1	0	Evaluar la respuesta
	si	0	no	Evaluar	2	0	0	
	no	0	no		2	0	0	
	no	0	no		2	0	0	
	no	0	no		2	0	0	
	no	0	no		2	0	0	
	no	0	no		2	0	0	

Figure 22. Assessment of the design of the relational database done by the teacher

Evaluación del ejercicio

Ejercicio no evaluado

La clave primaria de la tabla pedidos no coincide aunque el resto del ejercicio está bastante bien.

Enhorabuena!!

Comentarios al ejercicio

Nota del ejercicio 8

Guardar Evaluacion   volver atrás

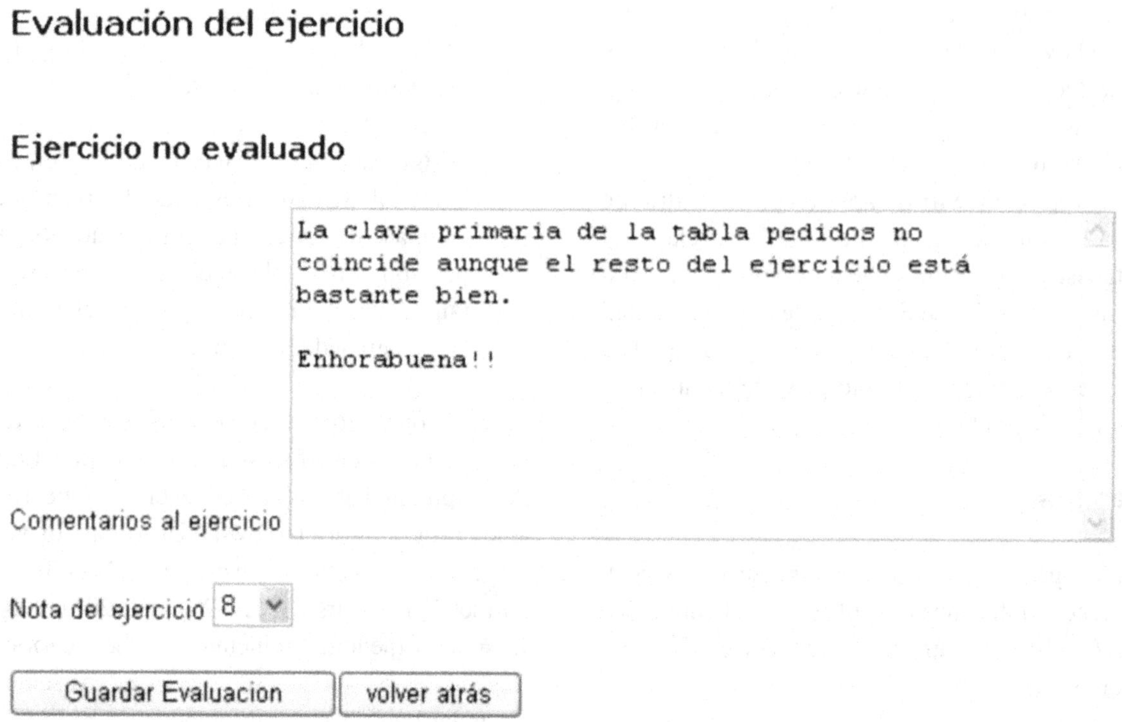

Figure 23. Assessment of and SQL query to be executed over the relational database done by the teacher

Consulta relacionada con la BBDD:

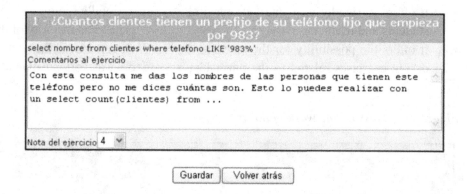

1 - ¿Cuántos clientes tienen un prefijo de su teléfono fijo que empieza por 983?

select nombre from clientes where telefono LIKE '983%'
Comentarios al ejercicio

Con esta consulta me das los nombres de las personas que tienen este teléfono pero no me dices cuántas son. Esto lo puedes realizar con un select count(clientes) from ...

Nota del ejercicio 4

Guardar   Volver atrás

learning process of the topics covered, i.e. the process of designing relational databases and executing SQL queries.

Some particular comments were: "This [Database – SQL] tool was very useful when beginning with relational databases and SQL", "I could practice to execute SQL queries over a relational database without having to install mysql in my own laptop", "Using the Database – SQL tool helped me to understand the theoretical basis of the normalization process when designing a relational database", "Using this [Database – SQL] tool was very useful to understand the way the SQL commands work".

Professors engaged in the performed experiences drew some conclusions regarding the behavior of the students when using the Database – SQL tool:

- Students felt encouraged to start the learning of the relational database design by themselves, reproducing and extending the examples given in class, without the fear of not being able to ask for the teacher advice.
- In the laboratory, the students tended to use the learning-support applications less, as they preferred to ask the professor.
- This database-SQL based tool is more used than other applications for web programming support (Antón-Rodríguez et al., 2012) used in the same subject as it provides more practical and understandable results.

FUTURE RESEARCH DIRECTIONS

This testing in a real scenario was aimed to collect feedback data and comments in order to improve the application tailoring it to the needs of the target users and enhancing their experience with the application. Feedback from students suggested a set of further developments to provide the application with an added value, which are the following:

- Add multilingual support. Moodle works with language packages which will facilitate the translation of the application into different languages.
- Allow the possibility to execute SQL queries without performing a previous exercise of database design.

Using these kind of Moodle-based innovative teaching applications, students obtain a better understanding of the potential of the topic studied, i.e., the web development.

CONCLUSION

In this chapter, we have presented an innovative Moodle-based tool to support the teaching and learning process of relational databases design, as well as the teaching and learning process of implementing SQL DML queries to be executed over relational databases, for engineering students. The experiences were carried out during two academic courses, 2010-2011 and 2011-2012, with very positive results.

Comparing to the initial reluctance of the students to use other tools available at the web applications development laboratory, the Database-SQL tool was welcomed as it was the only way to practice database design before the final test. This was not the case of other web programming tools developed for this subject such as a code validator for the JavaScript client-side scripting language, as the student can easily check if his code works properly without the help of such a tool.

Taking into consideration the results of the project, the main conclusions of the present work focusing on the pedagogic aspect, are, so far, the following:

- To support a course through a single virtual learning environment is preferable than to have to access different stand alone tools, both for teachers and students.
- To count with tailored educational tools, such as is the case of the Database – SQL tool for a web applications development course, is always an asset.
- The tools used in an e-learning project must be pedagogic and student-oriented.

REFERENCES

Antón-Rodríguez, M., Pérez-Juárez, M. A., Díaz-Pernas, F. J., Perozo-Rondón, F. J., Martínez-Zarzuela, M., & González-Ortega, D. (2012). Moodle-Based Software to Support the Learning of Web Programming. *International Journal of Knowledge Society Research, 3*(3), 16-28. doi: 10.4018/jksr.2012070102

Cheung, W., Li, E., & Yee, L. (2003). Multimedia learning system and its effect on self-efficacy in database modeling and design: an exploratory study. *Computers & Education, 41*(3), 249-270. doi: 0360-1315(03)00048-410.1016/S

Churcher, C. (2012). *Beginning Database Design. From Novice to Professional*. United States of America: Apress. doi:10.1007/978-1-4302-4210-9

Domínguez, C., & Jaime, A. (2010). Database design learning: A project-based approach organized through a course management system, *Computers & Education, 55*(3), 1312-1320. doi:10.1016/j.compedu.2010.06.001

Law, K. M. Y., Lee, V. C. S., & Yu, Y. T. (2010) Learning motivation in e-learning facilitated computer programming courses. *Computers & Education, 55*(1), 218-228. doi: 10.1016/j.compedu.2010.01.007

Martínez-González, M. M., & Duffing, G. (2007). Teaching databases in compliance with the European dimension of higher education: Best practices for better competences. *Education and Information Technologies, 12*(4), 211-228. doi: 10.1007/s10639-007-9047-3

Sancho-Thomas, P., Fuentes-Fernández, R., & Fernández-Manjón, B. (2009) Learning teamwork skills in university programming courses. *Computers & Education, 53*(2), 517-531. doi: 10.1016/j.compedu.2009.03.010

Sumathi, S., & Esakkirajan, S. (2007). *Fundamentals of Relational Database Management Systems*. Berlin: Springer; doi:10.1007/978-3-540-48399-1

Thomas, P. G., & Paine, C. B. (2000). *How student learn to program: Observation of practical work based on tasks completed*. Research Report 2000/03, Department of Computing. The Open University. Retrieved July 10, 2014 from http://www.researchgate.net/publication/221424279_How_Students_Learn_to_Program_Observations_of_Practical_Tasks_Completed/file/50463517eb57513342.pdf

KEY TERMS AND DEFINITIONS

DDL: Acronym for Data Definition Language that is the part of the SQL language that includes the statements used to define the database structure or schema.

DML: Acronym for Data Manipulation Language that is the part of the SQL language used to implement the Create Retrieve Update Delete (CRUD) functionality over a repository.

Moodle: Acronym for Modular Object-Oriented Dynamic Learning Environment, a free popular software e-learning platform.

Normalization: A process in which the relations of a relational database are systematically examined looking for anomalies and, when detected, those anomalies are removed by splitting up the relation into two new, related, relations.

Relational Database: A paradigm for the databases design that that was born in 1970 when E.F. Codd, a researcher at IBM, wrote a paper outlining the process of defining such a database which allows to easily find specific information as well as to sort information based on any field and to generate reports that contain only certain fields from each record.

SQL: Acronym for Structured Query Language, a special computer language used to create relational databases and that is the standard for database interoperability and the foundation for all of the popular Database Management Systems (DBMS) available today, from Access to Oracle.

Web Application: It is any software application that runs in a web browser or that is created by using a browser-supported programming language. It is stored on a remote web server and delivered over the Internet to the user web browser. Modern web sites allow the capture, processing, storage and transmission of customer data for immediate and recurrent use. Some common examples of web applications are webmail such as Gmail, online shops such as Amazon, Content Management Systems (CMS) such as Drupal or Learning Management Systems (LMS) such as Moodle.

Chapter 11
ZatLab:
Programming a Framework for Gesture Recognition and Performance Interaction

André Baltazar
Catholic University of Portugal, Portugal

Luís Gustavo Martins
Catholic University of Portugal, Portugal

ABSTRACT

Computer programming is not an easy task, and as with all difficult tasks, it can be faced as tedious, impossible to do, or as a challenge. Therefore, learning to program with a purpose enables that "challenge mindset" and encourages the student to apply himself in overcoming his handicaps and exploring different theories and methods to achieve his goal. This chapter describes the process of programming a framework with the purpose of achieving real time human gesture recognition. Just this is already a good challenge, but the ultimate goal is to enable new ways of Human-Computer Interaction through expressive gestures and to allow a performer the possibility of controlling (with his gestures), in real time, creative artistic events. The chapter starts with a review on human gesture recognition. Then it presents the framework architecture, its main modules, and algorithms. It closes with the description of two artistic applications using the ZatLab framework.

INTRODUCTION

There is so much information in a simple gesture. Why not use it to enhance a performance? We use our hands constantly to interact with things. Pick them up, move them, transform their shape, or activate them in some way. In the same unconscious way we gesticulate in communicating fundamental ideas: stop; come closer; go there; no; yes; and

so on. Gestures are thus a natural and intuitive form of both interaction and communication (Watson, 1993). Children start to communicate by gestures (around 10 months age) even before they start speaking. There is also ample evidence that by the age of 12 months children are able to understand the gestures other people produce (Rowe & Goldin-meadow, 2009). For the most part gestures are considered an auxiliary way of

DOI: 10.4018/978-1-4666-7304-5.ch011

communication to speech, tough there are also studies that focus on the role of gestures in making interactions work (Roth, 2001).

It is also important to understand that whereas all gestures derive from a chain of movements, not all movements can be considered gestures (Kendon, 1994). Gestures are the principal non-verbal, cross-modal communication channel, and they rely on movements for different domains of communication (Volpe, 2005). Looking at the Merriam-Webster dictionary[1], one will find the word "gesture" means a movement usually of the body or limbs that expresses or emphasizes an idea, sentiment, or attitude, as well as the use of motions of the limbs or body as a means of expression.

Gestures and expressive communication are therefore intrinsically connected, and being intimately attached to our own daily existence, both have a central position in our (nowadays) technological society.

However, the use of technology to understand gestures is still somehow vaguely explored, it has moved beyond its first steps but the way towards systems fully capable of analyzing gestures is still long and difficult (Volpe, 2005). Probably because if in one hand, the recognition of gestures is somehow a trivial task for humans, in other, the endeavor of translating gestures to the virtual world, with a digital encoding is a difficult and ill-defined task. It is necessary to somehow bridge this gap, stimulating a constructive interaction between gestures and technology, culture and science, performance and communication. Opening thus, new and unexplored frontiers in the design of a novel generation of multimodal interactive systems.

This chapter describes the entire process of learning how to program and implement a framework that enables the recognition of gestures in real-time and their use for artistic purposes. Therefore, first one will review the literature on gesture research, followed by the framework proposal, implementation and application.

BACKGROUND

Introduction

As Godoy (Godøy & Leman, 2009) refers, there is no clear definition of what a gesture is: "Given the different contexts in which gestures appear, and their close relationship to movement and meaning, one may be tempted to say that the notion of gesture is too broad, ill-defined, and perhaps too vague." This framework is focused on gesture recognition, so there is intrinsically a demand for the explanation and definition of the terms that are not well clarified.

This section is dedicated to the understanding and definition of a gesture and how it can be captured and recognized. It will also discuss the previous works published on this research field and present a review and technologically comparison of the different Motion Capture (MoCap) systems available nowadays. This section will provide valuable input for the development of the proposed framework.

Gestures

The human movement (Zhao & Badler, 2001) can be involuntary, subconscious, that occurs for biological or physiological purposes (e.g. blinking, breathing, balancing), or voluntary, conscious like those task-driven actions such as speaking or running to get somewhere. There is also a wide class of movements that fall in between these two, having both the voluntary and involuntary qualities. Such movements are the ones that occur in an artistic performance or music concert and perhaps unconsciously with other activities. These can range from leg and foot coordination enabling walking, till the communicative gestures, such as facial expressions, expressive limb gestures and postural attitude. The communicative gestures are the focus of this work and thus, their definition is of central importance.

A good perspective on how to distinguish movement from gesture is given by Kurtenbach and Hulteen (Wachsmuth & Fröhlich, 1998), they state that "A gesture is a motion of the body that contains information. Waving goodbye is a gesture. Pressing a key on keyboard is not a gesture because the motion of a finger on its way to hitting a key is neither observed nor significant. All that matters is which key was pressed. Pressing the key is highlighted as the meaning-bearing component, while the rest of the movement of the person is considered irrelevant.".

Actually, there is no single universally accepted definition of what a gesture actually is. Depending on the domain of research one will find different meanings (Zhao & Badler, 2001). These domains can range from the psychological-linguistic, to the cognitive science or the performative arts. In the following subsections the different approaches are explained.

Gestures in the Psychological-Linguistic Domain

In psychological-linguistic domain, there are three authors that have made significant contributions, following the seminal work David Efron started in the 40s (re-issued later (Efron, 1972)). They are Kendon (Kendon, 1970, 1980, 1994), McNeill & Levy (D McNeill & Levy, 1982; David McNeill, 1985, 1992), and Rimé & Schiaratura (Feldman & Rimé, 1991; Rimé, 1982).

Kendon, presented the following definition: "...for an action to be treated as a gesture it must have features which make it stand out as such". Although this is not clearly a definition, it suggests the analysis of features as classification characteristics. Observing the relations between speech and gesture, he proposed his gesticulation theory. A gesture is the "nucleus of movement with definite form and enhanced dynamic qualities (...) preceded by a preparatory movement and succeeded by a movement which either moves the limb back to is

rest position or repositions it for the beginning of a new gesture phrase." ((Kendon, 1980) pp.34).

Gestures in the Cognitive Science Domain

The cognitive science domain is a research area also related to psychology but with a strong branch on Artificial Intelligence. The research consists in building cognitive models in order to understand human behavior. If the model can reproduce human behavior under certain assumptions, it will also provide answer about human behavior in different assumptions. By changing these assumptions one can achieve different explorations and thus, different results. The speech and gesture relation has been broadly studied in the cognitive science context (Feyereisen & de Lannoy, 1991), but yielded contradictory hypotheses. These still need to be further investigated and reviewed. Maybe with different approaches from psychology, neurophysiology and even pathology, some day one will be able to delineate the functioning of communicative gesture.

Gestures in the Performing Arts Domain

Gestures are seen as the most appropriate mean of expression for theater and dance. Performers use gestures to communicate to an audience, either if is a comedy or a tragedy, either if a character is good or evil. Thus, through gestures, actors enhance the emotional content of their stories and characters.

For the contemporary dance and avant-garde theater the gesture is not simply a complement or a decoration. It is yes, the source, the cause and the conductor thread (Royce, 1984).

In this performative domain, gestures can have different interpretations due to culture specifications. In ballet, the gesture is based in Greco-Roman ideals of posture and movement. Standing straight, with slow, expansive and gracious movements will portray an elegant and graceful ballerina, while narrow, clumsy and rough movements will be seen as ugly and poor. Also in a play, the director must plan the combined movement of the cast, treating the movement as an extension of the line, mass and form. The actors themselves must be aware the quantity of movement used in a gesture, and how much space they are occupying in a stage, in order to transmit energy or weakness. The length of a gesture, either short or long, its intensity, either strong or soft, everything will add and convey emotional content. One wrong gesture can ruin a character or all the stage dynamics.

Thus, adequately planned, chosen and executed, gestures can create a mood, or a state of mind and arouse an emotional response from the audience (Dietrich, 1983).

Also in the music research field, body movement has been often related to the notion of gesture. The reason is that many musical activities (performance, conducting, dancing) involve body movements that evoke meanings, and therefore these movements are called gestures (Godøy & Leman, 2009).

To summarize, the study of gesture is a broad research field, with long branches extending from the rather philosophical, theoretical approaches, till the more technological, experimental areas. This gives a cross-disciplinary nature to the research (what is good) but also adds to the difficulty on defining precisely what is a gesture. What is common with the different approaches is that a gesture implies expression, communication and a purpose. Is the voluntary act of synthesizing movements to achieve a goal, fulfill an intention.

Recognizing Gestures

Gesture recognition consists in recognizing meaningful expressions of motion by a human, either to communicate or to interact with the environment.

Typically, the meaning of a gesture can be dependent on:

- **The Spatial Information:** Where it occurs;
- **The Temporal Information:** When and how fast it occurs;
- **Pathic Information:** The path it takes;
- **Symbolic Information:** The sign it makes; and
- **Affective Information:** Its emotional quality.

Indeed, gestures can involve the hands, arms, face, or even the entire body. They can be static, where the user assumes a certain pose, or dynamic, where the user treads a set of poses through time. Some gestures can also have both static and dynamic elements.

To detect and recognize all this range of gestures one needs to specify where it begins and where it ends in terms of frames of movement, both in time and space. So the automatic recognition of gestures implies the temporal or spatial segmentation of the movement.

Besides, in order to determine the relevant aspects of a gesture, the human body position, the angles and rotations of its joints as well as their kinetic information (velocities, accelerations) need to be determined. This can be done, either by using sensing devices attached to the user, or using cameras and Computer Vision (CV) techniques.

Next section will provide a review of previous works developed in the area of gesture recognition, with particular emphasis for the performative arts.

Previous Works

The field of human movements and gesture analysis has, for a long time now, attracted the interest of many researchers, choreographers and dancers. Thus, since the end of the last century, a significant corpus of work has been conducted relating movement perception with music (Fraisse, 1982). The important role of the human body in complex processes such as action and perception, and the interaction of mind and physical environment has been acknowledged originating new concepts such as embodiment (the argument that the motor system influences our cognition, just as the mind influences bodily actions) and enactive (the human mind organizes itself through interaction with the environment) (Varela, Thompson, & Rosch, 1993). Along with these relatively new concepts, many approaches have been proposed to translate the human physical movement and gesture into digital signals for further observation, study or plainly so that one can use them to control musical parameters in algorithmic music composition systems.

Already in the 90s, Axel Mulder (Mulder, 1994) characterized three techniques for tracking/capturing human movements that still remains an important reference. Accordingly to him, the human movement tracking systems can be classified as inside-in, inside-out and outside-in systems.

Inside-in systems are defined as those that employ sensors and sources that are both on the body (e.g. a glove with piezo-resistive flex sensors). The sensors generally have small form-factors and are therefore especially suitable for tracking small body parts. Whilst these systems allow for capture of any body movement and allow for an unlimited workspace, they are also considered obtrusive and generally do not provide 3D world based information.

Inside-out systems employ sensors on the body that sense artificial external sources (e.g. a coil moving in a externally generated electromagnetic field), or natural external sources (e.g. a mechanical head tracker using a wall or ceiling as a reference or an accelerometer moving in the earth gravitational field). Although these systems provide 3D world-based information, their workspace and accuracy is generally limited due to use of the external source and their form factor restricts use to medium and larger sized body parts.

Outside-in systems employ an external sensor that senses artificial sources or markers on the body, e.g. an electro-optical system that tracks reflective markers, or natural sources on the body

(e.g. a video camera based system that tracks the pupil and cornea). These systems may suffer from occlusion, and a limited workspace, but they are considered the least obtrusive. Due to the occlusion it is hard or impossible to track small body parts unless the workspace is severely restricted (e.g. eye movement tracking systems). The optical or image based systems require sophisticated hardware and software and may be therefore expensive.

Following this least obtrusive Outside-In technique, several projects with the purpose of creating and controlling electronic music have been developed since the mid 1990s. Early works of composers Todd Winkler (Winkler, 1995) and Richard Povall (Povall, 1998), or the choreographer Robert Weschler work with Palindrome[2]. Also, Mark Coniglio continued development of his Isadora[3] programming environment, plus the groundbreaking work Troika Ranch[4] has done in interactive dance, stand out as important references on how video analysis technologies have provided interesting ways of movement-music interaction.

Other example of research in this field is the seminal work of Camurri, with several studies published, including:

- An approach for the recognition of acted emotional states based on the analysis of body movement and gesture expressivity (Castellano, Villalba, & Camurri, 2007). By using non-propositional movement qualities (e.g. amplitude, speed and fluidity of movement) to infer emotions, rather than trying to recognize different gesture shapes expressing specific emotions, they proposed a method for the analysis of emotional behavior based on both direct classification of time series and a model that provides indicators describing the dynamics of expressive motion cues;
- The Multisensory Integrated Expressive Environments (a. Camurri, Volpe, Poli, & Leman, 2005), a framework for mixed reality applications in the performing arts such

as interactive dance, music, or video installations, addressing the expressive aspects of nonverbal human communication;

- The research on the modeling of expressive gesture in multimodal interaction and on the development of multimodal interactive systems, explicitly taking into account the role of non-verbal expressive gesture in the communication process (A. Camurri, Mazzarino, & Ricchetti, 2004). In this perspective, a particular focus is on dance and music as first-class conveyors of expressive and emotional content;
- The Eyesweb software (A. Camurri et al., 2000), one of the most remarkable and recognized works, used toward gestures and affect recognition in interactive dance and music systems.

Also Bevilacqua, at IRCAM-France worked on projects that used unfettered gestural motion for expressive musical purposes (Bevilacqua, Müller, & Schnell, 2005; Bevilacqua & Muller, 2005; Dobrian & Bevilacqua, 2003). The first involved the development of software to receive data from a Vicon motion capture system and to translate and map it into music controls and other media controls such as lighting (Dobrian & Bevilacqua, 2003). The second (Bevilacqua et al., 2005) consisted in the development of the toolbox "Mapping is not Music" (MnM) for Max/MSP, dedicated to mapping between gesture and sound. And the third (Bevilacqua & Muller, 2005) presents the work of the a gesture follower for performing arts, which indicates in real-time the time correspondences between an observed gesture sequence and a fixed reference gesture sequence.

Likewise, Nort and Wanderley (Nort, Wanderley, & Van Nort, 2006) presented the LoM toolbox. This allowed artists and researchers access to tools for experimenting with different complex mappings that would be difficult to build from scratch (or from within Max/MSP) and which can be combined to create many different control possibilities. This includes rapid experimentation of mapping in the dual sense of choosing what parameters to associate between control and sound space as well as the mapping of entire regions of these spaces through interpolation.

Schacher (Schacher, 2010) searched answers for questions related to the perception and expression of gestures in contrast to pure motion-detection and analysis. Presented a discussion about a specific interactive dance project, in which two complementary sensing modes were integrated to obtain higher-level expressive gestures. Polloti (Polotti & Goina, 2011) studied both sound as a means for gesture representation and gesture as embodiment of sound and Bokowiec (Bokowiec, 2011) proposed a new term, "Kinaesonics", to describe the coding of real-time one-to-one mapping of movement to sound and its expression in terms of hardware and software design.

Another important work, also published in 2011, is the one of Gillian (Gillian, Knapp, & O'Modhrain, 2011). He presented a machine learning toolbox that has been specifically developed for musician-computer interaction. His toolbox features a large number of machine learning algorithms that can be used in real-time to recognize static postures, perform regression and classify multivariate temporal gestures.

Also in 2009, the author made part of the project "Kinetic controller driven adaptive and dynamic music composition systems"[5]. One of the aims of the project was to utilize video cameras as gestural controllers for real-time music generation. The project included the development of new techniques and strategies for computer-assisted composition in the context of real-time user control with non-standard human interface devices. The research team designed and implemented real-time software that provided tools and resources for music, dance, theatre, installation artists, interactive kiosks, computer games, and internet/web information systems. The accurate segmentation of the human body was an important issue for increased gestural control using video cameras. In the International Computer Music Conference (ICMC) of 2010 the author published a paper (Baltazar, Guedes, Gouyon, & Pennycook, 2010), presenting an algorithm for real-time human body skeletonization for Max/MSP. This external object for Max/MSP was developed to be used with the technology available at that time, a computer webcam capturing video in two dimensions. The algorithm was inspired by existing approaches and added some important improvements, such as means to acquire a better representation of the human skeleton in real-time.

The output of the algorithm could be used to analyze in real-time the variation of the angles of the arms and legs of the skeleton, as well as the variation of the mass center position. This information could be used to enable humans to generate rhythms using different body parts for applications involving interactive music systems and automatic music generation. Nevertheless, the common CV problems of image segmentation using a two dimensional webcam, reduced the applications of the algorithm.

By the end of 2010 a new sensor was launched with three dimensions video capture technology, that changed the way the human body could be tracked, the Microsoft Kinect camera (Zeng & Zhang, 2012). The Kinect impact has extended far beyond the gaming industry. Being a relatively cheap technology, many researchers and practitioners in computer science, electronic engineering, robotics, and even artists are leveraging the sensing technology to develop creative new ways to interact with machines. Being for health, security or just entertainment purposes. For instance, Yoo (Yoo, Beak, & Lee, 2011) described the use of a Microsoft Kinect to directly map human joint movement information to MIDI.

Also, using a Kinect, the author published a first version of the framework in ARTECH 2012 conference (Baltazar, Martins, & Cardoso, 2012). The paper described a modular system that allows the capture and analysis of human movements in an unintrusive manner (using a

custom application for video feature extraction and analysis developed using openFrameworks). The extracted gesture features are subsequently interpreted in a machine learning environment (provided by Wekinator (Fiebrink, Trueman, & Cook, 2009)) that continuously modifies several input parameters in a computer music algorithm (implemented in ChucK~ (Wang, Cook, & others, 2003). The paper published at ARTECH was one of the steps for the framework presented in the following section of this chapter.

ZATLAB: A FRAMEWORK FOR GESTURE RECOGNITION

The research on the topic of gesture recognition poses challenging demands on the development of software modules and tools so that any proposed hypothesis and algorithms can be objectively implemented and evaluated. The prototypes developed are also important to establish a starting point for future research, therefore enabling the further improvement and validation of the algorithms implemented.

Inevitably, during the development of this project a great deal of work has been invested into software development. Therefore, this section presents the main design requirements and the implementation strategies taken towards the development of a software framework for the analysis of gestures. It also describes in detail the major software contributions.

The framework described in this chapter will take the view that perception primarily depends on the previous knowledge or learning. Just like humans do, the framework will have to learn gestures and their main features so that later it can identify them. It is however planned to be flexible enough to allow learning gestures on the fly. In this particular case, while developing a framework to be used on a stage, by a dancer or performer, one wanted to allow as much freedom of movements as possible without being intrusive on the scene.

The less the performer had to change is routine (by wearing sensors, markers or specific clothes) the better. That, together with the low cost of the technology (that allows the framework to reach to a broader number of performers), lead to the decision of using the optical \ac{MOCAP} option instead of others. The challenge of choosing this path resides on the development of sensor and \ac{CV} solutions, and their respective computational algorithms.

Designed to be efficient, the resulting system can be used to recognize gestures in the complex environment of a performance, as well as in "real-world" situations.

An overview of the proposed gesture recognition framework is presented in Figure 1. Summarized descriptions of the main blocks that constitute the proposed system are presented in this section. More detailed discussions about each of the processing stages will appear in the subsequent sections.

The ZtS is a modular framework that allows the capture and analysis of human movements and the further recognition of gestures present in those movements.

Thus, using the optical approach, the Data Acquisition Module will process data from a Microsoft Kinect or a Vicon Blade MoCap. However it can be easily modified to have input from any type of data acquisition hardware. The data acquired will go through the Data Processing Module. Here, it is processed in terms of movement analysis and feature extraction. This will allow providing a visual representation of the skeleton captured and its respective movements features. This module has also access to the database where it can record or load files. These can include: gestures, an entire captured performance, or features extracted from the movements. Once the features are extracted, these are processed by the Gesture Recognition Module using two types of Machine Learning (ML) algorithms: DTW and HMM (explained in the following sections). If a gesture is detected, it is passed to the Processing Module and this will store it, represent it or pass it to the Trigger Output Module.

In the Trigger Output Module the selected movement features or the detected gestures are mapped into triggers. These triggers can be continuous or discrete and can be sent to any program that supports the OSC communication protocol (Wright, Freed, Lee, Madden, & Momeni, 2001).

In the next sections the different modules are presented in detail.

Data Acquisition Module

The human body tracking is one of the key elements of this system. The acquisition of human movements should be as accurate as possible, to ensure a proper analysis of their features and a correct gesture recognition. But the technology chosen must also be available and affordable to a broad range of performers. Also it should be the least intrusive possible. This arises some issues to solve and decisions to make. In a previous research, the author developed a similar module using a 2D webcam, whose output was then analyzed using image segmentation algorithms (as described in the Section 'Previous Works' (Baltazar et al., 2010)). Not being as accurate as one intended, another solution had to be taken.

More recently, with the Microsoft Kinect, it became possible to obtain a full-body detection using the depth information combined with the video signal. When compared with the previous webcam version, it can be said that it becomes simpler to detect and track a foreground object/person. The "traditional" CV tracking problems, such as light constraints or background/foreground separation can be solved using this new hardware.

Another advantage, that is very important in the scope of this framework, it is its portability. Not only it can be used in almost every environment imaginable (indoors, outdoors, good or bad light conditions, crowded places) but also, this sensor can be considered (almost) a Plug & Play technology. After some drivers and software

Figure 1. The ZatLab framework architecture diagram

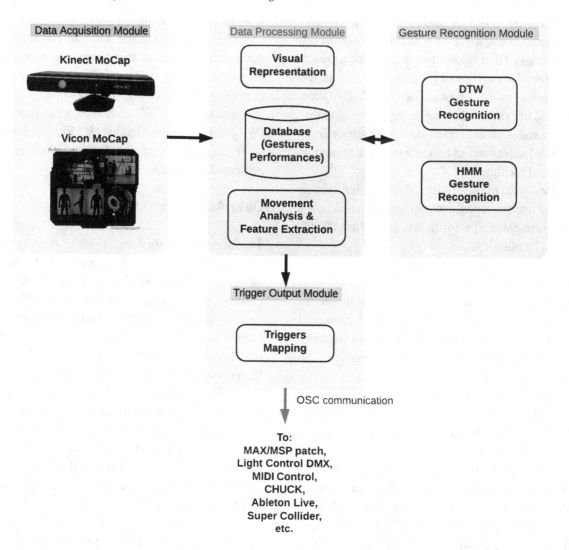

installations, and computer teaks to make it work native, one just needs to plug it to the USB port and start working with it. To users/performers that are not keen to informatics, there is also the alternative to download applications that already have the drivers and software packages embedded, which will work instantly, such as the Synapse[6].

Altogether the Kinect provides a good solution for the framework: it is portable, reasonably cheap, and has high performance tracking capabilities.

There is also a higher end method for detection, the Vicon MoCap system. With the advantages

of remarkable tracking and low latency. It has, nevertheless, explicit disadvantages, such as: the cost, the rather complex and somewhat fixed setup for several infrared cameras and the necessity of wearing a special suit equipped with reflective markers.

Another disadvantage is that Vicon Blade only allows the real-time transmission of data to other commercially developed programs of their company or with companies that have established sharing protocols. Also, the transmission is made in a proprietary protocol. Consequently, in the case of this work, the real-time OSC transmission between the Vicon Blade and the ZtS (or any other external program) had to be developed.

This application, named ofxViconOSC, developed within the scope of this project, that can stream, in real-time the data from a Vicon system to any computer, is now available to the scientific community at the Centro de Investigação em Ciência e Tecnologia das Artes (CITAR) website[7].

Having these two technologies available at CITAR, the framework developed should allow working with both.

In summary, this module consists on the acquisition of the real-world data to the virtual-world. It is independent of the hardware chosen to acquire the human movements, but is preset to work with a Microsoft Kinect and a Vicon Blade. In this module the hardware messages are decoded into human body joints to feed the Data Processing Module, presented next.

Data Processing Module

This module is the core of the framework, it will process and redirect the data to other modules keeping the framework functioning properly and effectively.

This receives the skeleton joints data from the aforementioned Data Acquisition Module and processes it for three different purposes:

1. **Visual Representation:** The GUI provides a real-time, intricate but intuitive visual feedback to the user. Not only displays the skeleton of the user as if he was in front of a mirror (a virtual mirror in this case), but it can also display different panels of information. These range from the gestures previously recorded (with velocity and acceleration information attached), the gesture that was recognized, what triggers are setup and if a movement trigger was activated or not. The Figures 2 and 3 present different views of the ZtS GUI.

2. **Database Management:** The database allows the user to record and load several types of files. It is organized in the following folders:

   a. **Performances:** The user can record an entire performance (e.g. a dance, a presentation, etc). It records the several skeleton joints data sequence in a text file. It allows reproducing exactly what was done by the user, thus enabling the review, setup and adjustment of triggers in offline mode (for instance, can be used to record a dance rehearsal, review it and setup some gesture triggers to use on the next rehearsal or in the presentation of the dance performance).

   b. **Gestures:** The user can record a set of gestures for training the recognition algorithms or for gesture notation purposes. Different from the performance recording, hence will be recording only the segment of data that represent the gesture and its main features (for instance, the circles presented in Figure 2 can be recorded in the database for future use).

   c. **Gesture Models:** When the user trains the gesture recognition algorithms, he is creating a gesture model. This model contains the features of the recognition algorithms, necessary for the recognition of a similar gesture. This folder stores the model files.

   d. **Drawings:** The user can use the framework in a more lateral purpose for free drawing (like for instance, a virtual board). In this folder the user can store the drawings. The files are stored with a single identifier name consisting on the data and time of the start of recording.

3. **Movement Analysis and Feature Extraction:** Having in mind the results of previous researches (Al-Hamadi, Elmezain,

Figure 2. The GUI in development mode and the respective control panel; on the control panel one can see the DTW Mode is activated and the triggers are being sent to "localhost" and port 12345. Next to the gesture is presented its index and some statistics about it, in this case its average speed and acceleration. On the top right corner one can see the algorithm just recognized gesture "1".

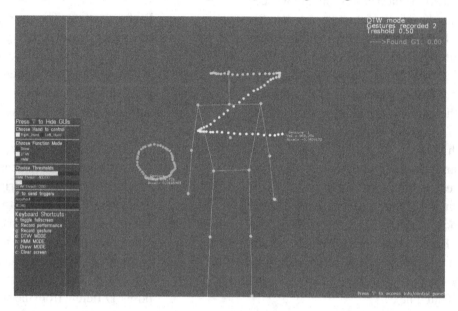

Figure 3. The application of the framework in FestivalIN (further described in next section); the different color particles indicate triggers have been activated (in this case sound triggers).

& Michaelis, 2010), the movement features chosen to compute are the ones provided by the Physics kinematic equations[8] to describe movement along with the orientation angle of the gesture path, described next.

From the data acquired one already has the information of the coordinates and the respective timestamp t for each joint of the human body. Therefore, the following features can be computed.

a. **Time:** For a given movement segment, its total time can be easily computed by subtracting the first sample time-stamp t_1 from the last sample time-stamp t_n:

$$T = t_n - t_1$$

b. **Displacement:** Knowing all the coordinates of the movement segment, the total displacement D can be calculated by summing the relative difference among $coord_i$ and the previous $coord_{i-1}$, from the first sample (i = 1) till the last (n).

$$D = \sum_{i=1}^{n} \left\| coord_i - coord_{i-1} \right\|$$

c. **Velocity:** Also, the velocity and acceleration can be computed. The average velocity will be defined as the quotient of the displacement Δd and the interval time Δt. In the case of consecutive frames (where the Δt is very small) we can assume this is the instantaneous velocity v_i.

$$v_i = \frac{\left| coord_i - coord_{i-1} \right|}{t_i - t_{i-1}}$$

And the average velocity can be computed as the sum off all the v_i divided by the number of samples n:

$$v_{avg} = \frac{\sum_{i=1}^{n} \left\| v_i \right\|}{n}$$

d. **Acceleration:** Similarly, the instantaneous acceleration can be approximated by the average acceleration over a small interval Δt.

$$a_i = \frac{v_i - v_{i-1}}{t_i - t_{i-1}}$$

And the average acceleration can be computed as:

$$a_{avg} = \frac{\sum_{i=1}^{n} \left\| a_i \right\|}{n}$$

All the features are extracted within a motion segment. These features are very important to describe the joint movements. Although with these features one is already able to visualize and extract relevant information from the data, the direction of movement the joint takes at each frame is also a key feature for the ML algorithms (explained in the next section). This feature will allow not only to detect immediately if the movement is done from left to right, but also if it is a simple line or something more complex like a circle or a square.

e. **Direction of Movement:** The angle or direction of movement can be calculated using the known coordinates at consecutive frames and applying the arc-tangent function. This is given by the following equation and the result is given in degrees (in this case computed only in two dimensions: Δx is the displacement along the x axis and Δy is the displacement along the y axis).

$$\phi = \arctan \frac{\Delta y}{\Delta x}$$

ϕ ranges from $0°$ till $360°$. This would create a tremendous range of data to be analyzed, in real-time, by the ML algorithms (Al-Hamadi et al., 2010). Also, measuring the direction of the movement in single unit degrees could lead to additional noise in the data. Therefore, it is necessary to normalize the data to an observable "codeword". This can be done by dividing the total range of the angles in 12 equally separated spaces (12 spaces allow to understand differences in increments of $30°$). So, the direction of movements is classified accordingly to the degrees belonging to a determined interval.

The framework is setup to work with these 12 symbols, but it can be easily adapted to work with more or less. See Table 1 and Figure 4 for better understanding this angle based "codeword".

Having all the features extracted, these are passed to the Gesture Recognition Module, explained next.

Gesture Recognition Module

The gesture recognition in Human-Computer Interaction (HCI) has many similarities with other areas of research. Being encompassed in a more general area of pattern recognition, stand out, in particular, the similarities with speech or handwriting recognition. Being these areas already more developed in scientific terms, it is natural to try to mirror the various techniques applied in these areas to gesture recognition (Corradini, 2001).

Table 1. Angles codeword table

Angle	Codeword Value	Angle	Codeword Value
[0°, 30°]	0	[181°, 210°]	6
[31°, 60°]	1	[211°, 240°]	7
[61°, 90°]	2	[241°, 270°]	8
[91°, 120°]	3	[271°, 300°]	9
[121°, 150°]	4	[301°, 330°]	10
[151°, 180°]	5	[331°, 359°]	11

Figure 4. Examples of gestures recorded and their associated angle orientation codeword; in the case of the circle all the orientation values are present, but the timestamped sequence will reveal if it was executed in clockwise or counter-clockwise motion.

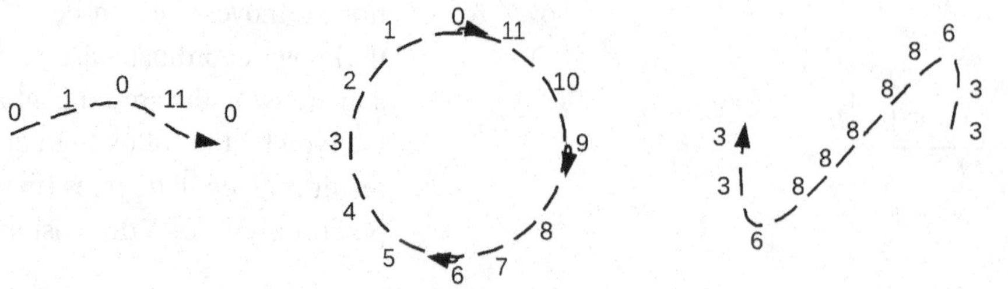

Considering a gesture G can be described as a sequence of feature vectors, it can be assumed that the best way to describe it is to gather N sequences (prototypes) of that gesture (performed in different ways). Therefore, when in recognition mode, an unknown input can be compared against each one of these N prototypes and, taking into account the measures and criteria chosen, a degree of similarity can be assigned.

Although it has a high computational cost, a large set of reference patterns N should be used for this comparison, representing each gesture G. The biggest problem with this approach is the choice of a suitable distance measure. The simplest way to define it is by calculating the distances between the corresponding samples of the reference and the unknown input sequences and accumulate the result. Unfortunately, gestures have a variable spatio-temporal structure. They vary when performed by different people and even the same user is not able to perform a gesture exactly the same way several times in a row. This means that, depending on both the speed of the movement performance and the user, the recorded gesture signals can be stretched or compressed.

Therefore, to compare two signals permitting them to have different lengths requires dynamic programming. Learning from speech recognition, since speech shares the varying temporal structure of gestures, an algorithm often used in that field is the Dynamic Time Warping (DTW) (Lawrence Rabiner & Juang, 1993). The DTW algorithm performs a time alignment and normalization by computing a temporal transformation allowing two signals of different lengths to be matched.

Another alternative of dynamic programming is the statistical and probabilistic approach, such as Hidden Markov Model (HMM). It is a rich tool used for gesture recognition in diverse application domains. Probably, the first publication addressing the problem of hand gesture recognition is the seminal paper by Yamato (Yamato, Ohya, & Ishii, 1992). In his approach, a discrete HMM

and a sequence of vector-quantized (VQ)-labels have been used to recognize six different types of tennis strokes.

In this section, one will discuss the principles of both the algorithms working on the Gesture Recognition Module, the DTW and the HMM.

The DTW

When two signals with temporal variance must be compared, or when looking for a pattern in a data stream, the signals may be stretched or shrunk along its time axis in order to fit into each other. A comparison made after these operations can give false results because we may be comparing different relative parts of the signals. The DTW is one of the methods to solve this problem (Ten Holt, Reinders, & Hendriks, 2007). The algorithm calculates the distances between each possible pair of the two signals taking into account their associated feature values. With these measured distances it builds a matrix of accumulated distances and finds the path that guarantees the minimum distance between signals. This path represents the best synchronization of both signals and thus, the minimum feature distance between their synchronized points.

Consequently, the DTW has become popular by being extremely efficient as the time-series similarity measure which minimizes the effects of shifting and distortion in time, allowing "elastic" transformation of time series in order to detect similar shapes with different phases. It has been used in various fields, such as speech recognition (Lawrence Rabiner & Juang, 1993), data mining (Keogh & Ratanamahatana, 2005), and movement recognition (Corradini, 2001; Gillian et al., 2011).

To explain this implementation, first it is important to realize how to proceed in order to recognize a gesture. Regarding a case-study example of an user using his right hand to record and test gesture recognition. This relies in two main procedures:

1. **Recording Gestures:** When recording a gesture, a **vector_of_features** is incremented, at each frame, with several feature values, for instance x, y, z, ϕ where x, y, z are the coordinates and ϕ is the orientation angle of the hand movement. So when the user decides to record a gesture he will really be recording the sequence of movement features he is performing. The user can record as many gestures he wants, thus creating a database of several of these **vector_of_features** stored in a **vector_of_gestures**. This database will be the reference to which the forthcoming "test" gestures will be compared. Refer to Figure 5 to a graphical explanation of the recording procedure.

2. **Recognizing:** Having at least one gesture recorded on the database, the system enters in recognition mode. At each frame the **vector_of_test** will be fed with the same features the previous **vector_of_features**.

This vector stores the data, keeping thus a real-time array of features (with size N - the double of space the biggest gesture recorded).

Once it gets N feature samples, the system will cyclically divide the movement input at regular intervals creating several **vector_of_test** that will keep charging (**vector_to_dtw**). The system performs the DTW distance of each one of this **vector_of_test** against each **vector_of_features** stored in the **vector_of_gestures**. When the DTW distance to one of the gestures recorded is lower than a determined threshold, the input sequence is recognized as a gesture. Refer to Figure 6 to a graphical explanation of the procedure.

In this case, you can realize the signal being tested in slightly bigger than **Gesture 1** (in Figure 4), nevertheless, is the same gesture in shape. Therefore, despite some distance between both signals, the DTW algorithm will detect it as being similar to Gesture 1 (as intended).

Figure 5. The sequence of gesture features are accumulated in a vector. When the user records the gesture, this sequence will be stored as a new gesture in the vector_of_gestures.

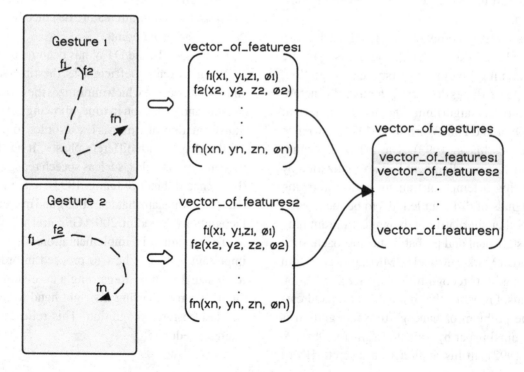

Figure 6. A movement is tested through the DTW distance in order to find if it is present in the Gestures Database. Relating to the previous Figure 5 when testing the entire movement (in blue) it would result in finding the stored Gesture 1 (vector_of_features1).

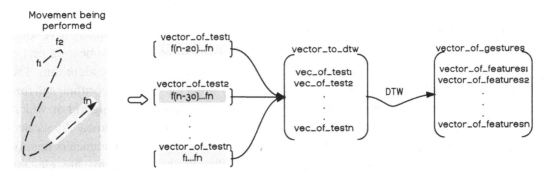

The key point of this algorithm is the construction of the DTW cost matrix. This is built by iteratively finding the minimum Euclidean Distance amongst the components of both vector signals, hence finding the optimal warping path, also named minimum warping distance.

Breaking down into a detailed description each component of **vector_of_test** will be tested against each component of **vector_of_features**. Once the minimum pair-wise distance is found, this distance will be stored in the cost matrix, and proceed to the next component. This cycle repeats until all the components have been analyzed and the cost matrix built. By summing all these minimum distance values along the cost matrix, one will have the shortest warping path, or the minimum distance of the signals. The implementation code was done based on Lemire (Lemire, 2009) approach to DTW algorithm.

The HMM

HMM (LR Rabiner, 1989; Yamato et al., 1992) are powerful statistical models for representing sequential or time-series data, and have been successfully used in many tasks such as speech recognition, protein/DNA sequence analysis, robot control, and information extraction from text data. HMM have also been applied to hand and face recognition (Nefian & Hayes III, 1998).

The HMM is rich in mathematical structures and has been found to efficiently model spatio-temporal information in a natural way. The model is termed "hidden" because all that can be seen is only a sequence of observations (symbols). It also involves elegant and efficient algorithms, such as Baum-Welch and Viterbi (Viterbi, 1967) for evaluation, learning and decoding.

Formally, an HMM is defined as a quintuple S, V, Π, A, B (LR Rabiner, 1989) where $S = \{s_1, ..., s_N\}$ is a finite set of N hidden states (that model a gesture); $V = \{v_1, ..., v_M\}$ is a set of M possible symbols (e.g. features of the gesture) in a vocabulary; $\Pi = \{\pi_i\}$ are the initial state probabilities; $A = \{a_{ij}\}$ are the state transition probabilities; $B = \{b_i(v_k)\}$ are the output or emission probabilities.

Therefore, each HMM is modeled and expressed as $\lambda = (\Pi, A, B)$ where the parameters are:

- π_i: The probability that the system starts at state i at the beginning;
- a_{ij}: The probability of going from state i to state j;
- $b_i(v_k)$: The probability of generating symbol v_k at state i.

The generalized topology of an HMM is a fully connected structure, know as an *ergodic* model, where any state can be reached from any other state. When employed in dynamic gesture recognition, the state index transits only from left to right with time.

The global structure of the HMM recognition is constructed by training of each HMM $(\lambda_1, \lambda_2, ..., \lambda_M)$, whereby insertion (or deletion) of a new (or existing) HMM is easily accomplished. λ corresponds to a constructed HMM model for each gesture and M is the total number of gestures being recognized.

When working with HMM there are three basic problems to solve:

1. **Evaluation:** Given a model and a sequence of observations, how do we compute the probability that the observed sequence was produced by the model? Namely, one has to evaluate the probability of an observed sequence of symbols $O = o_1 o_2, ..., o_t$ (where $o_i \in V$) given a particular HMM (λ), e.g. $p(O|\lambda)$. This is extremely useful, in this case having several competing "models" of gestures, this will allow to find which gesture "model" best matches the observations (of the gesture being performed live).

2. **Decoding:** This is to uncover the hidden part of the model, i.e. to find the state sequence that illustrates best the model. In other words, to find the most likely state transition path associated with an observed sequence. Having a sequence of states $q = q_1, q_2, ..., q_t$ we will want to find $q^* = \arg\max_q p(q \hat{} O|\lambda)$.

3. **Training:** Is the crucial part of HMM, since it will allow adapting the model parameters to the observed training sequence, hence creating the best models for the gestures performed. In other words, is to adjust all the parameters of our model λ to maximize

the probability of generating an observed set of sequences O, this is, to find $\lambda^* = \arg\max_\lambda p(O|\lambda)$.

These three problems already have solutions. The first is solved by implementing part of the Forward-Backward iterative algorithm. The second by using the Viterbi algorithm, and the third by using the Baum-Welch algorithm, which uses the Forward and Backward probabilities calculated previously to update the parameters iteratively.

Although the algorithms are elegant and sophisticated, their implementation is not very straightforward. Consequently, the next paragraphs will explain how these work together in gesture recognition. Specifically the ***HMM class*** was developed with 3 modes of operation: Train, Evaluate, Test (decode). These are called by using the pointer to the class and choosing the operation mode wanted (1-for testing, 2 - for evaluating, 3- for training). This implementation was based in (Liu, 2009) and (LR Rabiner, 1989).

Again, for a gesture to be recognized, first one will have to "teach" the algorithm how the gesture look like and how it is executed. In the previous DTW approach, one is able to do direct and immediate comparison of signals. In the case of HMM, being a probabilistic model build upon statistics, the "teaching" is not so forthcoming. It will involve the creation of a training set of gestures for each one we wish to detect. Recalling the same case-study proposed before, imagine a user using his right hand to record and test gesture recognition. In order to do so, this module operates in the following fashion.

1. **Record Gesture Samples:** To train a HMM of a gesture first one needs to create several instances of the same gesture. Thus, using a similar method to the one explained before (Figure 4) one will be recording, at each frame, several feature values of the user movement (kept in **vector_of_features**). The

user will record several identical samples of the same gesture being each one stored in a **vector_of_gestures**.

2. **Create a New HMM:** Having a reasonable amount of examples of the same gesture (defined by the user), when the order to train a new HMM is made, this has to be created and initialized.

For each new HMM the user can dynamically choose the number of hidden states (N_{states}). For instance to create a new HMM with a **vector_of_gestures** and N_{states} one would do:

a. **vec_hmm_models.push_back(new HMM(vector_of_gestures, N_{states}));**
This creates a new instance of **HMM class** with a new position in the pointer **vec_hmm_models** to it. The matrices of this new HMM are initiated following the next rules:

a. The initial states probability (matrix N_{states} x 1) is initiated as $1/N_{states}$ to give an equal probability distribution amongst the states.

b. Considering the gesture is done in one continuous, fluid movement, the transition probability between states should have more weight between the adjacent ones, thus the state transition probability matrix (a_{ij} of size N_{states} x N_{states}) is initiated as exemplified on Table 2.

c. At last, the state output matrix ($N_{observations}$ x N_{states}), that allows to relate the observed output data ($N_{observations}$) to the state transition, is initiated by distributing equally the probabilities of the output: $1/N_{observations}$.

3. **Train a HMM:** Having the new HMM created, the system will train it using the samples provided. To do so, the **vector_of_gestures** will be passed to the Baum-Welch algorithm by calling the HMM class with the respective operation mode (mode 3, for training):

a. **vec_hmm_models[last]->RunHMM(3, vector_of_gestures);** the train routine will breakdown the **vector_of_gestures** in its constituents (**vector_of_features**). These features are the observed data and with it the algorithm performs a statistical evaluation of the data sequence that will lead to the update of the emission and transition probabilities matrices, modeling thus the hidden states for the gesture performed.

Computing the Baum-Welch

The algorithm takes sequences of observations as input and estimates the new values of transition matrix (a_{ij}) and emission matrix ($b_i(v_k)$) that maximize the probability for the given observations. It runs iterations over the input data and terminate when convergence or certain threshold condition is met, for instance: number of iterations, difference in parameter changes.

The algorithm takes two passes over the data. In the first pass, it uses forward algorithm to construct α probabilities (the pseudo-code for this algorithm is explained in the following section (Computing the Likelihood). In addition to the α probabilities, the algorithm runs a similar backward algorithm to construct β probabilities. The backward probability $\beta(t, i)$ is the probability of seeing observation from o_{t+1} to the end, given that we are in state j at time t.

Based on the α and β probabilities, one can compute the expected number (counts) of transitions ($\xi(i, j)$) from state i to state j at a given observation t ($\gamma(t, i)$).

Part of the pseudo-code for Baum-Welch algorithm is presented in Listing 1. The α probabilities are updated after calling the forward function at line 2. The remaining code computes $\xi(i, j)$ and $\gamma(t, i)$ counts.

Table 2. The state transition probability matrix initialization example; the probability is divided amongst adjacent states. The N -ish state is connected to the first, closing thus the probabilities loop.

State	0	1	2	N
0	0, 5	0, 5	0	0
1	0	0, 5	0, 5	0
2	0	0	0, 5	0, 5
N	0, 5	0	0	0, 5

With $\xi(i, j)$ and $\gamma(t, i)$ computed, the a_{ij} and $b_i(v_k)$ matrices are updated.

4. **Verify the Model:** Having the model constructed with its respective emission and transition matrices one can verify if the training was done properly. This is accomplished using the Viterbi algorithm (computer implementation explained next). This algorithm will provide the sequence of hidden states in respect to the HMM built:
   a.   vec_hmm_models[last]->RunHMM(2, 0);

Computing the Viterbi

The Viterbi algorithm finds the most likely path of states that generate the observations. Instead of summing over all $\alpha, \beta, \gamma, \xi$ to 0 probabilities (like Baum-Welch algorithm does), Viterbi algorithm finds the maximum one and keeps a pointer to trace the state that leads to the maximum probability. The pseudo-code for Viterbi algorithm is given in Listing 2. The input to the algorithm is a sequence of observations and output is a sequence of the most likely states that generate the observation.

5. **Recognizing:** Once having a trained HMM the system can enter in test mode. Again, like in the DTW case (Section ofxDTW) the **vector_of_test** will be fed with the same features of the previous samples used to train the model. In this case the vector will be continuously tested against the trained HMM:

Listing 1. The pseudo-code for the Baum-Welch algorithm

```
1  initialize all cells of α, β, γ, ξ to 0
2  calculate likelihood ← Forward(o)
3  β(o_T,1) = 1 // base case t = T, end of sequence
4  for t = o_T to o_1 //cycle to compute the Backward algorithm
5     for i = 1 to N
6        do γ(t,i) = γ(t,i) + (α((t,i) · β(t,i)/likelihood)))
7           for j = 1 to N
8              do β(t,i) = β(t,i) + β(t+1,i)α_{ji}b_{it}
9                 ξ(j,i) = ξ(j,i) + (α(t,j)β(t+1,i)α_{ji}b_{it}/likelihood)
```

Listing 2. The pseudo-code for the Viterbi algorithm

```
1  initialize all cells of α to 0
2  α(o₁, s) = 1  // base case t = 1, there are no preceding states
3  for t = o₂ to oₜ  // cycle to compute the Viterbi algorithm
4     for i = 1 to N
5        for j = 1 to N
6           if α(t-1, j)aᵢⱼbᵢₜ > αMax(t, i)
7              then αMax(t, i) = α(t-1, j)aᵢⱼbᵢₜ
8                   MaxPointer(t, i) = j
9  Seq_of_states = sequence(MaxPointer)
10 return Seq_of_states
```

a. **vec_hmm_models[last]->RunHMM(1, vector_of_test);**

If there are more than one HMM trained, the **vector_of_test** is iteratively tested against all the models $likelihood \leftarrow Forward(o)$ of the **vec_hmm_models[M]**. The highest likelihood HMM is returned by the Forward Algorithm (computer implementation next).

This test is done in regard to each trained model emission and transition probabilities matrices. If the observed test sequence matches the probabilities previously calculated for the model matrices, the likelihood of that sequence will be maximized. Therefore, if that returned likelihood is high enough to surpass a user-defined threshold, the gesture is recognized as belonging to that respective model.

Computing the Likelihood

To compute the likelihood, the Forward algorithm computes the $\beta(o_T, 1) = 1$ for the sequence of O observations and N hidden states. This can be viewed as a matrix, where each cell $t = o_T$ is the probability of being in state

$$\gamma(t, i) = \gamma(t, i) + \left(\alpha \left((t, i) \cdot \beta(t, i) / likelihood \right) \right)$$

while seeing the observations until

$$\beta(t, i) = \beta(t, i) + \beta(t+1, i) \alpha_{ji} b_{it}.$$

An overview of Forward algorithm is shown in the pseudo-code below (Listing 3). The input to the algorithm is a sequence of observations

$$\xi(j, i) = \xi(j, i) + \left(\alpha(t, j) \beta(t+1, i) \alpha_{ji} b_{it} / likelihood \right)$$

The output is the likelihood probability for the observation. The algorithm makes the assumption the first observation in sequence is the start state, and the last observation is the end state.

The Gesture Recognition Module is of paramount importance for this framework. The recognition algorithms (DTW and HMM) can be used in simultaneous or individually, providing different modes of training and recognition.

When a gesture is recognized, this is communicated to the Processing Module that will redirect the information to the Triggers Output Module. Next is the description of this module.

Listing 3. The pseudo-code for the Forward algorithm

```
1  initialize  all  cells  of  α  to  0
2  α(o₁, s) = 1  //base case t=1, there  are  no  preceding  states
3  for  t = o₂  to  o_T  //cycle  to  compute  the  Forward  algorithm
4    for  i = 1  to  N
5      for  j = 1  to  N
6        do  α(t, i) = α(t, i) + α(t − 1, j)a_{ij}b_{it}
7  likelihood = α(o_T, N)
8  return  likelihood
```

Triggers Output Module

Paraphrasing Newton third law of movement, "For every action, there is an equal and opposite reaction". This module is responsible for the re-action. It may not be opposing neither equal, but it is definitely a reaction, in this case to a gesture performed.

This module has the setup of what will be the framework reaction to a gesture recognized. This can be internal or external. Internally it can react by generating visual contents on the GUI such as images, information or drawings. And externally it can control anything that directly assumes OSC communication protocol, what nowadays is pretty common.

OSC (Wright et al., 2001) was originally developed to facilitate the distribution of control structure computations to small arrays of loosely coupled heterogeneous computer systems. A common application of OSC is to communicate control structure computations from one client machine to an array of synthesis servers. OSC is a 'transport-independent' network protocol, meaning that OSC data can be carried by any general-purpose network technology. Today most implementations use the main Internet protocols (UDP and TCP/IP) via Ethernet or wireless network connections. Thus,

most of the programs used in the performative arts domain (and other domains) allow communication through \ac{OSC}, these range from sound and music control programs, video or light setup and display tables, till computers and robotic hardware.

Therefore, is possible to control a vast amount of events with a gesture. One just have to decide on the trigger mapping and respective OSC syntax.

For each gesture trained in the framework a trigger is assigned. It can be discrete (triggering only events each time gesture is recognized) or continuous (controlling events such as sound pitch or modulation accordingly to a velocity or coordinate value). The triggers can be further customized by the user, but are preset to work in the following fashion:

1. **Discrete Triggering:** Each gesture trained for recognition is associated with a single identifier trigger, matching the gesture index (e.g. Gesture 1, Gesture 2, etc.). When a gesture is recognized a trigger message is sent through OSC, using the following syntax:

```
Gesture index, joint, coord_X,
coord_Y, coord_Z, Avg. Velocity, Avg.
Acceleration
```

2. **Continuous Triggering:** The default configuration for continuous triggering consists on maintaining a constant communication of the joints kinematic features. For instance, the left hand OSC message will be:

```
HandL, coord_X, coord_Y, coord_Z,
Inst. Velocity, Inst. Acceleration
```

In order to create an interesting result one needs to map the triggers to the respective events. As reviewed in Background Section, there are several strategies to do the mapping of the triggers to expressive events. The choice of which to apply is done by the users of the framework. This is, the framework allows the association of triggers to gestures, therefore when the gesture is performed and recognized the trigger is sent. What the user does with that trigger is depends on his creativity or purpose. For instance, on the applications described on the following Section, the triggers were mapped internally to the emission of visual particles and externally to the control of sound events.

This section discussed some of the requirements, choices and the major contributions towards the development of an open source software platform for the computational analysis of gestures.

Some implementation details about the main building blocks of the framework proposed were described, where the efficiency, flexibility and code reusability aspects taken into consideration during the software development, were highlighted. Next section presents two artistic uses of the framework.

Framework Applications

Introduction

This section presents the artistic applications of the framework. Namely its use in an Interactive Opera, in collaboration with Miso Music Portugal,

and the use of the framework as a public interactive installation in the Festival of Creativity and Innovation, in Lisbon, 2013.

Using ZtS in an Artistic Performance

MisoMusic Portugal[9] was commissioned to create an interactive multimedia Opera (to debut in September 2013), by the renown Polish Festival *Warsaw Autumn*[10] (Warszawska Jesień).

Knowing the work developed in the scope of this project, MisoMusic proposed the use of the ZtS framework in the Opera to control real-time audio samples and the direct sound input of the voice of one performer. But before entering on further details about the developments made, the following section will describe briefly the Opera, named "A Laugh to Cry". This will set the benchmark for the work developed in the ZtS framework.

About the Opera "A Laugh to Cry"

A *Laugh to Cry* explores some primary concerns, which have always haunted human beings, and reveals them from the perspective of our contemporary globalized world. The opera is shaped like a meditation on the hegemonic power of the destruction of memory, the devastation of the Earth and even the collapse of humanity. It evolves in the fringes between dream and reality, between the visible and invisible, being divided in several acts where five characters, two sopranos, one bass and two narrators (a female and a male voice), live and dwell constantly between these two parallels. The opera also involves seven acoustic instruments: flute, clarinet, percussion, piano, violin, viola, cello, as well as live electronics and extended video scenography.

A *Laugh to Cry* pursues Miguel Azguime goal, as poet and composer, to grasp an ideal balance between language and music, to merge the language semantic and metaphorical components with its sonic values, in order to achieve his concept of "speech as music and music as speech". A *Laugh to Cry* extends Miguel Azguime research on voice analysis, re-synthesis and processing, aiming at creating a dynamic continuum between timbre, harmony, rhythm and voice spectra.

System Requirements

The framework had to be tailored to the composer/performer (Miguel Azguime) needs. Specifically, he wanted to control sound samples and live voice input with his movements and gestures. In this case, the framework was adapted with several triggers that controlled sounds in a MAX/MSP[11] patch (this patch was developed by a fellow researcher, André Perrotta).

The framework went through a series of tests and refinements, in particular to respond to the composer choices and performer abilities.

In the end the ZtS framework enabled several types of sound control:

- The trigger of sound samples with the movement velocity of the hands of the performer;
- The cycle through eight banks of sound samples by performing a gesture;
- The trigger of capturing a sound action (sound sample or live voice input). The performer was able to freeze a sound when he performed a holding hands pose. This enabled the performer to control the captured sound in terms of pitch, reverb, feedback and loudness. When he wanted he just needed to do a more sudden movement with both hands (exceeding a pre-determined hand movement velocity threshold) to release the sound.

In Figure 7 one can see the hardware setup. A Microsoft Kinect was used to capture the human body and an Apple MacMini running the ZtS was hidden under a black cloth. The framework was sending the control triggers to the sound computer on the technical regie at 25 meters of distance. One setup a Local Area Network to enable the triggers transmission. Also, in this case, the performer wanted the visual feedback to make sure he was in the right position, so there was a 15 inch LCD on stage (also hidden from the audience).

The framework ended up being used for the solo of one of the main Opera characters, performed by Miguel Azguime himself. The ZtS framework travelled with the Opera throughout the entire tour. In the first performances the setup was done by the author of the framework, which also supervised its function during the Opera. Since everything ran smoothly on the first three performances of the Opera (two in Lisbon and one in Poland), for the Sweden leg of the tour (four more presentations) one of the Opera technicians received a brief formation on how to do the setup and execute the ZtS. Important to realize that he did the setup alone and operated the framework on those four shows without any problem, thus revealing the usability of the framework.

In sum, the result of the developments made especially for the Opera use was very interesting. The relation between human movement/gestures and sound manipulation was immediately perceived by the audience, therefore creating a particular arouse during that part of the piece. Of course the principal credit goes to the performer, in this case Miguel, which learned very quickly to interact and get exactly what he wanted from the framework, when he wanted, thus enabling him to add extra layers of emotion and enhancement to the solo he performed.

In the following section is the statement Miguel gave regarding the use of the framework.

Evaluation

Once the Opera presentations were finished, one asked Miguel Azguime, the author/performer and main user of the ZtS framework, to answer

Figure 7. The setup used for the opera "A Laugh to Cry"; on the top left image is the view from the technical sound area. The top right and left bottom images present the view of the ZtS setup. The last photo illustrates the view Miguel had when using the system.

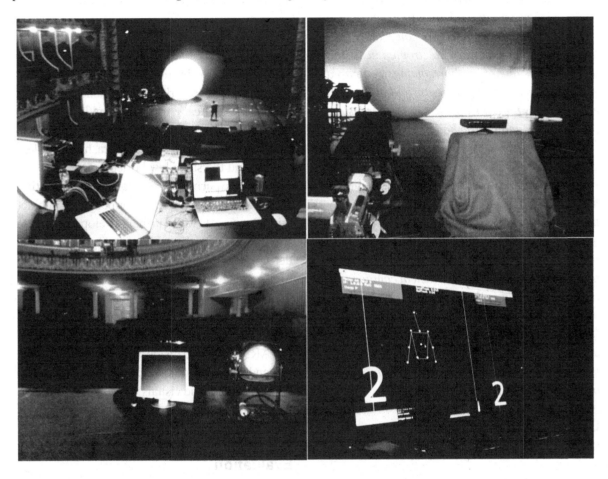

a few questions about the system and to transmit his opinion about it. Here is a literal quote of the text he sent.

Since the beginning, in the design of the opera "The Laugh to Cry", were implicit certain technological aspects and modes of interaction, which had not been possible to research, develop and use in previous works. In particular the relationship sound - gesture took this project a clear role that was intended to develop and the Zatlab System developed by André Baltazar came precisely to meet this desire, having been adapted to respond to musical, performative and expressive purpose

I intended for a crucial moment of the opera and true climax of the symbolic and narrative discourse thereof.}

Playwright and musical composition itself for this decisive moment in the opera were designed to take advantage of the interaction with the system and conditioned by the type of gestural control offered by the same.

A clear perception to the public that the gesture is that of inducing sound, responsiveness of the system to allow clarification of musical and expressive speech, effectively ensuring the alternation between sudden, rapid, violent gestures, sounds on the one hand and modular suspensions by gesture in total control of the sound processing parameters on the other, constituted a clear enrichment both in terms of communication (a rare cause and effect approach in the context of electronic music and it certainly is one of its shortcomings compared with music acoustic instruments) and in terms of expression by the ability of the system to translate the language and plastic body expression.

Clearly, as efficient as the system may be, the results thereof and eventual artistic validation, are always dependent on composite music and the way these same gestures are translated into sound (or other interaction parameters) and therefore is in crossing gesture with the sound and the intersection of performance with the musical composition (in this case) that is the crux of the appreciation of Zatlab. However, regardless of the quality of the final result, the system has enormous potential as a tool sufficiently open and malleable in order to be suitable for different aesthetic, modes of operation and different uses.

Using ZtS in a Public Interactive Installation

Another application of the system consisted in making it as an interactive installation at FestivalIN[12], Lisbon. The FestivalIN was announced as the biggest innovation and creativity aggregating event being held in Portugal, precisely in Lisbon at the International Fair of Lisbon. It is described as a unique event that integrates, in a practical, dynamic and consistent way, the core concepts associated to Creativity and Innovation.

It presents itself as an absolutely innovative event, anchoring sensorial experiences (physical and virtual interactions), crossing different areas of the Creative Industries. It is a space, which involves people, ideas and experiences and promotes, both nationally and internationally, Portugal most creative possessions, boosting its authors, creators and entrepreneurs in a worldwide scale.

System Requirements

Departing from the developments made to the Opera, the framework was adapted to be more responsive and easy to interact with. The users were able to trigger and control sound samples, much like Miguel did on the Opera, however they did not had the same level of control.

Since the purpose was to install the application at a kiosk and leave it there for people to interact with, the visuals were further developed to create some curiosity and attract users. The human body detection algorithm was also customized in order to filtrate the control, amongst the crowd, to only the person closer and centered to the system.

Figure 8. presents the setup and some interactions with the system. The closet was provided by CITAR. This stored inside a MacMini running the ZtS and had a custom fit opening for a Microsoft Kinect. Outside the visuals were displayed in a 32 inch LCD and the sound was provided by a stereo setup provided by the FestivalIn organization.

Evaluation

The response to the system was very good, in particular amongst the children. All day long there was someone playing with it. The fact that the people were detected immediately either if they were just passing by or really wanted to interact was a key factor to the system popularity. The persons saw their skeleton mirrored on the screen and wave at it, therefore triggering sounds and building up the users' curiosity. Soon enough they understand the system response to their gestures and were engaged, interacting and creating musical expressions.

Figure 8. The setup used for FestivalIn; on the left, the cabinet provided by CITAR, you can notice the Kinect bellow the LCD TV. On the right top, the visuals when someone interacted and left bottom a kid playing with the system.

CONCLUSION

The goal of this research is to foster the use of gestures, in an artistic context, for the creation of new ways of expression. Consequently, the approach taken envisioned the study of the gesture: its understanding, how to capture it (in a non intrusive way) and how to recognize it (in real-time).

Following this study, one concluded the gesture recognition is a rather simple task for the average person, but its automatically recognition, by a machine, is a much more complex task. Therefore, this chapter proposes a flexible and extensible computer framework for recognition of gestures in real-time.

Designed to be causal and efficient, the resulting system can be used to capture and recognize human body gestures, in real-time, paving the way

to applications such as interactive installations, computer music interaction, performance events controlling, amongst others.

The main advantage of this framework against other works developed in this area is to have a fully functional pipeline of integrated modules, allowing the human movement capture, movement feature extraction, gesture training and its recognition, all in a single application. Consequently, enabling a more straightforward use (especially by the artistic community).

The proposed system is based in a relatively cheap MoCap system (Microsoft Kinect) and is developed to work without any third party installations besides the respective capture device drivers.

The recognition process is then based in ML algorithms, namely DTW and HMM.

This chapter also described two artistic applications of the framework. One was an interactive artistic installation and the other was its use in an interactive Opera. These applications sustain the artistic relevance of the framework.

In particular regarding its application in the Opera, one can conclude the framework was successfully applied in performance context, recognizing the performer gestures, in real-time, and triggering events. Being the performers the ultimate users of the framework, one reckons their opinion is very important. Therefore the fact that Miguel Azguime (the Opera performer) considers the use of the framework "constituted a clear enrichment (to the performance) both in terms of communication and in terms of expression" leads to the conclusion the main goal one proposed to achieve (using gestures, in an artistic context, for the creation of new ways of expression) was accomplished.

A software implementation of the system described in this chapter was also made available as free and open source software. Together with the belief that this work showed the potential of gesture recognition, it is expected that the software implementation may stimulate further research in this area as it can have significant impact in many HCI applications such as interactive installations, performances and Human-Computer Interaction *per se*.

FUTURE WORK

After a great deal of investment in the area of algorithm development, which has given rise to the implementation of the framework proposed, there are nevertheless several lines of future work that are now possible to anticipate.

In regard to the present software implementation one of the main improvements that can be accomplished is the further development of the GUI in order to make the framework even more intuitive and easy to work with.

Also, the current version still requires the prior specification of the number states to train each new HMM. This is a limitation of the current implementation, but the framework is flexible enough to include new approaches to an automatic estimation of the number of hidden states for each HMM.

It would be also interesting to apply it on works previous made (when there were not 3D cameras available) and incorporate some of the features analysis into the framework, works like the human movement rhythm analysis done by Guedes or explore the emotion contained in the gesture has Camurri intended.

The motivation for this research was drawn from performative art domain. However, it was always kept in mind that the proposed concepts and methods could be used in other domains. Thus, the main opportunity for future research comes from extending this framework to other domains and requirements. For instance, one has the future goal of applying these methods in benefit to the hearing impaired community.

REFERENCES

Al-Hamadi, A., Elmezain, M., & Michaelis, B. (2010). Hand Gesture Recognition Based on Combined Features Extraction. *International Journal (Toronto, Ont.)*, 1–6. Retrieved from http://www.academia.edu/download/30613967/v6-1-1.pdf

Baltazar, A., Guedes, C., Gouyon, F., & Pennycook, B. (2010). *A Real-time human body skeletonization algorithm for MAX / MSP / JITTER*. ICMC.

Baltazar, A., Martins, L., & Cardoso, J. (2012). ZATLAB: A Gesture Analysis System to Music Interaction. In *Proceedings of 6th International Conference on Digital Arts (ARTECH 2012)*. Retrieved from http://www.inescporto.pt/~jsc/publications/conferences/2012ABaltazarARTECH.pdf

Bevilacqua, F., & Muller, R. (2005). A gesture follower for performing arts. In *Proceedings of the International Gestur*, (pp. 3–4). Academic Press. Retrieved from http://www.sdela.dds.nl/cinedebate/gesturalfollower.pdf

Bevilacqua, F., Müller, R., & Schnell, N. (2005). MnM: a Max/MSP mapping toolbox. In *Proceedings of the 2005 conference on New interfaces for musical expression* (pp. 85–88). Academic Press.

Bokowiec, M. A. (2011). V! OCT (Ritual): An Interactive Vocal Work for Bodycoder System and 8 Channel Spatialization. In Proceedings of NIME 2011 (pp. 40–43). NIME.

Camurri, A., Hashimoto, S., Ricchetti, M., Ricci, A., Suzuki, K., Trocca, R., & Volpe, G. (2000). EyesWeb: Toward Gesture and Affect Recognition in Interactive Dance and Music Systems. *Computer Music Journal*, *24*(1), 57–69. doi:10.1162/014892600559182

Camurri, A., Mazzarino, B., & Ricchetti, M. (2004). Multimodal analysis of expressive gesture in music and dance performances. *Gesture-Based*. Retrieved from http://link.springer.com/chapter/10.1007/978-3-540-24598-8_3

Camurri, a., Volpe, G., Poli, G. De, & Leman, M. (2005). Communicating expressiveness and affect in multimodal interactive systems. *IEEE Multimedia*, *12*(1), 43–53. doi:10.1109/MMUL.2005.2

Castellano, G., Villalba, S., & Camurri, A. (2007). Recognising human emotions from body movement and gesture dynamics. *Affective Computing and Intelligent*, 71–82. Retrieved from http://link.springer.com/chapter/10.1007/978-3-540-74889-2_7

Corradini, A. (2001). Dynamic time warping for off-line recognition of a small gesture vocabulary. In *Proceedings of Recognition, Analysis, and Tracking of Faces and Gestures in Real-Time Systems*, (pp. 82–89). IEEE. doi:10.1109/RAT-FG.2001.938914

Dietrich, J. E. (1983). Play Direction (2nd ed.). Prentice Hall. Retrieved from http://amazon.com/o/ASIN/0136833349/

Dobrian, C., & Bevilacqua, F. (2003). Gestural control of music: using the vicon 8 motion capture system. In Proceedings of the 2003 conference on New interfaces for musical expression (pp. 161–163). National University of Singapore. Retrieved from http://dl.acm.org/citation.cfm?id=1085753

Efron, D. (1972). *Gesture, Race and Culture*. Mouton and Co.

Feldman, R. S., & Rimé, B. (Eds.). (1991). Fundamentals of Nonverbal Behavior (Studies in Emotion and Social Interaction). Cambridge University Press. Retrieved from http://amazon.com/o/ASIN/052136700X/

Feyereisen, P., & de Lannoy, J.-D. (1991). Gestures and Speech: Psychological Investigations (Studies in Emotion and Social Interaction). Cambridge University Press. Retrieved from http://amazon.com/o/ASIN/0521377625/

Fiebrink, R., Trueman, D., & Cook, P. R. (2009). A metainstrument for interactive, on-the-fly machine learning. In Proc. NIME (Vol. 2, p. 3). Retrieved from http://www.cs.dartmouth.edu/~cs104/BodyPartRecognition.pdf

Fraisse, P. (1982). Rhythm and Tempo. In D. Deutsch (Ed.), *The Psychology of Music* (pp. 149–180). Academic Press. doi:10.1016/B978-0-12-213562-0.50010-3

Gillian, N., Knapp, R. B., & O'Modhrain, S. (2011). A machine learning toolbox for musician computer interaction. In *Proceedings of the 2011 International Coference on New Interfaces for Musical Expression (NIME11)*. NIME.

Godøy, R. I., & Leman, M. (2009). *Musical Gestures: Sound, Movement, and Meaning*. In R. I. Godøy & M. Leman (Eds.), *Musical Gestures Sound Movement and Meaning* (p. 320). Routledge. Retrieved from http://www.amazon.jp/dp/0415998875

Kendon, A. (1970). Movement coordination in social interaction: Some examples described. *Acta Psychologica*, *32*(0), 101–125. doi:10.1016/0001-6918(70)90094-6 PMID:5444439

Kendon, A. (1980). Gesticulation and speech: two aspects of the process of utterance. In M. R. Key (Ed.), *The Relationship of Verbal and Nonverbal Communication* (pp. 207–227). The Hague: Mouton.

Kendon, A. (1994). Do Gestures Communicate? A Review. *Research on Language and Social Interaction*, *27*(3), 175–200. doi:10.1207/s15327973rlsi2703_2

Keogh, E., & Ratanamahatana, C. A. (2005). Exact indexing of dynamic time warping. *Knowledge and Information Systems*, *7*(3), 358–386. doi:10.1007/s10115-004-0154-9

Lemire, D. (2009, June). Faster Retrieval with a Two-Pass Dynamic-time-warping lower bound. *Pattern Recognition*, 1–26. Retrieved from http://www.sciencedirect.com/science/article/pii/S0031320308004925

Liu, C. (2009). cuHMM: A CUDA implementation of hidden Markov model training and classification. *The Chronicle of Higher Education*.

McNeill, D. (1985). So you think gestures are nonverbal? *Psychological Review*, *92*(3), 350–371. doi:10.1037/0033-295X.92.3.350

McNeill, D. (1992). *Hand and {Mind}: What {Gestures} {Reveal} about {Thought}*. Chicago: University of Chicago Press.

McNeill, D., & Levy, E. (1982). Conceptual Representations in Language Activity and Gesture. In R. J. Jarvella & W. Klein (Eds.), *Speech, Place, and Action* (pp. 271–295). Chichester, UK: Wiley.

Mulder, A. (1994, July). Human movement tracking technology. *Hand*, 1–16.

Nefian, A. V., & Hayes, M. H., III. (1998). Hidden Markov models for face recognition. In *Proceedings of Acoustics, Speech and Signal Processing*, (Vol. 5, pp. 2721–2724). IEEE.

Polotti, P., & Goina, M. (2011). *EGGS in Action*. NIME.

Povall, R. (1998). Technology is with us. *Dance Research Journal*, *30*(1), 1–4. doi:10.2307/1477887

Rabiner, L. (1989). Tutorial on Hidden Markov Models and Selected Applications in speech Recognition. *Proceedings of the IEEE*. Retrieved from http://ieeexplore.ieee.org/xpls/abs_all.jsp?arnumber=18626

Rabiner, L., & Juang, B.-H. (1993). Fundamentals of Speech Recognition. Prentice Hall. Retrieved from http://amazon.com/o/ASIN/0130151572/

Rimé, B. (1982). The elimination of visible behaviour from social interactions: Effects on verbal, nonverbal and interpersonal variables. *European Journal of Social Psychology*, *12*(2), 113–129. doi:10.1002/ejsp.2420120201

Roth, W.-M. (2001). Gestures: Their Role in Teaching and Learning. *Review of Educational Research, 71*(3), 365–392. doi:10.3102/00346543071003365

Rowe, M. L., & Goldin-meadow, S. (2009). development. *First Language, 28*(2), 182–199. doi:10.1177/0142723707088310 PMID:19763249

Royce, A. P. (1984). *Movement and Meaning: Creativity and Interpretation in Ballet and Mime.* Indiana Univ Pr. Retrieved from http://amazon.com/o/ASIN/0253338883/

Schacher, J. C. (2010). Motion To Gesture To Sound : Mapping For Interactive Dance. Academic Press.

Ten Holt, G. A., Reinders, M. J. T., & Hendriks, E. A. (2007). Multi-dimensional dynamic time warping for gesture recognition. In *Proceedings of Thirteenth Annual Conference of the Advanced School for Computing and Imaging* (Vol. 119). Academic Press.

Van Nort, D., Wanderley, M. M., & Van Nort, D. (2006). The LoM Mapping Toolbox for Max/MSP/Jitter. In *Proceedings of the International Computer Music Conference.* Academic Press.

Varela, F. J., Thompson, E., & Rosch, E. (1993). *The Embodied Mind: Cognitive Science and Human Experience.* MIT Press. Retrieved from http://books.google.pt/books?id=QY4RoH2z5DoC

Viterbi, A. J. (1967). Error bounds for convolutional codes and an asymptotically optimum decoding algorithm. *IEEE Transactions on* Information Theory, *13*(2), 260–269. doi: doi:10.1109/TIT.1967.1054010

Volpe, G. (2005). Expressive Gesture in Performing Arts and New Media: The Present and the Future. *Journal of New Music Research, 34*(1), 1–3. doi:10.1080/09298210500123820

Wachsmuth, I., & Fröhlich, M. (Eds.). (1998). Gesture and Sign Language in Human-Computer Interaction. In *Proceedings of International Gesture Workshop,* (*Vol. 1371,* p. 198). Springer.

Wang, G., Cook, P., & Associates. (2003). ChucK: A concurrent, on-the-fly audio programming language. In *Proceedings of International Computer Music Conference* (pp. 219–226). Academic Press. Retrieved from http://nagasm.org/ASL/icmc2003/closed/CR1055.PDF

Watson, R. (1993). A survey of gesture recognition techniques technical report tcd-cs-93-11. *Department of Computer Science, Trinity College.* Retrieved from http://citeseerx.ist.psu.edu/viewdoc/download?doi=10.1.1.51.9838&rep=rep1&type=pdf

Winkler, T. (1995). Making motion musical: Gesture mapping strategies for interactive computer music. In *Proceedings of ICMC* (pp. 261–264). ICMC.

Wright, M., Freed, A., Lee, A., Madden, T., & Momeni, A. (2001). Managing complexity with explicit mapping of gestures to sound control with osc. In *Proceedings of International Computer Music Conference* (pp. 314–317). ICMC.

Wu, Y., & Huang, T. (1999). Vision-based gesture recognition: A review. *Urbana,* 103–115. Retrieved from http://link.springer.com/content/pdf/10.1007/3-540-46616-9_10.pdf

Yamato, J., Ohya, J., & Ishii, K. (1992). Recognizing Human action in Time-sequential Images using Hidden Markov Model. *Computer Vision and Pattern.* Retrieved from http://ieeexplore.ieee.org/xpls/abs_all.jsp?arnumber=223161

Yoo, M. J., Beak, J. W., & Lee, I. K. (2011, June). Creating Musical Expression using Kinect. *Visual Computing,* 324–325. Retrieved from http://visualcomputing.yonsei.ac.kr/papers/2011/nime2011.pdf

Zeng, W., & Zhang, Z. (2012). *Multimedia at Work Microsoft Kinect Sensor and Its Effect*. Academic Press.

Zhao, L., & Badler, N. (2001). *Synthesis and acquisition of laban movement analysis qualitative parameters for communicative gestures*. Retrieved from http://repository.upenn.edu/cis_reports/116/

KEY TERMS AND DEFINITIONS

Computer Vision: Consists in the estimation of several properties of physical objects, based on their two dimensional (projection) images through the use of computers and cameras. With its beginnings in the early 1960s, it was thought to be an easy problem with a solution probably possible over a short time period. However, it revealed to be a task far more difficult. Since those early days CV has matured from a small research topic to a complete field of research and application (Aggarwal, 2011).

Human Computer Interaction: A discipline concerned with the design, evaluation and implementation of interactive computing systems for human use and with the study of major phenomena surrounding them. Because HCI studies a human and a machine in communication, it draws from supporting knowledge on both the machine and the human side. On the machine side, techniques in computer graphics, operating systems, programming languages, and development environments are relevant. On the human side, communication theory, graphic and industrial design disciplines, linguistics, social sciences, cognitive psychology, and human performance are relevant (Chairman-Hewett, 1992).

Machine Learning (ML): Derives from the artificial intelligence field. It is concerned with the study of building computer programs that automatically improve and/or adapt their performance through experience. ML can be thought of as "programming by example" and has many common aspects with other domains such as statistics and probability theory (understanding the phenomena that have generated the data), data mining (finding patterns in the data that are understandable by people) and cognitive sciences. Instead of the human programming a computer to solve a task directly, the goal of ML is to devise methods by which a computer program is able of come up with is own solution to the task, based only on examples provided (Grosan & Abraham, 2011).

ENDNOTES

Some CV techniques are described in this chapter, including some algorithms developed and published by the author, e.g. (Baltazar et al., 2010).

[1]   http://www.merriam-webster.com/dictionary/gesture?show=0&t=1384961916

[2]   http://www.palindrome.de

[3]   http://www.troikatronix.com/isadora.html

[4]   http://www.troikaranch.org/

[5]   http://smc.inescporto.pt/kinetic/

[6]   http://synapsekinect.tumblr.com

[7]   http://artes.ucp.pt/citar/

[8]   http://www.physicsclassroom.com/class/1dkin/u1l6a.cfm

[9]   Music Portugal Cultural Association, which has the status of Portuguese Public Utility Institution, was born as an extension of Miso Ensemble, to develop and promote contemporary musical creation in Portugal and Worldwide. Its founders are Paula and Miguel Azguime, composers, performers and directors that since the foundation of the Miso Ensemble in 1985, develop their work tirelessly in the field of new music, contributing actively to expand the contemporary way.

[10]   http://warszawska-jesien.art.pl/en/wj2013/home

[11]   http://cycling74.com/products/max/

[12]   http://www.festivalin.pt

Chapter 12
Design a Computer Programming Learning Environment for Massive Open Online Courses

Ricardo Queirós
Polytechnic Institute of Porto, Portugal & CRACS/INESC TEC, Portugal

ABSTRACT

Teaching and learning computer programming is as challenging as it is difficult. Assessing the work of students and providing individualised feedback is time-consuming and error prone for teachers and frequently involves a time delay. The existent tools prove to be insufficient in domains where there is a greater need to practice. At the same time, Massive Open Online Courses (MOOC) are appearing, revealing a new way of learning. However, this paradigm raises serious questions regarding the monitoring of student progress and its timely feedback. This chapter provides a conceptual design model for a computer programming learning environment. It uses the portal interface design model, gathering information from a network of services such as repositories, program evaluators, and learning management systems, a central piece in the MOOC realm. This model is not limited to the domain of computer programming and can be adapted to any area that requires evaluation with immediate feedback.

INTRODUCTION

The evolution of e-learning in the last decades has been astonishing. In fact, e-learning seems to be constantly reinventing itself, finding new uses for technology, creating new tools, discovering new concepts. Platforms for supporting e-learning have been evolving for some years, exploring many approaches and producing a great variety of solutions.

These solutions make the learning and teaching more efficient and productive, but they usually lack effective real-time monitoring to learning process (Henda, 2013).

In the meantime many universities and institutions are using platforms for Massive Online Open Courses (MOOCs), characterised with a great diversity of topics and a huge number of enrolments. However, the real-time feedback is important for the effectiveness of MOOCs. We

DOI: 10.4018/978-1-4666-7304-5.ch012

state that novice students in an e-learning system might feel being isolated from the teachers and other students, because of the lack of essential interactions components in the system design (Jonas & Burns, 2013). This issue leads to a negative impact on the students' outcome. With well-designed synchronous virtual classrooms and collaborative tools it is possible to reduce this negative impact (Nedeva & Dineva, 2010).

This issue augments when we talk about complex domains. Learning complex skills is hard. A good example is the computer programming domain. Introductory programming courses are generally regarded as difficult and often have high failure and dropout rates (Ala-Mutka, 2005), (O'Kelly & Gibson, 2006) and (Robins et al, 2003). Many educators claim that "learning through practice" is by far the best way to learn computer programming and to engage novice students (Jonas & Burns, 2013), (Eckerdal, 2009). Practice in this area boils down to solving programming exercises. Nevertheless, solving exercises is only effective if students receive an assessment on their work. Assessing the work of students and providing individualised feedback to all students is time-consuming for teachers and frequently involves a time delay. The existent tools and specifications prove to be insufficient in complex evaluation domains where there is a greater need to practice (Rongas & Kaarna, 2004).

This paper presents a conceptual design model for learning environments regarding complex domains. Specifically, we focus on the computer programming domain. This environment uses the portal interface design model gathering information from a network of services such as repositories and program evaluators. These services will improve the responsiveness of the environment, a crucial success factor in massive courses.

The design model includes also the integration with learning management systems, a central piece in the MOOC realm, endowing this way the model with characteristics such as scalability, collaboration and interoperability.

The remainder of this paper is organised as follows: the next section presents a brief survey on integration specifications such as, the digital repositories interoperability specification and the learning tools interoperability specification. Next, we present the conceptual model of a learning environment for a complex domain such as the computer programming domain. In the following section we propose a graphical user interface for such model focusing on the user profiles and actions, screen layout and implementation details. Finally, we conclude with a summary of the main contribution of this work and a perspective of future work.

INTEGRATION SPECIFICATIONS

The current generation of e-learning platforms values the interchange of learning objects and learners' information through the adoption of standards that brought content sharing and interoperability to eLearning. Learning Objects (LO) are units of instructional content that can be used, and most of all reused, on web based eLearning systems. Despite its success in the promotion of the standardization of eLearning content, it is not enough to ensure interoperability, which is a major user concern with the existing systems. The definition of common protocols and interfaces for the communication among systems is also an important issue to address.

In the last few years there have been initiatives (Leal & Queirós, 2010) to adapt Service Oriented Architectures (SOA) to e-learning. These initiatives, commonly named e-learning frameworks, had the same goal: to provide flexible learning environments for learners worldwide. Usually they are characterized by providing a set of open interfaces to numerous reusable services organized in genres or layers and combined in service usage models.

While eLearning frameworks are general approaches for e-learning system integration, several authors proposed service oriented approaches specifically targeted to the LMS. In fact, there are several references in the literature to middleware components for LMSs integration in SOA based eLearning systems. Apostolopoulos proposes a middleware component (Apostolopoulos & Kefala, 2003) to address the lack of integration of eLearning services. In this approach the eLearning components are implemented as agents maintained in a local management information base, and can communicate with the agent manager through the SNMP protocol. Costagliola develop an architecture (Casella et al, 2007) based on a middleware component and use Web Services to integrate different software components and improve interoperability among different systems. The middleware component enables the student learning process traceability since it has been developed to be compliant with SCORM. Al-Smadi presents a service-oriented architecture (Al-Smadi & Gutl, 2010) for a generic and flexible assessment system with cross-domain use cases. All these approaches have in common the need of a modification of LMS for each specific vendor, with the implementation of a new module or building block. To the best of the authors' knowledge there are no references in the literature to the use of a common standards supported by the major LMS vendors as a means to integrate the LMS in a service oriented network of learning environments.

Other e-learning interoperabiliy initiatives (for instance, NSDL, POOL, OKI, EduSource, IMS DRI, IMS LTI) appeared in the last. We detail the last two ones in the following subsections.

Digital Repositories Interoperability

The IMS DRI provides recommendations for common repository functions, namely the submission search and download of LOs. It recommends exposing these functions as SOAP web services. Although not explicitly recommended, other web service interfaces may be used, such as the Representational State Transfer (REST). SOAP web services are usually action oriented, especially when used in Remote Procedure Call (RPC) mode and implemented by an off-the-shelf SOAP engine such as Axis. REST web services are object (resource) oriented and implemented directly over the HTTP protocol, mostly to put and get resources. The reason to provide two distinct web service flavours is to encourage the use of the repository by developers with different interoperability requirements. A system requiring a formal an explicit definition of the API in Web Services Description Language, to use automated tools to create stubs, will select the SOAP flavour. A lightweight system seeking a small memory footprint at the expense of a less formal definition of the API will select the REST flavour. The following paragraphs detail the main functions. The **Submit/Store** function uploads an LO to a repository and makes it available for future access. This operation receives as argument an IMS CP compliant file and an URL generated by the Reserve function. This operation validates the LO conformity to the IMS Package Conformance and stores the LO in the internal database. To send the LO to the server we could use, in the REST flavour, the PUT or the POST HTTP methods.

The **Search/Expose** function enables the eLearning systems to query the repository using the XQuery language, as recommended by the IMS DRI. This approach gives more flexibility to the client systems to perform any queries supported by the repository's data. To write queries in XQuery the programmers of the client systems need to know the repository's database schema. These queries are based on both the LO manifest and its usage reports, and can combine the two document types. The client developer needs also to know that the database is structured in collections. A collection is a kind of a folder containing several resources and sub-folders. From the XQuery point of view the database is a collection of manifest files. For each manifest file there is a nested collection containing the usage reports. As

Figure 1. The IMS LTI framework

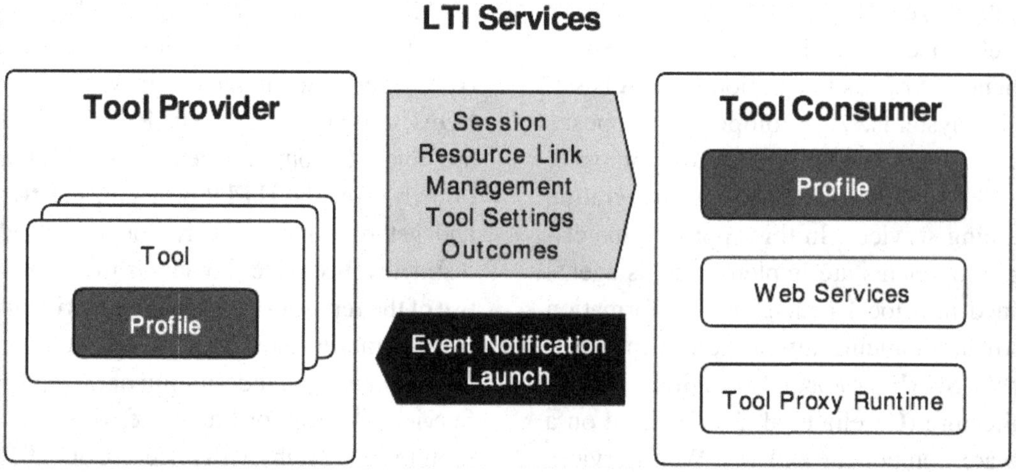

LTI Services

an example of a simple search, suppose you want to find all the titles of LOs in the root collection whose author is Manzoor. The XQuery file would contain the data.

The **Report/Store** function associates a usage report to an existing LO. This function is invoked by the LMS to submit a final report, summarizing the use of an LO by a single student. This report includes both general data on the student's attempt to solve the programming exercise (e.g. data, number of evaluations, success) and particular data on the student's characteristics (e.g. gender, age, instructional level). With this data, the LMS will be able to dynamically generate presentation orders based on previous uses of LO, instead of fixed presentation orders. This function is an extension of the IMS DRI. The **Alert/Expose** function notifies users of changes in the state of the repository using a RSS feed. With this option a user can have up-to-date information through a feed reader. Next, we present an example of a GET HTTP request.

Learning Tools Interoperability

A common interoperability standard that is increasingly supported by major LMS vendors is the IMS Learning Tools Interoperability (IMS LTI) specification. It provides a uniform standards-based extension point in LMS allowing remote tools and content to be integrated into the LMS. The main goal of the LTI is to standardize the process for building links between learning tools and the LMS. There are several benefits from using this approach: educational institutions, LMS vendors and tool providers by adhering to a clearly defined interface between the LMS and the tool, will decrease costs, increases options for students and instructors when selecting learning applications and also potentiates the use of software as a service (SaaS).

The LTI has 3 key concepts as shown in Figure 1 (Gilbert, 2010): the Tool Provider, the Tool Consumer, and the Tool Profile.

The Tool Provider is a learning application that runs in a container separate from the LMS. It publishes one or more tools through the Tool Profiles. The Tool Profile is an XML descriptor that describes how a tool integrates with a tool consumer. It is composed by information about the tool metadata, vendor information, resource and event handlers and menu links. The Tool Consumer publishes a Tool Consumer Profile (XML descriptor of the Tool Consumer's supported LTI

Figure 2. Conceptual model

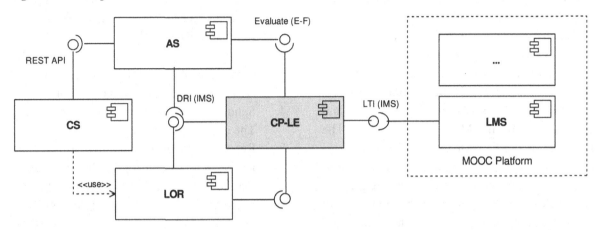

functionality that is read by the Tool Provider during deployment), provides a Tool Proxy Runtime and exposes the LTI services.

The IMS launched also a subset of the full LTI v1.0 specification called IMS Basic LTI. This subset exposes a single (but limited) destination between the LMS and the application as shown in Figure 1.

For instance, there is no provision for accessing run-time services in the LMS and only one security policy is supported. Basic LTI also supports a basic security model based on the OAuth protocol. This protocol aims to secure the message interactions between the Tool Consumer and the Tool Provider. It requires a key and a shared secret to sign messages. The key is sent with each message, as well as an OAuth-generated signature based on the key. The Tool Provider verifies the secret based on the provided key and re-computes the signature and compares the recomputed signature with the transmitted signature to verify the sender's credentials.

CONCEPTUAL MODEL

Typically, a conceptual model represents entities and relationships between them regarding a specific domain. Therefore, we present the conceptual model for the design of a computer programming teaching/learning environment. The aim of this conceptual model is to express the meaning of domain concepts and the correct relationships between different concepts. The model for the computer programming learning environment (CP-LE) is depicted by the UML component diagram in Figure 2 composed by the following concepts:

- Learning Objects Repository (LOR) to store/retrieve exercises;
- Assessment System (AS) to evaluate students exercises;
- Learning Management System (LMS) to present the exercises to students;
- Converter System (CS) to convert between different exercise formats.

The CP-LE has a two-fold goal: to coordinate the systems and services of this network and to interface with users, both teachers and students. On the LMS side the choice fell on Moodle since it is a popular and open source LMS, arguably the most popular LMS nowadays (Cole & Foster, 2007), (Davis & Wagner, 2009). This LMS has made efforts to support interoperability with other e-learning systems at two levels: content (e.g. IMS CP, SCORM, IMS CC) and communication (e.g.

IMS LTI). Also successfully tests were made with Sakai LMS on this network evidencing the interoperable characteristics of the proposed approach.

The LOR system selected was CrimsonHex (Queirós & Leal, 2013)—a software for the creation of repositories of programming exercises. The exercises are described as learning objects and complying with the IMS CC specification. The repository also adheres to the IMS DRI specification to communicate with other systems. Other software for repositories were analysed (e.g. Flori, HarvestRoad Hive, IntraLibrary) but none of them met the domain requirements for the content and communication interoperability and most of them follow a commercial development model.

The AS system selected was Mooshak (Leal & Silva, 2003). Mooshak is an open source system for managing programming contests on the Web including automatic judging of submitted programs. One of the most important reasons for its selection was the support of web services.

The CS system selected was BabeLO (Queirós & Leal, 2013). This system converts formats of programming exercises among systems. At the time of writing this dissertation no other system was found with these characteristics.

The integration of the CP-LE component with the other systems must rely on content and communication standards. Using content and communication standards we can abstract the use of specific systems for each type of system. For instance, we can use on this network any repository as long it supports the IMS CC specification to formalize the description of programming exercises and it implements the IMS DRI specification for communication with other services.

In this particular scenario the teacher starts by setting a number of activities in the LMS, including the resolution of programming exercises. To select the relevant programming exercises the teacher:

1. Searches for relevant exercises in the repository. Then, the learner

2. Tries to solve the exercises set be the teacher using an experimentation environment (e.g. Eclipse IDE). The IDE

3. Recovers exercises descriptions from the repository showing them to the student. After coding the program the learner

4. Send an attempt to the evaluation engine. The evaluation engine

5. Recovers test cases from the repository. The learner may submit repeatedly, integrating the feedback received from the evaluation engine. In the end, the evaluation engine

6. Sends a grade to the LMS that records it and reports the LO usage data back to the repository.

Repositories

Learning objects repositories are an essential part of service oriented platforms in eLearning since they provide content to several types of services. The need for this kind of repositories is growing as more educators are eager to use digital educational contents and more of it is available. Several surveys show that users are concerned with issues that are not completely addressed by the existing systems, such as interoperability. Thus, a desired feature of a repository is the support for a standard and automatic communication with other systems.

The repository used in this work was the crimsonHex. It was developed as part of the EduJudge project (Leal & Queirós, 2010) to act as a programming problem repository service. The Core component of the repository exposes the main features, both to external services, such as the LMS and the AS, and to internal components, respectively: the Web Manager, to allow the creation, revision, uploading/downloading of LO and related metadata, enforcing compliance with controlled vocabularies; and the Importer, to populate the repository with existing legacy repositories.

The Core component of the crimsonHex repository provides a minimal set of operations exposed as web services—in SOAP and REST flavours—and based in the IMS DRI specification.

Assessment Systems

The purpose of a programming exercise evaluator is to mark and grade exercises in computer programming courses and in programming contests. By exposing its functions as services, an evaluator of this kind is able to participate in business processes integrating different system types such as Programming Contest Management Systems, Learning Management ystems, Integrated Development Environments and Repositories.

In order to formalize the definition of this service we used an eLearning framework. An eLearning framework aims to adapt SOA to eLearning providing flexible learning environments for learners worldwide. The new service—Evaluate Programming Exercise—models the evaluation of an attempt to solve a programming exercise defined as a learning object and produces a detailed report. This evaluation report includes information to support exercise assessment, grading and/or ranking by client systems.

This service exposes its functions as SOAP and REST web services. The three types of request handled by this service are:

- **ListCapabilities:** Provides the client systems with the capabilities of a particular evaluator;
- **EvaluateSubmission:** Allows the request of an evaluation for a specific programming exercise;
- **GetReport:** Allows a requester to get a report for a specific evaluation using a ticket.

More details about the definition of this service can be found elsewhere (Leal & Queirós, 2010).

Integrated Development Environments

Experimenting environments–environments for practicing on a learning subject to consolidate learning–are another type of specialized services to be integrated in learning processes. These environments need a user interface to interact with learners and application interfaces to be integrated on the learning process. In some cases they will have to be developed for specific domain, while in other they can be adapted from existing systems.

Take the computer language programming domain as an example. An Integrated Development Environment (IDE) is arguably the best place for a student to practice by solving programming exercises, but any tool on a CLMS will hardly be a match. Surely, an IDE lacks the features to communicate with other specialized services, but this shortcoming may be overcome using plugins, similar to those described in the previous subsection for Moodle.

One approach is to use rich web editors such as Ace. Ace is an embeddable code editor written in JavaScript. It matches the features and performance of native editors such as Sublime, Vim and TextMate. It can be easily embedded in any web page and JavaScript application. Ace is maintained as the primary editor for Cloud9 IDE and is the successor of the Mozilla Skywriter (Bespin) project.

A GUI PROPOSAL

In this section we propose a possible GUI for the learning environment. In the design of the Web component one of our major concerns was usability, and to promote it we followed established user interface design principles (Shneiderman, 1998). The main feature of the resulting design is the use of a single screen common to all user profiles. This type of design breaks with the traditional structure of web interfaces used by other systems (A. Co-Lab, 2003). To design this user interface we started with the identification of task and usage profiles, task objects and task actions. Then we selected a suitable interaction style and finally we created a screen layout.

User Profiles and Actions

At the beginning of the design process we identified the following task profiles:

- **Administrator:** A person responsible for the management of the system configurations such as user accounts and repository settings;
- **Teacher:** A person responsible for a set of activities related with the resource management such as the authoring of two type of resources: expository (e.g. video, PDF, or HTML files) and evaluation resources (programming exercises) and the submission of the resources in the repository. The submission will be enforced to comply with controlled vocabularies defined in meta-data standards (IEEE LOM) and possible extensions. This class of users will also receive the exercises solved by students and the automatic feedback generated by the assessment system;
- **Student:** A person that browses the resources and solve exercises.

We assume that users will have different usage profiles. On one hand, many will be novice or first-time users, especially among students. On the other hand, we expect some users, especially teachers and old students, to use it frequently, tending to become experts in its use. After the identification of users and usage profiles we proceeded to identify the tasks they need to perform on this interface. We clearly identified expository and evaluation resources as our task objects, each

with a number of associated task actions, depending on user profiles. Task actions over resources include: viewing, downloading, solving, voting, sharing, and commenting. A typical pedagogical learning process is the classroom assignment in a Computer Science course.

For instance, when a student starts solving an exercise, the CP-LE component automatically creates a project. A project contains source code and related files for building a program in a specific programming language. Thus, a set of predefined files need to be generated for the project creation. These files are related with the chosen programming language.

After the automatic creation of the project the student reads the exercise description and solves it in a specialized Web editor (e.g. AceEditor). The student should test the code locally by executing the teachers' test cases and is encouraged to create new ones. If new test cases are created, a validation step is performed to verify that they meet the specification defined by the teacher in the authoring phase. After testing, the student should submit the solution to the Assessment System where the submission is checked against the complete test set provided by the teacher. The report on the evaluation returned by the AS is presented to the student. The student may submit repeatedly, integrating the feedback received from the AS. In the end of this cycle, the CP-LE component reports the exercise usage data back to the repository and the grade results back to the LMS.

Screen Layout

To define the screen layout we sought an interaction style balancing intuitiveness and expressiveness. We first considered direct manipulation of task objects. Although it provides a convenient way to select objects, it is not possible to map all the identified task actions to basic mouse interaction (click, point and drag). We found form filling adequate for entering data for the complex tasks, such as search, commenting and solving.

Finally, we decided to blend these two interaction styles, using a form of direct manipulation for task object selection and form-filling for executing task actions.

Based on this blended interaction style we defined a screen layout—a single screen with specific areas for task object selection and task actions. Task object selection is needed by all users, although selectable content depends on the user's profile, thus it can be implemented by a common tree-based control. Different task actions require specific forms or panels that also share a common control on the users interface. Since the number of task actions is comparatively small we chose a tabbed control to aggregate them. The tab configuration shown to users depends both on their profile and on the current task object selection.

Figure 3 shows the user interface layout of the computer programming learning environment with two main areas: selection on the left side and action on middle. In the selection area the user navigates through the repository structure to select task objects. In the action area the user executes task actions (e.g. view videos, solve exercises) on the selected task objects. Secondary areas in this layout are the header, used for authentication and registration, and the right side, used for statistics and chat.

As a rule, all available task actions are enabled, thus helping novice users to recognise which are the available actions. However, some of these task actions can be executed directly over selected task objects without requiring additional data. In general, these task actions are meant for frequent users and will be bound to contextual menus on the tree-control, as well as to accelerator keys.

IMPLEMENTATION

The learning environment was developed using an Ajax framework to enable the implementation of the single screen design resulting from the last section. We selected the Google Web Toolkit (GWT), an open source Java software development framework that allows a rapid development of

Figure 3. Screen layout

AJAX applications in Java When the application is deployed, the GWT cross-compiler translates Java classes of the GUI to JavaScript files and guarantees cross-browser portability. The framework supports also asynchronous remote procedure calls. This way, tasks that require high computational resources (e.g., complex searching within the repository) can be triggered asynchronously, increasing the user interface's responsiveness. The complex controls required by the selection and action areas are provided by SmartGWT, a GWT API's for SmartClient, a Rich Internet Application (RIA) system.

The Web component is organised in two main packages: the back-end (server) and the front-end (client). The back-end includes all the service implementations triggered by the user interface. These implementations rely on the gateway class for managing the communication with the Web services. A single class implementing the Gateway design pattern concentrates the interaction with the core component.

The integration of the pivot component in the LMS relies on the LTI specification. The basic workflow for using Basic LTI starts when the Teacher (or LMS administrator) adds the tool as a Basic LTI tool into their course structure as a resource link using the LMS control panel. The Teacher sets the URL, secret, and key as metadata for the resource link. When the students select the tool, the LMS uses the URL, secret, and key information to launch the student into the CP-LE in an iframe or new browser window. The CP-LE component receives a launch request that includes user identity, course information, role information, and the key and signature. The launch information is sent using an HTTP form generated in the user's browser with the Basic LTI data elements in hidden form fields and automatically submitted to the external tool using JavaScript. The following is a subset of the information that the LMS (Tool Consumer) sends to the CP-LE (Tool Provider):

```
resource_link_id=1 //An unique iden-
tifier for the resource in the LMS.
resource_link_title= My First Exer-
cise // Title of the resource
resource_link_description= Descrip-
tion... //Description of the re-
source.
user_id=2 // User identifier
user_image=myPhoto.gif // Profile
picture
roles= Instructor,Administrator //
List of one or more user roles.
context_title=Course Fullname 101 //A
title of the context (e.g. course in-
formation).
```

All these data items are included on the POST data when a Basic LTI launch is performed. These data items can be used, for instance, to personalize the frontend of the tool providers. To extend these fields it is necessary to prefix all fields not described herein with "ext_".

CONCLUSION

This paper presents a conceptual model for the design of a learning environment for the teaching and learning process in complex domains such as computer programming. The design model is suitable for integration in MOOC platforms where there are a large number of enrolments and, at the same time, a large number of dropouts due to lack of teacher support. The adaptation to MOOC platforms is guaranteed with the integration of systems that provide automatic assessment giving to the student a higher autonomy to proceed in the course without the need to wait for teachers' feedback.

The model could be adapted to other complex domains. Playing business games in management courses or simulating a human patient in life sciences courses, or simulating an electronic circuit in electronics courses are examples of complex learning domains that require the use of special evaluators. Currently we have Petcha (a CP-LE component) running at ESEIG—an Engineering School—with promising results.

Regarding future work we expected to include other services in this network with the inclusion of a plagiarism tool to avoid plagiarism and ensure good scholarly practices and a resources sequencing tool. Sequencing of exercises is another topic that can be explored in the future and it is closely related with pedagogical issues during the construction of a learning scenario. Several standards appeared in recent years trying to cope this topic but fail due its complexity for e-Learning systems to implement. One research path is to deliver exercises to students dynamically according with their profiles, knowledge evolution and course goals. An intended addition is a sequencing and adaptation tool to guide the student through a collection of expository and evaluation resources. The CP-LE component will report the exercise assessment to this new tool that will use it to propose the appropriate content or exercise to the student.

We concluded that a pivot component integrated in the LMS is a promising approach to the task of coordinating a heterogeneous network of e-learning systems. The pivot component can have its own user interface for interaction with students, as is required for the resolution environment, that is embed in the LMS user interface. It can also control the invocation of remote web services, such as those exposed by the repository of learning objects and evaluation engine. Finally, it can summarize the activity of the student as a grade and report it back to the grade book of the LMS.

Unfortunately, we must conclude also that the LMS support of LTI standard in not mature enough for using this approach in the near future.

Most LMS vendors, and in particular those we tested, support only the Basic LTI. Thus, the grade reporting feature could not be fully implemented in our integration and validation setup. Moreover, we had to perform custom installations of both LMSs, mixing code from a stable distribution and code under development just to have Basic LTI.

A full and stable support of LTI in major LMS vendors will encourage us to implement a more sophisticated version of the approach described in this paper. Instead of embedding the resolution environment on the LMS the student should be able to use and Integrated Development Environment (IDE) such as Eclipse. We plan to develop an IDE plug-in to create a programming exercise resolutions environment. It will complement the standard code programming features of an IDE with reading exercise descriptions from the repository, submitting code them to the evaluation engine and displaying feedback to the student. In this future work we will split the coordination task among the pivot component integrated in the LMS and the plug-in on the IDE. Also, the LMS must communicate with a local service on the student's machine (hosted on the IDE) rather than on the cloud. Still, this variant is a step towards to integrate in this network the best of bread for each task.

REFERENCES

Al-Smadi, M., & Gutl, C. (2010). *SOA-based architecture for a generic and flexible e-assessment system*. EDUCON. doi:10.1109/EDUCON.2010.5492537

Ala-Mutka, K. (2005). A survey of automated assessment approaches for programming assignments. *Journal of Computer Science Education, 15*(2), 83–102. doi:10.1080/08993400500150747

Apostolopoulos, T. K., & Kefala, A. S. (2003). *An e-learning service management architecture.* ICALT.

Casella, G., Costagliola, G., Ferrucci, F., Polese, G., & Scanniello, G. (2007). A SCORM thin client architecture for e-learning systems based on web services. *International Journal of Distance Education Technologies*, *5*(1), 19–36. doi:10.4018/jdet.2007010103

Co-Lab, A. (2003). *Learning repositories included in learning repository investigation.* Retrieved from http://www.academiccolab.org/resources/DraftRepositoriesList.pdf

Cole, J., & Foster, H. (2007). *Using Moodle: Teaching with the Popular Open Source Course Management System* (2nd ed.). O'Reilly Media. Retrieved from http://www.amazon.com/exec/obidos/redirect?tag=citeulike07-20&path=ASIN/059652918X

Davis, C. C. B., & Wagner, E. (2009). *The Evolution of the LMS: From Management to Learning - Deep Analysis of Trends Shaping the Future of eLearning (Tech. Rep.).* Sage Road Solutions, LLC.

Eckerdal, A. (2009). *Novice programming students' learning of concepts and practice.* (Unpublished Doctoral Dissertation). Uppsala University.

Gilbert, T. (2010). Leveraging sakai and ims lti to standardize integrations. In *Proceedings of 10th Sakai Conference.* Academic Press.

Henda, B.-A. (2013). Monitoring activities in an e-learning 2.0 environment: A multi-agents system. In *Proceedings of Eighth International Conference on Internet and Web Applications and Services.* ICIW.

Jonas, N. C., & Burns, D. (2013). Using e-learning to educate health professionals in the management of children's pain. In *Proceedings of 6th International Conference Creativity Engagement in Higher Education.* Academic Press.

Leal, J. P., & Queirós, R. (2010). *From eLearning Systems to Specialised Services. In A New Learning Paradigm: Competition Supported by Technology.* Barcelona: Sello Editorial.

Leal, J. P., & Silva, F. M. A. (2003). Mooshak: A web-based multi-site programming contest system. *Software, Practice & Experience*, *33*(6), 567–581. doi:10.1002/spe.522

Nedeva, E. D., & Dineva, S. (2010). Overcome disadvantages of e-learning for training English as foreign language. In *Proceedings of The 5thInternational Conference on Virtual Learning.* Academic Press.

O'Kelly, J., & Gibson, J. P. (2006). Robocode & problem-based learning: A non-prescriptive approach to teaching programming. *SIGCSE Bulletin*, *38*(3), 217–221. doi:10.1145/1140123.1140182

Queirós, R., & Leal, J. P. (2013). crimsonHex: A learning objects repository for programming exercises. *Software, Practice & Experience*, *43*(8), 911–935. doi:10.1002/spe.2132

Queirós, R., & Leal, J. P. (2013). BabeLO - An Extensible Converter of Programming Exercises Formats. *IEEE Transactions on Learning Technologies*, *6*(1), 38–45. doi:10.1109/TLT.2012.21

Robins, A., Rountree, J., & Rountree, N. (2003). Learning and teaching programming: A review and discussion. *Computer Science Education*, *13*(1), 137–172. doi:10.1076/csed.13.2.137.14200

Rongas, T., & Kaarna, A. (2004). Classification of computerized learning tools for introductory programming courses: Learning approach. In Kinshuk et al. (Eds.), *ICALT*. IEEE Computer Society. Retrieved from http://dblp.uni-trier.de/db/conf/icalt/icalt2004.htmlRongasKK04

Shneiderman, B. (1998). Designing the Users Interface -Strategies for Effective Human-Computer Interaction (3rd ed.). Boston, MA: Addison-Wesley.

ADDITIONAL READING

Al-Khalifa, H. S., & Davis, H. C. (2006). The evolution of metadata from standards to semantics in e-learning applications. In Proceedings of the seventeenth conference on Hypertext and hypermedia (HYPERTEXT '06). ACM, New York, NY, USA, 69-72. DOI= http://doi.acm.org/10.1145/1149941.114995610.1145/1149941.1149956

Alario, C., & Wilson, S. (2010, 15-17 November). 2010). Comparison of the main alternatives to the integration of external tools in different platforms. In *Iceri2010 proceedings (3466-3476)*. IATED.

Aroyo, L., & Dolog, P., jan Houben, G., Kravcik, M., Naeve, A., Nilsson, M., & Wild, F. (2006). Interoperability in personalized adaptive learning. *Journal of Educational Technology & Society*, 9(2), 4–18.

Ashford-Rowe, K., & Malfroy, J. (n.d.). E-learning benchmark report: Learning management system (lms) usage (Tech. Rep.). Sydney.

Barker, P., & Campbell, L. M. (2010). Metadata for learning materials: An overview of existing standards and current developments. *Technology, Instruction. Cognition and Learning*, 7(3-4), 225–243.

Barret, H. (2010). Electronic portfolios in stem - what is an electronic portfolio. Retrieved from http://www.scribd.com/doc/40206175/E-Portfolio-Definition

Benford, S., Burke, E., Foxley, E., Gutteridge, N., & Zin, A. (2011). Early experiences of computer-aided assessment and administration when teaching computer programming. *Research in Learning Technology*, 1(2).

Bersin, H. C. O. K. M. D., J. (2009). Learning management systems 2009: Executive summary. Bersin & Associates.

Blumenstein, M., Green, S., Nguyen, A., & Muthukkumarasamy, V. (2004). An experimental analysis of game: A generic automated marking environment. *SIGCSE Bulletin*, 36(1), 67–71. doi:10.1145/1026487.1008016

Borg, W. R., & Gall, M. D. (2007). Educational research; an introduction, by walter r. borg and meredith d. gall (8th ed. ed.) [Book]. McKay New York. Britain, L. O., S. (1998). A Framework for Pedagogical Evaluation of Virtual Learning Environments (Tech. Rep.). Retrieved from http://www.leeds.ac.uk/educol/documents/00001237.htm

Burguillo, J. C. (2010, September). Using game theory and competition-based learning to stimulate student motivation and performance. *Computers & Education*, 55(2), 566–575. doi:10.1016/j.compedu.2010.02.018

Chae, G. B., Chandra, S., Mann, V., & Nanda, M. G. (2004). Decentralized orchestration of composite web services. In Proceedings of the 13th international world wide web conference on alternate track pa-pers & posters 134-143. New York, NY, USA: ACM.

Cheang, B., Kurnia, A., Lim, A., & Oon, W.-C. (2003, September). On automated grading of programming assignments in an academic institution. *Computers & Education, 41*(1), 121–131. doi:10.1016/S0360-1315(03)00030-7

Curbera, F., Duftler, M., Khalaf, R., Nagy, W., Mukhi, N., & Weerawarana, S. (2002, March). Unraveling the Web services web: An introduction to SOAP, WSDL, and UDDI. *IEEE Internet Computing, 6*(2), 86–93. doi:10.1109/4236.991449

Dagger, D., O'Connor, A., Lawless, S., Walsh, E., & Wade, V. P. (2007). Service-Oriented E-Learning Platforms: From Monolithic Systems to Flexible Services. *IEEE Internet Computing, 11*(3), 28–35. doi:10.1109/MIC.2007.70

Daly, C. (1999, June). Roboprof and an introductory computer programming course. *SIGCSE Bulletin, 31*(3), 155–158. doi:10.1145/384267.305904

Donello, J. (2002). Theory & practice: Learning content management systems. *ELearningMag.*

Douce, C., Livingstone, D., & Orwell, J. (2005, September). Automatic test based assessment of programming: A review. *Journal of Educational Resources in Computing, 5*(3), 4, es. doi:10.1145/1163405.1163409

Eckerson, W. W. (1995). Three tier client/server architecture: Achieving scalability, performance, and efficiency in client server applications. Open Information Systems, 10(1).

Edwards, S. H., Borstler, J., Cassel, L. N., Hall, M. S., & Hollingsworth, J. (2008). Developing a common format for sharing programming assignments. *SIGCSE Bulletin, 40*(4), 167–182. doi:10.1145/1473195.1473240

Edwards, S. H., & Pugh, W. (2006, March). Toward a common automated grading platform. In *Birds-of-a-feather session at the 37th sigcse technical symposium on computer science education.*

Ellis, R. K. (2009). *Field guide to learning management systems.* ASTD Learning Circuits.

Engels, S., Lakshmanan, V., & Craig, M. (2007, March). Plagiarism detection using feature-based neural networks. *SIGCSE Bulletin, 39*(1), 34–38. doi:10.1145/1227504.1227324

Erl, T. (2005). *Service-oriented architecture - concepts, technology and design.* Upper Saddle River, NJ: Prentice Hall.

Esteves, M., Fonseca, B., Morgado, L., & Martins, P. (2010, March). Improving teaching and learning of computer programming through the use of the Second Life virtual world. British Journal of Educational Technology. Retrieved from doi: .10.1111/j.1467-8535.2010.01056.x

Farance, F., & Tonkel, J. (1999). Ltsa specification - learning technology systems architecture, draft 5 (Tech. Rep.). IEEE. Retrieved from http://ltsc.ieee.org/wg1/files/ltsa05:pdf

Fay, E. (2010). Repository software comparison: Building digital library infrastructure at lse. *Ariadne, 64.* Retrieved from http://www.ariadne.ac.uk/issue64/fay/

Fernandez, J. L., Carrillo, J. M., Nicolas, J., Toval, A., & Carrion, M. I. (2011). Trends in e-learning standards. *International Journal of Computers and Applications, 353*(1), 49–54.

Fielding, R., & Taylor, R. (2002). Principled design of the modern web architecture. *ACM Trans. Internet Technol.* 2(2), 115-150. DOI= http://doi.acm.org/10.1145/514183.51418510.1145/514183.514185

Friesen, N. (2004a). *Metadata in practice (chap. Semantic and Syntactic Interoperability for Learning Object Metadata).* Chicago, IL: ALA Editions.

Friesen, N. (2004b). Editorial - a gentle introduction to technical elearning standards. *Canadian Journal of Learning and Technology, 30*(3).

Friesen, N. (2005). *Interoperability and learning objects: An overview of e-learning standardization*. Interdisciplinary Journal of Knowledge and Learning Objects.

Gomes, A., & Mendes, A. J. (2007). Learning to program - difficulties and solutions. Proceedings of the International Conference on Engineering Education. Retrieved from http://icee2007.dei.uc.pt/proceedings/papers/411.pdf

Gray, L. (2008). Effective practice with e-portfolios: Supporting 21st century learning. JISC. Retrieved from http://www.jisc.ac.uk/media/documents/publications/effectivepracticeeportfolios.pdf

Gross, P., & Powers, K. (2005). Evaluating assessments of novice programming environments. In Proceedings of the first international workshop on Computing education research (ICER '05). ACM, New York, NY, USA, 99-110. DOI= http://doi.acm.org/10.1145/1089786.108979610.1145/1089786.1089796

Guerreiro, P., & Georgouli, K. (2008). Enhancing elementary programming courses using e-learning with a competitive attitude. [IJIE]. *International Journal of Internet Education, 10*(1), 38–46.

Gutierrez Rojas, I. Agea, Crespo Garcia, R. M., Pardo, A., & Delgado Kloos, C. (2009). Assessment interoperability using qti. In Interactive conference on computer aided learning.

Harasim, L. (2006). A History of E-learning: Shift Happened. Retrieved from 2 doi: 210.1007/978-1-4020-3803-7

Hoel, T., & Mason, J. (2011). Expanding the scope of metadata and the issue of quality. In 19th international conference on computers in education. Retrieved from http://hoel.nu/publications/ICCEworkshop paper Hoel Mason2011/final.pdf

Ihantola, P., Ahoniemi, T., Karavirta, V., & Seppala, O. (2010). Review of recent systems for automatic assessment of programming assignments. In *Proceedings of the 10th koli calling international conference on computing education research*, 86-93). New York, NY, USA: ACM. Retrieved from http://doi.acm.org/10.1145/1930464.1930480

Jackson, D., & Usher, M. (1997). Grading student programming using assyst. In In technical symposium on computer science education. Proceedings of the 28th sigcse, 335 -339.

Jenkins, T. (2002). On the Difficulty of Learning to Program. In 3rd annual conference of ltsn-ics, Loughbourgh. Retrieved from http://www.ics.ltsn.ac.uk/pub/conf2002/tjenkins.pdf

Jerman-Blazic, B., & Klobucar, T. (2005). Privacy provision in e-learning standardized systems: Status and improvements. *Computer Standards & Interfaces, 27*(6), 561–578. http://www.qou.edu/arabic/researchProgram/eLearningResearchs/privacyp.pdf doi:10.1016/j.csi.2004.09.006

Juedes, D. (2003). Experiences in web-based grading. In In *33rd asee/ieee frontiers in education conference*, 5-8.

Kati Clements, J. M. P. Agueda Gras-Velázquez. (n.d.). Educational resources packaging standards scorm and ims common cartridge - the users point of view. In Search and exchange of e-learning materials 2010 proceedings.

Klenin, A. (2011). Common problem description format: Requirements. ACMICPC World Final CLIS (Competitive Learning Institute Symposium).

Kumar, P., Samaddar, S., Samaddar, A., & Misra, A. (2010). Extending ieee ltsa e-learning framework in secured soa environment. In 2nd international conference on education technology and computer (icetc). doi:10.1109/ICETC.2010.5529417

Kurilovas, E. (2012). European learning resource exchange: A platform for collaboration of researchers, policy makers, practitioners, and publishers to share digital learning resources and new e-learning practices. In P. O. P. A. Cakir (Ed.), Social development and high technology industries: Strategies and applications. IGI-Global; Retrieved from http://www.igi-global.com/chapter/social-development-high-technology-industries/58723, doi:10.4018/978-1-61350-192-4.ch014

Lahtinen, E., Ala-Mutka, K., & Jarvinen, H.-M. (2005, June). A study of the difficulties of novice programmers. *SIGCSE Bulletin, 37*(3), 14–18. doi:10.1145/1151954.1067453

Lawrence, A. W., Badre, A. M., & Stasko, J. T. (1994). Empirically evaluating the use of animations to teach algorithms. Proceedings IEEE Symposium on Visual Languages, 48-54. Retrieved from http://citeseerx.ist.psu.edu/viewdoc/download?doi=10.1.1.25.8514rep=rep1type=pdf

Leal, J. P., & Queirós, R. (2009), Defining Programming Problems as Learning Objects, *Proceedings of International Conference on Computer Education and Instructional Technology*, Venice, Italy.

Leal, J. P., & Queirós, R. (2012). A Comparative Study on LMS Interoperability. In I. Management Association (Ed.), Virtual Learning Environments: Concepts, Methodologies, Tools and Applications, 1613-1630. Hershey, PA: Information Science Reference. doi: doi:10.4018/978-1-4666-0011-9.ch804

Levensaler, L., & Laurano, M. (2010). *Talent management systems 2010: Market realities, implementation experiences and solution provider profiles*. Bersin & Associates.

Luck, M., & Joy, M. (1999). A secure online submission system. *Softw. Pract. Exper.* 29(8), 721-740. DOI=.10.1002/(SICI)1097-024X(19990710)29:8

Malita, L. (2009). E-portfolios in an educational and ocupational context. *Procedia: Social and Behavioral Sciences, 1*(1), 2312–2316. doi:10.1016/j.sbspro.2009.01.406

Malmi, L., Karavirta, V., Korhonen, A., & Nikander, J. (2005). Experiences on automatically assessed algorithm simulation exercises with different resubmission policies. J. Educ. Resour. Comput. 5, 3, Article 7, DOI= http://doi.acm.org/10.1145/1163405.116341210.1145/1163405.1163412

Mandal, A. K., Mandal, C., & Reade, C. M. P. (2006). Architecture of an automatic program evaluation system. CSIE. Retrieved from http://sit.iitkgp.ernet.in/chitta/pubs/CSIEAIT06-p152.pdf

Mandal, C. V. L. R. C. M. P., Sinha. (2004). A web-based course management tool and web services. Electronic Journal of E-Learning. Retrieved from http://doi.acm.org/10.1145/1163405.1163412

Markiewicz, M. E., & de Lucena, C. J. P. (2001, July). Object oriented framework development. *Crossroads, 7*(1), 3–9. http://doi.acm.org/10.1145/372765.372771 doi:10.1145/372765.372771

Mason, R., & Rehak, D. (2003). Keeping the learning in learning objects. In A. Littlejohn (Ed.), Reusing online resources: a sustainable approach to e-learning, 20-34. London: Kogan Page.

Massart, D. a. (2010). Taming the metadata beast: Ilox. *D-Lib Magazine, 16*(1), 11–12.

McCallum, S. H. (2006). A look at new information retrieval protocols: Sru, opensearch/a9, cql, and xquery. In In world library and information congress. Retrieved from http://archive.ifla.org/IV/ifla72/papers/102-McCallum-en.pdf

McGreal, R. (2008). A typology of learning object repositories. In H. H. Adelsberger, Kinshuk, J. M. Pawlowski, & D. G. Sampson (Eds.), Handbook on information technologies for education and training, 5-28.

Meier, W. (2002). exist: An open source native xml database. In Web-services, and database systems, node 2002 web and database-related workshops (pp.169-183). Springer.

Mory, E. H. (2007). Feedback Research Revisited. In D. H. Jonassen (Ed.), *Handbook of research for educational communications and technology*. Association for Educational Communications and Technology.

Nichani, M. (2001). Lcms = lms + cms [rlos] - how does this a ect the learner? the instructional designer? ELearningPost.

Nielsen, J. (1994). Usability engineering. San Francisco, Calif.: Morgan Kaufmann Publishers. Retrieved from http://www.worldcat.org/search?qt=worldcatorgallq = 0125184069

Nielson, F., Nielson, H. R., & Hankin, C. (1999). *Principles of program analysis*. Secaucus, NJ, USA: Springer-Verlag New York, Inc. doi:10.1007/978-3-662-03811-6

O'Kelly, J., & Gibson, J. P. (2006, June). Robocode & problem based learning: A non-prescriptive approach to teaching programming. *SIGCSE Bulletin*, *38*(3), 217–221. doi:10.1145/1140123.1140182

Ochoa, X., & Duval, E. (2009). Quantitative analysis of learning object repositories, *AACE*, 2(3). Retrieved from http://ieeexplore.ieee.org/lpdocs/epic03/wrapper.htm?arnumber=5184802

Ochoa, X., Klerkx, J., Vandeputte, B., & Duval, E. (2011). On the use of learning object metadata: The globe experience. In *Ec-tel* (pp. 271–284). DBLP; http://dblp.uni-trier.de doi:10.1007/978-3-642-23985-4_22

Oliveira, L., & Moreira, F. (2010). Personal learning environments: Integration of web 2.0 applications and content management systems. In 11th European conference on knowledge management.

Oncu, C. H. S., & Cakir, H. (2011). Research in online learning environments: Priorities and methodologies. *Computers & Education*, *57*(1), 1098–1108. doi:10.1016/j.compedu.2010.12.009

Pantel, C. (n.d.). A framework for comparing web-based learning environments (Unpublished master's thesis). School of Computing Science, Simon Fraser University, Canada.

Pisan, Y., Richards, D., Sloane, A., Koncek, H., & Mitchell, S. (2003). Submit! A web-based system for automatic program critiquing. *In Proceedings of the australasian conference on computing education*, 20(1), 59-68.

Queirós, R., & Leal, J. P. (2012). Programming Exercises Evaluation Systems - An Interoperability Survey. In M. Helfert, M. J. Martins & J. Cordeiro (eds.), 1, 83-90. ISBN: 978-989-8565-06-8

Queirós, R., & Leal, J. P. (2012). PETCHA: a programming exercises teaching assistant. In Proceedings of the 17th ACM annual conference on Innovation and technology in computer science education (ITiCSE '12), 192-197. DOI= http://doi.acm.org/10.1145/2325296.232534410.1145/2325296.2325344

Queirós, R., & Leal, J. P. (2013). Making Programming Exercises Interoperable with PExIL. In J. Ramalho, A. Simões, & R. Queirós (Eds.) Innovations in XML Applications and Metadata Management: Advancing Technologies, 38-56. DOI: doi:10.4018/978-1-4666-2669-0.ch003

Queirós, R., & Leal, J. P. (2013). *Ensemble - An E-Learning Framework, Special issue on Cloud Education Environments at the Journal of Universal Computer Science.* JUCS; doi:10.3217/jucs-018-11-1454

Reek, K. A. (1989, February). The try system -or- how to avoid testing student programs. *SIGCSE Bull.*, 2(1), 112-116. DOI: http://doi.acm.org/10.1145/65294.71198

Rehak, M. R. D. R. (2003). Keeping the learning in learning objects. In Littlejohn, A. (Ed.) Reusing online resources: a sustainable approach to e-Learning, 22-30.

Reilly, W., Wolfe, R., & Smith, M. (2006, April). Mit's cwspace project: Packaging metadata for archiving educational content in dspace. *International Journal on Digital Libraries*, 6(2), 139–147. doi:10.1007/s00799-005-0131-2

Repository software survey. (2010). Repositories Support Project. Robertsson, E. (2002). Combining schematron with other xml schema languages (Tech. Rep.).

Rodriguez, E., Sicilia, M. A., & Arroyo, S. (2006). Bridging the semantic gap in standards-based learning object repositories. In *Proceedings of the workshop on learning object repositories as digital libraries current challenges*, 478-483.

Rogers, S. A. (2003). Developing an institutional knowledge bank at ohio state university: From concept to action plan. *Portal Libraries and the Academy*, 3(1), 125–136. doi:10.1353/pla.2003.0018

Romli, R., Sulaiman, S., & Zamli, K. (2010, june). Automatic programming assessment and test data generation a review on its approaches. In Information technology (itsim), 2010 international symposium, 3(1), 1186-1192. DOI: doi:10.1109/ITSIM.2010.5561488

Saikkonen, R., Malmi, L., & Korhonen, A. (2001, June). Fully automatic assessment of programming exercises. *SIGCSE Bulletin*, 33(1), 133–136. doi:10.1145/507758.377666

Schulte, C., & Bennedsen, J. (2006). What do teachers teach in introductory programming? In Proceedings of the second international workshop on computing education research, 17-28. New York, NY, USA: ACM. Retrieved from http://doi.acm.org/10.1145/1151588.1151593 doi:10.1145/1151588.1151593

Siddiqui, A., Khan, M., & Akhtar, S. (2008, August). Supply chain simulator: A scenario-based educational tool to enhance student learning. *Computers & Education*, 51(1), 252–261. doi:10.1016/j.compedu.2007.05.008

Simon, B., Massart, D., van Assche, F., Ternier, S., Duval, E., Brantner, S., & Miklos, Z. (2005). A simple query interface for interoperable learning repositories. In *Proceedings of the 1st workshop on interoperability of web-based educational systems*, 11-18.

Spacco, J., Hovemeyer, D., Pugh, W., Emad, F., Hollingsworth, J. K., & Padua-Perez, N. (2006, June). Experiences with marmoset: Designing and using an advanced submission and testing system for programming courses. *SIGCSE Bulletin*, 38(3), 13–17. doi:10.1145/1140123.1140131

Tang C.M., P. C., Yu Y. T. (2010). A review of the strategies for output correctness determination in automated assessment of student programs. In proceedings of global chinese conference on computers in education.

Tang, Y. Y. T. P. C. K., C. M. (2009a). An approach towards automatic testing of student programs using token patterns. In proceedings of the 17th international conference on computers in education (icce 2009), 1, 188-190.

Tang, Y. Y. T.. P. C. K., C. M. (2009b). Automated systems for testing student programs: Practical issues and requirements. In proceedings of the international workshop on strategies for practical integration of emerging and contemporary technologies in assessment and learning, 132-136.

Tastle, W. A. J., & Shackleton, P. (2005). E-learning in higher education: The challenge, eort, and return of investment. *International Journal on E-Learning.*

Team, J. (2006). *E-learning repository systems research watch (Tech. Rep.).* JISC.

Ternier, S., Massart, D., Totschnig, M., Klerkx, J., & Duval, E. (2010). The simple publishing interface (spi). *D-Lib Magazine, 16*(1), 9–10.

Tremblay, G., Guerin, F., Pons, A., & Salah, A. (2008, March). Oto, a generic and extensible tool for marking programming assignments. *Software, Practice & Experience, 38*(3), 307–333. doi:10.1002/spe.839

Truong, N. K. D. (2007). A web-based programming environment for novice pro- grammers (Doctoral dissertation, Queensland University of Technology). Retrieved from http://eprints.qut.edu.au/16471/

Tsunakawa, T. (2010). Pivotal approach for lexical translation (Unpublished doctoral dissertation). University of Tokyo.

Tzikopoulos, M. N. V. R., A. (2009). An overview of learning object repositories. In In t. halpin (ed.), selected readings on database technologies and applications. IGI Global.

Verhoe, T. (2008). Programming task packages: Peach exchange format. International Journal Olympiads. *Inform (Silver Spring, Md.), 2*(1), 192–207.

Wang, F. L., & Wong, T.-L. (2008). Designing programming exercises with computer assisted instruction. In Proceedings of the 1st international conference on hybrid learning and education, 283-293. Berlin, Heidelberg: Springer-Verlag. Retrieved from doi: doi:10.1007/978-3-540-85170-7_25

Ward, J. (2004). Unqualified dublin core usage in oai-pmh data providers. *OCLC Systems & Services, 20*(1), 40–47. doi:10.1108/10650750410527322

Wiedenbeck, S., Labelle, D., & Kain, V. N. R. (2004). Factors affecting course outcomes in introductory programming. In In *16th annual workshop of the psychology of programming interest group*, 97-109.

Williams, G. M. J. (2005). The evolution of e-learning. [Global.]. *Universitas*, 21.

Wilson, S., Blinco, K., & Rehak, D. (2004). Service-Oriented Frameworks: Modelling the infrastructure for the next generation of e-Learning Systems (Tech. Rep.). JISC Report. Retrieved from http://www.jisc.ac.uk/uploadeddocuments=AltilabServiceOrientedF rameworks.pdf

Xavier, J., & Coelho, A. (2011). Computer-based assessment system for e-learning applied to programming education. In *Iceri2011 proceedings, 3738-3747*. IATED.

KEY TERMS AND DEFINITIONS

Assessment Systems: Systems responsible for the evaluation of computer programs based on several evaluation models such as test cases.

Learning Object Repository: A type of a digital library. It enables educators to share, manage and use educational resources. A more narrow definition would also require that repositories implement a metadata standard.

Learning Tools Interoperability: A specification developed by IMS Global Learning Consortium. The principal concept of LTI is to establish a standard way of integrating rich learning applications (often remotely hosted and provided through third-party services) with platforms like learning management systems, portals, or other educational environments. In LTI these learning applications are called tools (delivered by tool providers) and the LMS, or platforms, are called tool consumers.

Massive Open Online Courses: A massive open online course (MOOC) is an online course aimed at unlimited participation and open access through the Web. In addition to traditional course materials such as videos, readings, and problem assets, MOOCs provide interactive user forums that help build a community for students, teachers and teaching assistants (TAs).

Compilation of References

Feldman, R. S., & Rimé, B. (Eds.). (1991). Fundamentals of Nonverbal Behavior (Studies in Emotion and Social Interaction). Cambridge University Press. Retrieved from http://amazon.com/o/ASIN/052136700X/

Abrial, J. R. (1996). *The B-Book: Assigning Programs to Meanings.* Cambridge, UK: Cambridge University Press. doi:10.1017/CBO9780511624162

Abrial, J. R. (2007). Formal methods: Theory becoming practice. *Journal of Universal Computer Science, 13*(5), 619–628.

Abrial, J. R. (2010). *Modeling in Event-B: System and Software Engineering.* Cambridge, UK: Cambridge University Press. doi:10.1017/CBO9781139195881

Accreditation Board of Engineering and Technology. (2008). *Criteria for accrediting engineering programs: Effective for evaluations during the 2008-2009 accreditation cycle.* Baltimore, MD: ABET Engineering Accreditation Commission.

ACM & IEEE Computer Society, The Joint Task Force on Computing Curricula. (2012). *Computer Science curricula 2013.* Retrieved February 23, 2014 from http://www.acm.org/education/CS2013-final-report.pdf

ACM. (2013). *Computing Science Curricula 2013: Curriculum Guidelines for Undergraduate Degree Programs in Computer Science* (Report from The Joint Task Force on Computing Curricula). Retrieved from Recommendations - Association for Computing Machinery: http://www.acm.org/education/CS2013-final-report.pdf

Adamo-Villani, N., Oania, M., & Cooper, S. (2012). Using a Serious Game Approach to Teach Secure Coding in Introductory Programming: Development and Initial Findings. *Journal of Educational Technology Systems, 41*(2), 107–131. doi:10.2190/ET.41.2.b

Adams, D., & Trefftz, C. (2004). Using XML in a compiler course. *ACM SigCSE Bulletin, 36*(3), 4–6. doi:10.1145/1026487.1008001

Afonso, R., & Pinheiro, V., (2011). *Modelos de periodização convencionais e contemporâneos.* Retrieved from http://www.efdeportes.com

Aguirre, S., Salvachua, J., Quemada, J., Fumero, A., & Tapiador, A. (2006). Joint degrees in e-learning systems: A web services approach. In *Proceedings of the 2nd IEEE International Conference on Collaborative Computing: Networking, Applications and Worksharing.* IEEE. Retrieved from http://jungla.dit.upm.es/ saguirre/publications/CollaborateCom20061:pdf

Aiken, A. (1996). *Cool: A portable project for teaching compiler construction.* SigPLan.

Airasian, P. W. (2000). *Assessment in the classroom: A concise approach* (2nd ed.). Boston: McGraw-Hill.

Airasian, P. W. (2001). *Classroom assessment: Concepts and applications* (4th ed.). Boston: McGraw-Hill.

Akinnaso, F. N. (1992). Schooling, Language and Knowledge in Literate and Nonliterate Societies. *Comparative Studies in Society and History, 34*(1), 68–109. doi:10.1017/S0010417500017448

Ala-Mutka, K. M. (2005). A Survey of Automated Assessment Approaches for Programming Assignments. *Computer Science Education*, *15*(2), 83–102. doi:10.1080/08993400500150747

Alario, C., & Wilson, S. (2010). Comparison of the main alternatives to the integration of external tools in different platforms. In Proceedings of ICERI 2010. IATED.

Al-Hamadi, A., Elmezain, M., & Michaelis, B. (2010). Hand Gesture Recognition Based on Combined Features Extraction. *International Journal (Toronto, Ont.)*, 1–6. Retrieved from http://www.academia.edu/download/30613967/v6-1-1.pdf

Al-Khalifa, H. S., & Davis, H. C. (2006). The evolution of metadata from standards to semantics in e-learning applications. In *Proceedings of Hypertext*, (pp. 69-72). Retrieved from http://doi.acm.org/10.1145/1149941.1149956

Almeida, C. (2012). *Mindstorms na aprendizagem da algoritmia e programação*. (Master Thesis). Universidade de Aveiro, Areiro, Portugal.

Almeida, J. B., Frade, M. J., Pinto, J. S., & de Sousa, S. M. (2011). *Rigorous Software Development. An Introduction to Program Verification*. London: Springer-Verlag. doi:10.1007/978-0-85729-018-2

Almstrum, V. L., Henderson, P. B., Harvey, V. J., Heeren, C., Marion, W. A., & Riedesel, C. et al. (2006). Concept inventories in computer science for the topic discrete mathematics. *ACM SIGCSE Bulletin*, *38*(4), 132–145. doi:10.1145/1189136.1189182

Alphonce, C. G. (2003). *"Killer Examples" for Design Patterns and Objects First*. Retrieved from http://www.cse.buffalo.edu/~alphonce/KillerExamples/OOPSLA2002/

Al-Smadi, C. M. (2010). Soa-based architecture for a generic and flexible e-assessment system. In Proceedings of Education Engineering (EDUCON). IEEE.

American Association for the Advancement of Science. (2005). *Invention and impact: Building excellence in undergraduate science, technology, engineering, and mathematics (STEM) education*. Retrieved from http://www.aaas.org/publications/books_reports/CCLI

Anderson, L., Krathwohl, D., Airasian, P., Cruikshank, K., Mayer, R., & Pintrich, P. et al. (2001). *A Taxonomy for Learning and Teaching and Assessing: A Revision of Bloom's Taxonomy of Educational Objectives*. New York: Addison Wesley Longman, Inc.

Anderson, R., Simon, B., Wolfman, S. A., VanDeGrift, T., & Yasuhara, K. (2004). Experiences with a tablet PC based lecture presentation system in computer science courses. *SIGCSE Bulletin*, *36*(1), 56–60. doi:10.1145/1028174.971323

Anjaneyulu, K. S. (1994). Bug analysis of Pascal programs. *SIGPLAN Notices*, *29*(4), 15–22. doi:10.1145/181761.181762

Antón-Rodríguez, M., Pérez-Juárez, M. A., Díaz-Pernas, F. J., Perozo-Rondón, F. J., Martínez-Zarzuela, M., & González-Ortega, D. (2012). Moodle-Based Software to Support the Learning of Web Programming. *International Journal of Knowledge Society Research*, *3*(3), 16-28. doi: 10.4018/jksr.2012070102

Apostolopoulos, T. K., & Kefala, A. S. (2003). An e-learning service management architecture. In Proceedings of ICALT (pp. 140-144). ICALT.

Appel, A., & Ginsburg, M. (2004). *Modern Compiler Implementation in C*. Cambridge University Press.

Appel, A., & Palsberg, J. (2002). *Modern Compiler Implementation in Java*. Cambridge University Press. doi:10.1017/CBO9780511811432

Aroyo, L., & Dolog, P., jan Houben, G., Kravcik, M., Naeve, A., Nilsson, M., & Wild, F. (2006). Interoperability in personalized adaptive learning. *Journal of Educational Technology & Society*, *9*(2), 4-18. Retrieved from http://www.ifets.info/journals/92=2:pdf

Astrachan, O., Mitchener, G., Berry, G., & Cox, L. (1998). Design patterns: An essential component of CS curricula. *SIGCSE Bulletin*, *30*(1), 153–160. doi:10.1145/274790.273182

Atchison, W. F., Schweppe, E. J., Viavant, W., Young, D. M., Conte, S. D., & Hamblen, J. W. et al. (1968). Curriculum '68: Recommendations for academic programs in computer science. *Communications of the ACM*, *11*(3), 151–197. doi:10.1145/362929.362976

Baker, L. J. (1995). *The effect of cooperative study groups on achievement of college-level computer science programming students*. (Unpublished doctoral dissertation). University of Texas, Austin, TX.

Baldwin, D. (1992). Using scientific experiments in early computer science laboratories. In *Proceedings of the 23rd SIGCSE Technical Symposium on Computer Science Education, SIGCSE'92* (pp. 102-106). New York, NY: ACM Press. doi:10.1145/134510.134532

Baltazar, A., Martins, L., & Cardoso, J. (2012). ZATLAB: A Gesture Analysis System to Music Interaction. In *Proceedings of 6th International Conference on Digital Arts (ARTECH 2012)*. Retrieved from http://www.inescporto.pt/~jsc/publications/conferences/2012ABaltazarARTECH.pdf

Baltazar, A., Guedes, C., Gouyon, F., & Pennycook, B. (2010). *A Real-time human body skeletonization algorithm for MAX / MSP / JITTER*. ICMC.

Balz, M., & Goedicke, M. (2010). Teaching Programming with Formal Models in Greenfoot. In *Proceedings of the 2nd International Conference on Computer Supported Education* (pp. 309-316). Valencia: INSTICC Press.

Bandura, A. (1997). *Self Efficacy: The exercise of control*. New York: WH Freeman and Co.

Bandura, A., & Locke, E. (2003). Negative self-efficacy and goal effects revisited. *The Journal of Applied Psychology*, 88(1), 87–99. doi:10.1037/0021-9010.88.1.87 PMID:12675397

Barak, M., Harward, J., Kocur, G., & Lerman, S. (2007). Transforming an introductory programming course from lectures to active learning via wireless laptops. *Journal of Science Education and Technology*, 16(4), 325–336. doi:10.1007/s10956-007-9055-5

Barker, P., & Campbell, L. M. (2010). Metadata for learning materials: an overview of existing standards and current developments. *Technology, Instruction, Cognition and Learning, 7*(3-4), 225-243. Retrieved from http://www.icbl.hw.ac.uk/publicationFiles/2010/TICLMetadata/TICLpaper.MetadataForEducationpostref:pdf

Barret, H. (2010). *Electronic portfolios in stem - what is an electronic portfolio*. Retrieved from http://www.scribd.com/doc/40206175/E-Portfolio-Definition

Barret, H. (n.d.). Categories of eportfolio tools (Tech. Rep.). JISC.

Barrett, H. (2005). *Researching Electronic Portfolios and Learning Engagement: The REFLECT Initiative*. TaskStream Inc.

Barrón-Estrada, M. Cabada, Ra., Cabada, Ro., & Garcia, C. (2010). A hybrid learning compiler course, Lecture Notes in Computer Science, 6248, 229–238.

Baturay, M. H., & Bay, O. F. (2010). The effects of problem learning on the classroom community perceptions and achievement of web-based education students. *Computers & Education*, 55(1), 43–52. doi:10.1016/j.compedu.2009.12.001

Beaubouef, T., & Mason, J. (2005). Why the high attrition rate for computer science students: Some thoughts and observations. *SIGCSE Bulletin*, 37(2), 103–106. doi:10.1145/1083431.1083474

Beck, K. (2000). *Extreme programming explained: Embrace change*. Boston, MA: Addison-Wesley Longman, Inc.

Beck, K. (2003). *Test-Driven Development: By Example*. Boston, MA: Addison-Wesley Longman, Inc.

Beck, L. L., & Chizhik, A. W. (2008). An experimental study of cooperative learning in CS1. In *Proceedings of SIGCSE of ACM Technical Symposium on Computer Science Education*, (pp. 205-209). ACM. doi:10.1145/1352135.1352208

Ben-Ari, M. (2001). Constructivism in computer science education. *Journal of Computers in Mathematics and Science Teaching*, 20(1), 45–73.

Ben-Ari, M., Bednarik, R., Levy, R., Ebel, G., Moreno, A., Myller, N., & Sutinen, E. (2011). A decade of research and development on program animation: The Jeliot experience. *Journal of Visual Languages and Computing*, 22(5), 375–384. doi:10.1016/j.jvlc.2011.04.004

Benaya, T., & Zur, E. (2008). Understanding Object Oriented Programming Concepts in an Advanced Programming Course. In R. Mittermeir & M. Syslo (Eds.), *Informatics Education - Supporting Computational Thinking* (pp. 161–170). Berlin: Springer-Verlag. doi:10.1007/978-3-540-69924-8_15

Benford, S., Burke, E., Foxley, E., Gutteridge, N., & Zin, A. (2011). Early experiences of computer-aided assessment and administration when teaching computer programming. *Research in Learning Technology*, *1*(2). Retrieved from http://www.researchinlearningtechnology.net/index.php/rlt/article/view/9481

Bennedsen, J., & Caspersen, M. E. (2005). An investigation of potential success factors for an introductory model-driven programming course. In *Proceedings of the first International workshop on Computing Education Research (ICER'05)* (pp. 155-163). Seattle, WA: ACM. doi:10.1145/1089786.1089801

Bennedsen, J. B., Caspersen, M. E., & Kölling, M. (2008). *Reflections on the Teaching of Programming: Methods and Implementations*. Springer Publishing Company, Inc. doi:10.1007/978-3-540-77934-6

Bennedsen, J., & Caspersen, M. E. (2003). Rationale for the Design of a Web-based Programming Course for Adults. In *Proceedings of the International Conference on Open and Online Learning (ICOOL'03)*. University of Mauritius.

Bennedsen, J., & Caspersen, M. E. (2006). Abstraction ability as an indicator of success for learning object-oriented programming? *SIGCSE Bulletin*, *38*(2), 39–43. doi:10.1145/1138403.1138430

Bergin, J., Caristi, J., Dubinsky, Y., Hazzan, O., & Williams, L. (2004). Teaching software development methods: The case of extreme programming. *SIGCSE Bulletin*, *36*(1), 448–449. doi:10.1145/1028174.971452

Berscia, W., & Miller, M. (2006). *What's Worth?* The Perceived Benefits of Instructional Blogging. *Electronic Journal for the Integration of Technology in Education*.

Bersin. (2009). *Learning management systems 2009: Executive summary*. Bersin & Associates.

Beug, A. (2012). *Teaching Introductory Programming Concepts: A Comparison of Scratch and Arduino*. (Master Thesis). California Polytechnic State University, San Luis Obispo, CA.

Bevilacqua, F., & Muller, R. (2005). A gesture follower for performing arts. In *Proceedings of the International Gestur*, (pp. 3–4). Academic Press. Retrieved from http://www.sdela.dds.nl/cinedebate/gesturalfollower.pdf

Bevilacqua, F., Müller, R., & Schnell, N. (2005). MnM: a Max/MSP mapping toolbox. In *Proceedings of the 2005 conference on New interfaces for musical expression* (pp. 85–88). Academic Press.

Biggs, J. B., & Collis, K. F. (1982). *Evaluating the quality of learning: the SOLO taxonomy (structure of the observed learning outcome)*. New York: Academic Press.

Bliven, B. (1924, June). Article. *The Century Illustrated Monthly Magazine*, *108*, 148.

Bloom, B. S., Engelhart, M. D., Furst, E. J., Hill, W. H., & Krathwohl, D. R. (1956). *Taxonomy of Educational Objectives, Handbook I: Cognitive Domain*. London, UK: Longmans, Green and Co Ltd.

Blumenstein, M., Green, S., Nguyen, A., & Muthukkumarasamy, V. (2004, June). An experimental analysis of game: A generic automated marking environment. *SIGCSE Bulletin*, *36*(1), 67–71. doi:10.1145/1026487.1008016

Bobrovnik, V.I. (2014). Structure and logical organization of current studies in track and field sports. *Pedagogics, Psychology, Medical-Biological Problems of Physical Training and Sports, 3*, 3-18.

Bokowiec, M. A. (2011). V! OCT (Ritual): An Interactive Vocal Work for Bodycoder System and 8 Channel Spatialization. In Proceedings of NIME 2011 (pp. 40–43). NIME.

Boulanger, J. L. (Ed.). (2012). *Formal Methods: Industrial Use from Model to the Code*. London: ISTE – John Wiley & Sons.

Bowen, J. P., & Hinchey, M. G. (2006). Ten Commandments of Formal Methods ... Ten Years Later. *IEEE Computer*, *39*(1), 40–48. doi:10.1109/MC.2006.35

Brassard, G., & Bratley, P. (1996). *Fundamentals of Algoritmics*. Hertfordshire, UK: Prentice-Hall.

Braught, G., Miller, C. S., & Reed, D. (2004). Core empirical concepts and skills for computer science. In *Proceedings of the 35th SIGCSE Technical Symposium on Computer Science Education, SIGCSE'04* (pp. 245-249). New York, NY: ACM Press. doi:10.1145/971300.971388

Bridgeman, S., Goodrich, M. T., Kobourov, S. G., & Tamassia, R. (2000). PILOT: An interactive tool for learning and grading. In *Proceedings of the 31st SIGCSE Technical Symposium on Computer Science Education, SIGCSE'00* (pp. 139-143). New York, NY: ACM Press. doi:10.1145/330908.331843

Britain, L. O. S. (1998). *A Framework for Pedagogical Evaluation of Virtual Learning Environments* (Tech. Rep.). Retrieved from http://www.leeds.ac.uk/educol/documents/00001237.htm

Brock, J., Bruce, R., & Reiser, S. (2009). Using Arduino for introductory programming courses. *Journal of Computing Sciences in Colleges*, 25(2), 129–139.

Burguillo, J. C. (2010). Using game theory and competition-based learning to stimulate student motivation and performance. *Comput. Educ., 55*(2), 566-575. Retrieved from doi: 10.1016/j.compedu.2010.02.018

Butcher, D. F., & Muth, W. A. (1985). Predicting performance in an introductory computer science course. *Communications of the ACM, 28*(3), 263–268. doi:10.1145/3166.3167

Byrne, P., & Lyons, G. (2001). The effect of student attributes on success in programming. *SIGCSE Bulletin, 33*(3), 49–52. doi:10.1145/507758.377467

Camurri, A., Mazzarino, B., & Ricchetti, M. (2004). Multimodal analysis of expressive gesture in music and dance performances. *Gesture-Based*. Retrieved from http://link.springer.com/chapter/10.1007/978-3-540-24598-8_3

Camurri, a., Volpe, G., Poli, G. De, & Leman, M. (2005). Communicating expressiveness and affect in multimodal interactive systems. *IEEE Multimedia, 12*(1), 43–53. doi:10.1109/MMUL.2005.2

Camurri, A., Hashimoto, S., Ricchetti, M., Ricci, A., Suzuki, K., Trocca, R., & Volpe, G. (2000). EyesWeb: Toward Gesture and Affect Recognition in Interactive Dance and Music Systems. *Computer Music Journal, 24*(1), 57–69. doi:10.1162/014892600559182

Carbone, A., & Ceddia, J., Simon, D'Souza, & Mason, R. (2013). Student Concerns in Introductory Programming Courses. In *Proceedings of the fifteenth Australasian Computing Education conference (ACE'13)* (pp. 41-50). Adelaide, Australia: ACE.

Carlson, P. A., & Berry, F. C. (2003). Calibrated peer review™ and assessing learning outcomes. In *Proceedings of the 33rd Annual Frontiers in Education Conference*. Piscataway, NJ: IEEE Digital Library doi:10.1109/FIE.2003.1264740

Casella, G., Costagliola, G., Ferrucci, F., Polese, G., & Scanniello, G. (2007). A scorm thin client architecture for e-learning systems based on web services. *International Journal of Distance Education Technologies, 5*(1), 19–36. doi:10.4018/jdet.2007010103

Caspersen, M. E. (2007). *Educating novices in the skills of programming.* (PhD Thesis). University of Aarhus, Aarhus, Denmark.

Castellano, G., Villalba, S., & Camurri, A. (2007). Recognising human emotions from body movement and gesture dynamics. *Affective Computing and Intelligent*, 71–82. Retrieved from http://link.springer.com/chapter/10.1007/978-3-540-74889-2_7

Castelo, J., Barreto, H., Alves, F., Mil-Homens, P., Carvalho, J., & Vieira, J. (1999). *Metodologia do treino desportivo.* Lisboa: Faculdade de Motricidade Humana - Serviço de edições.

Cegielski, C. G., & Hall, D. J. (2006). What makes a good programmer? *Communications of the ACM, 49*(10), 73–75. doi:10.1145/1164394.1164397

Cerone, A., Roggenbach, M., & Schlingloff, H., Schneider, & G. Shaikh, S. (2013). Teaching Formal Methods for Software Engineering – Ten Principles. In *Proceedings of Fun With Formal Methods, Workshop affiliated with the 25th Int.Conf. on Computer Aided Verification*. Saint Petersburg: Academic Press.

Chae, G. B., Chandra, S., Mann, V., & Nanda, M. G. (2004). Decentralized orchestration of composite web services. In *Proceedings of the 13th international world wide web conference on alternate track papers & posters*, (pp. 134-143). New York, NY: ACM. doi: 10.1145/1013367.1013390

Chambless, D. L., Beck, A. T., Gracely, E. J., & Grisham, J. R. (2000). Relationship of cognitions to fear of somatic symptoms: A test of the cognitive theory of panic. *Depression and Anxiety*, *11*(1), 1–9. doi:10.1002/(SICI)1520-6394(2000)11:1<1::AID-DA1>3.0.CO;2-X PMID:10723629

Chamillard, A. T. (2006). Using student performance predictions in a computer science curriculum. *SIGCSE Bulletin*, *38*(3), 260–264. doi:10.1145/1140123.1140194

Cheang, B., Kurnia, A., Lim, A., & Oon, W.-C. (2003, September). On automated grading of programming assignments in an academic institution. *Computers & Education*, *4*(1), 121–131. doi:10.1016/S0360-1315(03)00030-7

Chen, M.-Y., Wei, J.-D., Huang, J.-H., & Lee, D. T. (2006). Design and applications of an algorithm benchmark system in a computational problem solving environment. In *Proceedings of the 11th Annual Conference on Innovation and Technology in Computer Science Education, ITiCSE'06* (pp. 123-127). New York, NY: ACM Press. doi:10.1145/1140124.1140159

Cheung, W., Li, E., & Yee, L. (2003). Multimedia learning system and its effect on self-efficacy in database modeling and design: an exploratory study. *Computers & Education*, *41*(3), 249-270. doi: 0360-1315(03)00048-410.1016/S

Chloros, G., Zervas, P., & Sampson, D. G. (2010). Ask-lom-ap: A web-based tool for development and management of ieee lom application profiles. In Proceedings of ICALT, (pp. 138-142). ICALT. doi:10.1109/ICALT.2010.46

Christensen, H. B. (2004). Frameworks: Putting design patterns into perspective. *SIGCSE Bulletin*, *36*(3), 142–145. doi:10.1145/1026487.1008035

Churcher, C. (2012). *Beginning Database Design. From Novice to Professional*. United States of America: Apress. doi:10.1007/978-1-4302-4210-9

Cizek, G. J. (1999). *Cheating on tests: How to do it, detect it, and prevent it*. Mahwah, NJ: Lawrence Erlbaum.

Cizek, G. J. (2003). *Detecting and preventing classroom cheating: Promoting integrity in assessment*. Thousand Oaks, CA: Corwin Press.

Clancy, M. (2004). Misconceptions and attitudes that interfere with learning to program. In S. Fincher & M. Petre (Eds.), *Computer Science Education Research* (pp. 85–100). London, UK: Routledge.

Clancy, M. J., & Linn, M. C. (1999). Patterns and pedagogy. *SIGCSE Bulletin*, *31*(1), 37–42. doi:10.1145/384266.299673

Clark, J. (1906). The correspondence school—Its relation to technical education and some of its results. *Science*, *24*(611), 327–334. doi:10.1126/science.24.611.327 PMID:17772791

Clyde, L. A. (2005). Educational Blogging. *Teacher Librarian*, *32*(3), 43–45.

Cockburn, A. (2002). *Agile software development*. Boston, MA: Addison-Wesley Longman Inc.

Coffey, J. W. (2013). Integrating theoretical and empirical computer science in a data structures course. In In *Proceedings of the 44th SIGCSE Technical Symposium on Computer Science Education, SIGCSE'13* (pp. 23-27). New York, NY: ACM Press. doi:10.1145/2445196.2445211

Cohen, L., Manion, L., & Morrison, K. (2001). *Research Methods in Education* (5th ed.). New York: Routledge.

Co-Lab, A. (2003). *Learning repositories included in learning repository investigation*. Retrieved from http://www.academiccolab.org/resources/DraftRepositoriesList.pdf

Cole, J., & Foster, H. (2007). *Using Moodle: Teaching with the Popular Open Source Course Management System* (2nd ed.). O'Reilly Media. Retrieved from http://www.amazon.com/exec/obidos/redirect?tag=citeulike07-20&path=ASIN/059652918X

Collberg, C., Kobourov, S. G., & Westbrook, S. (2004). AlgoVista: An algorithmic search tool in an educational setting. In *Proceedings of the 35th SIGCSE Technical Symposium on Computer Science Education, SIGCSE'04* (pp. 462-466). New York, NY: ACM Press. doi:10.1145/971300.971457

Cook, C., Drachova, S., Hallstrom, J., Hollingsworth, J., Jacobs, D., Krone, J., & Sitaraman, M. (2012). A Systematic Approach to Teaching Abstraction and Mathematical Modeling. In *Proceedings of the 17th ACM Annual Conference on Innovation and Technology in Computer Science Education (ITiCSE'12)* (pp. 357-362). Haifa, Israel: ACM. doi:10.1145/2325296.2325378

Cormen, T. H., Leiserson, C. E., Rivest, R. L., & Stein, C. (2009). *Introduction to Algorithms* (3rd ed.). Cambridge, MA: The MIT Press.

Corradini, A. (2001). Dynamic time warping for off-line recognition of a small gesture vocabulary. In *Proceedings of Recognition, Analysis, and Tracking of Faces and Gestures in Real-Time Systems,* (pp. 82–89). IEEE. doi:10.1109/RATFG.2001.938914

Cristiá, M. (2006). Teaching formal methods in a third world country: what, why and how. In *Proceedings of the conference on Teaching Formal Methods 2006.* London: BCS London Office.

Crocker, D. (2004). Safe Object-Oriented Software: The Verified Design-By-Contract Paradigm In *Proceedings of the Twelfth Safety-critical Systems Symposium* (pp. 19-41) London: Springer-Verlag.

Crooks, S. M., Klein, J. D., Savenye, W., & Leader, L. (1998). Effects of cooperative and individual learning during learner-controlled computer-based instruction. *Journal of Experimental Education, 66*(3), 223–244. doi:10.1080/00220979809604406

Curbera, F., Duftler, M., Khalaf, R., Nagy, W., Mukhi, N., & Weerawarana, S. (2002). Unraveling the Web services web: an introduction to SOAP, WSDL, and UDDI. *IEEE Internet Computing, 6*(2), 86-93. doi:10.1109/4236.991449

Dagdilelis, V., & Satratzemi, M. (1998). DIDAGRAPH: Software for teaching graph theory algorithms. In *Proceedings of the 3rd Annual Conference on Innovation and Technology in Computer Science Education, ITiCSE'98* (pp. 64-68). New York, NY: ACM Press. doi:10.1145/282991.283024

Dagger, D., O'Connor, A., Lawless, S., Walsh, E., & Wade, V. P. (2007). Service-Oriented E-Learning Platforms: From Monolithic Systems to Flexible Services. *IEEE Internet Computing, 11*(3), 28-35. Retrieved from http://ieeexplore.ieee.org/xpls/abs/all:jsp?arnumber=4196172

Daly, C. (1999, June). Roboprof and an introductory computer programming course. *SIGCSE Bulletin, 31*(3), 155–158. doi:10.1145/384267.305904

Danielsiek, H., Paul, W., & Vahrenhold, J. (2012). Detecting and understanding students' misconceptions related to algorithms and data structures. In *Proceedings of the 43rd SIGCSE Technical Symposium on Computer Science Education, SIGCSE'12* (pp. 21-26). New York, NY: ACM Press. doi:10.1145/2157136.2157148

Dannels, D. P., & Martin, K. N. (2008). Critiquing critiques a genre analysis of feedback across novice to expert design studios. *Journal of Business and Technical Communication, 22*(2), 135–159. doi:10.1177/1050651907311923

Davis, C. C. B., & Wagner, E. (2009). *The Evolution of the LMS: From Management to Learning - Deep Analysis of Trends Shaping the Future of eLearning* (Tech. Rep.). Sage Road Solutions, LLC. Retrieved from http://www.loc.gov/standards/mets/mets-schemadocs.html

Davis, J., Wellman, B., Anderson, M., & Raines, M. (2009). Providing robotic experiences through object-based programming (PREOP). In *Proceedings of the 2009 Alice Symposium,* (pp. 1-5). Durham, NC: ACM. doi:10.1145/1878513.1878520

Deci, E. L., & Ryan, R. M. (1985). *Intrinsic Motivation and Self-determination in Human Behavior.* New York, NY: Plenum Press. doi:10.1007/978-1-4899-2271-7

Dehnadi, S. (2006). Testing Programming Aptitude. In P. Romero, J. Good, E. A. Chaparro, & S. Bryant. In *Proceedings of the 18th Annual Workshop of the Psychology of Programming Interest Group (PPIG'06)* (pp. 22-37). Brighton, UK: PPIG.

Demaille, A., Levillain, R., & Perrot, B. (2008). A set of tools to teach compiler construction. *ACM SIGCSE, 40*(3), 68–72. doi:10.1145/1597849.1384291

Denning, P. J. (2007). Computing as a natural science. *Communications of the ACM, 50*(7), 13–18. doi:10.1145/1272516.1272529

Denning, P. J., Comer, D. E., Gries, D., Mulder, M. C., Tucker, A. B., Turner, A. J., & Young, P. R. (1989). Computing as a discipline. *Communications of the ACM, 32*(1), 9–23. doi:10.1145/63238.63239

Denning, P. J., & McGettrick, A. (2005). Recentering computer science. *Communications of the ACM, 48*(11), 15–19. doi:10.1145/1096000.1096018

Denning, T., Griswold, W. G., Simon, B., & Wilkerson, M. (2006). Multimodal communication in the classroom: What does it mean for us? *SIGCSE Bulletin, 38*(1), 219–223. doi:10.1145/1124706.1121410

Derkach, V. N., & Yedinak, G. A. (2014). On the question of periodization training content and Paralympic athletes with disorders of the musculoskeletal system in the light of the general theory of sports training. *Pedagogics, Psychology, Medical-Biological Problems of Physical Training and Sports, 5.*

Dick, M., Bareiss, C., Carter, J., Joyce, D., Harding, T., & Laxer, C. (2003). Addressing student cheating: Definitions and solutions. *SIGCSE Bulletin, 35*(2), 172–184. doi:10.1145/782941.783000

Dietrich, J. E. (1983). Play Direction (2nd ed.). Prentice Hall. Retrieved from http://amazon.com/o/ASIN/0136833349/

Dijkstra, E. W. (1976). *A Discipline of Programming.* Englewood Cliffs, NJ: Prentice Hall.

Dijkstra, E. W. (1989). On the Cruelty of Really Teaching Computing Science. *Communications of the ACM, 32*(12), 1388–1404.

Dobrian, C., & Bevilacqua, F. (2003). Gestural control of music: using the vicon 8 motion capture system. In Proceedings of the 2003 conference on New interfaces for musical expression (pp. 161–163). National University of Singapore. Retrieved from http://dl.acm.org/citation.cfm?id=1085753

Domínguez, C., & Jaime, A. (2010). Database design learning: A project-based approach organized through a course management system, *Computers & Education, 55*(3), 1312-1320. doi:10.1016/j.compedu.2010.06.001

Donohue, B., Miller, A., Crammer, L., Cross, C., & Covassin, T. (2007). A standardized method of assessing sport specific problems in the relationships of athletes with their coaches, teammates, family, and peers. *Journal of Sport Behavior.*

Douce, C., Livingstone, D., & Orwell, J. (2005). Automatic test based assessment of programming: A review. *Journal of Educational Resources in Computing, 5*(3), 4, es. doi:10.1145/1163405.1163409

Duda, J., Chi, L., Newton, M.L., Walling, M.D., & Catley, D. (1995). Task and ego orientation and intrinsic motivation in sport. *Journal of Sport Psychology, 26,* 40–63.

Dyba, T., Arisholmk, E., Sjoberg, D. I. L., Hannay, J. E., & Shull, F. (2007). Are two heads better than one? On the effectiveness of pair programming. *IEEE Software, 24*(6), 12–15. doi:10.1109/MS.2007.158

Eagle, M., & Barnes, T. (2009). Experimental evaluation of an educational game for improved learning in introductory computing. In *Proceedings of the 40th ACM Technical Symposium on Computer Science Education (SIGCSE'09)* (pp. 321-325). Chattanooga, TN: ACM. doi:10.1145/1508865.1508980

Eap, T. M., Hatala, M., & Richards, G. (2004). Digital repository interoperability: design, implementation and deployment of the ecl protocol and connecting middleware. In *Proceedings of the 13th international world wide web conference on alternate track papers & posters,* (pp. 376-377). New York, NY: Academic Press. doi:10.1145/1013367.1013483

Ebel, G., & Ben-Ari, M. (2006). Affective effects of program visualization. In *Proceedings of the second International workshop on Computing Education Research (ICER'06)* (pp. 1-5). Canterbury, UK: ACM.

Eberlein, T., Kampmeier, J., Minderhout, V., Moog, R. S., Platt, T., Varma-Nelson, P., & White, H. (2008). Pedagogies of engagement in science: A comparison of PBL, POGIL, and PLTL. *Biochemistry and Molecular Biology Education*, *36*(4), 262–273. doi:10.1002/bmb.20204 PMID:19381266

Eckerdal, A. (2009). *Novice programming students' learning of concepts and practice*. (Unpublished Doctoral Dissertation). Uppsala University.

Eckerson, W. W. (1995). Three tier client/server architecture: Achieving scalability, performance, and efficiency in client server applications. *Open Information Systems, 10*(1).

Edwards, S. H., & Pugh, W. (2006, March). Toward a common automated grading platform. In *Proceedings of Birds-of-a-feather session at the 37th sigcse technical symposium on computer science education*. ACM.

Edwards, S. H., Borstler, J., Cassel, L. N., Hall, M. S., & Hollingsworth, J. (2008). Developing a common format for sharing programming assignments. *SIGCSE Bull., 40*(4), 167-182. doi: 10.1145/1473195.1473240

Edwards, H. M., Thompson, J. B., Halstead-Nussloch, R., Arnow, D., & Oliver, D. (2000). Report on the CSEET '99 Workshop: Establishing a Distance Education Program. *Computer Science Education*, *10*(1), 57–74. doi:10.1076/0899-3408(200004)10:1;1-P;FT057

Edwards, S. H. (2004). Using software testing to move students from trial-and-error to reflection-in-action. *SIGCSE Bulletin*, *36*(1), 26–30. doi:10.1145/1028174.971312

Efron, D. (1972). *Gesture, Race and Culture*. Mouton and Co.

Elgg. (n.d.). Retrieved May 14, 2014 from http://www.elgg.org

Ellis, R. K. (2009). *Field guide to learning management systems*. ASTD Learning Circuits.

Engels, S., Lakshmanan, V., & Craig, M. (2007, March). Plagiarism detection using feature-based neural networks. *SIGCSE Bull.*, *39*(1), 34-38. http://doi.acm.org/10.1145/1227504.1227324

Erl, T. (2005). *Service-oriented architecture - Concepts, technology and design*. Upper Saddle River, NJ: Prentice Hall.

Esteves, M., Fonseca, B., Morgado, L., & Martins, P. (2010). *Improving teaching and learning of computer programming through the use of the Second Life virtual world.British Journal of Educational Technology*. doi:10.1111/j.1467-8535.2010.01056.x

Fagin, B., & Merkle, L. (2003). Measuring the effectiveness of robots in teaching computer science. *SIGCSE Bulletin*, *35*(1), 307–311. doi:10.1145/792548.611994

Falchikov, N. (2005). *Improving assessment through student involvement: Practical solutions for aiding learning in higher and further education*. London: Routledge Falmer.

Farance, F., & Tonkel, J. (1999). *Ltsa specification - Learning technology systems architecture, draft 5* (Tech. Rep.). IEEE. Retrieved from http://ltsc.ieee.org/wg1/files/ltsa05:pdf

Fay, E. (2010). Repository software comparison: Building digital library infrastructure at lse. *Ariadne, 64*. Retrieved from http://www.ariadne.ac.uk/issue64/fay/

Feinerer, I., & Gernot, S. (2009). Comparison of tools for teaching formal software verification. *Formal Aspects of Computing*, *21*(3), 293–301. doi:10.1007/s00165-008-0084-5

Fernandez, J. L., Carrillo, J. M., Nicolas, J., Toval, A., & Carrion, M. I. (2011). Trends in e-learning standards. *International Journal of Computers and Applications*, *353*(1), 49–54. Retrieved from http://www.ijcaonline.org/dedce/number1/dece008.pdf

Feyereisen, P., & de Lannoy, J.-D. (1991). Gestures and Speech: Psychological Investigations (Studies in Emotion and Social Interaction). Cambridge University Press. Retrieved from http://amazon.com/o/ASIN/0521377625/

Fiebrink, R., Trueman, D., & Cook, P. R. (2009). A metainstrument for interactive, on-the-fly machine learning. InProc. NIME (Vol. 2, p. 3). Retrieved from http://www.cs.dartmouth.edu/~cs104/BodyPartRecognition.pdf

Fielding, R., & Taylor, R. (2000). Principled design of the modern web architecture. In *Proceedings of22nd International Conference on Software Engineering*, (pp. 407-416). Academic Press. doi:10.1145/337180.337228

Fincher, S., & Petre, M. (2004). *Computer Science Education Research*. RoutledgeFalmer, Taylor & Francis Group.

Fitzgerald, J., Bicarregui, J., Larsen, P. G., & Woodcock, J. (2013). Industrial Deployment of Formal Methods: Trends and Challenges. In A. Romanovsky & M. Thomas (Eds.), *Industrial Deployment of System Engineering Methods* (pp. 123–143). Berlin: Springer-Verlag. doi:10.1007/978-3-642-33170-1_10

Fitzgerald, J., Larsen, P. G., Mukherjee, P., Plat, N., & Verhoef, M. (2005). *Validated Designs for Object-oriented Systems*. New York: Springer.

Fonte, D., Vilas Boas, I., Cruz, D., Gançarski, A., & Henriques, P. (2012). Program Analysis and Evaluation using Quimera. In *Proceedings of ICEIS'2012 --- 14th International Conference on Enterprise Information Systems*, (pp. 209-219). ICEIS.

Fonte, D., Vilas Boas, I., Oliveira, N., Cruz, D., Gançarski, A., & Henriques, P. (2014). Partial Correctness and Continuous Integration in Computer Supported Education. In *Proceedings of CSEdu'2014: 6th International Conference on Computer Supported Education*. CSEdu.

Fonte, D., Cruz, D., Gançarski, A., & Henriques, P. (2013). A Flexible Dynamic System for Automatic Grading of Programming Exercises, OASIC.SLATE.2013*Symposium on Languages, Applications and Technologies*, *29*, 129-144.

Forišek, M., & Steinová, M. (2012). Metaphors and analogies for teaching algorithms. In *Proceedings of the 43th SIGCSE Technical Symposium on Computer Science Education, SIGCSE'12* (pp. 15-20). New York, NY: ACM Press. doi:10.1145/2157136.2157147

Fowler, M. (1999). *Refactoring: Improving the Design of Existing Code*. Boston, MA: Addison-Wesley Longman Inc.

Fraisse, P. (1982). Rhythm and Tempo. In D. Deutsch (Ed.), *The Psychology of Music* (pp. 149–180). Academic Press. doi:10.1016/B978-0-12-213562-0.50010-3

Friesen, N. (2004). *Metadata in practice (chap. Semantic and Syntactic Interoperability for Learning Object Metadata)*. Chicago, IL: ALA Editions.

Friesen, N. (2004). Editorial - a gentle introduction to technical elearning standards. *Canadian Journal of Learning and Technology*, *30*(3). Retrieved from http://www.cjlt.ca/index.php/cjlt/article/view/136

Friesen, N. (2005). *Interoperability and learning objects: An overview of e-learning standardization.Interdisciplinary Journal of Knowledge and Learning Objects*.

Fuller, U., Johnson, C. G., Ahoniemi, T., Cukierman, D., Hernán-Losada, I., & Jackova, J. (2007). Developing a computer science-specific learning taxonomy. *SIGCSE Bulletin*, *39*(4), 152–170. doi:10.1145/1345375.1345438

Gamma, E., Helm, R., Johnson, R., & Vlissides, J. (1995). *Design Patterns: Elements of Reusable Object-Oriented Software*. Boston, MA: Addison-Wesley Longman Inc.

Garett, N., Thoms, B., Soffer, M., & Ryan, T. (2007). Extending the Elgg Social Networking System to Enhance the Campus Conversation. In *Proceedings of DESRIST 2007*. DESRIST.

Gelfand, N., Goodrich, M. T., & Tamassia, R. (1998). Teaching data structure design patterns. *SIGCSE Bulletin*, *30*(1), 331–335. doi:10.1145/274790.274324

Gersting, J. L. (2000). Computer Science Distance Education Experience in Hawaii. *Computer Science Education*, *10*(1), 95–106. doi:10.1076/0899-3408(200004)10:1;1-P;FT095

Gilbert, T. (2010). Leveraging sakai and ims lti to standardize integrations. In *Proceedings of 10th Sakai Conference*. Academic Press.

Gillian, N., Knapp, R. B., & O'Modhrain, S. (2011). A machine learning toolbox for musician computer interaction. In *Proceedings of the 2011 International Coference on New Interfaces for Musical Expression (NIME11)*. NIME.

Giménez, O., Petit, J., & Roura, S. (2012). Jutge.org: An educational programming judge. In *Proceedings of the 43th SIGCSE Technical Symposium on Computer Science Education, SIGCSE'12* (pp. 445-450). New York, NY: ACM Press.

Ginat, D. (2003). The greedy trap and learning from mistakes. In *Proceedings of the 34th SIGCSE Technical Symposium on Computer Science Education, SIGCSE'03* (pp. 11-15). New York, NY: ACM Press. doi:10.1145/611892.611920

Ginat, D. (2007). Hasty design, futile patching and the elaboration of rigor. In *Proceedings of the 38th SIGCSE Technical Symposium on Computer Science Education, SIGCSE'07* (pp. 161-165). New York, NY: ACM Press. doi:10.1145/1268784.1268832

Ginat, D. (2008). Learning from wrong and creative algorithm design. In *Proceedings of the 39th SIGCSE Technical Symposium on Computer Science Education, SIGCSE'08* (pp. 26-30). New York, NY: ACM Press. doi:10.1145/1352135.1352148

Glass, G. V. (1976). Primary, secondary, and meta-Analysis. *Educational Researcher, 5*(10), 3–8. doi:10.3102/0013189X005010003

Godøy, R. I., & Leman, M. (2009). *Musical Gestures: Sound, Movement, and Meaning.* In R. I. Godøy & M. Leman (Eds.), *Musical Gestures Sound Movement and Meaning* (p. 320). Routledge. Retrieved from http://www.amazon.jp/dp/0415998875

Gomes, A., & Mendes, A. J. (2007). Learning to program - difficulties and solutions. In *Proceedings of the International Conference on Engineering Education.* Retrieved from http://icee2007.dei.uc.pt/proceedings/papers/411.pdf

Gomes, A., & Mendes, A. J. (2008). A study on student's characteristics and programming learning. In *Proceedings of the World Conference on Educational Multimedia, Hypermedia and Telecommunications (EDMEDIA'08)* (pp. 2895-2904). Vienna, Austria: AACE.

Gonzalez, G. (2006). A systematic approach to active and cooperative learning in CS1 and its effects on CS2. In *Proceedings of SIGCSE of ACM Technical Symposium on Computer Science Education,* (pp. 133 – 137). ACM. doi:10.1145/1121341.1121386

Gray, L. (2008). Effective practice with e-portfolios: Supporting 21st century learning. *JISC.* Retrieved from http://www.jisc.ac.uk/media/documents/publications/effectivepracticeeportfolios.pdf

Gray, W., Goldberg, N., & Byrnes, S. (2007). Novices and programming: Merely a difficult subject (why?) or a means to mastering metacognitive skills? *Journal of Educational Resources in Computing, 9*(1), 131–140.

Greenberg, I., Kumar, D., & Xu, D. (2012). Creative coding and visual portfolios for CS1. In *Proceedings of the 43rd ACM technical symposium on Computer Science Education* (SIGCSE'12) (pp. 247-252). Raleigh, NC: ACM. doi:10.1145/2157136.2157214

Gross, P., & Powers, K. (2005). Evaluating assessments of novice programming environments. In *Proceedings of the first international workshop on computing education research,* (pp. 99-110). New York, NY: ACM. Retrieved from http://doi.acm.org/10.1145/1089786.1089796

Gudzial, M. (2008). Education: Paving the way for computational thinking. *Communications of the ACM, 51*(8), 25–27. doi:10.1145/1378704.1378713

Guerreiro, P., & Georgouli, K. (2008, 01). Enhancing elementary programming courses using e-learning with a competitive attitude. *International Journal of Internet Education, 10.*

Gutierrez Rojas, I. A., Crespo Garcia, R. M., Pardo, A., & Delgado Kloos, C. (2009). Assessment interoperability using qti. In *Interactive conference on computer aided learning.* Retrieved from http://www.iicm.tugraz.at/CAF2009

Haberman, B., Averbuch, H., & Ginat, D. (2005). Is it really an algorithm – The need for explicit discourse. In *Proceedings of the 10th Annual Conference on Innovation and Technology in Computer Science Education, ITiCSE'05* (pp. 74-78). New York, NY: ACM Press. doi:10.1145/1067445.1067469

Hadjerrouit, S. (2008). Towards a Blended Learning Model for Teaching and Learning Computer Programming: A Case Study. *Information in Education, 7*(2), 181–210.

Hannay, J. E., Dybå, T., Arisholm, E., & Sjøberg, D. I. K. (2009). The effectiveness of pair programming: A meta-analysis. *Information and Software Technology, 51*(7), 1110–1122. doi:10.1016/j.infsof.2009.02.001

Hansen, S., Tuinstra, K., Pisani, J., & McCann, L. I. (2003). Graph Magic: A visual graph package for students. *Computer Science Education, 13*(1), 53–66. doi:10.1076/csed.13.1.53.13541

Harasim, L. (2006). *A History of E-learning: Shift Happened.* doi: doi:10.1007/978-1-4020-3803-7

Harman, K., & Koohang, A. (2006). *Learning objects: Standards, metadata, repositories, and LCMS.* Santa Rosa, CA: Informing Science Press.

Harrison, J. (2008). *Theorem Proving for Verification. Computer Aided Verification, LNCS* (Vol. 5123, pp. 11–18). Berlin: Springer-Verlag. doi:10.1007/978-3-540-70545-1_4

Hawi, N. (2010). Causal attributions of success and failure made by undergraduate students in an introductory-level computer programming course. *Computers & Education, 54*(4), 1127–1136. doi:10.1016/j.compedu.2009.10.020

Hearst, M., Kukich, K., Hirschman, L., Breck, E., Light, M., & Burge, J. et al. (2000). The debate on automated essay grading. *Intelligent Systems, 45*(2), 123–129.

Hedges, L. V., & Olkin, I. (1985). *Statistical methods for meta-analysis.* Orlando, FL: Academic Press.

Henda, B.-A. (2013). Monitoring activities in an e-learning 2.0 environment: A multi-agents system. In *Proceedings of Eighth International Conference on Internet and Web Applications and Services.* ICIW.

Henry, T. (2005). Teaching compiler construction using a domain specific language. *ACM SIGCSE, 37*(1), 7–11. doi:10.1145/1047124.1047364

Herron, M. (1971). The nature of scientific enquiry. *The School Review, 79*(2), 171–212. doi:10.1086/442968

Higgins, C. A., Gray, G., Symeonidis, P., & Tsintsifas, A. (2005). Automated assessment and experiences of teaching programming. *Journal of Educational Resources in Computing, 5*(1). http://doi.acm.org/10.1145/1163405.1163410

Hiltz, S. R., & Turoff, M. (2005). Education Goes Digital: The Evolution of Online Learning and The Revolution in Higher Education. *Communications of the ACM, 48*(10), 59–63. doi:10.1145/1089107.1089139

Hoel, T., & Mason, J. (2011). Expanding the scope of metadata and the issue of quality. In *Proceedings of 19th international conference on computers in education.* Retrieved from http://hoel.nu/publications/ICCEworkshop paper Hoel Mason2011/final.pdf

Howles, T. (2007). *A study of attrition and the use of student learning communities in the computer science introductory programming sequence.* (Unpublished doctoral dissertation). Nova Southeastern University.

Hundhausen, C. D., Douglas, S. A., & Stasko, J. T. (2002). A Meta-Study of Algorithm Visualization Effectiveness. *Journal of Visual Languages and Computing, 13*(3), 259–290. doi:10.1006/jvlc.2002.0237

Hwang, G.-J., Wu, P.-H., & Chen, C.-C. (2012). An online game approach for improving students' learning performance in web-based problem-solving activities. *Computers & Education, 59*(4), 246–1256. doi:10.1016/j.compedu.2012.05.009

Ihantola, P., Ahoniemi, T., Karavirta, V., & Seppala, O. (2010). Review of recent systems for automatic assessment of programming assignments. In *Proceedings of the 10th koli calling international conference on computing education research,* (pp. 86-93). New York, NY: ACM. Retrieved from http://doi.acm.org/10.1145/1930464.1930480

Ihantola, P., Ahoniemi, T., Karavirta, V., & Seppälä, O. (2010). Review of recent systems for automatic assessment of programming assignments. In *Proceedings of the 10th Koli Calling International Conference on Computing Education Research, Koli Calling 2010* (pp. 86-93). New York, NY: ACM Press. doi:10.1145/1930464.1930480

Islam, Md., & Khan, M. (2005). *Teaching compiler development to undergraduates using a template based approach.* Center for research on Bangla language processing (CRBLP), Brac University.

Ivers, K. S., & Barron, A. E. (1998). Using paired learning conditions with computer-based instruction to teach preservice teachers about telecommunications. *Journal of Technology and Teacher Education, 6*(2-3), 183–191.

Jackson, D., & Usher, M. (1997). Grading student programming using assyst. In Proceedings of technical symposium on computer science education, (pp. 335 -339). ACM.

Jafari, A., McGee, P., & Carmean, C. (2007). *A Research Study on Current CMS and Next Generation E-Learning Environment*. Next Generation Course Management System Group.

Janzen, D. S., & Saiedian, H. (2006). Test-driven learning: Intrinsic integration of testing into the CS/SE curriculum. *SIGCSE Bulletin*, *38*(1), 254–258. doi:10.1145/1124706.1121419

Jena, S. (2008). *Authoring and sharing of programming exercises*. (Unpublished master's thesis). San Jose State University. Retrieved from http://scholarworks.sjsu.edu/etdprojects=19

Jenkins, T. (2002). On the Difficulty of Learning to Program. In *Proceedings of 3rd annual conference of ltsn-ics*. Retrieved from http://www.ics.ltsn.ac.uk/pub/conf2002/tjenkins.pdf

Jenkins, T. (2002). On the difficulty of learning to program. In *Proceedings of the 3rd Annual Conference of the LTSN Centre for Information and Computer Sciences (vol. 4*, pp. 53-58). LTSN.

Jerman-Blazic, B., & Klobucar, T. (2005). Privacy provision in e-learning standardized systems: Status and improvements. *Computer Standards & Interfaces*, *27*(6), 561–578. doi:10.1016/j.csi.2004.09.006

Johnson, D. W., Johnson, R. T., & Stanne, M. B. (2000). *Cooperative learning methods: A meta-analysis*. Retrieved from http://www.tablelearning.com/uploads/File/EXHIBIT-B.pdf

Johnson, D. W., & Johnson, R. T. (1989). *Cooperation and competition: Theory and research*. Interaction Book Company.

Johnson, D. W., & Johnson, R. T. (2009). An educational psychology success story: Social interdependence theory and cooperative learning. *Educational Researcher*, *38*(5), 365–379. doi:10.3102/0013189X09339057

Johnson, D., Johnson, R., & Smith, K. (1998). Cooperative learning returns to college: What evidence is there that it works? *Change*, *30*(4), 26–35. doi:10.1080/00091389809602629

Jonas, N. C., & Burns, D. (2013). Using e-learning to educate health professionals in the management of children's pain. In *Proceedings of 6th International Conference Creativity Engagement in Higher Education*. Academic Press.

Jonassen, D. H. (2000). *Computers as Mindtools for Schools* (2nd ed.). Upper Saddle River, NJ: Merrill.

Jones, C. G. (2004). Test-driven development goes to school. *Journal of Computing Sciences in Colleges*, *20*(1), 220–231.

Juedes, D. (2003). Experiences in web-based grading. In *Proceedings of 33rd ASEE/IEEE Frontiers in Education Conference*. IEEE. doi:10.1109/FIE.2003.1266003

Kacer, B., Weinholtz, D., & Rocklin, T. (1990). Individual versus small group instruction of computer applications: A quantitative and qualitative comparison. *Journal of Computing in Teacher Education*, *9*(1), 6–12.

Kaczmarczyk, L., East, J. P., Petrick, E. R., & Herman, G. L. (2010). Identifying Student Misconceptions of Programming. In *Proceedings of the 41st ACM Technical Symposium on Computer Science Education (SIGCSE'10)* (pp. 107-111). Milwaukee, WI: ACM. doi:10.1145/1734263.1734299

Kalaian, S., & Kasim, R. (2013). Multilevel Meta-Analysis: Effectiveness of Small-Group Learning Methods Compared to Lecture-Based Instruction in Science, Technology, Engineering, and Mathematics College Classrooms. In SAGE Research Methods Cases. London: SAGE Publications. doi: doi:10.4135/978144627305014531371

Kalaian, S. A., & Kasim, R. M. (2008). Applications of Multilevel Models for Meta-analysis. In A. O'Connell & B. McCoach (Eds.), *Multilevel Analysis of Educational Data* (pp. 315–343). Charlotte, NC: Information Age Publishing, Inc.

Kalaian, S. A., & Kasim, R. M. (2014). A meta-analytic review of studies of the effectiveness of small-group learning methods on statistics achievement. *Journal of Statistics Education*, 22(1). Retrieved from www.amstat.org/publications/jse/v22n1/kalaian.pdf

Kati Clements, J. M. P., & Gras-Velazquez, A. (n.d.). Educational resources packaging standards scorm and ims common cartridge - The users point of view. In Proceedings of Search and exchange of e-learning materials. Academic Press.

Kazimoglu, C., Kiernan, M., Bacon, L., & MacKinnon, L. (2011). Understanding Computational Thinking before Programming: Developing Guidelines for the Design of Games to Learn Introductory Programming through Game-Play. *International Journal of Game-Based Learning*, 1(3), 30–52. doi:10.4018/ijgbl.2011070103

Kazimoglu, C., Kiernan, M., Bacon, L., & Mackinnon, L. (2012). A Serious Game for Developing Computational Thinking and Learning Introductory Computer Programming. *Procedia-Social and Behavioral Journal*, 47, 991–1999.

Keeler, C. M., & Anson, R. (1995). An assessment of cooperative learning used for basic computer skills instruction in the college classroom. *Journal of Educational Computing Research*, 12(4), 379–393. doi:10.2190/1E43-Y7G4-PXRV-KHDC

Kelleher, C., & Pausch, R. (2005). Lowering the barriers to programming: A taxonomy of programming environments and languages for novice programmers. *ACM Computing Surveys*, 37(2), 83–137. doi:10.1145/1089733.1089734

Kendon, A. (1970). Movement coordination in social interaction: Some examples described. *Acta Psychologica*, 32(0), 101–125. doi:10.1016/0001-6918(70)90094-6 PMID:5444439

Kendon, A. (1980). Gesticulation and speech: two aspects of the process of utterance. In M. R. Key (Ed.), *The Relationship of Verbal and Nonverbal Communication* (pp. 207–227). The Hague: Mouton.

Kendon, A. (1994). Do Gestures Communicate? A Review. *Research on Language and Social Interaction*, 27(3), 175–200. doi:10.1207/s15327973rlsi2703_2

Keogh, E., & Ratanamahatana, C. A. (2005). Exact indexing of dynamic time warping. *Knowledge and Information Systems*, 7(3), 358–386. doi:10.1007/s10115-004-0154-9

Kett, J. (1994). *Pursuit of Knowledge Under Difficulties: From Self-Improvement to Adult Education in America, 1750-1990*. Stanford, CA: Stanford University Press.

Khuri, S., & Holzapfel, K. (2001). EVEGA: An educational visualization environment for graph algorithms. In *Proceedings of the 6th Annual Conference on Innovation and Technology in Computer Science Education, ITiCSE'01* (pp. 101-104). New York, NY: ACM Press. doi:10.1145/377435.377497

Kinnunen, P., & Malmi, L. 2006. Why students drop out CS1 course? In *Proceedings of the second International workshop on Computing Education Research (ICER'06)* (pp. 97-108). Canterbury, UK: ACM.

Klenin, A. (2011). Common problem description format: Requirements. In *Proceedings of ACMICPC World Final CLIS (Competitive Learning Institute Symposium)*. ACMICPC.

Koile, K., & Singer, D. (2006). Improving learning in CS1 via tablet-PC-based in-class assessment. In *Proceedings of the Second International Workshop on Computing Education Research (ICER'06)* (pp. 119-126). Canterbury, UK: ACM. doi:10.1145/1151588.1151607

Kolikant, Y. B.-D. (2005). Students' alternative standards for correctness. In *Proceedings of the First International Workshop on Computing Education Research, ICER'05* (pp. 37-43). New York, NY: ACM Press.

Kommers, P. A. M., Jonassen, D. H., & Mayes, T. M. (Eds.). (1992). *Cognitive Tools for Learning*. Heidelberg, Germany: Springer-Velag. doi:10.1007/978-3-642-77222-1

Koprivica, V. (2012). Block Periodization - A Breakthrough or a misconception. *Sport Logica*, 8(2), 93–99.

Korečko, Š., & Dancák, M. (2011). Some Aspects of BKPI B Language Compiler Design. *Egyptian Computer Science Journal*, 35(3), 33–43.

Korečko, Š., Sorád, J., & Sobota, B. (2011). An External Control for Railway Traffic Simulation, In *Proceedings of the Second International Conference on Computer Modelling and Simulation* (pp. 68-75). BrnoUniversity of Technology.

Krushkov, H., Krushkova, M., Atanasov, V., & Krushkova, M. (2009). A computer –based tutoring system for programming. In *Proceedings of Mathematics and Mathematical Education*. Academic Press.

Kulkarni, C., Wei, K. P., Le, H., Chia, D., Papadopoulos, K., & Cheng, J. et al. (2013). Peer and self-assessment in massive online classes. *ACM Transactions on Computer-Human Interaction, 20*(6), 33. doi:10.1145/2505057

Kumar, P., Samaddar, S., Samaddar, A., & Misra, A. (2010). Extending ieee ltsa e-learning framework in secured soa environment. In *Proceedings of 2nd international conference on education technology and computer (icetc)*. doi:10.1109/ICETC.2010.5529417

Kurilovas, E. (2012). European learning resource exchange: A platform for collaboration of researchers, policy makers, practitioners, and publishers to share digital learning resources and new e-learning practices. In P. O. P. A. Cakir (Ed.), Social development and high technology industries: Strategies and applications. IGI-Global. Retrieved from http://www.igi-global.com/chapter/social-development-high-technology-industries/58723

Ladenberger, L., Bendisposto, J., & Leuschel, M. (2009). Visualising Event-B Models with B-Motion Studio *Proceedings of Formal Methods for Industrial Critical Systems, 5825*, 202–204. doi:10.1007/978-3-642-04570-7_17

Lahtinen, E., Ala-Mutka, K. A., & Järvinen, H. M. (2005). A Study of the difficulties of novice programmers. In *Proceedings of 10th Annual SIGSCE Conference on Innovation and Technology in Computer Science Education* (pp. 14-18). Monte da Caparica, Portugal: ACM. doi:10.1145/1067445.1067453

Lahtinen, E., Ala-Mutka, K., & Jarvinen, H.-M. (2005, June). A study of the difficulties of novice programmers. *SIGCSE Bull., 37*(3), 14-18. doi:10.1145/1151954.1067453

Lancaster, T., & Culwin, F. (2004). A Comparison of Source Code Plagiarism Detection Engines. *Computer Science Education, 14*(2), 101–112. doi:10.1080/08993 400412331363843

Larsen, P. G., Fitzgerald, J., & Riddle, S. (2009). Practice-oriented courses in formal methods using VDM++. *Formal Aspects of Computing, 21*(3), 245–257. doi:10.1007/s00165-008-0068-5

Laurillard, D. (1987). The different forms of learning in psychology and education. In J. Richardson, M. Eysenck & D. Warren-Piper (Eds.), Students Learning (pp. 198-207). Buckingham, UK: Open University Press.

Laurillard, D. (2012). *Teaching as a Design Science*. New York, NY: Routledge.

Lauwers, T., Nourbakhsh, I., & Hamner, E. (2009). CSbots: design and deployment of a robot designed for the CS1 classroom. In *Proceedings of the 40th ACM Technical Symposium on Computer Science Education (SIGCSE'09)*. Chattanooga, TN: ACM. doi:10.1145/1508865.1509017

Law, K. M. Y., Lee, V. C. S., & Yu, Y. T. (2010) Learning motivation in e-learning facilitated computer programming courses. *Computers & Education, 55*(1), 218-228. doi: 10.1016/j.compedu.2010.01.007

Lawrence, A. W., Badre, A. M., & Stasko, J. T. (1994). Empirically evaluating the use of animations to teach algorithms. In *Proceedings of Visual Languages 1994 IEEE Symposium*, (pp. 48-54). IEEE. Retrieved from http://citeseerx.ist.psu.edu/viewdoc/download?doi=10.1.1.25.8514rep=rep1type=pdf

Lazaridis, V., Samaras, N., & Zissopoulos, D. (2003). Visualization and teaching simplex algorithm. In *Proceedings of the 3rd IEEE International Conference on Advanced Learning Technologies, ICALT'03* (pp. 270-271). Athens, Greece: IEEE Computer Society Press. doi:10.1109/ICALT.2003.1215078

Le Lann, G. (1997). An Analysis of the Ariane 5 Flight 501 Failure - A System Engineering Perspective. In *Proceedings of the 1997 International Workshop on Engineering of Computer-Based Systems*. IEEE. doi:10.1109/ECBS.1997.581900

Leal, J. P., & Queirós, R. (2012). A Comparative Study on LMS Interoperability. In Virtual Learning Environments: Concepts, Methodologies, Tools and Applications (pp. 1613-1630). Hershey, PA: Information Science Reference. doi: doi:10.4018/978-1-4666-0011-9.ch804

Leal, J. P., & Queirós, R. (2009), Defining Programming Problems as Learning Objects. In *Proceedings of International Conference on Computer Education and Instructional Technology*. Venice, Italy: Academic Press.

Leal, J. P., & Queirós, R. (2010). *From eLearning Systems to Specialised Services.In A New Learning Paradigm: Competition Supported by Technology*. Sello Editorial.

Leal, J. P., & Silva, F. M. A. (2003). Mooshak: A web-based multi-site programming contest system. *Software, Practice & Experience, 33*(6), 567–581. doi:10.1002/spe.522

Lecomte, T. (2009). Applying a Formal Method in Industry: A 15-Year Trajectory. *Proceedings of Formal Methods for Industrial Critical Systems, 5825*, 26–34. doi:10.1007/978-3-642-04570-7_3

Lecomte, T., Servat, T., & Pouzancre, G. (2007). Formal Methods in Safety-Critical Railway Systems. In *Proceedings of 10th Brasilian Symposium on Formal Methods*. Ouro Preto.

Lee, D., Rodrigo, M., Baker, R., Sugay, J., & Coronel, A. (2011). Exploring the relationship between novice programmer confusion and achievement. In *Proceedings of the 4th International Conference on Affective Computing and Intelligent Interaction (ACII'11)* (pp. 175-184). Memphis, TN: Springer-Verlag. doi:10.1007/978-3-642-24600-5_21

Lemire, D. (2009, June). Faster Retrieval with a Two-Pass Dynamic-time-warping lower bound. *Pattern Recognition*, 1–26. Retrieved from http://www.sciencedirect.com/science/article/pii/S0031320308004925

Leuschel, M., & Butler, M. (2003). ProB: A model checker for B. In *Proceedings of FME 2003: Formal Methods*, (LNCS), (vol. 2805, pp. 855–874). Berlin: Springer-Verlag. doi:10.1007/978-3-540-45236-2_46

Levensaler, L., & Laurano, M. (2010). *Talent management systems 2010: Mar-ket realities, implementation experiences and solution provider profiles*. Bersin & Associates.

Li, Z. (2006, November). Exploring effective approaches in teaching principles of compiler. *The China Papers*.

Liang, Y., Liu, Q., Xu, J., & Wang, D. (2009, Dec.). The recent development of automated programming assessment. In *Computational intelligence and software engineering*, (pp. 1-5). IEEE. Retrieved from http://ieeexplore.ieee.org/stamp/stamp.jsp?tp=arnumber=5365307

Linden, G. (n.d.). *Learning JavaScript Crunchzilla Code Monster*. Retrieved from http://www.crunchzilla.com/

Linn, M. C., & Clancy, M. J. (1992). The case for case studies of programming problems. *Communications of the ACM, 35*(3), 121–132. doi:10.1145/131295.131301

Linn, M. C., & Dalbey, J. (1985). Cognitive consequences of Programming Instruction: Instruction, Access and Ability. *Educational Psychologist, 20*(4), 191–206. doi:10.1207/s15326985ep2004_4

Lister, R. (2000). On blooming first year programming and its blooming assessment. In *Proceedings of the Australasian Conference on Computing Education (ACSE'00)* (pp. 158-162). Melbourne, Australia: ACM. doi:10.1145/359369.359393

Lister, R., Adams, E., Fitzgerald, S., Fone, W., Hamer, J., Lindholm, M., … Thomas, L. (2004) A multi-national study of reading and tracking skills in novice programmers. *ACM SIGCSE Bulletin, 36*(4).

Lister, R., Adams, E. S., Fitzgerald, S., Fone, W., Hamer, J., & Lindholm, M. et al. (2004). A multinational study of reading and tracing skills in novice programmers. *SIGCSE Bulletin, 36*(4), 119–150. doi:10.1145/1041624.1041673

Lister, R., Simon, B., Thompson, E., Whalley, J. L., & Prasad, C. (2006). Not seeing the forest for the trees: Novice programmers and the SOLO taxonomy. *SIGCSE Bulletin, 38*(3), 118–122. doi:10.1145/1140123.1140157

Liu, C. (2009). cuHMM: A CUDA implementation of hidden Markov model training and classification. *The Chronicle of Higher Education*.

Liu, S., Takahashi, K., Hayashi, T., & Nakayama, T. (2009). Teaching Formal Methods in the context of Software Engineering. *ACM SIGCSE Bulletin, 41*(2), 17–23. doi:10.1145/1595453.1595457 lok Lee, F., & Heyworth, R. (2000). *Problem complexity: A measure of problem difficulty in algebra by using computer*. Academic Press.

Lucas, J., Naps, T. L., & Roessling, G. (2003). Visual-Graph - A graph class designed for both undergraduate students and educators, In *Proceedings of the 34th SIGCSE Technical Symposium on Computer Science Education, SIGCSE'03* (pp. 167-171). New York, NY: ACM Press. doi:10.1145/611892.611960

Luck, M., & Joy, M. (1999). A secure on-line submission system. In Software - practice and experience, (pp. 721-740). Academic Press.

Lu, J., & Fletcher, G. (2009). Thinking about computational thinking. In *Proceedings of the 40th ACM technical symposium on Computer Science Education (SIGCSE'09)* (pp. 260-264). Chattanooga, TN: ACM. doi:10.1145/1508865.1508959

MacDonald, P., & Ciesielski, V. (2002). Design and evaluation of an algorithm animation of state space search methods. *Computer Science Education, 12*(4), 301–324. doi:10.1076/csed.12.4.301.8622

Major, L., Kyriacou, T., & Brereton, O. (2012). Systematic literature review: Teaching novices programming using robots. *IET Software, 6*(6), 502–513. doi:10.1049/iet-sen.2011.0125

Malita, L. (2009). E-portfolios in an educational and ocupational context. *Procedia: Social and Behavioral Sciences, 1*(1), 2312–2316. doi:10.1016/j.sbspro.2009.01.406

Malmi, L., Karavirta, V., Korhonen, A., & Nikander, J. (2005, September). Experiences on automatically assessed algorithm simulation exercises with different resubmission policies. *Journal of Educational Resources in Computing, 5*(3), 7, es. doi:10.1145/1163405.1163412

Mandal, A. K., Mandal, C., & Reade, C. M. P. (2006). Architecture of an automatic program evaluation system. *CSIE*. Retrieved from http://sit.iitkgp.ernet.in/ chitta/pubs/CSIEAIT06-p152.pdf

Mandal, C. V. L. R. C. M. P., & Sinha. (2004). A web-based course management tool and web services. *Electronic Journal of E-Learning, 2*. http://doi.acm.org/10.1145/1163405.1163412

Margolis, J., & Fisher, A. (2003). *Unlocking the Clubhouse: Women in Computing*. Cambridge, MA: The MIT Press.

Markiewicz, M. E., & de Lucena, C. J. P. (2001, July). Object oriented framework development. *Crossroads, 7*(1), 3–9. doi:10.1145/372765.372771

Martens, R., Vealley, S., & Burton, D. (1990). *Competitive anxiety in sport*. Champaign, IL: Human Kinetic.

Martin, J. J., & Gill, D. L. (1991). *The relationships among competitive orientation, sport-confidence, self-efficacy, anxiety, and performance*. Academic Press.

Martín-Albo, J., Núñez, J. L., & Navarro, J. G. (2009). Validation of the Spanish version of the Situational Motivation Scale (EMSI) in the educational context. *The Spanish Journal of Psychology, 12*(2), 799–807. doi:10.1017/S113874160000216X PMID:19899680

Martin, C., & Hughes, J. (2011). Robot dance: edutainment of engaging learning. In *Proceedings of the 23rd Psychology of Programming Interest Group (PPIG'11)*. York, UK: PPIG.

Martínez-González, M. M., & Duffing, G. (2007). Teaching databases in compliance with the European dimension of higher education: Best practices for better competences. *Education and Information Technologies, 12*(4), 211-228. doi: 10.1007/s10639-007-9047-3

Martin, R. C. (2003). *Agile Software Development: Principles, Patterns, and Practices*. Upper Saddle River, NJ: Prentice Hall.

Martins, S., Mendes, A. J., & Figueiredo, A. D. (2012). A Context for Learning Programming Based on Research Communities. *Cadernos de Pedagogia do Ensino Superior, 4*, 3–22.

Mason, R., & Rehak, D. (2003). Keeping the learning in learning objects. In A. Littlejohn (Ed.), *Reusing online resources: A sustainable approach to e-learning*, (pp. 20-34). London: Kogan Page. Retrieved from http://oro.open.ac.uk/800/

Massart, D. A. (2010). Taming the metadata beast: Ilox. *D-Lib Magazine, 16*(1), 11–12. Retrieved from http://www.dlib.org/dlib/november10/massart/11massart.html

Matocha, J. (2002). Laboratory experiments in an algorithms course: technical writing and the scientific method. In *Proceedings of the 32nd ASEE/IEEE Frontiers in Education Conference, FIE'02* (pp. T1G 9-13). Champaign, IL: Stipes Publishing. doi:10.1109/FIE.2002.1157917

Matthews, M. R. (1994). *Science teaching: The role of history and philosophy of science.* New York: Routledge.

Matthews, R., Hin, H., & Choo, K. (2009). Multimedia learning object to build cognitive understanding in learning introductory programming. In *Proceedings of the 7th International Conference on Advances in Mobile Computing and Multimedia (MoMM'09)* (pp. 396-400). Kuala Lumpur, Malaysia: ACM. doi:10.1145/1821748.1821824

Mayer, R. E. (1981). The Psychology of How Novices Learn Computer Programming. *ACM Computing Surveys*, *13*(1), 121–141. doi:10.1145/356835.356841

McCallum, S. H. (2006). A look at new information retrieval protocols: Sru, opensearch. In *World library and information congress*. Retrieved from http://archive.ifla.org/IV/ifla72/papers/102-McCallum-en.pdf

McCracken, D. D. (1989). Three "lab assignments" for an algorithms course. In *Proceedings of the 20th SIGCSE Technical Symposium on Computer Science Education, SIGCSE'89* (pp. 61-64). New York, NY: ACM Press.

McDowell, C., Werner, L., Bullock, H., & Fernald, J. (2002). The effects of pair-programming in an introductory programming course. In *Proceedings of the 33rd ACM Technical Symposium on Computer Science Education.* ACM. doi:10.1145/563351.563353

McGill, M. (2012). Learning to program with personal robots: Influences on student motivation. *ACM Transactions on Computers Education*, *12*(1), 4.

McGreal, R. (2008). A typology of learning object repositories (H. H. Adelsberger, Ed.). Academic Press.

McNeill, D. (1985). So you think gestures are nonverbal? *Psychological Review*, *92*(3), 350–371. doi:10.1037/0033-295X.92.3.350

McNeill, D. (1992). *Hand and {Mind}: What {Gestures} {Reveal} about {Thought}.* Chicago: University of Chicago Press.

McNeill, D., & Levy, E. (1982). Conceptual Representations in Language Activity and Gesture. In R. J. Jarvella & W. Klein (Eds.), *Speech, Place, and Action* (pp. 271–295). Chichester, UK: Wiley.

McWhorter, W. (2008). *The Effectiveness of Using Lego Mindstorms Robotics Activities to Influence Self-Regulated Learning in a University Introductory Computer Programming Course.* (Doctoral Dissertation). University of North Texas.

McWhorter, W., & O'Connor, B. (2009). Do LEGO® Mindstorms® motivate students in CS1? In *Proceedings of the 40th ACM technical symposium on Computer Science Education (SIGCSE'09)* (pp. 438-442). Chattanooga, TN: ACM. doi:10.1145/1508865.1509019

Mead, J., Gray, S., Hamer, J., James, R., Sorva, J., Clair, C., & Thomas, L. (2006). A cognitive approach to identifying measurable milestones for programming skill acquisition. *SIGCSE Bulletin*, *38*(4), 182–194. doi:10.1145/1189136.1189185

Mehta, J. I. (1993). *Cooperative learning in computer programming at the college level.* (Unpublished doctoral dissertation). University of Illinois, Chicago, IL.

Mehta, D., Kouri, T., & Polycarpou, I. (2012). Forming project groups while learning about matching and network flows in algorithms. In *Proceedings of the 17th Annual Conference on Innovation and Technology in Computer Science Education, ITiCSE'12* (pp. 40-45). New York, NY: ACM Press. doi:10.1145/2325296.2325310

Meier, W. (2002). Exist: An open source native xml database. In Web-services, and database systems, node 2002 web and database-related workshops, (pp. 169-183). Springer.

Mernik, M., & Zumer, V. (2003). An educational tool for teaching compiler construction. *IEEE Transactions on Education*, *46*(1), 61–68. doi:10.1109/TE.2002.808277

Mertler, C. A. (2001). Designing scoring rubrics for your classroom. *Practical Assessment, Research & Evaluation*, *7*(25).

Milne, I., & Rowe, G. (2002). Difficulties in learning and teaching programming – views of students and tutors. *Education and Information Technologies*, *7*(1), 55–66. doi:10.1023/A:1015362608943

Mobbs, R. (n.d.). *TU100: Sense and the SenseBoard, an introduction*. Retrieved from http://www.youtube.com/watch?v=xmYS1slSUuM

Montgomery, K. (2001). *Authentic assessment: A guide for elementary teachers*. New York: Longman.

Mora, M. C., Sancho-Bru, J. L., Iserte, J. L., & Sánchez, F. T. (2012). An e-assessment approach for evaluation in engineering overcrowded groups. *Computers & Education, 59*(2), 732–740. doi:10.1016/j.compedu.2012.03.011

Morgado, C., Sampaio, B., & Barbosa, F. (2013). Building collaborative quizzes. In *Proceedings of the 13th Koli Calling International Conference on Computing Education Research* (Koli Calling '13). ACM.

Morgado, C., & Barbosa, F. (2013). A Structured Approach to Problem Solving in CS1/2. *International Journal of Advanced Computer Science, 7*(3), 355–362.

Morgan, G., Stephanou, A., & Simpson, B. (2000). *Aptitude Profile Test Series: Manual*. Retrieved from http://www.acer.edu.au

Mory, E. H. (2007). Feedback Research Revisited. In D. H. Jonassen (Ed.), *Handbook of research for educational communications and technology*. Association for Educational Communications and Technology.

Motil, J., & Epstein, D. (2000). *JJ: a Language Designed for Beginners (Less Is More)*. Retrieved from http://www.ecs.csun.edu/~jmotil/TeachingWithJJ.pdf

Moura, I., & van Hattum-Janssen, N. (2011). Teaching a CS introductory course: An active approach. *Computers & Education, 56*(2), 475–48. doi:10.1016/j.compedu.2010.09.009

Mow, I. T. (2008). *Issues and Difficulties in Teaching Novice Computer Programming. Innovative Techniques in Instruction Technology, E-learning, E-assessment, and Education* (pp. 199–204). Springer Netherlands. doi:10.1007/978-1-4020-8739-4_36

Mulder, A. (1994, July). Human movement tracking technology. *Hand*, 1–16.

Muller, O., Haberman, B., & Ginat, D. (2007). Pattern-Oriented Instruction and its Influence on Problem Decomposition and Solution Construction. In *Proceedings of the 12th Annual Conference on Innovation and Technology in Computer Science Education (ITiCSE'07)* (pp. 151–155). Dundee, UK: ACM. doi:10.1145/1268784.1268830

Naps, T., Roessling, G., Almstrum, V., Dann, W., Fleischer, R., & Hundhausen, C. et al. (2003). Exploring the role of visualization and engagement in computer science education. *ACM SIGCSE Bulletin, 35*(4), 131–152. doi:10.1145/782941.782998

Naps, T., Rößling, G., Anderson, J., Oshkosh, W., Cooper, S., & Koldehofe, B. et al. (2003). Evaluating the educational impact of visualization. *SIGCSE Bulletin, 35*(4), 124–136. doi:10.1145/960492.960540

National Research Council. (2001). *Educating teachers of science, mathematics, and Technology: New practices for the new millennium*. Washington, DC: National Academy of Sciences. Retrieved from http://www.nap.edu

National Science Board. (2003). *The science and engineering workforce realizing America's potential* (NSB 03-69). Retrieved from http://www.nsf.gov/nsb/documents/2003/nsb0369/nsb0369.pdf

National Science Foundation. (1996). *Shaping the future: New expectations for undergraduate education in science, mathematics, engineering, and technology*. Washington, DC: Advisory Committee to the National Science Foundation Directorate for Education and Human Resources.

Nedeva, E. D., & Dineva, S. (2010). Overcome disadvantages of e-learning for training English as foreign language. In *Proceedings of The 5thInternational Conference on Virtual Learning*. Academic Press.

Nefian, A. V., & Hayes, M. H., III. (1998). Hidden Markov models for face recognition. In *Proceedings of Acoustics, Speech and Signal Processing*, (Vol. 5, pp. 2721–2724). IEEE.

Nguyen, D., & Wong, S. B. (1999). Patterns for decoupling data structures and algorithms. *SIGCSE Bulletin, 31*(1), 87–91. doi:10.1145/384266.299693

Nicol, D., & MacFarlane-Dick, D. (2004). *Rethinking Formative Assessment in HE: a theoretical model and seven principles of good feedback practice*. Quality Assurance Agency for Higher Education.

Nielsen, J. (1994). *Usability engineering*. San Francisco, CA: Morgan Kaufmann Publishers. Retrieved from http://www.worldcat.org/search?qt=worldcatorgallq=0125184069

Nielson, F., Nielson, H. R., & Hankin, C. (1999). *Principles of program analysis*. Secaucus, NJ: Springer-Verlag New York, Inc. doi:10.1007/978-3-662-03811-6

Nitko, A. J., & Brookhart, S. M. (2010). *Educational Assessment of Students*. Englewood Cliffs, NJ: Pearson.

Norman, D. (1983). Some observations on mental models. In D. Gentner & A. Stevens (Eds.), *Mental Models* (pp. 7–14). Hillsdale, NJ: Erlbaum.

Ochoa, X., & Duval, E. (2009). Quantitative analysis of learning object repositories. *AACE*. Retrieved from http://ieeexplore.ieee.org/lpdocs/epic03/wrapper.htm?arnumber=5184802

Ochoa, X., Klerkx, J., Vandeputte, B., & Duval, E. (2011). On the use of learning object metadata: The globe experience. In Ec-tel, (pp. 271-284). Academic Press.

Office of Science and Technology Policy. (2006). *American competiveness initiative*. Domestic Policy Council. Retrieved from http://ostp.gov/html/ACIBooklet.pdf

O'Kelly, J., & Gibson, J. P. (2006, June). Robocode & problem based learning: A non-prescriptive approach to teaching programming. *SIGCSE Bulletin, 38*(3), 217–221. doi:10.1145/1140123.1140182

Oliveira, L., & Moreira, F. (2010). Personal learning environments: Integration of web 2.0 applications and content management systems. In *Proceedings of 11th European conference on knowledge management*. Academic Press.

Oliveira, N., Henriques, P., Cruz, D., & Varanda Pereira, M. (2009). VisualLISA: Visual Programming Environment for Attribute Grammars Specification. In *Proceedings of the International Multiconference on Computer Science and Information Technology -- 2nd Workshop on Advances in Programming Languages (WAPL'2009)*, (pp. 689-696). WAPL.

Oliveira, N., Varanda Pereira, M., Henriques, P., Cruz, D., & Cramer, B. (2010). VisualLISA: A Visual Environment to Develop Attribute Grammars. *Related Technologies and Applications, 7*(2), 266–289.

Oncu, C. H. S., & Cakir, H. (2011). Research in online learning environments: Priorities and methodologies. *Computers & Education, 57*(1), 1098–1108. doi:10.1016/j.compedu.2010.12.009

Pacheco, A., Henriques, J., Almeida, A. M., & Mendes, A. J. (2008). A study on basic mathematics knowledge for the enhancement of programming learning skills. In *Proceedings of the IEEIII08 - Informatics Education Europe III*. Venice, Italy: Academic Press.

Pantel, C. (n.d.). *A framework for comparing web-based learning environments*. (Unpublished master's thesis). School of Computing Science, Simon Fraser University, Canada.

Papamanthou, C., & Paparrizos, K. (2003). A visualization of the primal simplex algorithm for the assignment problem. In *Proceedings of the 8th Annual Conference on Innovation and Technology in Computer Science Education, ITiCSE'03* (p. 267). New York, NY: ACM Press. doi:10.1145/961511.961631

Pisan, Y., Richards, D., Sloane, A., Koncek, H., & Mitchell, S. (2003). Submit! A web-based system for automatic program critiquing. *Proceedings of the Australasian Conference on Computing Education, 20*(1), 59-68. Retrieved from http://dl.acm.org/citation.cfm?id=858403.858411

Piteira, M., & Costa, C. (2013). Learning Computer Programming - Study of difficulties in learning programming. In *Proceedings of the ISDOC 2013 International Conference on Information Systems and Design of Communication* (pp. 75-80). Lisboa, Portugal: ACM. doi:10.1145/2503859.2503871

Polotti, P., & Goina, M. (2011). *EGGS in Action*. NIME.

Povall, R. (1998). Technology is with us. *Dance Research Journal, 30*(1), 1–4. doi:10.2307/1477887

Preiss, B. R. (1999). Design patterns for the data structures and algorithms course. *SIGCSE Bulletin, 31*(1), 95–99. doi:10.1145/384266.299696

Priebe, R. (1997). *The Effects of cooperative learning in a second-semester university computer science course.* Paper presented at the Annual Meeting of the National Association for Research in Science Teaching. New York, NY.

Prince, M. (2004). Does active learning work? A review of the research. *The Journal of Engineering Education, 93*(3), 223–231. doi:10.1002/j.2168-9830.2004.tb00809.x

Qin, Z., Johnson, D. W., & Johnson, R. W. (1995). Cooperative versus competitive efforts and problem solving. *Review of Educational Research, 65*(2), 129–143. doi:10.3102/00346543065002129

Qualls, J., Grant, M., & Sherrell, L. (2011). CS1 Students' Understanding of Computational Thinking. *Journal of Computing Sciences in Colleges, 26*(5), 62–71.

Queirós, R., & Leal, J. P. (2012). PETCHA: A programming exercises teaching assistant. In *Proceedings of the 17th ACM annual conference on Innovation and technology in computer science education (ITiCSE '12).* ACM. Retrieved from http://doi.acm.org/10.1145/2325296.2325344

Queirós, R., & Leal, J. P. (2012). Programming Exercises Evaluation Systems - An Interoperability Survey. Academic Press.

Queirós, R., & Leal, J. P. (2013). Making Programming Exercises Interoperable with PExIL. In J. Ramalho, A. Simões, & R. Queirós (Eds.), Innovations in XML Applications and Metadata Management: Advancing Technologies, (pp. 38-56). Hershey, PA: Information Science Reference. doi: doi:10.4018/978-1-4666-2669-0.ch003

Queirós, R., & Leal, J. P. (2013). BabeLO - An Extensible Converter of Programming Exercises Formats. *IEEE Transactions on Learning Technologies, 6*(1), 38–45. doi:10.1109/TLT.2012.21

Queirós, R., & Leal, J. P. (2013). crimsonHex: A learning objects repository for programming exercises. *Software, Practice & Experience, 43*(1), 911–935. doi:10.1002/spe.2132

Queirós, R., & Leal, J. P. (2013). *Ensemble - An E-Learning Framework, Special issue on Cloud Education Environments at the Journal of Universal Computer Science.* JUCS. doi:10.3217/jucs-018-11-1454

Quinn, J., Pena, C., & McCune, L. (1996). The effects of group and task structure in an instructional simulation. In *Proceedings of the 1996 National Convention of the Association for Educational Communications and Technology.* Indianapolis, IN: Academic Press.

Rabiner, L. (1989). Tutorial on Hidden Markov Models and Selected Applications in speech Recognition. *Proceedings of the IEEE.* Retrieved from http://ieeexplore.ieee.org/xpls/abs_all.jsp?arnumber=18626

Rabiner, L., & Juang, B.-H. (1993). Fundamentals of Speech Recognition. Prentice Hall. Retrieved from http://amazon.com/o/ASIN/0130151572/

Rahmat, M., Shahrani, S., Latih, R., Yatim, N. F. M., Zainal, N. F. A., & Rahman, R. A. (2011). Major problems in basic programming that influence student performance. *Journal Procedia – Social and Behavioral Sciences, 59,* 287-296.

Ramani, K. V., & Rama Rao, T. P. (1994). A graphics based computer-aided learning package for integer programming: The branch and bound algorithm. *Computers & Education, 23*(4), 261–268. doi:10.1016/0360-1315(94)90014-0

Rankin, Y., Gooch, A., & Gooch, B. (2008). The impact of game design on students' interest in CS. In *Proceedings of the 3rd international conference on Game development in computer science education (GDCSE'08)* (pp. 31-35). Miami, FL: ACM. doi:10.1145/1463673.1463680

Raudenbush, S. W., & Bryk, A. S. (2002). *Hierarchical linear models: Applications and data analysis methods* (2nd ed.). Thousand Oaks, CA: Sage Publications, Inc.

Raudenbush, S. W., Bryk, A. S., Cheong, Y., & Congdon, R. T. (2004). *HLM 6: Hierarchical linear and nonlinear modeling.* Chicago, IL: Scientific Software International.

Raymond, E. S. (2001). *The Cathedral and the Bazaar: Musings on Linux and Open Source by an Accidental Revolutionary.* Cambridge, MA: O'Reilly & Associates.

Reed, D., Miller, C. S., & Braught, G. (2000). Empirical investigation through the CS curriculum. In *Proceedings of the 31st SIGCSE Technical Symposium on Computer Science Education, SIGCSE'00* (pp. 202-206). New York, NY: ACM Press.

Reed, J. N., & Sinclair, J. E. (2004). Motivating study of Formal Methods in the classroom. In C. N. Dean & R. T. Boute (Eds.), *TFM 2004 (LNCS)*, (Vol. 3294, pp. 32–46). Berlin: Springer-Verlag. doi:10.1007/978-3-540-30472-2_3

Reek, K. A. (1989, February). The try system -or- how to avoid testing student programs. *SIGCSE Bulletin*, *2*(1), 112–116. doi:10.1145/65294.71198

Rehak, M. R. D. R. (2003). Keeping the learning in learning objects. In A. Littlejohn (Ed.), Reusing online resources: A sustainable approach to e-Learning, (pp. 22-30). Academic Press.

Reilly, W., Wolfe, R., & Smith, M. (2006, April). Mit's cwspace project: Packaging metadata for archiving educational content in dspace. *Int. J. Digit. Libr.*, *6*(2), 139-147. 10.1007/s00799-005-0131-2

Repository Software Survey. (2010). Repositories Support Project. In *Combining schematron with other xml schema languages* (Tech. Rep.). Academic Press.

Rimé, B. (1982). The elimination of visible behaviour from social interactions: Effects on verbal, nonverbal and interpersonal variables. *European Journal of Social Psychology*, *12*(2), 113–129. doi:10.1002/ejsp.2420120201

Robins, A., Rountree, J., & Rountree, N. (2003). Learning and Teaching Programming: A Review and Discussion. *Computer Science Education*, *13*(2), 137–172. doi:10.1076/csed.13.2.137.14200

Robotiky – Play & Learn. (n.d.). Retrieved from robotiky.com

Rodriguez, E., Sicilia, M. A., & Arroyo, S. (2006). Bridging the semantic gap in standards-based learning object repositories. In *Proceedings of the workshop on learning object repositories as digital libraries current challenges*, (pp. 478-483). Academic Press.

Rogers, S. A. (2003). Developing an institutional knowledge bank at ohio state university: From concept to action plan. *Portal Libraries and the Academy*, *3*(1), 125-136. Retrieved from http://muse.jhu.edu/content/crossref/journals/portallibrariesandtheacademy=v003=3:1rogers:html

Romli, R., Sulaiman, S., & Zamli, K. (2010, June). Automatic programming assessment and test data generation a review on its approaches. In Proceedings of Information technology (ITSIM). Academic Press. doi:10.1109/ITSIM.2010.5561488

Rongas, T., & Kaarna, A. (2004). Classification of computerized learning tools for introductory programming courses: Learning approach. In Kinshuk et al. (Eds.), *ICALT*. IEEE Computer Society. Retrieved from http://dblp.uni-trier.de/db/conf/icalt/icalt2004.html-RongasKK04

Rongas, T., Kaarna, A., & Kalviainen, H. (2004). Classification of computerized learning tools for introductory programming courses: Learning approach. In *Proceedings of ICALT*. IEEE Computer Society. Retrieved from http://dblp.uni-trier.de/db/conf/icalt/icalt2004.htmlRongasKK04

Rößling, G. (2010). A Family of tools for supporting the learning of programming. *Algorithms*, *3*, 168-182. Retrieved from http://www.mdpi.com/1999-4893/3/2/168/pdf

Roth, W.-M. (2001). Gestures: Their Role in Teaching and Learning. *Review of Educational Research*, *71*(3), 365–392. doi:10.3102/00346543071003365

Rowbottom, D. J. (2000). Periodization of Training. Philadelphia: Lippincott Williams & Wilkins.

Rowe, M. L., & Goldin-meadow, S. (2009). development. *First Language*, *28*(2), 182–199. doi:10.1177/0142723707088310 PMID:19763249

Rowe, N. C. (2004). Cheating in online student assessment: Beyond plagiarism. *Online Journal of Distance Learning Administration*, *7*(2).

Royce, A. P. (1984). *Movement and Meaning: Creativity and Interpretation in Ballet and Mime*. Indiana Univ Pr. Retrieved from http://amazon.com/o/ASIN/0253338883/

Ryan, R. M., & Deci, E. L. (2000). Self-determination theory and the facilitation of intrinsic motivation, social development, and well-being. *The American Psychologist*, *55*(1), 68–78. doi:10.1037/0003-066X.55.1.68 PMID:11392867

Ryan, R. M., & Deci, E. L. (2000). Intrinsic and extrinsic motivations: Classic definitions and new directions. *Contemporary Educational Psychology, 25*(1), 54–67. doi:10.1006/ceps.1999.1020 PMID:10620381

Sadler, P., & Good, E. (2006). The impact of self- and peer-grading on student learning. *Educational Assessment, 11*(1), 1–31. doi:10.1207/s15326977ea1101_1

Sahni, S. (2005). *Data Structures, Algorithms, and Applications in Java* (2nd ed.). Summit, NJ: Silicon Press.

Saikkonen, R., Malmi, L., & Korhonen, A. (2001, June). Fully automatic assessment of programming exercises. *SIGCSE Bulletin, 33*(1), 133–136. doi:10.1145/507758.377666

Salleha, S., Shukura, Z., & Judib, H. (2013). Analysis of Research in Programming Teaching Tools: An Initial Review. In *Proceedings of 13th International Educational Technology Conference*, (pp. 127 – 135). Kuala Lumpur, Malasya: Science Direct, Elsevier. doi:10.1016/j.sbspro.2013.10.317

Salleh, N., Mendes, E., & Grundy, J. C. (2011). Empirical studies of pair programming for CS/SE teaching in higher education: A systematic literature review. *IEEE Transactions on Software Engineering, 37*(4), 509–525. doi:10.1109/TSE.2010.59

Sampson, D. G., Zervas, P., & Chloros, G. (2012). *Supporting the process of developing and managing lom application profiles: The ask-lom-ap tool.IEEE Transactions on Learning Technologies.*

Sánchez-Torrubia, M. G., Torres-Blanc, C., & Escribano-Blanco, M. A. (2010). GRAPHs: A learning environment for graph algorithm simulation primed for automatic fuzzy assessment. In *Proceedings of the 10th Koli Calling International Conference on Computing Education Research, Koli Calling 2010* (pp. 62-67). New York, NY: ACM Press. doi:10.1145/1930464.1930473

Sancho-Thomas, P., Fuentes-Fernández, R., & Fernández-Manjón, B. (2009) Learning teamwork skills in university programming courses. *Computers & Education, 53*(2), 517-531. doi: 10.1016/j.compedu.2009.03.010

Sanders, I. (2002). Teaching empirical analysis of algorithms. In *Proceedings of the 33th SIGCSE Technical Symposium on Computer Science Education, SIGCSE 2002* (pp. 321-325). New York, NY: ACM Press.

Santos, A., Gomes, A., & Mendes, A. J. (2010). Integrating New Technologies and Existing Tools to Promote Programming Learning. *Algoritms, 3*(2), 183–196. doi:10.3390/a3020183

Santos, A., Gomes, A., & Mendes, A. J. (2013). A taxonomy of exercises to support individual learning paths in initial programming learning. In *Proceedings of the 43rd Annual Frontiers in Education (FIE'13) Conference*. FIE. doi:10.1109/FIE.2013.6684794

Schacher, J. C. (2010). Motion To Gesture To Sound : Mapping For Interactive Dance. Academic Press.

Schleimer, S., Wilkerson, D., & Aiken, A. (2003). Winnowing: local algorithms for document fingerprinting. In *Proceedings of the 2003 ACM SIGMOD Int. Conf. on Management of Data*. ACM doi:10.1145/872757.872770

Schlenkrich, L., & Sewry, D. A. (2012). Factors for Successful Use of Social Networking Sites in Higher Education. *Journal of Social Studies Research, 5*.

Schn. Donald A & RIBA Building Industry Trust (1985). The design studio: An exploration of its traditions and potentials. London: Royal Institute of British Architects.

Scholtz, J., & Wiedenbeck, S. (1992). The role of planning in learning a new programming language. *International Journal of Man-Machine Studies, 37*(2), 191–214. doi:10.1016/0020-7373(92)90085-Y

Schulte, C., & Bennedsen, J. (2006). What do teachers teach in introductory programming? In *Proceedings of the second international workshop on computing education research*, (pp. 17-28). New York, NY: ACM. Retrieved from http://doi.acm.org/10.1145/1151588.1151593

SCORM. (n.d.a). Retrieved May 15, 2014 from http://scorm.com/scorm-explained/

Sendag, S., & Odabasi, H. F. (2009). Effects of an online problem based learning course on content knowledge acquisition and critical thinking skills. *Computers & Education, 53*(1), 132–141. doi:10.1016/j.compedu.2009.01.008

Seymour, S. R. (1994). Operative computer learning with cooperative task and reward structures. *Journal of Technology Education, 5*(2), 40–51.

Shackelford, R. L., & Badre, A. N. (1993). Why can't smart students solve simple programming problems? *International Journal of Man-Machine Studies, 38*(6), 985–997. doi:10.1006/imms.1993.1045

Shaffer, C.A., Cooper, M.L., Alon, A.J.D., Akbar, M., Stewart, M., Ponce, S., & Edwards, S.H. (2010). Algorithm visualization: The state of the field. *ACM Transactions on Computing Education, 10*(3), article 9.

Shepard, T., Lamb, M., & Kelly, D. (2001). More testing should be taught. *Communications of the ACM, 44*(6), 103–108. doi:10.1145/376134.376180

Sherstov, A. A. (2003). Distributed visualization of graph algorithms. In *Proceedings of the 34th SIGCSE Technical Symposium on Computer Science Education, SIGCSE'03* (pp. 376-380). New York, NY: ACM Press. doi:10.1145/611892.612011

Shneiderman, B. (1998). Designing the Users Interface -Strategies for Effective Human-Computer Interaction (3rd ed.). Boston, MA: Addison-Wesley.

Siddiqui, A., Khan, M., & Akhtar, S. (2008, August). Supply chain simulator: A scenario-based educational tool to enhance student learning. *Comput. Educ., 51*(1), 252-261. 10.1016/j.compedu.2007.05.008

Siegfried, R. (1998). The Jason programming language, an aid in teaching compiler construction. In *Proceedings of ESCCC-98*. ESCCC.

Siemens, G. (2003). *Open Source Content in Education: Part 2 – Developing, Sharing, Expanding Resources*. Retrieved May 12, 2014, from http://www.elearnspace.org/Articles/open_source_part_2.htm

Silva, J. L., Ribeiro, Ó. R., Fernandes, J. M., Campos, J. C., & Harrison, M. D. (2010). The APEX Framework: Prototyping of Ubiquitous Environments Based on Petri Nets. In *Human-Centred Software Engineering (LNCS),* (Vol. 6409, pp. 6–21). Berlin: Springer-Verlag. doi:10.1007/978-3-642-16488-0_2

Simon, B., Massart, D., van Assche, F., Ternier, S., Duval, E., Brantner, S., & Miklos, Z. (2005). A simple query interface for interoperable learning repositories. In *Proceedings of the 1st workshop on interoperability of web-based educational systems*, (pp. 11-18). Academic Press.

Soh, L. (2006). Implementing the jigsaw model in CS1 closed labs. In *Proceedings of the ACM Technical Symposium on Computer Science Education*. Bologna, Italy: ACM. doi:10.1145/1140124.1140169

Soloway, E. (1986). Learning to program = learning to construct mechanisms and explanations. *Communications of the ACM, 29*(9), 850–858. doi:10.1145/6592.6594

Soule, T., & Heckendorn, R. (2011). COTSBots: Computationally powerful, low-cost robots for Computer Science curriculums. *Journal of Computing Sciences in Colleges, 27*(1), 180–187.

Spacco, J., Hovemeyer, D., Pugh, W., Emad, F., Hollingsworth, J. K., & Padua-Perez, N. (2006, June). Experiences with marmoset: Designing and using an advanced submission and testing system for programming courses. *SIGCSE Bulletin, 38*(3), 13–17. doi:10.1145/1140123.1140131

Spielberger, C. D. (1985). Assessment of state and trait anxiety: Conceptual and methodological issues. *Southern Psychologist, 2*(4), 6–16.

Spohrer, J. C., & Soloway, E. (1986). Novice mistakes: Are the folk wisdoms correct? *Communications of the ACM, 29*(7), 624–632. doi:10.1145/6138.6145

Spohrer, J. C., Soloway, E., & Pope, E. (1985). A goal/plan analysis of buggy pascal programs. *Human-Computer Interaction, 1*(2), 163–207. doi:10.1207/s15327051hci0102_4

Springer, L., Stanne, M. E., & Donovan, S. S. (1999). Effects of small-group learning on undergraduates in science, mathematics, engineering, and technology: A meta-analysis. *Review of Educational Research, 69*(1), 21–51. doi:10.3102/00346543069001021

Stachel, J., Marghitu, D., Brahim, T., Sims, R., Reynolds, L., & Czelusniak, V. (2013). Managing Cognitive Load in Introductory Programming Courses: A Cognitive Aware Scaffolding Tool. *Journal of Integrated Design and Process Science. Computer Science, 17*(1), 37–54.

Stallman, R. (1999). *The GNU Project*. Retrieved May 12, 2014, from http://www.gnu.org/gnu/thegnuproject.html

Stone, J., & Clark, T. (2011). The Impact of Problem-Oriented Animated Learning Modules in a CS1-Style Course. In *Proceedings of the 42th ACM technical symposium on Computer Science Education (SIGCSE'11)* (pp. 51-56). Dallas, TX: ACM. doi:10.1145/1953163.1953182

Stone, J., & Clark, T. (2013). Engaging Students with Animated Learning Modules for Introductory Computer Science. In *Proceedings of the World Conference on E-Learning in Corporate, Government, Healthcare and Higher Education*. Las Vegas, NV: Association for the Advancement of Computing in Education (AACE).

Stray, C. (2001). The shift from oral to written examination: Cambridge and Oxford. *Assessment in Education: Principles, Policy & Practice, 8*(1), 33–50. doi:10.1080/09695940120033243

Striewe, M., & Goedicke, M. (2010). Visualizing data structures in an e-learning system. In Csedu, 172-179.

Sumathi, S., & Esakkirajan, S. (2007). *Fundamentals of Relational Database Management Systems*. Berlin: Springer; doi:10.1007/978-3-540-48399-1

Tang, C. M. P. C., & Yu, Y. T. (2010). A review of the strategies for output correctness determination in automated assessment of student programs. In Proceedings of global Chinese conference on computers in education. Academic Press.

Tang, Y. Y. T. P. C. K. C. M. (2009). An approach towards automatic testing of student programs using token patterns. In *Proceedings of the 17th international conference on computers in education*. Academic Press.

Tang, Y. Y. T. P. C. K. C. M. (2009). Automated systems for testing student programs: Practical issues and requirements. In *Proceedings of the international workshop on strategies for practical integration of emerging and contemporary technologies in assessment and learning*. Academic Press.

Tastle, W. A. J., & Shackleton, P. (2005). E-learning in higher education: The challenge, eort, and return of investment. *International Journal on E-Learning*.

Ten Holt, G. A., Reinders, M. J. T., & Hendriks, E. A. (2007). Multi-dimensional dynamic time warping for gesture recognition. In *Proceedings of Thirteenth Annual Conference of the Advanced School for Computing and Imaging* (Vol. 119). Academic Press.

Ternier, S. (2008). *Standards Based Interoperability for Searching in and Publishing to Learning Object Repositories* [Interoperabiliteit voor het publiceren en ontsluiten van leerobjecten in repositories met gebruik van standaarden]. (Doctoral dissertation). K.U.Leuven. Retrieved from https://lirias.kuleuven.be/handle/123456789/242045

Ternier, S., Massart, D., Totschnig, M., Klerkx, J., & Duval, E. (2010). The simple publishing interface (spi). *D-Lib Magazine, 1*(6), 9–10. Retrieved from http://www.dlib.org/dlib/september10/ternier/09ternier.html

Thomas, P. G., & Paine, C. B. (2000). *How student learn to program: Observation of practical work based on tasks completed*. Research Report 2000/03, Department of Computing. The Open University. Retrieved July 10, 2014 from http://www.researchgate.net/publication/221424279_How_Students_Learn_to_Program_Observations_of_Practical_Tasks_Completed/file/50463517eb57513342.pdf

Tichy, W. F. (1998). Should computer scientists experiment more? *IEEE Computer, 31*(5), 32–40. doi:10.1109/2.675631

TinCanAPI. (n.d.). Retrieved May 16, 2014 from http://tincanapi.com/overview/

TIOBE Programming Community Index for April. (2014). Retrieved from http://www.tiobe.com/index.php/content/paperinfo/tpci/index.html

Tomai, E., & Reilly, C. (2014). The impact of math preparedness on introductory programming (CS1) success. In *Proceedings of the 45th ACM Technical Symposium on Computer Science Education (SIGCSE'14)* (pp. 711-711). Atlanta, GA: ACM. doi:10.1145/2538862.2544292

Tombari, M., & Borich, G. (1999). *Authentic assessment in the classroom: Applications and practice.* Upper Saddle River, NJ: Merrill.

Tomlinson, C. A. (2011). One to Grow On / Every Teacher a Coach. In *Coaching* (pp. 92–93). The New Leadership Skill.

Tremblay, G., Guérin, F., Pons, A., & Salah, A. (2008, March). Oto, a generic and extensible tool for marking programming assignments. *Softw. Pract. Exper., 38*(3), 307-333. doi: 10.1002/spe.v38:3

Trtteberg, H., & Aalberg, T. (2006). *JExercise: A specification-based and test-driven exercise support plugin for Eclipse.* Academic Press.

Truong, N. K. D. (2007). *A web-based programming environment for novice programmers* (Doctoral dissertation). Queensland University of Technology. Retrieved from http://eprints.qut.edu.au/16471/

Tsunakawa, T. (2010). *Pivotal approach for lexical translation.* (Unpublished doctoral dissertation). University of Tokyo, Tokyo, Japan.

Tzikopoulos, M. N. V. R. A. (2009). An overview of learning object repositories. In T. Halpin (Ed.), Selected readings on database technologies and applications. IGI Global.

Underwood, J., & Szabo, A. (2003). Academic offences and e-learning: Individual propensities in cheating. *British Journal of Educational Technology, 34*(4), 467–477. doi:10.1111/1467-8535.00343

United Nations (2009). *Universal declaration of human rights.* Author.

US National Research Council and Committee on Developments in the Science of Learning with additional material from the Committee on Learning Research and Educational Practice. (2000). How People Learn: Brain, Mind, Experience, and School (2nd ed.). Washington, DC: National Academy Press.

Van Nort, D., Wanderley, M. M., & Van Nort, D. (2006). The LoM Mapping Toolbox for Max/MSP/Jitter. In *Proceedings of the International Computer Music Conference.* Academic Press.

Van Rooij, S. (2009, June). Adopting Open-Source Software Applications in Higher Education: A Cross-Disciplinary Review of the Literature. *Review of Educational Research, 79*(2), 682–701. doi:10.3102/0034654308325691

Vansteenkiste, M., & Deci, E. L. (2003). Competitively contingent rewards and intrinsic motivation: Can losers remain motivated? *Motivation and Emotion, 2*(7), 273-299. 10.1023/A:1026259005264

Varanda Pereira, M., Oliveira, N., Cruz, D., & Henriques, P. (2013). Choosing Grammars to support Language Processing Course, OASIcs.SLATE.2013*Symposium on Languages, Applications and Technologies, 29*, 155-169.

Varela, F. J., Thompson, E., & Rosch, E. (1993). *The Embodied Mind: Cognitive Science and Human Experience.* MIT Press. Retrieved from http://books.google.pt/books?id=QY4RoH2z5DoC

Varlamis, I., & Apostolakis, I. (2006). The present and future of standards for e-learning technologies. *Interdisciplinary Journal of Knowledge and Learning Objects, 2*(1). Retrieved from http://www.ijello.org/Volume2/v2p059-076Varlamis.pdf

Velázquez-Iturbide, J. Á., & Debdi, O. (2011). Experimentation with optimization problems in algorithm courses. In *Proceedings of the International Conference on Computer as a Tool, EUROCON'11.* Lisbon, Portugal: Universidade de Lisboa. doi:10.1109/EUROCON.2011.5929294

Velázquez-Iturbide, J. Á., Martín-Torres, R., & González-Rabanal, N. (2013). OptimEx: un sistema para la experimentación con algoritmos de optimización. In *Proceedings of SIIE13 XV International Symposium on Computers in Education* (pp. 30-35). Viseu, Portugal: Universidade de Viseu.

Velázquez-Iturbide, J. Á., Paredes-Velasco, M., & Debdi, D. (2013). GreedExCol: una herramienta educativa basada en CSCL para el aprendizaje de algoritmos voraces. In Proceedings of XV Simposio Internacional de Tecnologías de la Información y las Comunicaciones en la Educación (SINTICE 2013), Libro de Actas (pp. 96–103). Madrid, Spain: SCIE.

Velázquez-Iturbide, J.Á. (2013). An experimental method for the active learning of greedy algorithms. *ACM Transactions on Computing Education, 13*(4), article 18.

Velázquez-Iturbide, J. Á. (2014). *Una evaluación cualitativa de la comprensión de la optimalidad. Serie de Informes Técnicos DLSI1-URJC, 2014-03.* Madrid, Spain: Departamento de Lenguajes y Sistemas Informáticos I, Universidad Rey Juan Carlos.

Velázquez-Iturbide, J. Á., Debdi, O., Esteban-Sánchez, N., & Pizarro, C. (2013). GreedEx: A visualization tool for experimentation and discovery learning of greedy algorithms. *IEEE Transactions on Learning Technologies, 6*(2), 130–143. doi:10.1109/TLT.2013.8

Velázquez-Iturbide, J. Á., Pareja-Flores, C., Debdi, O., & Paredes-Velasco, M. (2012). Interactive experimentation with algorithms. In S. Abramovich (Ed.), *Computers in Education* (Vol. 2, pp. 47–70). New York, NY: Nova Science.

Ventura, P. R. Jr. (2005). Identifying predictors of success for an objects-first CS1. *Computer Science Education, 15*(3), 223–243. doi:10.1080/08993400500224419

Verdú, E., Regueras, L., Verdú, M., Leal, J., & Castro, J. (2012). A distributed system for learning programming online. *Computers & Education, 58*(1), 1–10. doi:10.1016/j.compedu.2011.08.015

Verhoe, T. (2008). Programming task packages: Peach exchange format. *International Journal Olympiads In Informatics, 2*(1), 192–207.

Viterbi, A. J. (1967). Error bounds for convolutional codes and an asymptotically optimum decoding algorithm. *IEEE Transactions on* Information Theory, *13*(2), 260–269. doi: doi:10.1109/TIT.1967.1054010

Voisinet, J. C., Tatibouet, B., & Hammad, A. (2002). jBTools: An experimental platform for the formal B method. *Proceedings of PPPJ, 2,* 137–140.

Volpe, G. (2005). Expressive Gesture in Performing Arts and New Media: The Present and the Future. *Journal of New Music Research, 34*(1), 1–3. doi:10.1080/09298210500123820

Wachsmuth, I., & Fröhlich, M. (Eds.). (1998). Gesture and Sign Language in Human-Computer Interaction. In *Proceedings of International Gesture Workshop, (Vol. 1371,* p. 198). Springer.

Wang, F. L., & Wong, T.-L. (2008). Designing programming exercises with computer assisted instruction. In *Proceedings of the 1st international conference on hybrid learning and education.* Berlin: Springer-Verlag. Retrieved from doi:10.1007/978-3-540-85170-7_25

Wang, G., Cook, P., & Associates. (2003). ChucK: A concurrent, on-the-fly audio programming language. In *Proceedings of International Computer Music Conference* (pp. 219–226). Academic Press. Retrieved from http://nagasm.org/ASL/icmc2003/closed/CR1055.PDF

Ward, J. (2004). Unqualified dublin core usage in oai-pmh data providers. *OCLC Systems & Services, 20*(1), 40-47. 10.1108/10650750410527322

Wathen, D., Baechle, T. R., & Earle, R. W. (2008). Periodization. In Human kinetics (3rd ed.). National Strength & Conditioning Association.

Watson, R. (1993). A survey of gesture recognition techniques technical report tcd-cs-93-11. *Department of Computer Science, Trinity College.* Retrieved from http://citeseerx.ist.psu.edu/viewdoc/download?doi=10.1.1.51.9838&rep=rep1&type=pdf

Weber, S. (2004). *The Success of Open Source.* Cambridge, MA: Harvard University Press.

Weinberg, R. S., & Gould, D. (2003). *Fundations of sport and exercise Psychology.* Champaingn, IL: Human Kinectics.

Wiedenbeck, S., Labelle, D., & Kain, V. N. R. (2004). Factors affecting course outcomes in introductory programming. In *Proceedings of 16th annual workshop of the psychology of programming interest group,* (pp. 97-109). Academic Press.

Wiedenbeck, S., Fix, V., & Scholtz, J. (1993). Characteristics of the mental representations of novice and expert programmers: An empirical study. *International Journal of Man-Machine Studies, 39*(5), 793–812. doi:10.1006/imms.1993.1084

Williams, L. A., & Kessler, R. R. (2001). Experiments with Industry's "Pair-Programming" Model in the Computer Science Classroom. *Computer Science Education, 11*(1), 7–20. doi:10.1076/csed.11.1.7.3846

Williams, L. A., & Tomayko, J. (2002). Agile Software Development. *Computer Science Education, 12*(3), 167–168. doi:10.1076/csed.12.3.167.8613

Williams, L., Wiebe, E., Yang, K., Ferzli, M., & Miller, C. (2002). In support of pair programming in the introductory computer science course. *Computer Science Education, 12*(3), 197–212. doi:10.1076/csed.12.3.197.8618

Wilson, S., Blinco, K., & Rehak, D. (2004, July). *Service-Oriented Frameworks: Modelling the infrastructure for the next generation of e-Learning Systems* (Tech. Rep.). JISC Report. Retrieved from http://www.jisc.ac.uk/uplo adeddocuments=AltilabServiceOrientedFrameworks:pdf

Wilson, B. C., & Shrock, S. (2001). Contributing to success in an introductory computer science course: A study of twelve factors. *SIGCSE Bulletin, 33*(1), 184–188. doi:10.1145/366413.364581

Wing, J. (2008). Five deep questions in computing. *Communications of the ACM, 51*(1), 58–60. doi:10.1145/1327452.1327479

Wing, J. M. (2006). Computacional Thinking. *Communications of the ACM, 49*(3), 33–35. doi:10.1145/1118178.1118215

Winkler, T. (1995). Making motion musical: Gesture mapping strategies for interactive computer music. In *Proceedings of ICMC* (pp. 261–264). ICMC.

Winslow, L. E. (1996). Programming pedagogy—a psychological overview. *SIGCSE Bulletin, 28*(3), 17–22. doi:10.1145/234867.234872

Woodcock, J., Larsen, P. G., Bicarregui, J., & Fitzgerald, J. (2009). Formal methods: Practice and experience. *ACM Computing Surveys, 41*(4), 19:1-19:36.

Wright, M., Freed, A., Lee, A., Madden, T., & Momeni, A. (2001). Managing complexity with explicit mapping of gestures to sound control with osc. In *Proceedings of International Computer Music Conference* (pp. 314–317). ICMC.

Wu, Y., & Huang, T. (1999). Vision-based gesture recognition: A review. *Urbana*, 103–115. Retrieved from http://link.springer.com/content/pdf/10.1007/3-540-46616-9_10.pdf

Wu, M. (2005). Teaching graph algorithms using online Java package IAPPGA. *ACM SIGCSE Bulletin, 37*(4), 64–68. doi:10.1145/1113847.1113879

Xavier, J., & Coelho, A. (2011, 14-16 November). 2011). Computer-based assessment system for e-learning applied to programming education. In Proceedings of ICERI201, (pp.3738-3747). IATED.

Yamato, J., Ohya, J., & Ishii, K. (1992). Recognizing Human action in Time-sequential Images using Hidden Markov Model. *Computer Vision and Pattern*. Retrieved from http://ieeexplore.ieee.org/xpls/abs_all.jsp?arnumber=223161

Yeh, K. C. (2009). Using an Educational Computer Game as a Motivational Tool for Supplemental Instruction Delivery for Novice Programmers in Learning Computer Programming. In *Proceedings of the Society for Information Technology & Teacher Education International Conference* (pp. 1611-1616). Charleston, SC: AACE.

Yoo, M. J., Beak, J. W., & Lee, I. K. (2011, June). Creating Musical Expression using Kinect. *Visual Computing*, 324–325. Retrieved from http://visualcomputing.yonsei.ac.kr/papers/2011/nime2011.pdf

Zahradník, D., & Korvas, P. (2012). *The Introduction into Sports Training*. Brno: Masaryk University.

Zeil, S. J. (2011). *ALGAE - Algorithm Animation Engine, Reference Manual Version 3.0, 2011*. Retrieved from http://www.cs.odu.edu/~zeil/AlgAE/referenceManual.pdf

Zeng, W., & Zhang, Z. (2012). *Multimedia at Work Microsoft Kinect Sensor and Its Effect*. Academic Press.

Zhao, L., & Badler, N. (2001). *Synthesis and acquisition of laban movement analysis qualitative parameters for communicative gestures*. Retrieved from http://repository.upenn.edu/cis_reports/116/

About the Contributors

Ricardo Queirós is an assistant professor at the School of Industrial Studies and Management (ESEIG) in Vila do Conde, which is responsible for courses in the area of ICT and Programming Languages. He is a PhD student of the Doctoral Program in Computer Sciences in the Faculty of Sciences of the University of Porto (FCUP). His scientific activity is related with e-Learning Standards and Interoperability, Languages for XML, Architectural Integration, with focus on the development of e-Learning Systems. He is an associated member of the Center for Research in Advanced Computing Systems (CRACS)—an INESC-Porto Associated Laboratory—and a founding member of KMILT (Knowledge Management, Interactive, and Learning Technologies) research group.

* * *

Míriam Antón-Rodríguez received the MS and PhD degrees in Telecommunication Engineering from the University of Valladolid, Spain, in 2003 and 2008, respectively. Since 2004, she is an assistant professor in the School of Telecommunication Engineering and a researcher in the Telematics and Imaging Group of the Department of Signal Theory, Communications, and Telematics Engineering. Her teaching and research interests include both applications on the Web and mobile applications mainly in learning, health, and socio-legal fields, bio-inspired algorithms for data mining, and neural networks for artificial vision. She is author or co-author of many publications in journals and of contributions to conferences.

André Baltazar was born in Oporto, Portugal. He concluded his Master's Degree in Electrical and Computing Engineering (Telecommunications and Multimédia) in 2009 and immediately started working at INESC-Porto as a researcher for the Kinetic Project. He is concluding his PhD in the Doctoral Program in Science and Art Technology at Catholic University of Portugal (UCP). He is a Researcher at the Research Center for Science and Technology in the Arts (CITAR), Porto, Portugal, and an Invited Assistant Professor at the Informatics Department of the School of Management and Industrial Studies (ESEIG-IPP) Porto. His research interests are mainly focused on the topic of gesture recognition and how can that be used on the field of Computer Music.

Amine Bitar is an Assistant Professor in the Department of Computer Science at the University of Balamand, Lebanon. He received his PhD in Computer Science in 2007. His thesis work focused on methods to facilitate users query results in search engines. He joined the University of Balamand in 2007. His main research interests focus on search engines, databases, Internet safety, mobile education, and using open source technologies in education. Recently, he conducted research projects on integrating open source social networking technologies in higher education. Dr. Bitar is a member in several executive, research, and organizing committees, as well a member in Ma3bar (Arab Center for the Support of Open Source Software) steering committee. He is also a reviewer in different international conferences and journals. He is a committee and jury member of several national programming contests.

Miguel Boavida works at Polytechnic Institute of Setúbal where he teaches Database Programming, Web Technologies, and Interface Design. Over the past ten years, his main line of research was related with the design of Sport's Information Systems and the development of Training Management System. As an expert in Sport's Technology, Miguel worked in several sports, mostly at an elite level. Miguel was one of the founders of SportTools, the first Portuguese Company working in Sport's Technology. He was also involved in the creation of the Master's course "Biomedical Engineering: Sport and Rehabilitation," teaching the Training Management Systems classes. Miguel's career in sport was mostly related with sailing, as he lived all his life in Lisbon, near the sea. Since 2003, Miguel is the Technical Coordinator of the Seawoman Project, an International Sailing Project focused on the development of new training strategies and transnational cooperation of sailing resources.

Luis Coelho holds a degree in Electronics Engineering and a PhD in Signal Processing. He has been widely involved with both public and private organizations in projects in the areas of computer science and signal processing mainly focused on the healthcare sector. He develops his research activities in the same areas where he collaborates in conferences and journals as author and reviewer. He currently teaches at the Polytechnic Institute of Porto and is the coordinator of the Biomedical Engineering Degree, which creates a strong motivation for the development of new and innovative teaching/learning paradigms.

Daniela Carneiro da Cruz got in 2007 a degree in Mathematics and Computer Science, at University of Minho, and in October 2011, she got a PhD degree in Computer Science, also at University of Minho, under the MAPi Doctoral Program. She teaches different courses in the areas of Compilers and Formal Development of Language Processors and Programming Languages and Paradigms (Procedural, Logic, and OO). As a researcher of gEPL, Daniela is working on the application of semantic-based slicing techniques to programs with contracts. She has also been involved in different research projects, such as CROSS – An Infrastructure for Certification and Re-engineering of Open Source Software; Hermes – Learning and Populating Ontologies from Textual Sources (bilateral Brasil-Portugal joint-research project); Quixote – Problem Domain Models to inter-relate Operational and Behavioral views in software systems (bilateral Argentina-Portugal joint-research project); PCDSL – Program Comprehension for Domain Specific Languages (bilateral Slovenia-Portugal joint-research project); and PCVIA (Program Comprehension by Visual Inspection and Animation).

Jorge de Carvalho is currently the Sport Department Director of Portuguese Institute of Sport and Youth. Since the early 1990s, Jorge is Lecturer in Faculty of the Human Kinetics, University of Lisbon, at the following classes: Special Education and Rehabilitation, Psychomotor Rehabilitation, and Sport Science. Since 2010, Jorge is also Lecturer for Adapted Physical Activity class in Polytechnic Institute of Setúbal. Jorge is also an International Expert in Training Course in the Special Education and Rehabilitation, Sports for People with a disabilities and Paralympics in Brazil, Angola, Mozambique, Macau, S. Tome & Príncipe, Guinea Bissau, Cap Verde, and Portugal. In his sports life, Jorge was also Chief of

Mission from Portugal Paralympic Mission for Beijing 2008 Paralympic Games, Athens 2004, Sydney 2000, Atlanta '96, Barcelona '92. Previously, Jorge was involved in the Management of the Paralympic Team of the Seoul '88 and New York '84.

Anabela de Jesus Gomes (born 1971) concluded her PhD, MSc, and BSc, all in Informatics Engineering at the University of Coimbra, in 2010, 2000, and 1995, respectively. She is a Professor at the Department of Informatics Engineering of the Polytechnic Institute of Coimbra (DEIS-IPC) since 1997, where she has been teaching Digital Systems, Operating Systems, Informatics Technology, Computer Architecture, Multimedia, Programming, and Human Computer Interaction, and also has been supervising various projects and internships. She has been member of the jury panel for several projects and internships of the different degrees taught in DEIS-IPC. She has over 30 scientific articles in prestigious international journals and conferences. Her research work focuses mostly in the area of Programming Teaching and Learning, Learning Styles, Learning Taxonomies, Learning Theories, Psychology of Programming, and E-learning. Her work has been referenced in publications of other authors.

Ouafae Debdi received the Management Computing degree from the Universidad Rey Juan Carlos, Madrid, Spain, in 2007, and two MSc degrees in Computer Science and Statistics in 2008 and 2009, respectively. She is working toward the PhD degree at the Universidad Rey Juan Carlos and is currently a fellow researcher at the Laboratory of Information Technologies in Education. Her research interests include human-computer interaction and software for programming.

Francisco Javier Díaz-Pernas received the PhD degree in industrial engineering from Valladolid University, Valladolid, Spain, in 1993. From 1988 to 1995, he joined the Department of System Engineering and Automatics, Valladolid University, Spain, where he has worked in artificial vision systems for industry applications as quality control for manufacturing. Since 1996, he has been a professor in the School of Telecommunication Engineering and a Senior Researcher in Telematics and Imaging Group of the Department of Signal Theory, Communications, and Telematics Engineering. His main research interests are applications on the Web, intelligent transportation system, and neural networks for artificial vision. He is author or co-author of many publications in journals and of contributions to conferences.

Rúben Fernandes finished his bachelor degree in 1997 in Biopathology in the School of Allied Health Sciences of the Polytechnic Institute of Porto. In 1998, he entered in the Faculty of Sciences of University of Porto, and in 2002, completed his second bachelor degree in Biology. During the period 1997 to 1999, he was researcher at IPATIMUP where, besides investigating chromosomal alterations involved in carcinogenesis, has also participated in several science communication activities under the Ciência Viva program. From 2000 to 2002, he joined the laboratory of Cytogenetics at the Institute of Biomedical Sciences Abel Salazar as researcher, and from 2003 to 2004, received a grant in the Institute of Cell and Molecular Biology, University of Porto, for the laboratory of Molecular Neurobiology. In 2003, he entered the Doctoral program at the University of Vigo in Spain and finished his PhD Cum Laude in 2008 in the field of Biochemistry, Genetics, and Immunology, with a thesis regarding the biochemical and genetic mechanisms underlying the antibiotic resistance in enterobacteria. Currently, he is Adjunct Professor at the Porto School of Allied Health Sciences and coordinator of the Master's degree in Health Biochemistry is also is the coordinator of the departmental area of Biomedical Engineering in the School of Industrial Studies and Management. Since 2010, he is a senior researcher in the Centre of Pharmacology and Chemical Biopathology of the Faculty of Medicine of Porto with interest in the study of the contribution of metabolic syndrome in cancer and infection, and supervises 7 PhD students and more than 10 Master's students.

Nélio Folgôa is graduated from Polytechnic Institute of Setúbal in Industrial Computing and has also a Master's degree in Computer Management at the same Institute. Since 2006, Nélio taught in several computer science courses such as: Data Base Systems, Programing, Health Information Systems and Multimedia, among others. On several higher education courses, as well as Technological Specialization Courses (level 5), Nélio teach Multimedia Applications Development, his main area of research. Since 2005, Nélio was part of Technical Team from an International Sailing Project, focused on the development of new training methods in Match Racing discipline. On a personal level, Nélio is a practitioner of cycling in the specialty Cross-Country Marathon.

María Isabel Jiménez Gómez was awarded her Master's degree in Telecommunications Engineering in 2003 and her PhD in 2009 from the University of Valladolid, Spain. She is working as assistant professor at that university since October 2005. She has large experience in digital signal processing, and specifically in radar systems. In addition, she is researching in teaching innovative projects, collaborating with different researching groups. Recently, she has been incorporated in Industrial Engineering School at the same University of Valladolid, as a teacher and researcher, in the area of manufacturing processes engineering. She is author or co-author of various publications in journals and of contributions to conferences.

David González-Ortega received his MS and PhD degrees in telecommunication engineering from the University of Valladolid, Spain, in 2002 and 2009, respectively. Since 2003, he has been a researcher in the Telematics and Imaging Group of the Department of Signal Theory, Communications and Telematics Engineering. Since 2005, he has been an assistant professor in the Higher School of Telecommunication Engineering, University of Valladolid. His research interests include computer vision, image analysis, pattern recognition, neural networks, and real-time applications. He is author or co-author of many publications in journals and of contributions to conferences.

Pedro Rangel Henriques got a degree in Electrotechnical/Electronics Engineering at FEUP (Porto University) and finished a PhD thesis in Formal Languages and Attribute Grammars at University of Minho. In 1981, he joined the Computer Science Department of University of Minho, where he is a teacher/researcher. Since 1995, he is the coordinator of the Language Processing Group at CCTC (Computer Science and Technologies Center). He teaches many different courses in the broader area of programming: Programming Languages and Paradigms; Compilers, Grammar Engineering, and Software Analysis; and Transformation; etc. Pedro Rangel Henriques has supervised PhD (11), and MSc (29) theses, and more than 50 graduating trainingships/projects in the areas of: language processing (textual and visual) and structured document processing, code analysis, program visulaization/animation, and program comprehension, knowledge discovery from databases, data-mining, and data-cleaning. He is co-author of the *XML & XSL: Da Teoria a Prática* book, publish by FCA in 2002, has published 6 chapters in books, 26 journal papers, and has been enrolled in 28 R&D projects.

Sema A. Kalaian, Professor of Statistics and Research Methods in the College of Technology at Eastern Michigan University, was a recipient of the (1) "Best Paper" award from the American Educational Research Association (AERA), and (2) "Distinguished Paper Award" from the Society for the Advancement of Information Systems (SAIS). Over the years, Dr. Kalaian taught introductory and advanced statistical courses such as Research Methods, Research Design, Multivariate Statistics, Survey Research, Multilevel Modeling, Structural Equation Modeling, Meta-Analysis, and Program Evaluation. Professor Kalaian's research interests focus on the development of new statistical methods and its applications. Much of her methodological developments and applications have focused on the (a) development of the multivariate meta-analytic techniques for combining evidence from multiple primary studies, (b) applications of the meta-analysis methods to various projects in different fields of study, and (c) developments of statistical methods for analyzing Delphi survey data.

Rafa Kasim, prior to his joining the private sector as a statistician and research consultant and the faculty of Indiana Tech University, served as a professor of statistics and research design in the College of Education at Kent State University. Previously, he was a senior statistician at the Evaluation, Management & Training Associates Inc. (EMT). His research focused on the application of multilevel analysis to study the effects of educational and social contexts on educational outcomes and human development in large-scale longitudinal data sets. Some of Dr. Kasim's work has also addressed the issues of selection and attrition bias in multi-site large studies. He has collaborated on numerous studies in fields such as adult literacy, education, and substance abuse treatments. Some of his work appears in *Application of Multilevel Models* (book chapter), *Journal of Educational and Behavioral Statistics, Harvard Educational Review*, and *Advances in Health Sciences Education*.

Štefan Korečko graduated (MSc) with honors at the Department of Computers and Informatics of the Faculty of Electrical Engineering and Informatics at Technical University of Košice (DCI FEEI TU) in 2001. In 2006, he defended his PhD thesis, where he designed morphisms between the languages of Petri nets and B-Method. Since 2004, he is working as an assistant professor at DCI FEEI TU. His scientific research focuses on formal methods, Petri nets and B-Method in particular, their integration and use in software development, modelling, and simulation. He has 12 years of experience in teaching undergraduate formal methods courses, which include formal software development in B-Method.

José Paulo Leal is assistant professor at the department of Computer Science of the Faculty of Sciences of the University of Porto (FCUP) and associate researcher of the Center for Research in Advanced Computing Systems (CRACS). His main research interests are eLearning system implementation, structured document processing, and software engineering. He has a special interest on automatic exercise evaluation, in particular on the evaluation of programming exercises, and on Web adaptability. He has participated in several research projects in his main research areas, including technology transfer projects with industrial partners. He has over 60 publications in conference proceedings, journals, and book chapters.

Maria José Marcelino (born 1959) concluded her PhD in Informatics Engineering at the University of Coimbra, in 1999. She is a Professor at the Department of Informatics Engineering of the Faculty of Science and Technology of the University of Coimbra (DEI-FCTUC), since 1986, where she has been teaching Programming, Simulation, Internet Technologies, Information and Communication Technologies Applied to Education and Training, and also has been supervising various projects and internships. She has been member of the jury panel for several projects and internships of the different degrees taught at DEI-FCTUC. She has over 70 scientific articles in international journals and conferences. Her research work focuses mostly in the area of Programming Teaching and Learning, Learning Theories, Modeling and Simulation applied to Education, e-learning, and m-learning. Her work has also been referenced in publications of other authors.

Mario Martínez-Zarzuela received the MS and PhD degrees in telecommunication engineering from the University of Valladolid, Spain, in 2004 and 2009, respectively. Since 2005, he has been an assistant professor in the School of Telecommunication Engineering and a researcher in the Telematics and Imaging Group of the Department of Signal Theory, Communications, and Telematics Engineering. His research interests include parallel processing on GPUs, neural networks, and bio-inspired architectures for computer vision and image processing. He is author or co-author of many publications in journals and of contributions to conferences.

Luís Gustavo Martins is an Assistant Professor at the Sound and Image Department of the School of the Arts of the Catholic University of Portugal (UCP), and he is an Integrated Researcher at the Research Center for Science and Technology in the Arts (CITAR), Porto, Portugal. He received his PhD in Electrical and Computer Engineering at University of Porto, Portugal, in 2009, with a thesis on the topic of sound segregation in music signals. His research is mainly focused on audio content analysis, sound processing and synthesis, and his research interests include signal processing, machine learning, perception and cognition, Music Information Retrieval (MIR), and software development. More recently, he has been exploring the use of tangible and multitouch interfaces for sound and music exploration and interaction. He is the Principal Investigator (PI) of the Research Project, "A Computational Framework for Sound Segregation in Music Signals," funded by the Portuguese Foundation for the Science and Technology (FCT) and with reference PTDC/EIA-CCO/111050/2009. He is an active developer of the open source Marsyas audio processing software framework.

Antoine Melki is an Associate Professor of Computer Science at the University of Balamand, Lebanon. He had been in the field for the last 25 years during which he assumed a number of administrative duties in addition to teaching. He is currently the chairperson of the Department of Computer Science, the director of Instructional Technology Unit, which is an excellence center, and the coordinator of the Arab Center for the Support of Open Source Software. His research concentration is computing curriculum design and open education.

António José Mendes (born 1959) concluded his PhD in Electrical Engineering at the University of Coimbra, in 1996. He is Professor at the Department of Informatics Engineering of the Faculty of Science and Technology of the University of Coimbra (DEI-FCTUC), since 1983, where he has been teaching several courses, especially in the Introductory Programming area. Currently, he serves as Director of the Department. He has supervised two completed PhD thesis and several MSc dissertations. He is author or co-author of more than 100 papers published in international journals and conferences. His research work focuses mostly in the area of Computer Science Education (mostly introductory programming teaching and learning) and Distance Learning. Currently, he is the Director of the University of Coimbra Distance Learning Unit.

Maria Costa Neves is a Clinical Psychologist graduated from ISPA (the Higher Institute for Applied Psychology) and has a postgraduate degree in Neuropsychology from UCAE (University School of Advanced Studies from Oporto). From 1996 until 2002, Maria worked at Neuropsychology department at São José Hospital, where she could exercise clinical practice and was part of a research group that develop several studies about brain injuries and neuropsychological rehabilitation. After 2002, she started her own private clinical practice where she worked until present. In 2003, Maria started working in sport bringing some of her clinical experience in Neuropsychology to the field of elite sports. Since 2003, Maria managed an international sailing project focused on the development of new training strategies, including mental training, leadership development, and media exposure. In 2012 Paralympic Games, Maria was responsible for mental training and psychological management of two athletes from Portuguese Paralympic Boccia Team. Maria Costa Neves is the CEO of SportTools – Technology for Sport.

Nuno Oliveira received, from Universidade do Minho, a degree in Computer Science (2007) and a MSc in Informatics (2009), for his thesis "Improving Program Comprehension Tools for Domain Specific Languages." He participated in several projects with focus on Domain-specific Languages, Visual Languages, and Program Comprehension. Currently, he is a PhD fellow from the HASLab/INESC TEC group at Universidade do Minho, studying Architectural Reconfiguration of Interacting Services, under a research grant funded by FCT.

Maximialino Paredes-Velasco received the Computer Science degree from Universidad de Sevilla and the PhD degree in Computer Science from the Universidad de Castilla – La Mancha, Spain, in 1998 and 2006, respectively. He is currently with the Universidad Rey Juan Carlos as a full-time lecturer, where he is a researcher of the Laboratory of Information Technologies in Education (LITE). His research areas include software for and innovation in programming education, mobile computing, and human-computer interaction. Prof. Paredes is an affiliate of the Spanish Association for the Advancement of Computers in Education (ADIE).

Maria João Varanda Pereira received the MSc and PhD degrees in Computer Science from the University of Minho in 1996 and 2003, respectively. She is a member of the Language Processing group in the Computer Science and Technology Center at the University of Minho. She is currently an adjunct professor at the Technology and Management School of the Polytechnic Institute of Bragança and vice-president of the same school. She usually teaches courses under the broader area of programming: programming languages, algorithms, and language processing. As a researcher of gEPL, she is working with the development of compilers based on attribute grammars, automatic generation tools, visual languages, domain-specific languages, and program comprehension. She is author or coauthor of 13 journal papers and over 52 international conference papers. She has also been involved in several bilateral projects and in 2007 was responsible for PCVIA (Program Comprehension by Visual Inspection and Animation).

María Ángeles Pérez was awarded her Master's degree in Telecommunications Engineering in 1996 and her PhD in 1999 from the University of Valladolid in Spain. She has been working as a lecturer at that University since October 1996. She has experience in coordinating projects related to telematic applications for the Information Society, mainly concerning the application of ICT (Information and Communication Technologies) to the learning process (e-learning). She has also experience in the evaluation of pre-proposals, proposals and final reports of projects cofunded by the European Commission. She is author or co-author of various publications in journals and of contributions to conferences.

Ana M. Pessoa studied Physics and post-graduated in Computational Methods in Science and Engineering. She has developed transversal scientific interests, since earlier research in Computational and Theoretical Chemistry, namely in Heterogeneous Catalysis, to current Biomedicine areas, as diverse as mathematical models in biomechanisms, such as dermic diffusion, or medicinal activity of organic compounds. She also has authored or co-authored several textbooks and coordinated a collection of undergraduate textbooks, while maintaining continuous teaching activity. She launched in recent years the Make Bio Happen Workshops, an annual initiative that promotes interface between entrepreneurship and Biomedical Engineering.

Martinha Piteira has an extended experience in Usability and e-Learning Systems. Since 2006, she is responsible for the management of the School of Technology's e-Learning platform from Polytechnic Institute of Setúbal. Martinha is also an active participant of the annual EUNIS (European University of Information System) e-Learning task force meeting as a school representative. In 2003, Martinha joined Polytechnic Institute of Setúbal, and since then, she has taught in several computer science courses, such as Data Base Systems, Usability and Accessibility, Programming, Health Information Systems, among others. Currently, Martinha is working in new research area related with the use of technology and new Learning Approach in Sports Science and High Performance Sport. Martinha Piteira has a Master's degree in Information System Management from ISCTE Lisbon University Institute, and at the present, she is a PhD student in Information Technology and Science at the same Institute.

Maria Ramires graduated from Lisbon University in Environmental Biology – Marine Variant and has also a Master's degree in Ecology and Environmental Management. During her Master's, Maria studied and developed a data management system to support birdwatching activity. In 2008, Maria started work at SportTools –Technology for Sport company, where Maria integrated several projects in field of software for sports such as Football, Tennis, Boccia, Rowing, and Sailing, among others. At SportTools, Maria is also responsible to linking the company to universities and other learning institutes. Since 1996, Maria is an athlete in Sailing sport and competed in several national and international championships. In 2006, Maria won the Portuguese Women's Match Racing Championship, and during the 2008-2010 seasons, she competed in the high-level international circuit of Match Racing (Olympic discipline at that time). Maria Ramires is also a certified Sailing coach.

João Santos works at Polytechnic Institute of Setúbal, where he teaches Database Programming, Web Technologies, and Service-Oriented Architectures. For the past ten years, his main line of research has been related to the database design and system integration working in several areas from government platforms to sport. Regarding is work in sport, João was one of the founders of SportTools, the first Portuguese Company working in Sport's Technology. He was also involved in the creation of the Master's course "Biomedical Engineering: Sport and Rehabilitation," teaching the Data Management in Sport. Since 2002, João was responsible for the analysis and development of several applications at the Portuguese Parliament, mostly related with the management of the parliamentary activities. He currently participates in several of this projects as advisor, expert in Data Base System, and Technical Coordinator.

Ján Sorád graduated (MSc) at the department of Computers and Informatics of the Faculty of Electrical Engineering and Informatics at Technical University of Košice in 2013. During his study, he was the principal developer of the modified Train Director and TS2JavaConn and continues to contribute to the tools even after the graduation. Nowadays, he works as a Java developer of an intelligent information system for flight training management support, called AVIS.

J. Ángel Velázquez-Iturbide received the Computer Science degree and the PhD degree in Computer Science from the Universidad Politécnica de Madrid, Spain, in 1985 and 1990, respectively. He is currently with the Universidad Rey Juan Carlos as a Professor, where he is the leader of the Laboratory of Information Technologies in Education (LITE). His research areas are software for and innovation in programming education, software visualization, and human-computer interaction. He is the lead investigator of the Spanish research grant "AlgoTools: Cognitive Tools for Active Learning of Algorithms." Prof. Velázquez is an affiliate member of IEEE Computer Society and IEEE Education Society, and a member of ACM and ACM SIGCSE. He is the President of the Spanish Association for the Advancement of Computers in Education (ADIE).

Index